The Way It Was

THE WAY IT WAS

COMPILED & EDITED
BY PAUL GANNON

PUBLISHED BY PAUL GANNON
CONNEMARA • IRELAND

Published 1999 by
Paul Gannon
Cloonluane, Renvyle, Co. Galway, Ireland

Design and typesetting
Jane Stark, Connemara Graphics

Printed in Spain by
GraphyCems
in association with
Ashford Press
Ballagh, Co. Limerick
Tel. 069 85255 Fax 069 85285

ISBN 978 0 9536214 0 8

Contents

For Collette, Luke and Amy

FOREWORD

It is my great pleasure to be asked to write the foreword to this fine production. The format is unique and original. It gives us an insight into the views and ideas of the personalities involved. We can read their hearts and minds and come to understand and appreciate how they viewed and dealt with the social and economic progress of that magical part of Ireland where they were all destined to live out their lives.

Connemara has been written about and painted; it has known great joy and equally, it has felt the pain of emigration when young men shed bitter tears at Galway's Ceannt Station in the 50s. Although the stories in this book come from West Connemara, they are nevertheless reflective of rural Irish society generally during this bygone era. People from all parts of rural Ireland will most likely identify with the subject matter of this book because it probably mirrors the social history of their own regions during the earlier part of this century.

'The Way It Was' is an attempt by Paul to write a definitive work. The verdict is yours; read on.

Paud Kennelly
Author of 'My Connemara' and 'More of My Connemara'

ACKNOWLEDGEMENTS

I wish to thank the following people for making this book possible:
My wife, Collette, for believing in me;
My parents, Paddy and Mary Gannon, who paid for my education and gave me my love of history and community;
My good friend, Míchael O'Sullivan, for the conversation in Carlow;
Linda O'Malley, for the use of the recording equipment;
Paud Kennelly for writing the foreword;
Tracey and Breda at Connemara West;

THE CONTRIBUTORS:–
John Gannon (RIP), Kate Conneely, Mickey Walsh, Ann Dodd, Dr Albert Flynn, Michael Gannon, Thomas O'Sullivan, Sr Phyl Clancy, Michael Flaherty, Tom Feneran, Marty Conneely, Eamonn Mac an Ríogh, Festy Mortimer, Carmel Mortimer, Joseph O'Toole, Kathleen O'Brien, Michael King, Mary Roe, Kirstin Klein, Joe Heaney, Martin O'Malley (RIP), Mary Teresa O'Malley, Fr Stephen Ludden, Fr Michael Keane, John Nee, Canon Michael Mooney (RIP), Mary Roe, Patrick Kelly (RIP), Barbara Joyce, Penny O'Malley, Thomas O'Malley, Nora Burke, Fr Dom Paul McDonnell, Mary Salmon, Gerry Salmon, Kathleen Faherty, Michael B. O'Brien, Christy Kenneally, Declan Lynch, Marge Aylward, Mary Zita King, Paul Harman, Alan Harman, Paddy Clancy, Shelley Horgan, Brian and Geraldine Deane, Tom Connolly, Sean Kelly, Eamonn Guy, Mary Guy, Gerald Bartley, Ina Allen, Mary Kane (RIP), Paddy Gannon, Michael Lavery, P. J. Conroy, Margaret Mitchell, Pete Lee (RIP), Del Allen (RIP), Barbara Flaherty, Sadie McDonnell, Teresa Bradley, Molly Fitzpatrick (RIP), Maggie O'Malley (RIP), Frances Nugent, Stephen Cosgrave (RIP), Gerry Lidwell, John Walsh, Michael O'Neill, Michael John King, Francie Mannion, Jenny Conboy, Nora McNamara, Gabriel McNamara, Mr Coen (RIP), Pauline McDonnell., Martin Conneely (RIP), Martin Conroy, John Joyce (RIP), Mike O'Malley (RIP), Matthew O'Malley, Margaret Conway, Margaret O'Malley (RIP), Peter J. McDonnell (RIP).

Special thanks to Sharon Coyne for her patience and perseverance.

And lastly, my thanks to Jane Stark of Connemara Graphics – a true professional and a pleasure to work with.

Paul Gannon

INTRODUCTION

He always sat directly in front of his beloved fire which he used to build so beautifully and with so much care. Tending to his fire was one of his greatest pleasures in life, and I could watch him for an eternity because he took such a scientific approach to the whole task. Sometimes we would sit for ages just staring into the heart of it, both of us lost in our own thoughts yet glad of each other's company. He was a great conversationalist and I was forever asking him about the old days. Football was always our favourite theme. He had a great memory and could recall events as if it was only yesterday. Sometimes he would afford himself a wry smile as he recalled certain matches and incidents. His memories went back seventy years or more. He was the last of his generation of footballers and I knew it was incumbent upon me to write it all down for future generations. He was happy for me to write his story and when I read it back to him he listened with great pride and satisfaction. Two months later he passed away peacefully. Shortly before he died, my son Luke was born, but fate decreed that John and Luke would never meet. This was a cause of great sadness to me, but I was also overcome with a great sense of relief that John's story did not die with him and that one day Luke would be able to read it for himself.

During the past year I have been privileged to meet with so many wonderful people, and my retrospective journey has been an exciting one, and one of the most fulfilling experiences of my life. I will be eternally grateful to all the people who made this book possible. Thank you for your interest, your patience, your tolerance and, most of all, for your goodwill and encouragement. You gave me the will and the confidence to persevere and you kept me focused. I have always loved history, and if the book contributes in some small way to helping us understand the social evolution of rural Ireland throughout the twentieth century, then it has been a worthwhile venture and I will be forever happy that I was called upon to produce it.

Paul Gannon
October 1999

The Emergency

I remember the day the War started. It was in September 1939. I was cutting oats along with my uncle. We were cutting with two hooks. A man passed along coming from Tully. He put 'God Bless' on the work and when he was going he said the war had started. That is the first we had heard of it. Then he went on unconcerned. You would think it was a boxing match that had started. I did not know anything about it and it had no effect on me but I know my uncle stood up and he spent a good while looking into space. He realised what had happened.

We were always kept in contact with the war through newspapers. We used to get the *Irish Press* and the *Irish Independent* but we could not really rely on them because there was a lot of propaganda. One side was claiming victory and the other denying it. You would not know who to believe. The same thing is going on today. The only person I remember having a radio at the time was the school teacher.

A few mines came ashore during the war years. I remember one outside Cashleen that came in on a green island called Inis Brúin. Another one came into Gurteen. I saw three more myself going along the cliffs of Achill one Sunday. They blew up the ones on Inis Brúin and Gurteen. The blasts shook the whole house. We thought the house was going to come in on top of us.

A lot of timber came ashore, mostly white deal, red deal and bales of teak. I remember it being piled high in Cloone Strand. They drew it away in asscarts and horsecarts. Men even came up from Westport in lorries and brought lorry loads of it away. It was worth their while travelling all that distance because timber was so scarce and this was the only way you would get it. Collecting driftwood could be dangerous on account of the mines being washed ashore. It was a risky sort of a game. Timber was very handy for a man building a house but there was very little building going on around here during the war. It was also used for roofing stables and in the making of gates and carts.

Barrels of petrol came ashore and some people thought they were barrels of rum. I remember a couple of fellows got a barrel and brought it home where they put in into the barn. They had no light, only a candle as they tried to tap the barrel. The next thing didn't the barrel go up in a blaze. Luckily enough, there was one old man present who had a wet bag which he threw on the barrel to extinguish the flames. He had suspected it was a barrel of petrol having come across them previously in World War I. Bales of rubber, each of them about two hundredweight came ashore. I remember myself and my brother, Tommy, (Lord have mercy on him), we got two bales. As we went further along the shore we saw that another fella had four bales of rubber got. More bales came in along Gurteen. A local man took them into Galway on a lorry and got £2 a bale for them. We got £4 for our two bales. It was a good sum of money to get but we knew the rubber was worth a lot more than that. It was rubber in its raw state, you see, and rubber was very scarce.

One day an old man searching for timber on the White Strand found a dead body. It was a Scottish sailor. They found identification papers on him. He was a Catholic and they buried him the far west corner of Renvyle Cemetery. It was written on his tombstone that he was 'able bodied seaman James McDonnell'. In later years his people came over from Scotland to see where he was buried. Another fellow came ashore in Sailor's Land where they used to play football. He was a Canadian airman, a Captain Morrow. He was a Protestant and they buried him in the Protestant graveyard in Moyard.

I remember the time they flew aeroplanes from America into England. It was in October. I was digging potatoes and all day long the aeroplanes kept passing overhead in twos and threes. We didn't know what was happening. Later we learnt that the Americans couldn't bring the aeroplanes in by aircraft carrier because they might have been torpedoed in the Atlantic by the German U-boats. I remember also, one really fine day, sitting down on the bank looking out to sea. Suddenly, I spied this object on the horizon. I kept watching it and how it was rising up and coming nearer. At that stage I noticed a big cable hanging out of it. It resembled a parachute because I used to see pictures of parachutes in the paper. I thought they must be landing troops on Inis Turk. My sister was home from England at the time. She came out and

Paddy Joe Davin and Tom Kane on Local Defence Force duty in Renvyle during World War II.

was a while looking at it. She identified it as a barrage balloon because she had seen them over in England. That was the time of the air-raids in London and they had put them up as a defence against the German bombers. They were anchored to the ground by three or four hundred yards of steel cable with a series of electric wires attached designed to bring down bombers if they came into contact. Three of them broke from their anchors the day of an easterly gale and were blown across the Irish Sea. Two of them came down somewhere in the midlands but one of them continued on, across Mayo and out into the Atlantic. By that time the gale had eased off and the wind had veered around north westerly and didn't it blow the balloon in again.

We saw it coming in across Curragh and as it was coming in, it was getting bigger, so big that it resembled a small cloud with a tail hanging out of it. It knocked all the wire, stone and sod fences in Curragh, cutting a big trench through them. There wasn't a man or woman in Cashleen or Ardnagreevagh that wasn't coming after it as it came over. The anchor got caught in the scelp of a rock somewhere in Ardnagreevagh and with the snatch didn't it pull out the balloon. Well it made an all-merciful bang and the air or gas that was inside of it came out. It hit the ground and hopped like a football in on top of a small thatched cottage. It knocked the gable and chimney and broke the windows. There was a man inside the house, sitting down at the fire smoking his pipe. Stones, soot and mortar came down around him as the house shook. He ran out but where did he run but straight into the balloon. The crowd was gathering now at this time, they even came back from Letterfrack and as they arrived this man was within in the balloon and some of them were saying "That thing is

Members of the West Connemara Red Cross in 1942, outside St Joseph's Catholic Church in Clifden.

mad, there's Germans in that, stand out from it, they might be armed". The old man emerged out through a tear in the side of the balloon. He was awful bewildered, stunned and shocked. So the people told him what happened and he said "Wasn't it a quare place to drop it, Isn't there plenty of room up on Gannon's mountain?" I remember there was a lot of rope hanging out of the balloon. I got a good fair share of this rope that lasted me up to two years. Rope was very scarce during the war. As for the cable, well every man claimed whatever part of it lay on his land. They cut in up in pieces and brought it away with them. The Local Defence Force and Coastguards took over control of the balloon, otherwise the locals would have cut it up and divided it out among themselves. The guards came later and I heard the balloon was taken off to Galway. A local bard wrote a poem about the barrage balloon and these are the lines from the poem that I remember:

'Twas on the 15th November
In the afternoon,
As I was looking out to sea
I spied a barrage balloon
It quickly swept in from the sea
Across the lands of Pete Nee
And then it crossed with a might roar
Upon the house of Johnó Mór
It knocked the chimney and the gable
And completely demolished his old stable
The people they arrived from near and far
They came by bike and bus and car
The first man on the scene
Was Tom Seánín Kitty
He quickly surveyed the damage
And said it was a pity

We had ration books during the war because of the overall shortages. I don't think it was a very fair system of distribution because there were big families with a lot of small children who were getting the same allowances as big families where there were a lot of grown-ups. Sometimes families with small children who would not be badly in the want would give their ration book to families of grown ups who would be in the want. Each person was allowed two ounces of tea in the week. We never threw away the tealeaves. We would leave them there and stew them over again. We drank a coffee called Coffee Éireann. Indeed it was only a dusty substitute for coffee, the sweepings of the floor in comparison with the coffee we would get after the

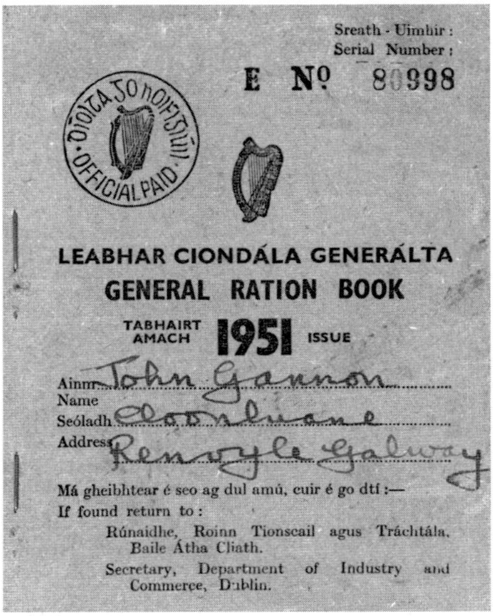

Sreath - Uimhir :
Serial Number :
E Nº 80998

OFFICIAL PAID

LEABHAR CIONDÁLA GENERÁLTA
GENERAL RATION BOOK
TABHAIRT AMACH 1951 ISSUE

Ainm / Name: John Gannon
Seóladh / Address: Cloonluane Renvyle Galway

Má gheibhtear é seo ag dul amú, cuir é go dtí :—
If found return to :
Rúnaidhe, Roinn Tionscail agus Tráchtála, Baile Átha Cliath.
Secretary, Department of Industry and Commerce, Dublin.

war. That's when we knew what right coffee was. Cocoa was great stuff if you could get it but it was scarce too. I recall a Van Houten's cocoa that came from Holland. We were allowed a half stone of flour in the week but we didn't always get it because the wholesalers were turning flour onto the black market leaving the retailer empty. This was going on a good while before the authorities got wind of it and put it right. The flour merchants stopped supplying the wholesalers and came up with some other better system of distribution. I remember people from our village going to Leenane where all they got was a half stone. Another man went to Maam. He only got a half stone of oatmeal. People cycled as far as Clifden, but travelling long distances in search of food was an accepted part of life during the emergency. People with no flour had to live on potatoes and were glad to have them. They used to make boxty. Having made a scraper out of tin they would use this to scrape down big potatoes. They would grind them out fine, put them in a cloth and squeeze the water out of them to make them dry. Then they would put boiled potatoes through them and make a class of a cake. This was boxty. You could cook it on an oven over the fire. It was really only potatoes in cake form but they liked it that way because you could drink a cup of tea with it. Potato cakes which were made from potatoes and flour (half-and-half) were much tastier. They had to be eaten hot to get the best result.

There was no rationing of tobacco but there were still shortages. I remember my brother Tommy going all the way to Claddaghduff to get some. I remember ten John Players cost 6p and you could get five Woodbines for 2p. Sweet Afton was another popular brand. However many people used to smoke tea and dried out dockleaves called *cupógs*. There wasn't much talk about drink because people didn't have the money in those years. If they had they'd be just as bad as they are today.

Paraffin wasn't awful scarce but I remember people used to still make their own candles using a class of lard they'd get ashore. They would make them in a bamboo. Split the bamboo first, join it then again and pull a string straight through the centre of it. Melt the lard and spill it into it. Leave it there and open it out again when it was set and you had the finished article. It used to burn bright with a brilliant light.

I remember before the war we were able to get a class of fertiliser called guano. It got its name from an uninhabited island in the Pacific, which we heard was a sanctuary for wild seabirds. They had been leaving their droppings on it for years. Some agricultural scientist came on the island and discovered that these droppings when mixed with a certain chemical made a great fertiliser. However, we couldn't get it during the war so people had to get as much redwrack seaweed as they could. You'd have to go out in wild rough weather in the middle of the night and compete to get your share of it. I remember heading out in the breakers and waves, out to my knees with a pitchfork. Many of the women did the same. We'd get it home and spread it out putting some stable manure through it. People sowed some wheat but mostly oats. I remember the government passed an Emergency Tillage Bill. This meant that people with arable land had to sow a certain amount of it. If they didn't they could be brought to court and fined. Looking back now, they were hard times but there was no fear of famine. When things straightened out and you got your ration it wasn't too bad.

There wasn't much in the line of recreational activities or social life, as we know it today. I spent many an evening kicking a rag football. Often when I'd tire of that I'd go into the house and play on the accordion. I remember groups of young ones would sit along the road talking. They would meet at crossroads, find a dry spot along a fence and spend the evening telling cracks. There used to be card playing in different houses. Then there were certain houses that held country dances. It cost sixpence to get into these dances. The majority of the young lads didn't ever have the sixpence so they would be around outside in the street. I used to get in free because I could play the accordion. There was no such thing as hired musicians in those years. My favourite tune was a reel called *The Heather Breeze*.

As the war dragged on during those years, for the most part we did not really pass too much notice. We didn't really take sides with Ireland being neutral but I suppose deep down we were hoping that England would win the war. We figured the devil you know is probably better than the devil you don't know.

Remembered by John Gannon and written by Paul Gannon

Dear Editor

Dear Editor,
I wish to congratulate you on your interesting newsletter. It gives us all a chance to voice our opinions. The letters will give the younger generation an insight into the life in Connemara in the 30s and 40s. I finished in Moyard NS in the early 30s and helped on our small farm for a while until I got work as a cook in a rectory. I often walked to Clifden on a Saturday to do the shopping. Once I got a seat on top of a load of cabbage plants which were being brought for sale at the market where there was a plentiful supply of potatoes, vegetables and fresh fish, all local produce.

During the war years, the home produced food kept people from starving. If I remember correctly, three-and-a-quarter pounds of flour was allowed per person per week, half a pound of sugar and half an ounce of tea. The flour was like sawdust. In order to stretch a ration, oatmeal was mixed with it; that, too, was of poor quality. We had no rural electrification. Candles and paraffin were strictly rationed. Often the only light on a long winter's night was from a bog deal stick in the open fire. By then I had a bicycle but I found it next to impossible to get tyres or tubes. One day I got to work with a couple of friends and packed the back tyre with hay. It was bumpy riding but it kept me on the road for three months until Mikie Manning got a tyre and tube for me. Those born in post war years will never realise what we, the older generation, lived through.

Thank God times are better for all of us now.
Continued Success,
Sincerely yours,
Kate Conneely.

SAVING THE SOD

Mickey Walsh

The Turf Scheme in Creeragh, which began in June 1942, was only one of several turf schemes organised around Ireland during the war years. The Minister for Industry and Commerce at the time was Séan Lemass and the huge shortage of imported coal forced him into the initiative. I was unemployed at the time, like so many of the local men and I was anxious for work. I cycled over to Creeragh to meet Michael Coyne, the ganger, and was taken on straight away. Both he and Paddy McDonnell, the other ganger, were gangers on the roadworks for the County Council and it was the County Council who administered all the turf schemes around the country. I remember there were about fifty men employed on the Creeragh scheme, which ran until 1945. Most of these men came from Lettergesh, Rossroe and Kylemore. The section of Creeragh mountain, chosen by the Council, covered about forty acres. Tommy Bodkin, John Coyne and Martin Coyne had the rights to this commonage and it was they who gave the Council permission to go ahead and open up the bogs for mass production.

All of the men on the scheme either walked or cycled to work. I remember having a Rudge bicycle at the time. The eight mile cycle usually took me about three quarters of an hour but I often had problems with bad tyres. It was impossible to buy new ones in those days on account of the war. We worked five-and-a-half days a week from 8 a.m to 5 p.m. each day. Lunch was a simple affair, usually consisting of homemade bread and butter and a bottle of tea. There was no machinery for doing any of the work. The turf was cut with sleáns and brought out to the side of the main road in cleaves. I remember, I had the biggest cleave on the scheme at one point and a friend of mine, Mattie Coyne, took pity on me and made me a hazel cleave which was much smaller and lightened the burden somewhat. Every man was expected to bring his own cleave. The cleaves were made from white sally rods. I remember the Salruck men, in particular, being very talented at cleave-making. I gave my old cleave to a man named Tommy Staunton who was in need of one. It was to prove too much for Tommy for he was the oldest man on the job. There were no donkeys used because the bog was too soft. Every cleave had a rope hanger attached to it which we suspended on our shoulder when carrying out a full load. I often walked up to a quarter of a mile with a full cleave of turf. It was hard work alright but the fact that there were so many men working together and that we were not unfairly rushed by the gangers made this work that little bit easier. Thinking back now I am sure it must have been an interesting spectacle for any passing visitors, the sight of this small army of men traversing the bogs with cleaves of turf on their backs. I do not think any of our young men today would put up with such labour, even if they were physically fit for it. I suppose it is probably a good thing that that kind of hardship is gone out of life for today's young people.

Most of the men were very good on the sleán but I had no experience at all of cutting turf. The first morning I started I was sent off spreading turf with a few others. All the men on the scheme were young and good workers. The gangers were very fair to us and I have no recollection of anyone ever being sacked. Every man did his best and I do not remember any particular individuals really standing out. We were all on the same rate of pay, ten-and-a-half shillings per day so there was no point in any man trying to be more productive than the next man. There was no overtime either. Overall the scheme ran very smoothly. As many as five or six lorries used to arrive at a time to bring the harvested turf back into Galway city. The men on the scheme all got on very well together and we all enjoyed the crack and the beautiful weather. I have fond memories of those summers and I wrote the following recitation in honour of all the men who worked on the Creeragh turf scheme:-

THE LONELY CREERAGH MIRE

On the lonely Creeragh mountain
Between Kylemore and Leenane
Where the wild bird rests and builds its nest
And where blooms the ceannabhán
A Turf Scheme there was started
Up in the month of June
To supply turf to the cities
To replace the foreign fuel.
They are a happy gang of men
Who on the bogs do toil,

Watched over by their gangers
Pat McDonnell and Michael Coyne
They worked with sleán, barrow and spade
And never seemed to tire
To save turf for their country
On the lonely Creeragh mire.
Too long we spent our money on dirty foreign coal,
Too long the neighbouring tyrant
Our country's riches stole,
But when trouble came upon them
They left us in the cold
Because all the coal in England they needed for their own;
But our own beloved country
Will not be without a fire
Where there are plenty of bogs in Ireland
And on lonely Creeragh mire.
Across the seas to England
Our young men used to roam,
Seeking for a living there
Denied to them at home.
They laboured hard
Their bread to earn
In city and in shire
For there was nothing heard of Turf Schemes then
Nor of lonely Creeragh mire.
Now to conclude and finish
I have nothing more to say
But for fine weather to dry the turf
That all my hearers pray.
Pray for the men who laboured there
That they may never tire;
God save dear old Ireland
And the turf at Creeragh mire.

In March 1944 I went to the labour exchange in Clifden to inform the manager that I was joining one of the Bord na Móna turf schemes up the country and that I wanted to sign off. I came to know about these schemes through one of Bord na Móna's own agents. These agents travelled all over the country recruiting young men for the schemes. I had enjoyed working on the Creeragh scheme but the prospect of travelling to live and work in a new place was more appealing to me at that time. Michael Laffey and John Walsh were to travel with me. I remember the three of us walking the fourteen miles to Clifden to catch the bus. We had free travel vouchers given to us by Bord na Móna. The bus brought us to Newbridge, Co Kildare. Newbridge was the main depot. After undergoing the compulsory medical examination we stayed the first night in the old navy barracks in Newbridge. The following morning we were brought by open lorry to Drummond, one of fourteen schemes that Bord na Móna had operating at the time.

There were people there from every county in Ireland. There was some daywork available but it was nearly all piecework. Every man could put himself under as much pressure as he wanted depending on how productive he intended to be. The man who was able to cut the most got the most wages and the man doing a small day's work got small wages. The turf was spread, footed, stacked and eventually loaded into lorries, which came down from Dublin. We worked from 8 a.m to 6 p.m. and for a half-day on Saturday. We worked in teams of three, one man cutting by hand and the other two wheeling. I was a wheeler. As the turfcutter fired the sods of the sleán, we caught them, filled our barrows and wheeled them off to spread out the contents. To maximise productivity we had a system whereby as I was pulling into the bank with an empty wheelbarrow the other wheeler was pulling out with a full load. This meant that the poor man on the sleán was never idle. The wheeling was tremendous exercise. I reckon it was every bit as good as those weights programmes that young men go on today.

There were big differences in the workmen. I remember Paddy Laffey from Culfin was untouchable on the sleán. An average worker could cut forty metres of turf in a day but Paddy Laffey was able to cut one hundred and twenty metres, three times as much. The average turfcutter had two wheelers attending him but Paddy Laffey always had five or six. I used to marvel at how he could keep going relentlessly without ever seeming to tire. He had such powerful arms and wrists and he had perfected the knack from plenty of practice. He stuck at it day after day, week after week for about six years. Sometimes the men used to have turf-cutting competitions among themselves. Bord na Móna used the metric system and the men were paid so much a metre. There was also plenty of overtime available and we often went out again after a day's work and took a plot of footing on piecework. It often took a few evenings to finish out such plots. The work on the scheme got much easier in the 1950s when the machines took over. Machines cut the turf and spread it and men footed it on piecework after that. Bord na Móna laid down small gauge railway lines through the bogs and brought in little locomotives for transporting the turf to the tipheads. From 1950 on I drove one of these locomotives. Some of the turf harvested in the 1950s was used in ESB power stations as well as domestically.

The first couple of years I was on the scheme the work only lasted from February to November and I was able to return home for a couple of months. However, from 1946 the scheme was all year round and we only had two weeks holidays altogether in the year. The work was very physically demanding in the forties before mechanisation but I was very fit. The wages were very good and we had great recreational facilities on the camp. Boxing, darts, table-tennis and rings were just some of the activities available in the recreation hall and of course every camp also had its own football field. I was never bored and enjoyed this army-like existence. There were four or five from the camp who played football with the local Ellistown club. They used to send a car for us every Sunday and we travelled all over Kildare playing matches. I developed a passionate interest in both hurling and football and went to watch many inter-county league matches in places like Newbridge, Portlaoise, Roscommon and Tuam. I was able to go to see Galway in Croke Park in 1956 when they defeated Cork to win the All-Ireland and I would have to rate Sean Purcell the finest footballer I have ever seen.

I always went home to Lettergesh for Christmas and for a week every summer at harvest time. The thing I missed most about home was the sea. However, I grew to love the landscape of the midlands also – the hawthorns in bloom, the little boreens, the fine land and the sweeping plains. The people of the Midlands were always very friendly and courteous towards me. Somehow, leaving my home place gave me more confidence and self-belief and I felt more fulfilled as a person there than I ever would have felt at home. The travelling gave me a broader perspective on life. I went on to spend sixteen years in Kildare working for Bord na Móna. I eventually returned home to Connemara in 1960. This was partly due to an unfortunate accident at work. I have no regrets about returning to Connemara but I enjoyed my time with Bord na Móna and I will always treasure all the happy memories.

Remembered by Mickey Walsh and written by Paul Gannon

The Captain of the Men of Death

Michael Gannon

The old people used to have a saying: "Consumption has no pity for blue eyes or golden hair."

TB was most commonly called consumption in the West of Ireland because it was so all-consuming. It swept all before it in families, even whole villages, and particularly institutions: orphanages, prisons, anywhere there were large collections of individuals living in substandard conditions of hygiene. This highly contagious disease was frequently passed on at country house dances long ago, where crowding, and rapid changes in temperature upon leaving the house for the damp night air, meant that many people inevitably became infected. TB was, at one time, the single greatest killer in Ireland since the Famine, with up to 8,000 deaths a year in the early 1900s. This figure decreased to 2,000–3,000 by the 1950s.

The disease itself affected many parts of the body. There was TB meningitis causing severe headaches and urinary TB that adversely affected the kidneys. The disease could also be found in a person's bones, heart or abdominal area. However, its most common form was in the lungs. The bacteria attacking the body brought on many symptoms including loss of appetite, loss of weight, cold sweats, great weakness and loss of energy. The symptoms varied according to which part of the body was infected but great weakness was by far the overwhelming symptom.

The bacteria were transmitted by infected milk and from person to person by droplet infection: spitting, coughing and sneezing. Ireland's temperate climate with its high humidity made the bacteria even more contagious. At one time in Ireland, public 'No Spitting' notices were common because TB could survive in dried sputum. The first sign of oncoming TB was a high temperature and a rosiness of the cheeks, which actually made the person appear very good-looking for a short time. This was, however, an almost certain sign of fairly advanced TB. There existed a belief that TB was hereditary (which it is not) and this contributed to the stigma or shame, which went with TB. This stigma lingered for decades after the disease was eradicated in the 1950s. Infected people were sent to sanitoria (e.g. Merlin Park) and those at home would never tell where they had gone, due to these feelings of shame. The first sanitoria or special TB hospitals were built in the 1920s. Although too few and too inadequate in their treatment to be of any real benefit to patients, they isolated TB sufferers and helped to prevent further spread of the disease. Patients were reluctant in the early days to be brought to these sanitoria, despite the severity of the disease.

Dr Noel Browne's Health and Building Programme in the late 1940s and early 1950s improved the conditions of the sanitoria. Patients' stays were still very long but they stood a better chance with improved facilities and medical treatment. Undoubtedly, however, the longevity of the stay did take its toll on families. Donal Kelly spent three years in Castlerea Sanatorium in Co Roscommon in the 1950s. "I can remember entire families being in the sanatorium. It was mainly young people who were inside and most of them went in thinking that they would end up dying there."

The initial treatment was rest and isolation but more advanced procedures were to follow. Numo Thorax was a procedure where air was pumped in between the chest wall and the lung in order to collapse the lung and thereby limit the progress of the disease. Patients who received this treatment were easily identifiable as they walked around with one shoulder up and one shoulder down, so to speak. There was very little physiotherapy available in the 1950s to help these patients. There was an operational procedure called thorocoplastics, which caused the permanent collapse of the lung, and usually entailed the removal of up to seven ribs from the patient. There were also more severe operations to remove the infected part of the lung and, in some cases, the whole lung.

Scientists eventually discovered a drug to tackle TB. It was called streptomycin. Early experiments with this drug showed toxic side effects. Many people who took it became deaf. Later on, newer drugs were given in combination which prevented side effects and enabled the drugs to do better. They could be taken for a shorter time with a good chance of recovery.

Barbara Flaherty spent sixteen months in Merlin Park in the 1950s. During this time she only saw her husband about once a month; she had one visit from her eldest daughter who was twelve and she never saw her other three daughters and her only son.

"I was ordered to rest completely except for going out to the toilet. For the first few months I was totally confined to bed. I spent most of the time listening to the radio with earphones on. Later on I was allowed out for a walk each day. This would last for about an hour. I used to walk around what we called the Merlin Block. I thought the outside air was so beautiful after being confined indoors for so long. I was also allowed to go to Mass on Sundays. The hardest part was seeing all the visitors coming in and being able to leave again while I was stuck in bed. I got very few visitors."

Mary Gannon, Barbara's daughter recalls her mother getting the disease. "The first indication I got that there was something wrong with my mother was when she stopped eating. She also started to feel very cold and would wear her coat inside the house. I remember then she had to go to meet a Dr McCann who was coming to Clifden on a certain date in the month. I had no idea what or where Merlin Park was until I was told by my mother, after her meeting with Dr McCann. There was no way at that time of getting to Galway. The only time I had ever been to Galway was when I went in an ambulance to get an x-ray. My father was lucky enough to get a lift in and out once a month, with a local councillor from Clifden who would be attending a Council meeting. He would be very excited as would the children but there was no chance of us going. I got in once to see my mother. I was twelve years old and I had to go to Galway to sit an exam for Preparatory College. After the exam I decided to visit my mother. I made enquiries about the location of Merlin Park and walked all the way out. It was like a long walk in the country in those days, long before that side of Galway City became so built up. When I finally arrived, the Sister in charge told me that no children were allowed in but I begged and begged and she finally relented. As I waited for my mother I remember being struck by the size of the place and the width of the corridors. This was to maximise the amount of fresh air coming in. When my mother saw me she got a terrible shock and became very distressed. I had been so desperate to see her but she appeared to be upset and overcome by seeing me. Sixteen months was a long time to be without one's mother yet by the standards of the 1940s and 1950s it was a relatively short stay."

Feichin Mulkerrins' from Claddaghduff earliest memory of TB was when he heard about people dying from it on Omey Island. "The people in the houses where somebody was dying from TB didn't want you to visit, for fear that you would catch the disease yourself. I remember the isolation room in Clifden Hospital. Once, after a patient died, they sealed the doors and windows and fumigated the room by pumping smoke through the keyhole. The walls of the room were later washed down and it was seven days before anyone was allowed in. I remember certain houses, where there was TB, being abandoned leaving everything intact. Nobody ever returned because they believed TB was still living in the building."

There can be no doubting the immense contribution that Dr Noel Browne made to the eradication of TB. In the 1940s and 1950s he was responsible for saving thousands of lives. His father died from TB when Noel was only ten years of age. His mother, who was also dying from TB and fearful of her family being split up and sent to workhouses and institutions, moved the family to London where the eldest daughter, Eileen, would look after them. She died when Noel was twelve. Later, his eldest sister died as did his younger brother following an operation. Noel always believed that his younger brother had the bad fortune to be chosen for an experiment that went wrong.

The change in Noel Browne's fortunes which was to follow was almost a fairytale one. His sister's employers agreed to sponsor his education in an English public school. He went on to eventually graduate as a doctor, specialising in TB. In 1947, at the age of thirty-two, he returned to Ireland. He was anxious to see changes in society and joined Sean McBride's Clann na Poblachta party. One year later, through good political fortune he became a TD and Minister for Health on his first day. No Minister in the history of the State has ever dealt as passionately or as successfully with the fight against TB as Noel Browne. He made one third of his Health Budget available for the eradication of TB. He borrowed money, which he mortgaged on the future income of the hospital sweepstakes, and he organised a huge building programme involving the construction of sanitoria to treat patients and isolate them, thereby reducing the rate of infection. Noel Browne lived into his eighties and continued to battle against poverty, ignorance and discrimination in Ireland on all fronts. He battled with both Church and State. He finally retired in Ballinahown in Connemara in the 1980s and many of his visions for a healthier, freer and more enlightened Ireland have since been realised. He died in 1997. *Go nd'ana Dia trócaire ar a anam.*

The incidence of TB since the 1950s has been very low. Improved domestic living conditions, good monitoring and vaccination systems and prompt treatment have collectively kept the disease at bay. However, in poorer parts of the world TB is still one of the greatest killers, often causing more deaths than one would find in wars, famines or natural disasters. TB in Ireland may now be just a memory but we must still be vigilant when it comes to basic health matters such as hygiene and a proper balanced diet. The TB story in this country is indeed one of the saddest episodes in the social history of our people and nowhere is this great sadness more borne out than in that heartbreaking song, *'There's a Graveyard in Tir Conaill'* the lyrics of which were inspired by the disease known as tuberculosis.

Based on the award winning documentary
'The Captain of the Men of Death'
by Michael Gannon for Connemara Community Radio

Humble Beginnings

Notice in *Connacht Tribune* Dated 16th January 1932:-

County Galway Board of Health and Public Assistance.
Erection of District Hospital at Clifden.
Clerk of Works Wanted.

Applications are invited from qualified engineers or architects holding a degree in engineering or architecture from the National University or a recognised school of architecture, for the position of clerk of works in connection with the erection of the above hospital at a salary of £5 5s 0d. per week, terminable on a week's notice from either side.

Applicants must be at least twenty-five years of age and have had previous experience in connection with the supervision of building works etc. Applications, accompanied by testimonials and proof of experience should reach me no later than 4 o'clock p.m. on Tuesday 26th instant, for submission to the commissioner acting as the Board of Health at a meeting the following day.

By Order: *S. O'Callcobair,* Secretary

The foundation stone was laid in 1932 by Canon McAlpine on a site purchased from Gerard Stanley, Clifden. The Canon was assisted on the day by Pappie Mannion. Pappie's reward for this effort was half-a-crown. Sadly no public representatives or members of the public were present. These were historic times in and around Clifden, for two years later on the 27th of April, 1935, the last train left Clifden Station.

Cunnane Construction Ltd. (Knock, Co Mayo) were the contractors who built the hospital with the help of the local people.

The hospital cost £14,000 to build, all of which was defrayed by the Hospital Trust Fund. The equipment for the hospital cost at least £500. The hospital was a long time built and remained vacant before the County Galway Hospital and Dispensaries Committee advertised for the various staff.

By the 19th of November 1935 all the necessary staff had been appointed. The staff consisted of:– Matron and Head nurse at a salary of £100 per annum without rations and apartments; two trained nurses at £75 per annum each all round; one cook at £25 per annum increased to £30 after three months satisfactory service; one wardsmaid at £18 per annum, increasing to £25 on the same lines as the cook; one porter who would act as gardener and ambulance driver at £2 per week with house, fire and light, (gate lodge). The matron and trained nurses were appointed by the local appointments commission and the hospital committee appointed the cook, wardsmaid and porter on a temporary basis.

Medical Officer	-	Dr Joseph Casey
Matron	-	Sr. Mercy (Byron)
Cook	-	Nora Coyne (Renvyle)
Ambulance Driver	-	Mr. Brian O'Toole
Nurses	-	Mary Ann Canavan, Fitzgerald, Fitzmorris
Wardsmaid	-	Mary Cafferty (Achill), Margaret Ward (Inishturbot)
First Patients	-	Mrs. Ellen Wallace (Kill), Mrs. Bridget Mullen (Streamstown), Andy McGrath (Sky Rd) and J. Conneely (Donloughan)

The hospital was financed and maintained by Galway County Council from 1935–1971. The County Manager at that time was Mr O'Flynn. In 1971 the Health Board took over the running of the Health Services in Counties Galway, Mayo and Roscommon.

The hospital was a great boost to Connemara because after 1922 (when the workhouse was burned down), people who needed hospitalisation were transferred to Central Hospital in Galway, (UCHG) 50 miles; St Brendan's, Loughrea, 70 miles and St Bridgid's, Ballinasloe, 90 miles.

The services provided in 1935 were:-

Medical service – people with pleurisy, pneumonia, rheumatic fever, strokes, hypertension, diabetes, arthritis etc, were admitted and treated.

Maternity service – all normal births were delivered safely and complicated cases were transferred to the Central Hospital, Galway.

Ambulance service – one ambulance served the entire area.

Researched and written by Ann Dodd

THE PRACTICE

There had always been a burning desire on the part of my father to enter the medical profession. However, for reasons best known to himself he never got to realise his childhood ambition. My decision in 1931 to pursue a career in medicine was probably more influenced by a desire to satisfy my father's wishes than by any great vocational impulse on my part. In 1931, a pass Leaving Certificate or pass Matriculation Certificate was sufficient for entry into the pre-medical course. I studied the basic sciences during those first few months, botany, biology, zoology, experimental physics, physiology, anatomy and organic chemistry, the latter being my favourite subject. In March 1932 I passed the pre-registration examination and qualified as a fully registered medical student.

Clinical training followed after two years and we spent a lot of time examining patients in the company of our professors. I admired Professors O'Malley and Fallon because they were so knowledgeable and had such great reputations. I looked up to them in terms of their ability but was somewhat taken aback initially by their sense of social detachment from the people under their care. I always understood that manner and personality were a very important part of being a doctor but we were never taught about that in college. We were never formally tutored in how to approach patients because I suppose it was probably assumed that we already had that ability.

When I graduated in June 1938 I knew that general practice was the area I wanted to specialise in because it would afford me the greatest amount of social interaction with the ordinary general public and it was in this context that I wanted to provide a medical service. My first appointment was a three month locum in Carna from July to October 1938. Carna, with its peripheral location, spartan dispensary facilities, rugged almost intimidating topography and native Irish language was initially quite a daunting prospect for a young graduate with no experience of doctoring outside of hospitals.

However, I settled in quickly enough and the local people were very friendly and helpful towards me. My weekly wage was £5 but the Carna people always liked to give a consideration. The consideration was usually a £1 for a home visit and a half crown at the surgery. I never asked for a consideration; it was always offered. I did my rounds on a bicycle and made a few trips to the offshore islands.

I always brought my black Gladstone bag (courtesy of the Department of Health) with me on my rounds. The bag contained surgical equipment including scalpel, syringes and stethoscope, ointments and dressings, pain relieving tablets including morphia and aspirin, iron tablets and vitamins. I always carried my thermometer in my inside jacket pocket.

My social life in Carna was mainly confined to the public house. I socialised with the teachers and nurses within the area. I do not think I ever had a drink with any of the native people of Carna. I suppose, when the other professional people in the area were not inclined to integrate with the locals I fell into the same boat. I often got the impression that the locals preferred this sort of social apartheid. Perhaps they felt it was appropriate. All of this was in stark contrast to the Renvyle/Letterfrack area in later years where the people were more forthcoming and where a tradition existed of always buying the doctor a drink.

The Carna experience taught me the importance of being considerate to sick people and also of staying calm and placid under stress, virtues that were not given appropriate priority in college.

In October 1938 I was appointed to the position of house surgeon in the Old Central Hospital in Galway. My weekly wage was £2 including room and board in the hospital. As house surgeon, I was expected to assist at operations and to perform minor surgery including the giving of anaesthetics. In July 1939 I left Galway to do a series of locums in Carrigaholt, Kilkee and Kilmihil. Being a native of Doonbeg, it was great to build up some general practice experience so close to home. In late 1939, shortly after getting married, my wife and I took the boat to England. I was anxious to build up my knowledge and experience in order to eventually secure my own practice back home. The wages were also substantially better in England. We moved to Lancashire and I did locums in Rochdale, Staffordshire and Warrington before eventually securing a position in a very busy practice in Manchester. The day ran from 9 a.m. to 8 p.m. I had a half-day off on Thursday and there were no surgeries on Sunday, although one was always on call. After morning surgery from 9 a.m. to 11 a.m. I went out on calls before returning for afternoon surgery which was later followed by an evening surgery. The job was much more demanding than any job I had ever had in Ireland. In November 1941 I was appointed to the position of Assistant to Dr McDonald, a Corkman, in his practice in Stoke-on-Trent. He paid me a weekly wage of £10, at least twice what I would have been on in Ireland. There were about three thousand patients on our list so I got considerable and much varied experience. I worked in Stoke for the next four years during which time I developed into a much more competent and confident general practitioner than I ever could have been had I elected to stay in Ireland. We were fortunate in that there was no rationing of medical supplies during the war. Having said that, however, we were handicapped somewhat by the unavailability of penicillin. Strangely enough, penicillin was available in Ireland because the US army had brought it into Northern Ireland and a lot of it was subsequently smuggled across the border. It was originally only available by injection and the patient had to be injected every four hours which was a tedious business. In later years, only one injection of a different form of the drug was required per day and ultimately oral penicillin was to become freely available to all. When I returned to Ireland to practise I always administered penicillin for tonsillitis, pneumonia and any serious infection or bug. Along with streptomycin, the advent of penicillin certainly contributed greatly to making general practice easier over the years.

The war did impact very negatively on social life and I was usually in bed by 11 p.m. in order to be bright and alert for the following morning. In any case, a different attitude prevailed in Stoke regarding the doctor going for a drink than that which prevailed in Ireland. It simply was not socially acceptable for the doctor to be out drinking and for the first time in my life I did experience feelings of embarrassment on meeting any of my patients in a public house. I suppose no patient likes to find his or her doctor under the influence, but I must add that I personally never experienced any hostility in this regard during my forty-five years of practice.

One outstanding memory I have of Stoke is how we used to be constantly inundated with people looking for National Health Certificates so as to avail of sick payment. I often spent an entire surgery session signing certificates without ever leaving my desk. By 1945 I had grown tired of England and was yearning to return home to run my own practice. During that final year I was continually on the lookout for a suitable position back in Ireland and when I saw a vacancy for the Renvyle Dispensary area advertised in the *Irish Independent* I decided to apply.

The interviews were held in O'Connell Street in Dublin and I was interviewed by a panel of four doctors representing the Local Appointments Commission. It was not a particularly difficult interview. However, because

Renvyle was considered to be a Gaeltacht area at that time I also had to undergo an oral Irish examination in front of a panel of very fluent elderly Irish speakers. They considered that my conversational Irish was not up to standard and I subsequently had to undergo a further examination. As luck would have it, the professor in charge happened to be a man by the name of Tomás O'Máille whose brother had been a regular patient of mine in Manchester. Professor O'Máille duly passed me as a fluent Irish speaker and I was appointed to the position of Dispensary Medical Officer for Renvyle. The annual salary was £350 with two additional allowances of £40 each, one on account of being resident in Connemara and the other in my capacity as Medical Officer of Health.

I travelled to Renvyle in my new little Ford car, which I had purchased in Dublin, after crossing over, for the princely sum of £130. I had never previously been to the Renvyle area and my initial impressions were anything but favourable. I was somewhat intimidated by the mountains and the vast expanses of bogland and I remember thinking that it was not altogether a very prosperous place. The Renvyle Dispensary area incorporated the four electoral districts of Ballinakill, Cleggan, Cois Killary and Renvyle. Its population was around two thousand and it would have been considered a relatively small practice, a stepping-stone to a more lucrative practice at some later stage. Such was my thinking early on, but fate decreed that I was not to move to a larger, more affluent dispensary area and ultimately I did not want to move. Shortly after I took up my appointment a vacancy arose in the Clifden Dispensary area. Clifden was considered to be one of the more lucrative practices at that time. However, I considered that the combination of dispensary and hospital would be too much of a workload and I did not bother to apply. My wife and I lodged in Kylemore Abbey, Ballyview Hotel in Letterfrack and Cartron House during the first few months until eventually the County Council provided me with my present house in Letterfrack, having purchased it for £3000 in 1946.

The main surgery, which was part of a small three-roomed cottage was located in Letterfrack. The middle bedroom served as the waiting room. The Home Assistants Officer also worked from this room.

A curtain was drawn across the middle of the room to conceal the bed. This was where the elderly couple who lived in the house slept. They spent most of their time in the kitchen on the east side of the house and the third room, on the west side served as the dispensary premises. It contained a table, two chairs, some wall presses, a small couch and a medical cabinet. Letterfrack surgery was held every Wednesday from 11 a.m. to 1 p.m. Tully surgery was every Friday from 11 a.m. to 1 p.m.

Despite the very basic nature of the dispensary it was very well stocked. I had no blood pressure apparatus but everything else was available to me, even items of equipment I would never use like a trachiostomy tube for performing throat operations and craniotomy forceps used in obstetrics. I had a substantial list of all the available drugs. These included Anadin, salicylicate of sodium which I used to give out for rheumatism, cough mixtures including syrup codeine phopa (a very potent cough sedative) and a variety of tonics. These tonics included iron and ammonium citrate, Easton's Syrup, Parrishes Food. Parrishes Food was the most popular tonic.

I was required to dispense my own drugs and medicines in very much the same manner that chemists do today. The old dispensaries all had weighing scales for weighing out solid drugs. They also had pestle and mortar for crushing solids. The solid drugs were supplied by Boileau and Boyd; the liquid medicines were supplied by Aerton-Saunders and Fannins were the principal suppliers of surgical instruments.

The most common cough mixture I used to make was a combination of two solid drugs, ammonium chloride and ammonium carbonate. These were weighed out in powder form, transferred into a 20 ounce glass tumbler where chlorodine and liquorice were added, bringing the mixture up to the 8 ounce mark. When the mixture was suitably prepared it was transferred subsequently into an 8 ounce bottle.

There was a humorous story once told about a dispensary doctor who, when confronted with a surgery full of people with coughs and colds, appeared out in the waiting room quite suddenly and dramatically, clutching two of the 80 ounce Winchester bottles. As his somewhat startled audience looked on he declared as follows "Those with coughs and spits take it out of this bottle but those with coughs and no spits take it out of this other bottle." One bottle was a cough suppressant and the other was a cough expectorant, designed to make them cough up the phlegm.

I also dispensed iron tablets, vitamins and antibiotics. I had responsibility for deciding on the quantity and the dose. I always had to be absolutely sure of my doses to protect against overdose. It may seem strange today but I can recall using strychnine in a stomach mixture to give the patient an appetite and also using arsenic in an iron mixture to give the patient a tonic.

The most common ailments of the day were colds, influenza, bronchitis and high temperatures. Diphtheria, a throat disease that affected children, was also common enough. I always sent these children straight to hospital because diphtheria can be fatal if not treated in time. I did experience many cases of tuberculosis and meningitis but thankfully I never misdiagnosed and was always able to get the child into Galway Hospital by ambulance in time. I was often called out to treat children who were experiencing asthma attacks. These occasions were always very stressful because it was impossible to predict what way the child would go. I usually gave the child an injection and got them into Galway Hospital by ambulance without delay. Nowadays most GPs have the use of nebulizers which are a source of great comfort to the patient. There were occasions when patients were brought to me in an unconscious state as a result of a road traffic accident. Thankfully in all of these cases I was able to transfer the patient to hospital with the help of the ambulance service which was based in Clifden.

A large percentage of my patients over the years suffered from stress, neurosis or depression. It was very hard to diagnose depression at times and there were no drugs to treat depression during the 40s and 50s. Barbiturates were the only tranquillisers available. Anti-depressants did not come on the scene until the 1960s. I often gave patients suffering from depression a tonic to bring home. There is no scientific basis for giving a person a tonic but my policy was never to tell the patients that they did not need something. I always gave them something to please them and send them home happy. There was no use telling them that there was nothing wrong with them since they would only go to some other general practitioner to get satisfaction.

The Home Assistants Officer worked for the County Council. His main function was to issue the red ticket or the black ticket to patients on my list. These tickets were only issued to people who were deemed by the Home Assistants Officer to be ill and in need of free medical treatment. The black ticket was for a surgery visit and the red ticket was for a home visit. Whenever a patient showed me either of these tickets it meant there was no charge. As soon as I had fulfilled my obligation to the patient the ticket then became obsolete and the next time the patient fell into bad health, he or she had to return to the Home Assistants Officer in order to be issued with a new ticket. The introduction of the medical card in the 1970s put an end to the red and black tickets.

In 1973 the then Minister for Health, Erskine Childers, was to significantly improve the status of dispensary doctors like myself when he introduced the 'fee-per-item-of-service' system. I still received a set wage but henceforth I also received additional payment for every item of service I gave. I was obliged to record all items of service and send in a monthly return. The fee per item service was too substantially improve my income during the 1970s. By 1973 I was running a very busy practice. I had 1300 medical card patients and 700 private patients. I employed Loretta Lydon as my first ever secretary. She stayed with me until 1977 when Ann Guy took over the position. When Ann moved on in 1979 she was succeeded by Teresa Bradley who remained with me until I retired in 1983. These three women looked after a lot of clerical and administrative work for me, which afforded me more time to concentrate on medical matters. All three were very professional in their approach and had the kind of manner and personality required to deal favourably with all the different types of patients who were on my list. The fee-per-item-of-service system has since been abolished and nowadays the general practitioner's payment is based on the capitation rate, i.e. the number of medical card patients on his or her list. It is a system which is more financially rewarding to the modern doctor and one which I was never able to avail of because I had already retired by the time it was introduced.

As with any profession there are always occupational hazards, which one has to put up with. In my case it was having to attend the District Court in Letterfrack. My position was compromised by having to give evidence against patients on my list for being drunk or involved in assault. I never relished this particular aspect of my work and still fondly remember one particular episode back in 1946 when a trip to the courthouse was avoided to the mutual benefit of almost everyone in the story.

In 1946 Dermot Gogarty was manager of Renvyle House Hotel. One of his guests that year was Lady Patricia Aherne. While out walking in Gurteen one day she came on a local man who was beating his donkey in an effort to get the donkey to be more productive. Shocked at what she was witnessing and unable to control her anger, Lady Patricia proceeded to inflict some degree of damage on the local man. He beat a hasty retreat home complaining of a mark behind his ear. His father duly put him to bed and sent for me. He knew that Lady Patricia Aherne was a wealthy woman and he was hoping to avail of my services to secure a successful legal action. In the meantime Garda Keating had been sent back to Renvyle House Hotel to take Patricia Aherne into custody for assault. He did not succeed in his mission however. The following morning Sergeant Connolly contacted me and asked me to interview and examine Lady Patricia Aherne at the hotel. I duly obliged and later that day I wrote out a medical certificate at Connolly's behest stating that Lady Patricia Aherne was unfit to make a statement on account of her pregnant condition. This certificate was right into Connolly's barrow because he had been got at by Dermot Gogarty to get around the case and get Lady Patricia Aherne out of her difficulty. With a little help from me he succeeded in doing this and was probably guest-of-honour later that evening. As for the poor man who had been assaulted, I am sure he probably made a remarkable recovery upon realising that all hopes of financial compensation had evaporated.

Patience, energy and knowledge are probably the three most necessary attributes required in a doctor. As dispensary doctors we were always subject to public criticism because of the very public nature of the service we provided. As the Chinese say, "If one is liked by everybody then enquiry is necessary and if one is disliked by everybody then enquiry is also necessary."

I served as a dispensary doctor for the Renvyle area for thirty-seven years and during that time I enjoyed a very good quality of life. I was privileged to work among a community of people who afforded me great respect as a professional and always made me feel that I was a very valued and very liked member of society. After I retired, I greatly missed the social contact with humanity and the buzz of being busy but I eventually warmed to the idea of retirement and I am very happy to be out of the medical business as the millennium approaches. People are far more demanding nowadays; they expect a lot from their local GP and a lot of this expectation in my view is quite unrealistic. The general public today is far more educated than it would have been in 1938 when I embarked on my medical journey and consequently they are far more perceptive, discerning and critical. Society is becoming more litigation happy and this is a very disturbing development for the medical profession.

Alternative medicine is becoming more and more popular and many GPs are now combining alternative medicine with orthodox medicine to satisfy public demand. Personally I think alternative medicine is designed for gullible people and I do not believe there is any credible basis for it. However, I do accept that people are entitled to shop around in their efforts to discover something to give them extra cause for optimism and I know there are many people out there who swear by alternative medicine.

I do not think there was any vocational compulsion on my part to become a doctor, yet once I really got into it I never considered any other career. Nowadays it is very common and very socially acceptable for people to change their career but in my day such practice would have been considered unusual. Once one entered a profession, one stuck to it and that was that. There was no more about it.

I derived greatest satisfaction as a doctor from getting people out of distress. Over the years it would be fair to say that many of the people who came to the surgery were not altogether too sick and that many more came with minor sicknesses which oft-times could cure themselves. Having said that, there are people who have told me that I was directly responsible for saving many lives down through the years. In the case of heart attacks, haemorrhages, ruptured varicose veins and arterial bleeding, these people may have a point and it is very kind of them to be so complimentary to me after all my years of service. There were patients who died under my care. I was probably not at fault for the majority of these deaths but always felt responsible nonetheless. The deaths of infants due to pneumonia or respiratory infection were particularly harrowing and always caused me to feel great pain and distress.

During my years in practice I did attend various medical seminars in Dublin and I also took courses from time to time. During these courses we would usually go around all the hospitals in Dublin and I always felt a great sense of renewal on such visits. It was great to meet up with other doctors to share ideas and exchange philosophies, but if the truth be known I did not mind the glorious isolation of West Connemara. I never missed associating with my colleagues on a more regular basis, maybe because I never considered it attractive to be associated exclusively with my own profession. I suppose I was always a bit cynical in my belief that doctors were never too enamoured of each other anyway.

In conclusion I would just like to add that I do reflect from time to time on what my life might have been like had I elected to travel the world and work in foreign lands with people of different nationalities. I think Africa would have had the greatest appeal for me because of its mystery, beauty and diversity. However it was not to be and I have no regrets. In any case, it is probably fair to say that medical practice and human nature are basically the same wherever one goes.

Remembered by Dr Albert Flynn and written by Paul Gannon

Into the Light

Many years before rural electrification arrived in Clifden, its townspeople were light years ahead, so to speak, thanks to the innovative genius of one of its most famous sons. Eddie King was a character, a very intelligent man, much loved by his clientele in the public house he ran in Clifden. The same public house still proudly bears his name over the door to this day. Back in the early 1920s it was a pub of some renown, a place where professional people and intellectuals liked to be seen. It was well known that Eddie kept a diary behind the counter. He had a habit of recording interesting ideas and items of information, which he often picked up by listening to his customers. On one occasion he overheard two engineers from the Marconi Station talking about the possibility of lighting up the town of Clifden. One engineer explained to the other that all that was required was a powerhouse near the waterfall fitted with a turbine. Eddie listened intently to the ensuing conversation and recorded the necessary information into the diary. Shortly after the burning of the Marconi Station in 1921, Eddie called an open meeting in the town to discuss the possibility of electrifying the town. The meeting drew a very positive response from all present and Eddie got the go-ahead from the people.

The first task was to erect a powerhouse at the waterfall overlooking the river. When this was eventually built, a canal was constructed diagonally across the road to facilitate the production of power using a turbine. The canal was one metre deep and half a metre wide. Eddie then decided to build dams with sluices on them to ensure a steady supply of water during a run of hot weather. The Owenglin River was selected for this purpose. Horses pulled galvanised sheets with bags of cement on them up the mountain. There was plenty of sand and gravel upriver to mix with the cement in the construction of the dams and sluice gates. Eddie employed a small army of men to carry out this work. He imported the turbines from England. The poles were erected with pick and shovel. All the poles were wired from the powerhouse. The people of the town had to wire their own homes and shops at their own expense. Eddie then fitted meter boxes in every house. He collected the money from the meter boxes himself. Eddie

Thomas O'Sullivan at the Powerhouse as it stands today.

supplied the town of Clifden with electric light from 1923 to 1953. When the ESB arrived they compensated Eddie for taking out his service. The ESB supplied Clifden with 3-phase power. They had no powerhouse. They first sourced their supply from the back rooms of the town hall.

Under the influence of Mr W. F. Row, the first engineer in charge of rural electrification and his successor Mr P. J. Dowling work began in 1946. The first pole in the rural electrification scheme was erected at Kilsallaghan in North Co Dublin on November 5th 1946. The first switch-on at a rural area took place the following January nearby in the village of Oldtown.

Every county was divided into rural areas of about 25 square miles (typically based on parish boundaries) and initially, one area in each county was chosen for connection. For example, Bansha was the first rural area in Co Tipperary to receive supply.

The first task was to set up a rural electrification office and to canvass households in the area to sign up for electricity supply. Many were enthusiastic but many were sceptical or fearful. The active support of organisations such as the ICA, Muintir na Tíre and local clergy was crucial in securing sufficient numbers to sign up and to make each area viable for the ESB.

As each area was canvassed the line crews moved in, surveying and pegging out the routes for the main lines, erecting poles.

Rural electrification had been envisaged in the original Shannon scheme, which was completed in 1929. This was built to supply the whole country. In the view of Dr Tom McLaughlin, the first Managing Director of the ESB, and initiator of the Shannon Scheme, rural electrification was seen as the application of modern science and engineering to raise the standard of rural living and to get to the root of the social evil of the flight from the land.

However, the financial resources were not available in the 1930s to plan for the early electrification of rural areas; electricity from the Shannon Scheme was supplied to towns and cities only.

In the late 1930s and 1940s the ESB and the Government drew up broad plans for rural electrification and the State agreed to subsidise it. However the continuation of the Second World War meant that no work could proceed until the end of the war.

At the same time people had to have their houses, farms and shops wired. As the project developed and people in newly connected areas spread the news about the changes that electricity brought, most resistance to getting electricity faded. The demand grew for connections and the pace of connections increased to a peak in the late 1950s.

The scale of the undertaking was enormous. It involved the erection of over 1 million poles. 75,000 miles of wire (enough to circle the world three times) and over 100,000 transformers, without the benefits of the mechanisation which we take for granted today. Sourcing of materials in the immediate post war years was a daunting task. The initial programme was substantially completed by 1962 with 282,000 houses connected. By 1976 the bulk of the work was completed with 420,000 houses connected, at a cost of £80m (£53m from the ESB and £27m from the state). The few remaining pockets were completed by 1978.

Written by Thomas O'Sullivan

Characters

When I was brought up in Clifden in the '30s and '40s it was a far cry from being a Mecca for money-spending tourists. In the 30s the inhabitants were just getting their lives together after the burning of Clifden by the Black and Tans and the aftermath of the Civil War. The '40s were no better as we tried to cope with the Emergency, rations and unemployment during World War II. Food and clothing were rationed but so, also, was money. There was not the cash flow in Clifden then as there is today. Money is not everything.

I believe that the greatest things in life are free, and we youngsters really enjoyed the freedom of Clifden and all that it had to offer to penniless kids. It was a great little town in which to spend one's childhood. I suppose I could describe it as an insular town – a place where everybody knew everyone else and suspected the stranger.

Today, parents are very concerned for the safety of their children and rightly so. Our parents had no fear for our safety. It was a great place to live and bring up a family. We roamed the streets, played on the beach, climbed the mountains, swam in the sea, walked and cycled the roads and the by-roads, and formed friendships that lasted for life.

The big event of the day was the arrival of the big red railway bus from Galway driven by Martin McEvady with his conductor Gabriel Burke. We met every bus, counted how many alighted, watched where they went, found out their business in the town and watched to see who hired Festy King's, Marty Mannion's or John Payne's car. People who came home on holidays were welcomed, strangers were eyed with suspicion and the great news of the day was the arrival of the school inspector. We went straight to the Convent, told the nuns and informed every teacher in the town that 'the Cigre' was on the bus. Everyone was in time for school the next day and all books and copies were in order. We sat up that night, revised all our spelling, tables and poetry. 'The Cigre' had no privacy of movement due to the petrol shortage during the war. Public transport was the order of the day.

Clifden in those days was full of characters – those unique Irish personalities who bring colour, humour and wit to every little town and village in Ireland. Clifden had a good quota of them. There was Pat Meledy, the butcher in Main Street known as 'Pat Ma' – the 'Ma' came from the sound of his sheep. My father died when I was only fourteen months, so 'Pat Ma' was the daddy-figure in my life. Pat wore an old tattered cap, a greasy waistcoat, and trousers that had seen better days. He had a fund of stories. He taught me how to play *Twenty-Five*, *Workhouse*, *Snap* and *Old Maid*. He cooked lambs' tails for me on his open fire. He bought bags of bulls' eyes for me, and fed me with porridge from his tin-plate. Pat was an old-age pensioner which entitled him to ten shillings every week. Every Friday he took me by the hand and brought me to the post office to collect his pension. The local assistant, Martha Ladley, handed Pat nine shillings and eleven pence and gave me a bright new penny. That made up the modest sum of ten shillings. Friday was our big day – Pat got his pension and I got mine. Every month he went on the train to a fair in Galway. He always brought me back a stick of Galway Rock. This was a pink sugar stick with Galway written all through it.

Pat Ma was my guardian, my hero and my friend. I remember when they laid him to rest. I was about ten years old then. P. K. Joyce brought me in Payne's car to Teamplandearg graveyard to see the last of Pat Ma. I cried for days after his burial.

Next door to Pat lived Mike Flaherty, known as 'Spick', because of the time he spent working in the workhouse. Spick had a little sweet shop. He sold us toffees covered with chocolates called 'Nobbies'. When we placed our order for a penny's worth of sweets he would always remark 'Sure yis nobbies'. He told us stories about his time in America and his adventures at the building of Brooklyn Bridge. He used to sit outside his shop door playing the flute. His favourite tunes were '*The Blackbird*' and '*The Stack of Barley*'.

A few doors down from Spick lived 'Auld King'. He had a long white beard and we kids were terrified of him. He was known locally as 'Coney Island', because of the many years he spent in America. Not many doors from him lived an old lady who also put the fear of God in us. She always dressed in black and used to threaten us with her stick. We called her 'Maggie Mick'. We used to shout in the door at her:

'Maggie Mick, Mick, Mick,
With your stick, stick, stick,
We're not afraid of you,
Or your dirty black shoe.

Another favourite haunt in Main Street was John William Lacey's shop. There we bought a supply of stink bombs and set them off in Sister Peter's class in the national school. All the perfumes of Arabia would not sweeten that classroom after our explosion of stink bombs. My Uncle Pat, known as 'The Flogger' was very fond of children. Half of the kids of the town gathered around his shop fire as he told story after story to us. We roasted sausages and bacon on the open fire in the bar. Every Sunday we trailed after him, burning furze bushes, picking cockles and mussels, roasting eggs on an open fire, counting cattle and many other things. Every Sunday during the summer he brought us on some mystery tour in the pony and trap. Ballinaleame, the home of his brother-in-law, John Edward Coneys, was always the favourite spot. The first stop was in Derrygimla where we got bags of sweets in Annie Cottingham's. Then we got lemonade and Kerry Cream biscuits in Tommie O'Flaherty's in Ballyconneely. I have very happy memories of my Uncle Pat.

Another favourite character of my childhood was Peter Downey. Peter had a big dray horse and a float. He delivered goods from the Railway Station to all the business people around the town. We all got our turns having a spin on the float. We waited until all the goods were delivered. Then we crowded into the empty float and got a spin around the town and back to the Railway Station. Peter was high on the list of our favourite people.

Another man we always teased and annoyed was Pat O'Connor. He did not give us sweets so he was condemned immediately. We shouted in his door at regular intervals:

'Pateen Skinner, Pateen Skinner,
Skin a flea for a halfpenny'.

We bought sweets from his neighbour Miss Bourke. Then we would rob the roses from her garden and bring them up to the nuns for the altar. From Miss Bourke's garden we crossed into Willie Lavelle's and stole the apples from his apple trees.

Another great character in Clifden was Johnnie Jennings. Johnnie was the local handyman. He seemed to be an authority on everything. He could paint houses, clean eave runs, replace slates after a storm. Johnnie seemed to be able to do everything. In my home he was even the family barber. On a Saturday night we lined up in the kitchen as Johnnie cut our hair. Newspaper was tucked inside our clothes as he cut away with a big sharp scissors. He, too, had a fund of stories, tricks and riddles. He performed all kinds of magic for us. Many a time he sent me around the town looking for the loan of the round square or the glass hammer.

Other characters that come to mind are Victor McDowell who walked on his heels and delivered papers for Bernard Ludden. Then there was Pep, Danny Hawkins, Mickileen the Weaver, Hector McDonagh who used to weigh us at the crane on the Square, Sweetie Lydon who sold us rainbow sweets at ten-a-penny, her brother, 'Twopence', the blacksmith and many more. All those colourful characters who brought so much happiness are gone to their final resting place.

Remembered and written by Phyl Clancy

DEAR OLD CLIFDEN TOWN

By day and night, though far away,
Fond memories come to me,
Of hillside green and vales serene
Of Erin o'er the sea.
There's not a place on all the face
Of Ireland's holy ground,
That I adore or think of more,
Than Dear Old Clifden Town.

I love that sweet old village street,
I know each dwelling there,
I clearly see in front of me
That little Market Square,
Where dealers they would meet each day
The monthly fair comes 'round
And there was fun for old and young
In Dear Old Clifden Town.

Each old time scene of peace serene,
I fondly now recall,
Though far away in dreams today,
I clearly see them all,
Some people love to tell you of
Great cities of renown,
But as for me just let me see,
My Dear Old Clifden Town.

And let me view, each one I knew,
Along the Cleggan side,
By Letterdeen and Clifden's Green,
My heart would ever bide.
There is not a spot that I have not,
In boyhood wandered round,
With friends of yore I'll meet no more,
In Dear Old Clifden Town.

I courted there a colleen fair,
With cheeks of rose's hue,
I'll never forget the day we met
Beneath the skies of blue,
But death's foul blow soon laid her
Beneath your silent mound,
Which made me stray far, far away
From Dear Old Clifden Town.

But still I'll pray for her each day
My blooming Irish Rose,
And turn to thee 'Sweet Grá Mo Chro'
In all my trails and woes,
And never again to roam I will
My Irish hillside brown,
My spirit will be with you still
My Dear Old Clifden Town.

Author Unknown
Given to me by Martin Conroy

I REMEMBER

I remember George Green, in black shiny suit and walking stick,
And Terry Foley, in an orange suit you could never call chic.
I remember Jerome McWilliams, reversing his lorry up Church Hill –
When he tried to drive up the normal way, it came to a standstill

I remember old Doctor Casey with his high hat on his head,
Revered by some he visited, to others, he brought a sense of dread.
I remember Harry Sullivan in his red convertible car
As he motored along Main Street, he beamed like a Hollywood star.

I remember Henry Canavan, repairing cars for Eddie King –
The antics of the old millionaire, and the havoc he would bring.
I remember old Jack Casey, and wonderful smells from his shop –
Tea chests, spices, dried fruit and the aroma of every drop.

I remember Owen Stankard's as the place for us to meet,
The place where we would gather, to give ourselves a treat.
I remember all the times, when we walked around the town
Aimlessly, endlessly talking, and sometimes acting the clown.

I remember Mrs Cullen and the wonderful things she could bake;
Taste buds leaped and danced as we ate the things she would make.
I remember May King and her long blond shining hair;
I remember Pappy Mannions where we bought things to wear.

I remember Francie Faherty licking his fingers to test the wires
When he ran Clifden Powerhouse, part of Eddie King's old empire.
I remember Jim King who drove the old Council lorry;
I remember Pat Joyce, who ran the Green Marble Quarry.

I remember John King in the Dole office at the end of town,
And Val King who lived opposite, a carpenter of some renown;
I remember Kevin Stanley, and the cows they milked every day;
I remember Percy also and his shop with its wonderful array.

I remember Crook, when he lived down in Market Street;
And his chequered roll of lino, where we tossed 'a penny a treat';
I remember Miss Lowery and her drapery shop;
I remember the post office where the buses used to stop.
I remember Guard Lonnergan and Sergeant Cassidy too,

And Charley the Kerryman, I can't remember his surname, can you?
I remember the FCA, and Jack Joyce's Hotel;
I remember how they used to train the soldiers there as well.

I remember Miss Durkin's kindness, when we were young;
I remember Miss Burke, and the flaming of the tongue.
I remember Claire King who lived down by the ball alley;
And further up by the old Church hall, I remember dear Miss Ladley.

I remember the Kerrigans, excellent tailors in their day,
And I remember the joiner, who lived across the way.
I remember John Mannion, our local TD,
He could sell you a bike, bury you and give advice for free.

I remember Pake Flaherty, who served as the court clerk;
I remember Guard Fox, who would wait for us in the dark.
I remember Tuppence the Blacksmith,
We passed his forge from school every day;
How his hammer rang on the anvil twice
As he produced that blacksmith's rhythm, in his inimitable way.

I remember Dr Willie who lived near Seaview,
And Doatie Lynch and John Joe, lived near there too;
Flannan Egan lived down by the quay;
Close by, cottages for lighthouse keepers home from the sea.

I remember Peter Carbery and his big American car,
His hackney carriage used to travel near and far;
And Mick Flanagan with his bakery and hire car as well –
A gentleman from Clifden, as those who knew will tell.

I remember Anthony Curran with his big old-fashioned horn,
Announcing all the latest happenings, and now and again to warn.
I remember Tommy Mullin and his barrels of salted fish;
He sold hardware and metal baths, and any kind of dish.

I remember Canon Cunningham and the nervous Father Ryan,
The stern Chancellor Corcoran, feared by all us kids at that time.
I remember Joe Packie, his bike shop, and Fox's mints at the dance –
One of Clifden's real characters, who always missed out on romance.

I remember Mike Mannings' garage and the Arch bar;
He would sell you a pram or a record, a drink, push bike or car,
A bottle of gas, a cooker, diesel, any petrol name the star,
Motorbike, van, lorry you name it, it was sold from the Arch Bar.

I remember the pictures, and Johnny Glynn
Trying to find fourpence, to get in,
Where Father Ryan used to intervene
When he saw romantic clinches coming on the screen.

He and Charley, combed the road to the beach
Searching for lovers they could not reach,
Trying to stop young folks sitting close to one another –
The fun couples had then, looking out for each other.

I remember the dump at Polladulla,
Sloping steeply down to the sea –
An eyesore when you travelled the Ballyconneely road,
Creating flotsam and jetsam where none should be.

I remember Paynes' pub and their Studebaker car,
And Festy King's small smoke-filled bar;
I remember the fire engine in Pat Skinner's store –
The tyres always flat had to be pumped before
They could attend a fire with urgency once more.

I remember a fire down in Peelers Row –
The engine would not start as the fire began to glow,
So they pumped the tyres and pushed it down
To the blazing fire, at the end of town.

By this time they'd received, a small pull start petrol pump,
So they dragged it to the fire and it started with a jump;
They connected the canvas hoses; water shot out of the spout.
Now they shouted, they'll put the blazing fire out!

Unfortunately no one inspected the canvas hoses for decay,
And the pinholes leaking water had got worse every day.
Then the canvas hose exploded with a real mighty slosh;
The onlookers got soaked in the ensuing backwash!

Pandemonium as they searched for a hose that did not leak,
The crowd standing speechless as the flames played hide and seek;
Then from the side of the tender, they pulled another hose,
And they screwed it on the pump by its heavy brass nose.

Up went a cheer as the water flowed free,
And they clapped their hands immediately.
The fire by now was failing fast,
And the water hopped and sizzled as it hit with a blast;
In the end they killed the fire, and saved the day,
And the crowd cheered again as they happily went on their way.

I remember Walter Donaldson's barber shop
Where we used to hate it when we were given the crop;
I remember George K. Ryan's first Morris Minor car
And McInerney's pub, with pieces of bacon hanging over the bar.

I remember Peter Downey with his shire horse and float;
I remember the old brig and Val King rebuilding his boat.
I remember Jer Sullivan and Mr Wilson too;
I remember Whales' house, and the swimming pool with water so blue.

I remember John R. Fox, who seemed to know everything;
Paddy Joe driving for Mannions, and the songs he used to sing.
I remember Mickleen Connelly who would say things he didn't mean;
And I remember the animal pound, down on the green.

I remember Packy Sweeney and his old Thames Trader van –
Loads of things, stacked on top from a chair to bags of bran.
I remember Martin McEvady driving the Clifden bus;
I remember Paddy Fury collecting tickets without any fuss.

I remember Maura McCarthy, on her stilettos climbing Church Hill,
And all the lads checking her out, just for the thrill.
I remember Marteen Mattie and Kelly the Showmaker too,
And I remember Lawn the postman and the things he used to do.

I remember Fear na Faithe and Willie Lavelle;
I can also remember bunter fishing with the Jeffries as well;
I remember the Ivy Hotel down by the waterfall,
And I remember Mrs Tierney as the nurse who used to call.

I remember Lena O'Halloran who owned the corner shop,
And I remember Paddy Bawn, who used to have a room on top.
I remember Maggie Ungie who had a shop in the town;
I remember Stephen Hehir who had a shop further down.

I remember Katie Aspell's, and the pipe where we used to drink;
I remember when it used to freeze, the road became a skating rink.
I remember Michael John Coyne ringing the church bell;
I remember PK in dark hat and coat, and taking snuff as well.

I remember James B the solicitor,
And the joiner who lived in Hulk Street.
I remember some kids at the national school,
Who came to school in bare feet.

I remember Danny Hawkins,
Whose trousers hung a long way from his shoes;
I remember Rene King writing the Connemara news.

I remember the Mulkerrins who lived out at Faul,
And I remember great dances at Clifden Town Hall.
I remember Josie and Kathleen, 'Come on Joe, she would cry'
As they walked out the Ballyconneely Road;
poor old Joe always followed with a sigh.

I remember Toby Joyce who always had sheep in his car,
And I remember the bookie office opposite the Arch Bar.
I remember Mrs PK who sold religious articles in her shop;
I remember Julia Curley who did the Clifden to Cleggan mail drop –
Her car was really ancient, with a carrier at the rear;
It had wooden spokes and a bulbous horn,
And she sometimes carried a fare.

I remember Matt Ryan, the nicest Postmaster the town has ever had;
I remember the great man's passing, and whole town being so sad.
I remember Dick Joyce and the wonderful Mrs Dick;
I remember Marty Conneely in London and Clifden,
And I still laugh today at all his wonderful tricks.

I remember Halloween nights, putting carbide in Alkaseltzer tins,
We would spit into the carbide,
And watch it blow the lid into smithereens.

I remember Lydon O'Neill's, delicious smells surrounding us there;
I remember Tommy Walshe's bakery and that wonderful aroma so rare.
I remember Tommy Mannion's pub and butcher shop;
I remember Bernie Lee singing at the top.

I remember McGinty's the contractors,
Coming to town to install new sewer pipes –
Oh, the havoc, and the chaos they caused, we had never seen the likes!
They all seemed to drive American cars –
Old wrecks if the truth be said –
Some were bought by local people
And ended up as chicken sheds.

I remember Paddy Festy's big Buick American car;
I remember Gerald Bartley, driving McEvaddy's Hillman Minx like a star;
I remember Dr Irwin in his Morris Minor car,
In plus fours and tweed jacket, this gentleman had travelled far.

I remember Brother Urban,
And our altar boys' excursion to Limerick –
We had never been so far from home,
And most of us were travel sick.

I remember Clancy's shop and bar,
Where you could buy your shopping and have a jar,
And the room where Mr Milne the dentist pulled our teeth
While we were stuck to the wicker chair he used for a seat.

I remember Slates and his old army coat,
And John Ryan selling the shop and buying a boat.
I remember Monto the bailiff chasing the lads off the mug!
And those that he caught Guard Fox gave a tug.

I remember Josie Guilfoyle,
A big man in every way –
He cooked for the Queen of Tonga
Folks used to say!

I remember Happy Mulkerrins,
And Mrs Emerson at the Livy Hotel;
Cindy that worked at Mikie Mannings,
Who could not speak English very well.

I remember Mrs Heanue warming her rear by the fire at school;
I remember the mirth as she tilted her skirt
And showed that long knickers could be really cool.

I remember Johnny 'O' and his mannerisms,
And the funny things he used say;
I remember Mickel the weaver,
Working down at the mill every day.

I remember Bernard Ludden always being busy –
He used to trot, never walk, every day;
He would serve his wonderful ice cream or a pint of beer,
Then talk about everything, while you waited to pay

I remember the whale, at the Wire Bridge,
Beaching itself on high ground,
And people coming to see this huge mammal
From miles and miles around.

I remember Paddy Foyle preferring girls at school,
And Eddie being the macho man playing Mr Cool;
Billy of course played with everyone,
And broke every rule.

I remember uncle Mikie at Dick's corner,
Chatting to Marty and Rory Lavelle,
Where often a big crowd would gather
To join in the chat as well.

I have so many precious memories of all the wonderful people I knew in Clifden while I was growing up and through my school years. I will never ever forget all those great characters who lived there and who will remain with me forever . . .

Written by Michael Flaherty

Fact, Fiction or Legend?

"Who are ye tellin'? Don't I know it, didn't I work there?" Lines uttered several times by the Dane. Clifden with its own Dane. By name, yes; by nationality, no – for he was as Irish as they come.

The story he referred to happened, around the turn of the century. I was present one evening, when he was in full flight. Being of an early age it became imprinted on my memory and I can recall that evening long ago as if it were yesterday. Most local elders and historians will remember or have heard of Duffy's Hotel or Kelly's Hotel. I don't know in what order it should be read. This majestic building stood on the site of the Clifden Community School. In fact it was used for a time as a secondary school before it fell into disrepair. Had the present laws regarding the protection of old, interesting buildings existed when it was decided to build a new school, this building could well be standing now, perhaps returned to its former splendour.

If you have stayed with me this far, and you fall into the category of an elder or an historian, and if I have jogged your memory, then you will recall that this building was haunted. According to the Dane, a young woman from well back the road worked in the hotel. Apparently the young woman, to quote the Dane, was interfered with. What he meant was, she was badly beaten and raped, beaten to the extent that her blood was spattered on the walls. That day the young woman was taken home where she was treated but she died some three months later as a result of her injuries.

There was no police inquiry into the case as the perpetrator was well-connected and, indeed, well known to the RIC, who were responsible for law and order then. However, justice appears to have been done to this man who, it seems, was a frequent visitor to the hotel, if you could call three visits a year frequent. Apparently unable to live with his conscience, he took his own life in the Salt Lake across the road in front of the hotel.

The room in which the deed was carried out was, from that day forth, locked up. It was said that the woman's blood stains could not be removed from the walls no matter how much washing or painting over was done.

For many years after this incident this bedroom door would burst open, as would the front door of the hotel, and a figure would be seen walking down the lawn, across the road and disappearing into the lake. This happened on the 28th day of February each year.

Written by Tom Feneran

A Strange Encounter

Let me take you back to a lovely spring evening about forty years ago. I was sitting on a rock beside Lough Sollagh which is situated just a few hundred yards below what is now the Alcock and Brown Memorial which stands on Errislannan hill overlooking Mannin Bay and the Marconi bog.

My reason for being on this rock was simply to keep an eye on one cow and a donkey. In those days, when water was scarce, it was the custom to drive the animals to the nearest lake for a drink and after wards they would graze along the lakeshore where the grass was always green and sweet – or so they say anyhow.

As I sat there looking out over Mannin bay and Slyne Head lighthouse in the distance, I noticed high above a very bright object in the sky. At first it looked like a pear-shaped balloon. Then, as it came closer over the coral beach at Errislannan, it started to hover in midair and a very bright telescopic pipe-like instrument shot down from the bottom of it.

I had never seen anything like it before. There was no noise coming from it, which I thought very strange. It did not look like a plane. "What could it be?" I thought to myself.

There was talk of flying saucers in those days but this strange object did not look like any of the saucers we had at home and I could not imagine those things flying anyway. This was huge and so bright that I froze with fear. Should I hide behind a rock or should I run home? Perhaps they would see me and follow me or take me away.

Then I saw it speed up and begin to head my way. It was going so fast that I thought it could not stop, but there it was right over the lake, yards from where I sat. It started to hover at about a hundred feet above my head and it sent out a beam of very bright light which blinded me. I tried to get up and run but could not see, and I seemed to be transfixed to the rock. My face and body felt very warm but I was more relaxed now. Then I felt this cold breeze all over me. I opened my eyes and I could see that the animals were still grazing, but the craft was still hovering above the lake and this silver pipe was coming down from above into the water. I did not feel afraid now and went on to watch what they would do.

I seemed to know in advance what was going to happen next. I looked at the animals; they were still grazing at the water's edge, not taking any notice. Suddenly a beam of light shot down from the craft towards the donkey and his head seemed to glow with a halo of light, though I could still see the rest of him. The light was only around his head and he seemed very still. After about thirty seconds it moved towards the cow's head, which again was not visible to me but the rest of her I could see. It then disappeared back into the craft. Both animals shook themselves and resumed grazing.

I could make out three or four peculiar-looking occupants of the craft. They looked like apes or gorillas, had short tails and all wore blue and green helmets and were about three feet tall.

The craft itself consisted of a large, dome-shaped capsule which appeared transparent at times as the different-coloured lights flashed on and off. It was now about a hundred feet above the lake's surface, moving very slowly with a very faint humming sound. Then suddenly a ball of light shot straight up out of the craft with great speed; they were waving at me and I waved back. Then the craft seemed to be beamed up rapidly towards the ball of light, which at this stage was very high in the sky. The two seemed to join up in a matter of seconds and disappeared into space. I then felt the donkey nudging me off the rock. They must have sent me to sleep to forget the whole thing. It was almost dark now and past time to go home.

Written by Marty Conneely

Pisreogs

When I was a child growing up in the 1920s, pisreogs were a fact of life. There were certain places where the children were not allowed to go in case the fairies would take them. If a woman had to go outside and leave a baby alone, the iron tongs were placed across the cradle to protect the baby from the fairies. If a child who seemed normal and thriving in its first few months of life became irritable and stopped developing in the normally expected manner, it was said that the fairies had taken the baby and left a changeling in its place. Often the same child did not survive more than one or two years and if it did it was retarded.

May morning was a day on which some women were reputed to go out early to take the first water from the spring well and three straws from the roof. By so doing they were supposed to take the butter from their neighbours. Another belief was that if a visitor came to the house while churning was in progress and left without putting a hand to the dash then he or she would take the butter.

On May morning also nobody wanted to be first to rise and because of this the morning cup of tea was often forsaken, as the turf fire was the only means of boiling water.

When finishing milking it was the custom to dip the thumb in the froth of the milk and make the sign of the cross on the cows thigh.

Fishermen generally were very superstitious. When going out to fish it was considered unlucky to meet a woman. Indeed, a red haired woman spelled disaster. I knew a man who often turned and missed his day's fishing because a red-haired woman from the village crossed his path.

There were certain places believed to be the path of the fairies where no one would build a hen house, much less a dwelling house.

Remembered and written by Kate Conneely

An Breo Bheag

Cursing stones were once a feature of some Connemara localities. Many people in the Renvyle area still remember two of the most popular or unpopular, as the case may be. An Breo Bheag was the name given to the Gurteen stone. It was, and still is, accepted in some quarters that if An Breo Bheag was turned three times in the name of the devil, a storm would follow. Two such storms are still often talked about; one is said to have occurred during a wedding on an island off Renvyle. Some people who were annoyed at not being invited to the wedding decided to get revenge by turning An Breo Bheag. The stone was duly turned and the storm which resulted marooned the guests on the island for the best part of a week.

A second occasion was when the Renvyle Stars football team crossed to Tullabawn to play Louisburg. Once again An Breo Bheag was used in Gurteen by somebody who had been omitted from the party and the team had a most uncomfortable journey back. The names of some members of the team who travelled to Tullabawn on that day in 1918 are given below.

It is said that the local priest persuaded the Ardnagreevagh people to bury their stone, while the Gurteen stone is placed in a less dangerous location. These stones were usually 'quern stones'. Querns were used long ago for grinding corn and many of them were to be found throughout the parish. The Irish word for a quern stone is 'breo' and by a strange coincidence 'breo' also has a second meaning. Yes, you've guessed it...storm! Could there be something in it?

RENVYLE STARS 1918

Phil Kane (Captain) Pat Faherty, Willie Hyland, Petie Sammon, Pappy Heanue, Michael L. Conneely, Tommie Kane, Tommie Faherty, Frank Kane, Peter Conneely, Eddie Diamond, Johnnie Walsh, Austin O'Malley and a Canavan.

Up the Killary

It was a pleasant summer's evening when the party of four arrived back in Rossroe harbour after their trip to Louisburg. The two women had gone down to visit Killageever Holy Well while the men were lobster fishing nearby. After they came ashore the women went to the house to make tea while the men carried on down to a sheltered inlet with their lobsters. They had storage pots in the inlet where they would leave the lobsters safe overnight.

Festy Mortimer

It was while they were attending to their work that they discovered all the herring. The biggest shoal they had ever seen had travelled all the way in to their little cove. They knew their luck was in and that they had stumbled on something very big.

Later that evening they bade farewell to the two women without telling them anything about their discovery. They were fearful that if they did, the women would spread the news and then all the local fishermen would be looking to share in the unexpected harvest. They told their own crowd only and joined up their biggest nets with those of two other men to ensure a bigger haul.

The word got around eventually, but not before the four men had enclosed the mouth of the inlet with their combination of big nets. It took them a full month to haul out all the herring, using four currachs and two yawls every day. Each currach could hold three thousand herring and the much bigger yawls had the capacity to carry eight thousand herring. Harry McKeown, proprietor of the Leenane Hotel who was also a fish buyer and exporter bought all the herring off the men for export.

This all happened in 1910, two years before I was born and the four men who enjoyed such good fortune that summer were Philip Coyne, my uncle George Mortimer, my father Michael Mortimer and my grandfather George Mortimer. My father told me years later that they made more money in that month than in all the years they had spent fishing before then.

I was nine years old in June 1921 when a British navy destroyer entered Rossroe harbour and the troops on board collected all the currachs which were then taken in tow up the Killary as far as Leenane. It was part of a great round up in the West Connemara area involving more than one thousand troops and police with planes to guide them. The purpose of the round up was to capture as many IRA men as possible. Many of the currachs which had been confiscated were subsequently damaged. Harry McKeown was to later organise a successful compensation claim against the British government. Perhaps it was just a coincidence but shortly after the claim went through the price of the salmon licence went up from £3 to £4. In 1921 it cost £7 to buy a currach.

Festy Mortimer's parents

My career in fishing started in 1926 when, at the age of fourteen, I was allowed to go to sea with my father and my two uncles George and John. In 1940 my father retired and was replaced by Tommy Dinny Kane. John Mortimer became the new skipper and when he died suddenly in 1944, I was given the responsibility of skippering the boat. I remained on as skipper until 1996. When George Mortimer later retired he was succeeded by John Joe Mortimer and in later years Peter Wallace became part of the crew.

The big Pattern day in Leenane, which usually fell on the 16th February each year, signalled the beginning of the salmon season. It ran until the 15th August although we sometimes didn't stay at the salmon that long. Nowadays the salmon season doesn't begin until the 10th June. We fished up the Killary all our lives. The fjord was divided up into fourteen stations and whichever crew got to a particular station first in the morning was then entitled to fish there for the day. During the '20s, '30s and '40s there would be a crew at every station from Monday to Friday. In accordance with the rules of the salmon licence there was no fishing allowed between 9 p.m. on Friday and 6 a.m on Monday. The fourteen stations were Doire na Sliogáin (the wood of the shells), Poll na nGabhar (the goat's hole), Poll Caitlín (Kathleen's hole), The Mark, Gob Gharraì (the point at the small garden), Teach Geal (the bright house), Coiléar Mór (the big quarry), Claí Gorm (the blue fence), Coiléar Beag (the small quarry), Leac Gharraí an Rí (the flat store at the king's garden – the king in question is Edward VII who visited Leenane in July 1903), Poll na Froganna (the Frog's Hole), Gob Nancy (Nancy's point), Bruach Buí (the yellow bank) and Dooneen.

The salmon season was always very unpredictable and could vary greatly from week to week. Most years we caught between four and five hundred in the season which was a fair return. My biggest ever haul of salmon in one day was 126 and the biggest salmon I ever caught weighed 52 pounds. He was probably the biggest fish ever caught in these parts. He was emptied and stuffed and can be seen on display in the Leenane Hotel to this day. At one time Patrick Coyne from Dawros used to make all the salmon nets for my crowd but after I took over I preferred to buy the mesh from Hamilton's in Leenane and then make up my own nets using my own rope and corks. During the '40s a thirty fathom net with a depth of 100 meshes cost about £12. It was expensive and I would not have bought that amount every year.

Up to about 1950 we were getting 10d to 1 shilling per pound while the summer salmon (those caught after June 15th) would fetch about 6d to 8d per pound. The salmon fisheries were all owned by the landlords in the area. They had all the rights covering the rivers and the lakes and in the case of Ballinahinch harbour, fishermen were not allowed to fish for salmon within one mile of the estuary of the Dawros River.

Up until 1968 all the fishermen up the Killary practised draftnet fishing. Where there was a crew of four, three men always went out in the currach, two to row and one to throw out the net, which would usually be piled in

Rossroe Pier

the stern of the boat. The draftnet we had would have been 180 yards long and 120 meshes deep. When the salmon would eventually show, the two oarsmen would try to circle the motion the salmon were on. The third man would cast out the net making sure not to get it caught in the currach because this would result in it tearing and this in turn would enable the salmon to escape. The fourth man on the shore held the end of the net to make sure that the salmon could not get through. Then, in due course, the whole crew would haul the net ashore until it all came to a very small haul. If there was a good catch of salmon we would have to slow down a bit, bring the bottoms in under the net and then bring it in double before finally emptying it into the boat. In 1946 I bought a second hand outboard engine for £50. This was a huge amount of money at the time but it made life a lot easier for all the crew.

In 1968 while on a visit to Dublin I happened to meet a friend of mine Wally McGurk who used to come to Rossroe on holidays. He told me that if enough pressure was brought to bear on the then Minister for Fisheries, Neil Blaney, we should have no problem getting drift netting introduced in West Connemara. At the time, drift netting was practised from Clare Island to Achill to the north of us and from Slyne Head to Galway to the south of us yet we were not allowed to fish in that way. Encouraged by Wally's optimism I subsequently organised a meeting of all the local fishermen in Tullycross Hall. Bobby Molloy also attended. The debate went on long into the night. Many of those present were afraid that the introduction of drift netting would put an end to draft netting because the salmon would not be able to get far enough in. Bobby Molloy attempted to allay some of these fears by telling the meeting that all fishermen would be limited to 800 yards of driftnet. At that time one could buy 100 yards of driftnet for around £30. The fishermen eventually agreed to lobby for the introduction of drift netting and later that year the Minister gave in to their wishes. It was a turning point for many of the fishermen, who now became more ambitious and invested in bigger boats. I did not consider it worth my while changing over and I stayed with the draft netting.

Tom Kane and Willie Lavelle setting off from Gurteen Quay in 1940.

A year later I bought the biggest boat ever to come into Rossroe Harbour. It was a 62 foot trawler which had originally been sunk near Blacksod Bay. Someone up in Blacksod had managed to refloat her using barrels and buoys and had brought her safely into harbour. She was an ideal boat for lobsters and in her time had made several runs from Belmullet to France. After buying her I had to replank her because she was in very poor condition. I never got the use out of her that I had hoped for, mainly because my sons married and moved away from Rossroe. I sold her eventually in 1975 because she had been too long lying idle. The buyer was from Galway and he paid me a lot more than I bought her for.

The herring and mackerel season ran from mid-April to the end of October. Most of the fish were salted and exported. In West Connemara this trade reached its peak in 1908 when the extension to Cleggan Pier was built. Barrels of Crowe salt were imported from Germany by rail to Clifden for salting the fish. At a later date the East Atlantic Co, in Dawros near Letterfrack used to bring the barrels of salt in by sea to Dawros. The fish were salted on the piers when they were landed and buyers or their agents would come to the piers to purchase the fish. The herring were always better left for two or three days before being salted but the mackerel had to be salted straight away.

Thomas Nee from Tully was the local buyer up until the mid-thirties when his brother-in-law Tommy Curley from Tullycross took over from him. Thomas Nee used to charter a boat from the Limerick Steamship Co to take the fish to Germany. The prices for herring and mackerel were roughly the same. We were paid around 2 shillings per 'long hundred' (126) of herring but this could drop to 1s 6d or occasionally rise to 2s 6d and these prices were obtained until the early 1950s without much change. The retail price of salt herrings was about 8 for 1 shilling.

Festy Mortimer at Rossroe

When we were counting out herring and mackerel we always counted in Irish and in threes. Every time we counted out one hundred, a tally of three fish was set aside to enable us to keep a record of the amount of hundreds counted. The additional twenty-six to make up the 'long hundred' we called 'a tally and a lámh'. We were throwing out a bit of good luck with the hundred and the extra fish were meant to compensate the buyer for any fish that might get damaged while in transit.

The lobster season ran from May to the end of October and lobsters were very plentiful up to about 1940. Most of those caught were exported to Billingsgate Market in London. Thomas Nee was also the buyer for lobsters and had storage tanks at Gurteen, Glassillaun and Dawros as well as a holding pond on the island of Glassillaun, the ruins of which can still be seen today. I remember my father used to get 8 shillings a dozen from Thomas Nee in the 1920s. I made all my own pots from sallyrods. By the mid '40s I was usually getting 11 shillings a dozen from Tommy Curley and I often had ten or eleven dozen lobsters for him. There was a tradition in those years whereby we used to give the buyer thirteen for the dozen. This meant, of course, that for every twelve sold, the buyer was getting an extra dozen free of charge. Curley's lorry usually arrived in Rossroe about three times a week.

A lot of bad feeling developed between the fishermen and the buyers over the lobsters. We had to wait until the return came back from Dublin before we'd be paid. There were many times when we received a lot less than the expected payment. One of the reasons a buyer would give was that a good few of the lobsters had died by the time they had reached Dublin on account of the heat. We never had any way of knowing for sure if this really was the case. Another excuse that was commonly given was that there had been a 'blue ticket'. What the significance of this blue ticket was I will never understand, but basically when the buyer told us this it meant that it had been a bad market. Again, we had no way of checking this out and more often than not our interpretation of the 'blue ticket' explanation was that there had been a fiddle. Looking back on those times I am convinced that we were deceived and underpaid on several occasions.

The lobster situation improved greatly, however, from the mid '40s on when a Frenchman named Mauger based in Cleggan became a buyer. He had proper storage facilities and we always got full payment. He paid us 30 shillings a dozen, which was three times better than what we had been accustomed to. At a later date Mauger started paying so much a pound instead of buying by the dozen. We were in the dark about this new arrangement initially and continued to sell by the dozen to Stephen 'Sailor' Flaherty who was a local agent for Mauger. Flaherty was subsequently selling to Mauger by the pound and by doing this he was nearly doubling his money. When we eventually became aware of what was going on, we sold directly to Mauger and realised a much more favourable return. Mauger also supplied the local fishermen with lobster pots free of charge. His coming onto the scene, when he did, was like a welcome breath of fresh air and he has always been good to any of the fishermen of West Connemara who have done business with him.

In the 1940s I was getting 3 shillings per hundredweight for winkles. They would be left on the shore at Rossore before being moved later to a collection point on the road. There were many occasions when Curley's lorry did not arrive as expected and the winkles died. The usual explanation given any time this happened was that 'the market was no good'. It was very frustrating to see absolutely no return on all the labour that had been put in. I sold clams and mussels to Mauger from time to time during the '40s and '50s and they usually realised £2 a stone. During the winter months I used to sometimes dredge for scallops in low tide. I usually kept the scallops for my own consumption, as I would consider them to be a real delicacy.

I made my first ever currach in 1938 for £3. The timber was all white deal, delivered to me by McKeown's lorry from Westport. I bought nine yards of canvas in Stanleys in Clifden at tenpence a yard and I also got nine yards of callico, rejects from the factory in Westport. I could usually get enough callico for four or five currachs at that time for as little as 5 shillings. With the £3 I received I was able to buy enough materials to make another two currachs. By the late 1940s I was charging £30 a currach, increasing to £60 by the late 1950s. Nowadays the price of a new currach is somewhere in the region of £900.

The first task in the making of a currach is to cut all the timber to suit. Having done this, the next task is to join all the frames together and to put in the stem, the stern and the seats. Ideally, the middle seat should be 15½ inches from the bottom of the currach with the seat nearer the stern at 13½ inches. When the body of the currach is complete the next step is to turn the whole structure upside down in order to bore the frames for the hoops at four inches apart all the way from stem to stern. After this the next job is to plank outside the hoops. The final part of the project involves covering the currach with canvas and tarring it. I was able to get tar in Tullycross and Leenane back in the early '40s for 1s 6d per gallon and somehow there was much better tar going back then than what is available today. Nowadays a gallon of tar would put me back £8.

I would consider that a good eye and patience are probably the two most important attributes required in fishing. Down through the years I have seen many young lads come and go mainly because they did not possess the necessary powers of concentration. They were far too easily distracted and had not the required self discipline to work at learning and developing a good eye. I developed great patience for fishing from spending so much time with the older crew members in the early years. I always admired the way they would stay at their station on the Killary for the whole of the day no matter how badly the fishing was going. They were able to stick it out when younger lads would get fed up and head home early. The experience I gained from fishing with my father and my uncles was invaluable and I hope I have passed some of this on to my own son, Feichin, who carries on a proud fishing tradition which has been in our family for many generations.

As a crew there were certain superstitions we abided by. For example, I would never put out a new currach without putting the sign of the cross on it with seawater and asking Almighty God to bring everyone home safe that would be in it. The crew would always say the following words, "In the name of the Father and of the Son and of the Holy Spirit, three men that never failed", before embarking on our day's work.

I have always loved and respected the sea and no matter how tough or frustrating the fishing got I would never dream of cursing the sea. I was always inclined to feel happier and more comfortable on water than on land particularly in good weather when being out at sea always made me feel livelier and more refreshed than I would have been had I remained ashore. Like so many other fishermen I never learnt to swim but having said that I was never afraid of the sea and the one time in my life that I did fall overboard I did not panic even though I went thirty feet below the currach. I could see the currach clearly above me, I waited for the rope which arrived down in a matter of seconds and I came up to safety along the rocks.

I had many great days on the sea and fishing has brought me great happiness and fulfilment over the years but there were dark days too. My first experience of a fishing tragedy was in 1923 when three Coyne brothers from Glassillaun were lost off Tullabawn and only one of the bodies was retrieved from the seas. That same year Phil Coyne and John McDonnell also from Glassillaun were lost when they turned over their currach while attempting to anchor the boat with a big stone. They had gone out that day to set nets for herring. Coyne's body was later found but not McDonnell's. The Cleggan Disaster in 1927 affected all of the local fishermen very deeply and we were never able to come to terms with the scale of it. My father and my uncles knew almost all of those men who were lost on that fateful night. Like the '20s, the '70s were tragic times with the loss of the Inishturbot men in 1974 and Martin Kerrigan and Petie Coyne in 1978. I will always be eternally grateful to God that he has spared my family from such loss down through the years.

Festy Mortimer painting currachs
PHOTO COURTESY OF GILES NORMAN PHOTOGRAPHY GALLERIES

As the beginning of a new century fast approaches I fear for the fishing industry locally. The picture I see is indeed a bleak one. In the case of the salmon there is too much poaching going on in the rivers and in the case of the Bundorragha and Erriff rivers which flow into the Killary there are not enough salmon to spawn. Those that escape the poachers are being taken by the Fisheries Board into a place where they can spawn but are then, in my opinion, let back out at the wrong time. They are being released in May at a time when the pollock are plentiful and the pollock are every bit as bad as the poachers. I often killed pollock in recent years with three or four salmon in them. The easy solution to the problem is for the Fisheries Board to release the young salmon either earlier or later but then again I have always found the Fisheries Board people to be too full of their own self-importance and too proud to take advice from the likes of me.

Killary is not the place it used to be sixty or seventy years ago. There are only four of the fourteen stations fished by the local fishermen of today, Gob Gharraí, Teach Geal, Claí Gorm and The Mark and now they are only allowed to fish four days a week. Every time I pass by and see all the rafts and blue buoys associated with mussel farming it makes me feel sick to the pit of my stomach. To me it is all just clutter and rubbish and it has destroyed what has always been my spiritual home. Today Killary is a place where shellfish no longer seem to be able to survive because of 'red tide'. There is a plentiful supply of coral on the Killary seabed. This coral has a red flower which upon bursting releases a poisonous red chemical into the water. The old people used to say that there was never any coral in the Killary before the British fleet came in for the visit of King Edward VII in 1903. Almost one hundred years later we seem to be suffering the consequences. Apart from Neil Blaney in 1968, I do not believe that any government minister ever since has done anything to really benefit the fishing industry in this country. Since we have become part of the European Union I feel that we have been sold out. The Spanish are supposed to leave twelve miles this side of them into the shore but they are doing what they like. They have been seen plenty of times at night fishing just off Crump Island and they are always gone by first light. Overall it is a sad state of affairs and it does not surprise me that so few of the younger generation in West Connemara today show any interest in making a living out of fishing.

I was able to rear a family of ten from fishing and making currachs in days gone by, but if I was starting out all over again today, as a young man, I know there is no way fishing and currach making alone would sustain me and that is what saddens me most of all after all these years.

Remembered by Festy Mortimer and written by Paul Gannon

KERRIGAN'S SONG

It's well that I remember on June the 24th,
When the three sailed out together from the quay of sweet Westport;
Through dark and gloom, they steered for home
without neither dread nor fear
And little did any of them think, their death it was so near.

At Cahir Isle she stood awhile and after doing good work,
Through splash and spray she made her way, to look for Inis Turk;
But the south-west gale it did prevail and on the waves she tossed
Till she became a total wreck upon the strand across.

O Blessed Virgin Mary, it was a terrible tale,
To see the mother of three orphans high dry on Mayo shore,
Her jet black hair like one in prayer as she lay on the strand,
Far from her native island home to Bofin she belonged.

Oh God be with Sean Kerrigan, I hope his soul's at rest
While his body lies in Achill far from his mothers breast.
I hear she's going to see him soon, I hope it won't be long,
To kneel and pray upon his grave, to sing to him a song.

This news caused great excitement when it spread around
From Westport quay to Belfast bay and from there to Achill Sound,
For the people were liked by everyone and its true to all that's past
But a few will say that on St. John's Day that Sean Kerrigan will be lost.

Author Unknown
Given to me by Festy Mortimer, who learnt the words from his mother

The Inishturbot Disaster

On the day of the All-Ireland Football Final in 1974 between Galway and Dublin a bunch of lads from Inishturbot travelled to Clifden to watch the game on television. For three of them it was their last journey. Patrick Stuffle, Patrick O'Toole and Michael Wallace were drowned on their way home. There were never any clues as to what caused the drowning. The first body was found about ten days later and the other two were found within the next two weeks. All three were found in different places.

Sergeant Sean Kelly in discussion with the late Festy Conneely during the search for bodies following the Inishturbot tragedy in 1974. Garda divers are in the background.

UNNAMED POEM

It's here I stand on a wave-washed strand;
I am gazing at the sea,
But the thoughts now running in my mind
They bring no joy to me.
I am thinking of three fishermen
Those waters did consume
And wondering like so many more
How they did meet their doom.

From Turbot Quay they went that day
A football game to see,
And landed on this very spot
Where now I chance to be.
They hauled their boat upon their backs
As they often did before;
It was little they thought
They'd never see their loved ones anymore.

To Clifden town it was their aim –
It was six miles away –
To watch on television
Their native county play.
Like every other Galway man
It was their great desire
To see the Galway football team
Bring home the Sam Maguire.

The day passed on and the night came on,
It was dark and raining too.
They hired a car to Eyrephort beach
And boarded the canoe.
Although the night was dark and wet
No danger was in sight;
It was many a night they crossed that way
On a dark and stormy night.

Those men fished for many years
In waters far and near,
And crossing over this narrow strip
They never had no fear.
We don't know how they met their doom
Or no one ever will;
Their boat was found next morning
Washed ashore near Fountain Hill.

When the news went around
that they were drowned
There was many silent tears;
It was the saddest tragedy
We have had in many years.
Our sympathy we do extend
And pray that God will find
Some comfort for their relatives
That they have left behind.

For several days beneath the sea,
In storm and in rain,
To get the bodies from the sea
The divers worked in vain;
They searched the shallows and the deep
And battled with the waves
In hope to bring the bodies
From their cold and watery graves.

From Cleggan Quay to Mannin Bay
A wide-spread search was made,
But as the days went into weeks
All hopes began to fade;
But God did hear the fervent prayers
And the bodies they were found
And buried with a blessing
In the family burial ground.

Their loss has left a loneliness
That everyone can feel;
They have left behind some wounded hearts
That only time could heal.
In their sandy graves near the angry waves
Their bodies now they lie,
But their souls have gone to rest with God
In the Home beyond the sky.

No more along the Clifden Bay
Will we hear their engine sound;
No more they'll set their nets or pots
Upon the fishing ground.
On All-Ireland Football Final days
As we sit to watch the score,
Our minds will sadly wander back
To nineteen-seventy-four.

Written by Joseph O'Toole.

VICTIMS OF THE GALE

On the 25th of October,
it being a rainy day,
But just as the evening came
it seemed to clear away,
Five Rossadillisk fishing boats set
Off for the fishing ground
And set their nets as usual
Just as the sun went down.

A storm arose so suddenly
No notice could be seen;
Neither the moon or stars were
Seen or any other sign.
To survive the gale it was in vain,
No open boat could stand;
Only one crew with God's own help
Did manage to make the land.

At daybreak the next morning
How sad it was to see
Four of the crew of Cloonan's boat
There washed up by the sea;
And when they were identified
They came there by mishap.
They were John Cloonan and his son,
Young Laffey and Delap.

They were brought into Cleggan
And laid there in a store
Awaiting for the coroner,
Who was there the day before.
He waited in the area till
The bodies were all found
And the verdict that he passed on them
Was accidentally drowned.

May God look to their parents,
To their wives and families,
And look to every other man
Depending on the seas
That night they spent in terror
On the Rossadillisk shore,
Awaiting for their loved ones
That they never will see no more.

During High Mass on Monday
For souls of those deceased,
Both Priest and congregation
Fell into silent tears.
The hardest heart it would relent
To have to weep and wail
To see before the altar
The victims of the gale.

They were carried through the chapel
Which grieves me to relate,
And placed upon a lorry
Outside the chapel gate.
The funeral was the largest
We had ever seen before,
Going down to Omey Island
Where they lie forever more.

Written by Joseph O'Toole

Tragedy at Sea

The dreadful Cleggan disaster happened on an October evening in 1927. The day had been wet with a wind from the south-east. Towards evening, the wind went southwest and it grew calm. There was a dark misty fog, and though the sharper weather observers said it might blow, all were not agreed on the point.

But if indications of a mere earthly order were few, those of a spiritual nature were not lacking to the same extent. As a 'Bofin crew of four left 'Bofin harbour they saw another boat following them with a crew of three. They were surprised at this, as there was no crew at the quay when they left. The following boat came at great speed, but it detoured so that it was at some distance from the first boat as it passed on its way. The crew of four could not recognise the others as they sped along. Cannon, the leader of the crew, said he did not like the looks of the boat and he advised his men to return. They were only just in when the storm came.

A crew from Errismore were fishing near Slyne Head. They saw a boat with a crew of three coming from the sea at great speed. The leader said it was not a 'right boat' and said they should go home. One of the crew was so frightened that he suggested not pulling in the nets. This was agreed on and they anchored the nets and fled. They had not reached shore when the storm burst. It got pitch dark and a shower came with the storm, and they found it very hard to land but still they succeeded. Next day they returned and found seven hundred – that is, 120 by 70 mackerel in the nets. (N.B. The old people of Renvyle say that there are never more or less than three in a phantom boat or under a phantom coffin. The three under a phantom coffin always walk two in front and one behind.)

There were October devotions in Cleggan church on the evening of the gale. When the wind arose it blew in the door of the church and was blowing out the candles. Some of the people looked around and seeing Laffey, a Cleggan fisherman, standing beside the door on the inside, beckoned to him to close the door. He did not move. A girl went down and closed the door and when she had done so she said to Laffey; "Isn't it a wonder you would not close the door?" He made no answer. She noticed nothing strange about him except that he was in oilers and was all wet. He was really at sea when he was seen at the church and was probably drowned by then. His body was never recovered. Local tradition has it that the sea will never be properly at rest again until all the bodies of those drowned are delivered up to the land.

The fishermen from Cleggan, Letter, and 'Bofin were fishing with driftnets for mackerel on that fatal night. The storm burst at nightfall; it came like a shot from a gun, so it gave little or no chance of escape. It got pitch dark as the shower came with the storm. Some fishermen cut the ropes and let the nets go; others threw out the grapnel to hold the nets and fled. Some drew in the nets, while a few had not let out the nets at all.

Tom and Mick Diamond from Letter made their way to the Ballinakill side of the bay with the greatest difficulty. They struck land in the dark and one of them was about to get out when a wave struck the side of the foundered boat and turned it over on top of both. They were so worn out that they could not escape. They were faced with death. But Peter O'Toole and another man came along with a lamp to see if anyone was in distress in the boat and they rescued the brothers. The Diamonds were unable to return home for two days and during that time they were mourned as lost.

There was great joy at their return. They still preserve pieces of the newspaper where their names appeared for the first and last time in print. One Cleggan crew and two Letter crews sheltered in a cave north of Cleggan tower. They managed to scramble up a rough path in the cliff and to drag the boats after them. One of the Cleggan men, Tom, managed to reach the top of the cliff. He went to the house of Captain Tulloch and got lights and help and so rescued the three crews. Tulloch brought the two Letter crews home in his car that night. Eighteen men lost their lives in that short-lived but terrible gale.

All those lost were natives of Cleggan and Bofin. This disaster put an end to driftnet fishing at Cleggan.

By kind permission of the Department of Irish Folklore.
University College Dublin.

THE LONELY ROCKS OF FRAOIL

Come all ye gallant seamen
Pray, to my song, give ear,
Concerning a brave fisherman
Who lived not far from here.
It being on the 2nd of October
The day being bright and clear
This fisherman named O'Malley
Set out for Inis Fraoil.

Aided by his two young sons,
He took the currach down;
With heart so light and spirits bright
He set out from Bun na hAbhainn.
The day being bright and sunny,
They quickly plied the oars
For to go and pull some crannach
As they often did before.

Across the deep blue ocean,
They pulled with might and main,
For to pull this precious seaweed
Which they'd sell to Mr. Kane.
They were only some hours at work
When the boys they got a fright,
For in from sea there came a fog
Which turned the day to night.

These boys, being only youngsters,
How must this brave man feel
As he stood in semi-darkness
On the lonely rocks of Fraoil.
The people on the mainland
They fell in deep dismay
And in the neighbouring houses
They all knelt down to pray.

They offered up the Rosary
As they often did before,
And they prayed to Him who stilled the waves:
Bring O'Malley safe to shore.
All praise be to his neighbours
And to his comrade Sean
Who kept the vigil by the fire
Til the day began to dawn.

Also to the local shopkeeper
Who supplied the fuel so dear,
Which helped to make the bonfire
Which was seen both far and near.
Likewise his wife and daughters –
Theirs was a sorry plight
As they watched out for their loved ones
All through that awful night.

No compass for to guide them
Or set their course aright,
As they watched from that bleak island
All through that awful night.
With dangers all around them
Where the breakers, break and roar,
When many a gallant seaman
Went down, to rise no more.

And then the fog it lifted
On the lonely rocks of Fraoil,
A light shone through the darkness
It shone out bright and clear.
Sometimes it seemed distant,
Sometimes it seemed near.
To know where the light came from
Those boys were at a loss;
How could they know it welcomed them
from the cliffs of Mullaghgloss.

It was nearly the next morning –
Just at the break of day –
The currach, it came skimming
Across the waters of the bay.
The cheer the neighbours gave him
Near brought the old cliffs down,
As O'Malley pulled his currach
Into dear old Bun na Habhainn.

Now to conclude and finish –
I have no more to say –
Long life to all brave fishermen
Whose livelihood is on the sea;
Terrible hours of hardship they have to undergo,
For they must brave the deep and treacherous sea
In their frail and light canoes.

Written by Mickey Walsh

THE FISHERMAN'S ESCAPE

One fine September morning, at the break of day,
Two stalwart brother fishermen, set out from Gurteen Quay.
The morning shone bright and clear,
No cloud was in the sky,
They baited their lobster pots,
Scarcely an hour had passed by,
When low a rainbow appeared in the sky.

The sky grew dark and dreary,
The waves began to rise,
The fishermen steered their boat for home,
But, alas too late were they,
A stormy south-westerly gale blew,
The sea was raging high.
They tried to decide what their best course now.

Said one unto the other,
'We'll alter course once more,
If we reach Fraoil island,
We'll safely reach the shore'
The rain lashed down, the storm kept on,
The distance was too great.
They scrambled onto a nearby rock,
Their currach with them did take.

The night fell black, the thunder cracked, the lightning flashed.
Those heroes watched and prayed,
They called on Christ to still the waves,
As yore on Galilee.
Their eyes were sore, their clothes were torn,
Their hands were swollen and numb.
Yet through the long and dreary night,
Onto the boat they clung.

At the break of day the salt spray was lashing o'er the rock.
One vain hope now, the sea to plough,
And try to reach some land.
A guiding hand led them safely on,
Right in on Glassillaun strand.

Written by Kate Conneely

The Merman in the Cove

(*extract from Connaught Tribune 1936*)

A remarkable story which seems to support the ancient belief in the existence of mermaids comes from Letterbeg, Renvyle, Connemara. Two fishermen from Letterbeg claim to have had an extraordinary encounter on Thursday – not with a mermaid, but with a 'merman'!

The men were Martin Heanue and Thomas Regan and their story is as follows:– While returning home from gunner-fishing at about 2 p.m. on Thursday, the fishermen noticed a strange object in a cove known locally as Fugha na mBan. Thinking it is was a windfall they approached to investigate. When within four or five yards of the object Heanue laid down his oars and knelt in the stern of the currach in order to grasp hold of it, while Regan backed in the currach.

The next moment Heanue got the fright of his life when the object turned round suddenly revealing the form and features of a man, growling in annoyance, and dived beneath the currach. Heanue jumped on his oars immediately and shouted to Regan to pull away.

The 'Apparition' arose again, however, and approached the boat threateningly. Regan raised his oar to strike it but Heanue, believing it to be something supernatural, shouted to him not to touch it. The men then rowed away with all speed, and the 'Apparition' pursued them for over two hundred yards, when it finally dived and disappeared.

DESCRIPTION OF 'CREATURE'

The fishermen described the 'Creature' as being slightly smaller than a full-grown man, with long fair hair and beard. Apart from the beard his face seemed perfectly smooth and fair. His eyebrows were bushy, but his face generally was not unpleasant. He had human arms and legs and swam with a breast-stroke, but partly on his side. He seemed to wear something like a skirt extending from his hips down to below his knees. This 'Garment' appeared to be loose fitting.

The whole story unquestionably sounds fantastic, but both fishermen are of a reliable type, and local superstition would not allow them to 'belie the sea'. Furthermore they were interviewed and cross-examined individually by a '*Connaught Tribune*' reporter and both versions coincided even to the smallest detail. Heanue believes that the monster 'was enchanted', but Regan, who is a world-war veteran, has no regard for such a theory.

A '*Connaught Tribune*' reporter was told locally that a somewhat similar monster was seen over thirty years ago by Mr Laurence Henry, late of Kylemore Castle while passing the cove in his steam launch. Mr Henry wanted to approach the cove and shoot it, but his crew 'mutinied', and refused to put the boat around.

THE MERMAN

One Thursday evening lately
While fishin' close at hand
They saw an object in a cove
Quite close to Padraic's land.

They thought it was a windfall
So they went to investigate
And what they found in it
To you I will relate.

Heanue thought to hit him
And it let a mighty roar
He told Reagan not to bother him
But to pull from the shore.

It dived beneath the curragh
And it rose the other side
Heanue thought to kill him
But the blow he did avoid.

Then the merman pursued them
And he followed like the wind
And they rowed over Leítir Bay
And they left him far behind.

Mike O'Malley

THE CHILDREN OF THE SEA

We are the children who live beside the sea.

We are the children who love the sea,
All summer long we play;
We laugh, skip and skip and run
Barefoot on sandy beaches.
We swim in waters blue
And fish in rock pools
For we are the children of the sea.

We watch the mackerel break,
Overhead the seagulls soar
While the dolphins leap and play
As they swim along the shore.
And when the day is over
We watch the evening sunset glow
On the shores of Killary
As the fishing boats come home
For we are the children of the sea.

And in the wintertime
When the wild waves rush to shore
We walk along the strand
Gathering shells of every hue.
And we long for summertime
And sunny days once more
For we are the children of the sea,
Yes, we are the children of the sea.

Written by Kathleen O'Brien

THE HERRING SILVER HUE

In County Galway long ago
When times were hard and food was scarce
There among the lovely hills,
There lived a fair and pleasant race,
The fishermen on deep sea blue
They caught the herring silver hue.

They fought to tend unyielding soil
And grew potatoes all the while;
They laboured hard from dawn till dusk
And prayed to God in their days of trial,
But in the morning and evening too
They caught the herring silver hue.

These days are gone as you can see,
There's bread enough for you and me
And houses grand beside the sea
In this mountain land so fair and free,
And the children that grow strong and true
They love the herring silver hue.

A mother sits by the open door
And thinks of one that never returned,
For beneath the deep sea wave
It's there he found a watery grave;
In life the thing he loved to do
Was fish for herring silver hue.

A lass she waits down by the shore
And sees the currachs sailing o'er,
For her fisher lad toils the live long day
To catch the fish within the bay,
When he returns with love so true
And lots of herring silver hue.

Old fishermen by grey stone walls
With weathered faces and fading eyes,
They look out towards the sea
And remember days that used to be,
Those days of youth and morning dew
When they chased the herring silver hue.

The Connacht land is fair and free,
No foreign bondage holds us now,
And the wind that blows down from the hills
Is sometimes wild and sometimes still,
And the trawlers on the deep sea blue
They trail the herring silver hue,
They trail the herring silver hue.

Written by Kathleen O'Brien

WILD OCEAN

The wild ocean where Viking ships once sailed,
Dark mountains towering against the sky:
White waves roll by the pier.
Old castles by the sea
Could tell of age-old Galway
When a noble race lived here.
The wind blows fierce in winter
And the trees are bare;
The air cold.
But however bleak, it's beautiful
On this rocky Renvyle shore.
And spring will bring wild flowers
That deck the meadows.
When summer is near
The fisherman fish for salmon
With faces brown and tangled hair.
People stroll on sandy beaches
And children play there.
The sun goes down in the western sea
And the seagulls fly over the wild ocean.

Written by Kathleen O'Brien

Last Postmaster

Michael King

My grandmother was postmistress in Errislannan post office going back to the turn of the century. When she retired, my uncle Donal King agreed to carry on as postmaster. I was twenty-two years of age in 1946 when he asked me if I would succeed him. I agreed to my uncle's request because I wanted to carry on the tradition of the Post Office being in our family and also because of the guaranteed monthly income that went with the appointment. I succeeded my uncle on the 1st of January 1947.

So much has changed over the past fifty years that when I finally decide to retire, Errislannan Post Office will officially close like many other small rural post offices all over Ireland. We are surplus to requirements in this new age of information technology, but because of an old agreement between the Department of Posts and Telegraphs and the Irish Postmasters' Union dating back to the 1950s, all postmasters can continue to keep their post offices open for business until they decide to retire. Only for this agreement I would have been closed down long ago along with many others like me.

Michael King (no relation) was the village postman in 1947. He would arrive at the post office every morning at 9.30 a.m. to collect the village post and transfer it to Ballinaboy post office where Thomas O'Malley would pick it up on his way to Clifden. Michael King would return to Ballinaboy post office at 3 p.m. to collect the incoming post from Thomas O'Malley on his return. He would deliver this around the village and usually returned to the post office by 4 p.m. each day. I would always get him to sign the letter bill, which was a record, of authentication and which is still in use today. I would stamp the letter bill and mark in the time of his arrival and departure. I was obliged to post a letter bill to Galway post office every day. Michael King would leave his bicycle, which was the property of the P & T at the post office overnight.

Sometimes, in the event of a big post the parcels would be delivered to

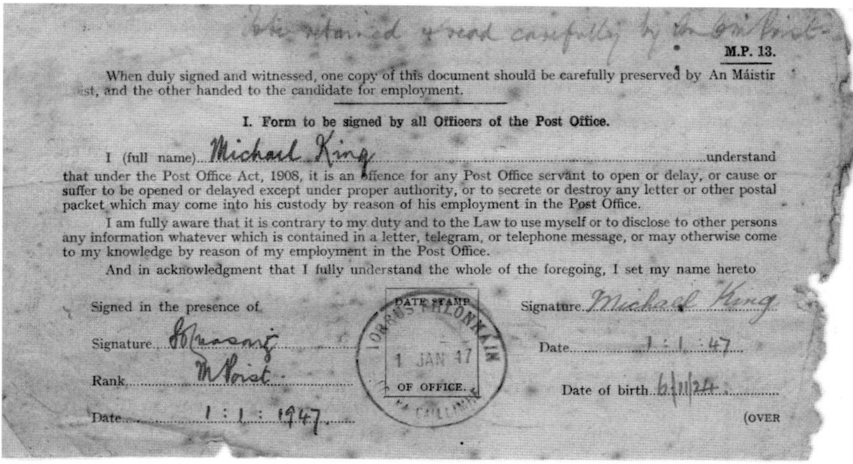

M.P. 13.

When duly signed and witnessed, one copy of this document should be carefully preserved by An Máistir ...ist, and the other handed to the candidate for employment.

I. Form to be signed by all Officers of the Post Office.

I (full name) Michael King understand that under the Post Office Act, 1908, it is an offence for any Post Office servant to open or delay, or cause or suffer to be opened or delayed except under proper authority, or to secrete or destroy any letter or other postal packet which may come into his custody by reason of his employment in the Post Office.

I am fully aware that it is contrary to my duty and to the Law to use myself or to disclose to other persons any information whatever which is contained in a letter, telegram, or telephone message, or may otherwise come to my knowledge by reason of my employment in the Post Office.

And in acknowledgment that I fully understand the whole of the foregoing, I set my name hereto

Signed in the presence of

Signature ...

Rank M Poist.

Date 1 : 1 : 1947.

DATE STAMP 1 JAN 47 OF OFFICE.

Signature Michael King

Date 1 : 1 : 47

Date of birth 6/11/24

(OVER

my post office from Ballinaboy by donkey and basket, and Michael King might have to make a couple of trips around the village to get everything delivered. It was very seldom that this occurred.

I always had a good relationship with the local postman and there was never any conflict between us although it was not uncommon at the time for postmasters and postmen not to get on. Nobody ever complained to me about our local postman. In any case, even if someone had complained, I had no authority to deal with the matter and all I could have done was to refer the matter to the postmaster in Clifden.

Padraig Joyce, was postmaster in Galway at the time and he was my direct superior. He usually arrived out every year to inspect my stocks and see that everything was in order. Sometimes he used to send the Clifden postmaster on his behalf. I was never given any notification of these visits. On such occasions the value of the unsold stock and the cash in hand were added up and had to reach a certain figure. In the late 1940s this figure was £70 but was to increase substantially over the next fifty years.

I usually sent in whatever cash I had received from my customers to

Marty Conneely at the Clifden Telephone Exchange, 1965.

Errislannan Post Office 1955

Galway post office, every week, in a registered official letter. In the late 19'40s this would only have amounted to £2 or £3. I was obliged to send in a monthly return making sure that my unsold stock and cash tallied. In 1947 I was paid a monthly wage of £6. The Clifden postmaster at the time would have been on about £10 a month.

I joined the Irish Postmasters' Union and did bring up a number of issues with the union over the years. One such issue was the fact that I was not authorised to give out Social Welfare payments. Some locals were upset that they could not collect their social welfare at their local post office so I brought it up at one of the union meetings in Maam Cross that year, but to no avail. The other side of the story, of course, was that there was probably a substantial number of people who preferred to collect their social welfare in Ballyconneely or Clifden because they could do a bit of shopping and go for a few drinks there, which was something they could not do in Errislannan. I also went to the union about the fact that certain local old age pensioners were collecting their pensions in other post offices. I was told that the IPU was powerless to help me because people were entitled to collect their pension in whatever post office they liked.

In the 1930s the pension was about seven shillings, rising to about £1 by 1950. The pension money usually arrived out every Wednesday from Galway in a small canvas bag. There would have been about £12 in it in the late 19'40s rising to about £25 by the late 1960s. At one time I was servicing about twenty old age pensioners and this made Friday a very busy day. Now there are only four pensioners left in the village. I was not authorised to issue money orders because my post office was deemed to be too small. Postal orders never exceeded £1 in the early days, at a cost of one penny to the customer. Stamps cost 2p each and it remained that way until the late 1950s. There have been many famous stamps over the years but my favourites were always those that depicted wildlife. I used to charge 5p for a registered letter although at that time they would not get to Galway city any quicker than an ordinary letter, which was very frustrating for the sender.

There was a standard charge of one shilling per telegram in the 1930s, but by the time I took over telegrams were priced on the basis of so much a word. I would ring the message through to Clifden post office and they would send it off from there. The first telegram I ever sent was for Mrs Brooks in Errislannan Manor. On average, I would probably have only sent out about ten telegrams per year in the '40s and '50s. I received no money for incoming telegrams. I was able to identify by the number of rings whether an incoming call was meant for Errislannan, Ballinaboy, Ballyconneely or Roundstone. One of the main services I gave in those years was delivering messages that came in by telegram to people in the locality. Very often the message had to do with somebody having died, either in Galway hospital or perhaps in England or America. I sold a lot of dog licences. It was customary for a guard to visit the village at least one a year to check that all dogs were fully licensed. The dog licence fee was five shillings as was the wireless licence, which came in during the 1950s. TV licences arrived in the 1960s and it is hard to believe that they now cost £70. I found that saving stamps did not really catch on in Errislannan until the late 1960s.

In all my years as postmaster of Errislannan post office I have always got my greatest fulfilment from giving my customers a good quality of service and also from maintaining good relations with them all. I would consider that my greatest achievement as a postmaster was to keep on friendly terms with all of my customers. I found non-locals more demanding as customers than locals. One had to dot every 'i' and cross every 't' so to speak. The non-local was also much more likely to complain about the post being slow. I much preferred dealing with locals.

Irish postman on his round.

The post office was a great meeting place; indeed, it was the only focal point locally and certainly it played a major role in the social life of Errislannan village right up to the end of the 1960s. As far as I was concerned, people could always delay as much as they liked, telling yarns and catching up on local gossip. I enjoyed having the place full of people and thrived on the banter and the conversation. I often used to make tea for customers. There was no sense of time in the old days. Many of my customers also confided in me. I heard about many a personal problem that I would have preferred not to have heard about, but there was no way out of it. I was always a very discreet person and my customers knew they could trust me not to pass on their troubles to any of their neighbours. I would love to have those times back again but without all the economic hardship. However, I know that society has developed and moved on so much in the intervening years that it is impossible to bring it all back. There is no hope for villages like Errislannan ever coming back to the way they were. Post offices like mine are not economically viable anymore and I do accept that it will soon be time for me to close the place down forever.

Being a postmaster all these years certainly had its drawbacks. It was a very restrictive occupation. I was very tied to the place and often it did not seem worth it, considering the paltry wages I was on. I remember at one stage working out how much I felt I should get in wages per hour and submitting it to the postmaster in Galway. I did not get any satisfaction. I never could afford to take a holiday because it would have been incumbent on me to pay the official who would be replacing me while I would be away. I was bitter enough about this state of affairs but powerless to do anything about it. There were many times when I would have preferred to have been working outdoors instead of being stuck inside and I do feel now that, if I was starting out all over again at the age of twenty-two, I would do something different with my life. However, I persevered all the years because I felt obliged to carry on providing a service which has been in my family now for the full duration of the twentieth century and that is something I will always be very proud of. I have seen many changes in the industry down through the years and I would consider that motorisation for postmen and computerisation have to be the two most significant developments during all that time.

Remembered by Michael King and written by Paul Gannon

Tom Post

Tom Post

People always liked my father because he was a jolly man and he always went with the mail to the door. I remember Annie Conroy telling me once – "I used to see him coming in the road. All you could see was the speck of the cap with parcels on the front of the carrier and him loaded down again at the back. They were sagging down off his back yet he would be always whistling, always jolly, no matter what sort of day it was. He was always happy." My father really loved his job. When he retired, he did not seem to really know where he was or what he was doing. I remember him going up to where the men would be cutting turf to talk to them and to see if he could get a bit of ease. He missed all the daily contact with people and they missed him. "The post is done now Tom Post is gone," a lot of them said afterwards.

He began his career as a postman in 1905, an employee of the British government of the day. He was paid six shillings a week starting off. After the foundation of the Irish Free State in 1921 he was working for the Dept of Post and Telegraphs and his conditions of service improved somewhat. By 1930 he was getting paid £3 a week.

Post was delivered five days a week in those days. He drove a big heavy post office bike with a big white carrier on the front.

Packie Conway outside Coyne's Post Office in Letterfrack, 1969. Also in picture are Mary Kelly, Julie Burns and John Mongan.

Meeting the postman on the 'Avenue' at Ballynahinch Castle: Petie Walsh (postman), Josie Flaherty, Martin Halloran, Jimmy Keane, Tom Joyce and Martin Lydon.

He always started his daily run at 8 a.m. He would collect the post at Ballyconneely, proceed to Ballinaboy P.O. and on to a post-box near the monastery, his final collection point en route to Clifden. Delia Wallace (Letterfrack) and Steve Mc Donagh (Cleggan) would meet him at Clifden post office. The bus would usually arrive from Galway at 1.30 p.m. and the three of them would sort through the incoming post before heading back out to their own areas. He would usually be back in Ballyconneely by about 3.30 p.m., having left post at Ballinaboy post office as well as to a few houses on his line.

He would usually stop at the gate of his own house in Derrygimla and my mother would bring him out some tea and bread. He could not eat inside and leave the post unattended nor was he allowed to bring the mail inside his own house.

On arrival in Ballyconneely Post Office, the post would have to be sorted again. Festy Nee delivered the Derrygimla post; Alfie McHale did the Dunloughan/Aillebrack run and my father delivered right down to the far end of Calla, at which point he would meet up with the Roundstone postman. I would estimate that he cycled about thirty miles every day at work. He often walked a further three to five miles across mountain boreens to deliver post to isolated houses. He was a great cyclist who often won bicycle races at sports meetings in Clifden. He developed a very high level of fitness because of the nature of his work. I remember on one occasion, having said goodbye to his sister, Winnie, at Clifden railway station, he borrowed a bicycle from someone in town and headed for Ballinahinch station, which he reached ahead of the train, in order to say farewell a second time.

The job was full of hardship in those days. It was often past midnight when my father returned home on account of the mail being so big, the lack of adequate lighting on the bike and, of course, adverse weather conditions. I can still picture him drying off in front of the open fire and how we would hardly be able to see him after a few minutes because the room would be covered in a cloud of steam. Despite all the hardship he was totally devoted to his work. He was very discreet and did not approve of any idle or derogatory talk. He often said to me, "If you ever become a postman, be honest, be straight and do your job right. Don't ever give anyone a chance to talk about you". He would never give mail to anyone else except the person whose name was on the envelope or parcel. I remember him heading off one night at 10.30 p.m. to deliver a letter to a man at the far end of Mannin, about six miles away. He had been unable to deliver it earlier in the day because the weather had been too bad, so he resolved to head over as soon as the weather cleared up. The fact that this did not happen until late at night made no difference to my father. There was no way he would have slept easily that night knowing that he had a letter belonging to someone in his own house. When he headed off into the black night my mother made no attempt to stop him because she understood the kind of man he was and how seriously he took his work. He used to always carry stamps in his wallet and he often stamped envelopes for people who had no money. He often ended up paying for these stamps himself when people would not come up with the money.

Delivering the post:
Mrs Mag Keaney of Cashel, 1932.

When my father retired in 1953 after forty-eight years service the postmaster in Galway, Mr. Joyce wanted me to take over from him. He appreciated my father's length of service, his obliging nature and, most of all, his honesty. However, I had seen him endure so much hardship in the job that I decided it was not for me. I always felt that the postal service got a lot more out of my father than he ever got out of it.

Shortly after my father retired, Fr Lynch bought a wallet for him. He gave it to a local man, Tommy Flaherty, and said to him, "I am giving you this wallet now, and I hope ye go out and collect for Tom Post. He was so long in the post and so faithful." The collection was duly organised and all the people of Errismore contributed, which showed how much they valued my father all those years. I haven't great time for postmen nowadays. Too many of them just do not have the personality for the job. They haven't a smile or a yarn and some of them are even reluctant enough to get out of the postal van and deliver the mail at the door. I do not believe that any postman ever again will treat the job in the same vocational manner that my father did, all those years ago.

Remembered by Matthew O'Malley and written by Paul Gannon

A Mercy Pilgrim Travels Back

Sr Phyl Clancy

'Twas the best of times – 'twas the worst of times'. I can echo the words of Charles Dickens in his novel 'A Tale of Two Cities' as I recall the days of my youth in the 1940s: 'Twas the best of times' – it certainly was! Life was simple, serene and secure. Simple, because we did not know the meaning of materialism. The Celtic Tiger did not arrive in Clifden until fifty years later. Serene! Life was quiet and peaceful. Everyone worked quietly and contentedly. Few had a steady job but all were working. The pay packet was small. There was no competition except on the football field or the ball alley. Life was secure. There was security within the family and the home. Married people took their marriage vows seriously – 'until death do us part'! Your partner was the one who shared your work place or who played *Twenty-Five* or *Whist* with you at the local card games. There was a spiritual dimension, too, to life. People attended Mass and the sacraments regularly. The family Rosary was recited in the home. People went on pilgrimage to Knock, Croagh Patrick and Lough Derg. Spain or the Canaries was not on their travel ticket.

'Twas the worst of times'. Yes it was. It was during World War II. Food and clothing were rationed. Money was scarce. My mother's widow's pension was five shillings per week. There were no steady jobs. Secondary education for the poorer classes, especially the boys, was nil. Because of the war in Europe the tourist trade was slack. People combed the shoreline for goods that were washed ashore from torpedoed ships. People from the hinterland of Cleggan, Letterfrack, Ballyconneely and Errismore could not travel into town because there was no petrol for cars or tyres for bicycles.

In such a society I spent my teenage years. I did the Leaving Certificate in the Convent Secondary School in 1948. What was I to do with my life? I often asked God what was He asking from me. I prayed for guidance. Some of my companions went nursing to England, others took up teaching posts as Junior Assistant Mistresses in the island schools or other small schools in the area. Many boys joined the National Army during the Emergency and later joined the Garda Siochana. Some went for the priesthood or religious life. My mother would have liked me to stay at home and help her to rebuild a declining business premises in Main Street.

After serious thought I opted for religious life. In the society in which I was brought up religious vocations thrived just as religious vocations thrive today in the Third World, which is a depressed society as Ireland was in the '40s.

I decided to join the Sisters of Mercy as they had formed me since childhood. I left Clifden in 1949 to join the Mercy Community in Swinford, Co Mayo. Lots of the neighbours called the night before I left to bid me goodbye. It was the general opinion around the town that I would be back in a month, so there were no tears shed. A neighbour gave me a gift of toilet soap. She said as she presented me the box, "There's three bars of soap and I'll give you three months!" I have used many a bar since then.

My good friend Eamonn Guy drove me to Swinford. When my family left that evening I saw my mother wiping away a tear as Eamonn drove out the Convent gate. I slept very little the first night. I looked around my cell (bedroom) from every angle. What I saw were plain white walls, a crucifix over the bed, a jug and basin and a small press. Religious life those days was not easy. We arose at 6 a.m. to the light of a candle. We called the others Sisters

Mercy Sisters – Receptions and Professions

on our turns. The mornings we gave the call we were up at 5.30 am. Our morning honorium was morning prayer and meditation at 6.30 am; Mass at 7.30 am; breakfast at 8 am and then each Sister had some house chore to complete. Cells were cleaned and beds made up before going to the school, the hospital or whatever the daily task was. In those days it was called a 'ministry'. and it was just a job to be done. We were expected to put the stamp of perfection on everything. Dinner was at 12.30 p.m; tea at 4 p.m; recreation from 4.30 – 5.15 p.m; evening prayer (the office) at 6 p.m. study and spiritual reading at 6.30 p.m; supper at 7 p.m; recreation at 8 p.m. night prayer at 9 p.m; lights out and silence at 10 p.m. According to the standards of the day the food was good and wholesome.

Meditations

After six months I received the habit of the Sisters of Mercy. We became Brides of Christ at a ceremony called 'Reception'. We dressed like brides, all in white satin and silk, complete with trail. Our families were invited to the ceremony. My mother nearly did not make it due to floods on the road near Kylemore. We wore a white veil for two years. At 'Reception' we got a new name. I was called Sister Mary Consilio. Two years after 'Reception' we had what was called 'First Profession'. At 'First Profession' we took temporary vows of poverty, chastity and obedience. After three years we were finally professed when we took vows for life.

Looking back on our honorium, the time we all should have enjoyed were the two periods of recreation, but we dreaded those periods. We were expected to make 'small talk', not to gossip and not to converse on any topics relating to the outside world. It was a great blessing when someone played the piano and we had a sing-song. If we were observed talking to the same person too often or frequently sitting beside the same person at recreation we were in trouble. This would be seen as a 'particular friendship' and such friendships were one of the major pitfalls of religious life. All our meals were eaten in silence except on special feast days.

We were always judged on our standards of work. If we were seen to be good workers, get good results in school, polish, shine and dust well, we were labelled as a 'good nun'. There was little sympathy for the weakling or the one in poor health. It was a lonely life. Today we hear so much about relationships. Sound friends and healthy relationships are the 'in thing' today, especially in religious life and the priesthood. As young Sisters we had no shoulder to cry on, no sympathetic listening ear, and no warm arms to give us a hug. We were expected to get all our consolation in the presence of the Blessed Sacrament. Having said that, we kept each other sane. We laughed and giggled at nothing; a strong sense of humour was our safety valve. Common sense told us that half the rules were crazy. Some found the rule of silence very difficult. Others valued it as an escape.

Having friends outside the circle of Mercy was greatly frowned on. If we were seen talking to the laity or 'seculars', as they were called, we were labelled as being 'a worldly Nun'.

We got two weeks holidays every summer. They were always spent at a seaside resort where the community rented a holiday home. Our companions were chosen for us. There were no choices or decisions to be made. All decisions were made at the top. We got home for five days every three years, accompanied by a companion. Sisters were never allowed out alone. When at home we had to stay in the local convent. I was lucky enough as the Convent in Clifden was just five minutes walking distance from my home. Other Sisters' homes were fifteen or twenty miles from the local Convent and their families had to hire a car to ferry them back and over every day. Any visitor who came to us outside an immediate family member had to leave the Convent after fifteen minutes. There were no visitors allowed after 4 p.m. or on the first Sunday of the month which was retreat Sunday. Sisters were rarely allowed to visit their sick parents and were never allowed to attend family funerals. There was no glamour attached to the life, even though Hollywood portrayed a different picture in their films '*Brides of Christ*' and '*Sister Act*'.

Then came Vatican II and Pope John opened all the doors and windows and they have not been closed since. Looking back on the regime, I can only describe it as one of 'control' and 'power'. It was supposed to keep us humble, but I think it was designed to make us dependent and infantile. In spite of the strict rules and regulations I marvel at how well people came through it.

The rules were so much in control that people could not think for themselves. It was a type of 'brain-washing', and yet in spite of that religious life produced brilliant women. Women who got first-class honours degrees in universities; who got first place in teacher training colleges; who were at the top of the medical profession; who were outstanding principals of schools, and matrons of hospitals; women who had an open heart and a listening ear for the poor and down-trodden. These were the women who educated our top politicians of today; our top legal advisors, psychologists, counsellors and consultants. Religious life may have been designed to make us immature and infantile but it never broke our spirits. It gave us a great chance in the educational field and developed our talents. Religious life produced artists, poets, writers, dramatists and musicians.

In the past, society had great respect for religion. It was a status symbol to have a priest or a nun in the family. Our families were proud of us. Maybe that was not a good thing either. Today we are part of a humbler Church. We may not have the great influx into religious life that we had in the past. I think the Holy Spirit is asking us to trust our laity to carry on His work – the people of God – *Pobail De* – whom He died to save. Together, I think we can build a better world and a humbler Church as we face the new Millennium. I have no doubt at all that God is still calling young boys and girls to the priesthood and religious life. He has never ceased to repeat the call 'Come follow me' as He did on the shores of Galilee to the fishermen. I wonder if our young people are listening to that call or are they so polluted with the noise from the disco, the pub and the telly that they do not hear.

I am glad I listened to that call fifty years ago. I am happy too that I have lived to experience both sides of the coin. As I said at the beginning, 'Twas the best of times –'twas the worst of times'. As I return to Clifden each year to 'the town I love so well' I say thank you Connemara for what you have been to me. Thank you for what you have done for me. Given the choice I would do it all again just as I did fifty years ago.

Remembered and written by Sr Phyl Clancy

Called to Serve

My reasons for becoming a priest probably originate in my formative years growing up in my home town of Clifden. My parents were hugely influential. They always had a very high moral standard of living and they had very high expectations for all their children. Our home was very much a home of prayer. Family prayer was very strong in rural Ireland in those times. Like so many other youngsters at that time I was somewhat in awe of the Mass ceremony. I loved serving Mass and helping the priest. I remember Canon Patrick Patterson who served in Clifden from 1932 to 1940 always gave the servers sixpence every Saturday as a reward for serving Masses during the week.

I attended St Jarlath's College, Tuam, from 1942 to 1946. The fee was £30 a year. In those days a lot of the students who attended St Jarlath's College went there with a view to becoming a priest. The school was looked upon as being a type of preparatory college for Maynooth. In 1946, along with four of my friends I sat for the Concursus. This was the special exam for entry into Maynooth. I sat for this exam mainly because my friends were doing likewise. It was not something I had thought too deeply about. My father who ran a grocery and bar business in Clifden had an expectation that I would ultimately return to Clifden to take over from him. I was very comfortable working in the business having spent all my school holidays helping out. Soon after sitting the Concursus, I was informed in writing by Archbishop Joseph Walsh of Tuam that I had been accepted for Maynooth. I had to confirm in writing that I would accept and I remember I was far from being convinced or definite about going. The economy was really struggling that year and I remember my father being very worried about being able to pay the fees. I talked it through with my parents and my father promised me the shop if things did not work out in Maynooth. The fact that this alternative had been guaranteed to me gave me a great feeling of security and I decided to give the priesthood a go.

I went to Maynooth in September 1946. The fee was £50 a year. We got home at Christmas and summer only and we had no contact with our families during the term. During our holidays we were obliged to visit our parish priest and offer our services to him. Canon Con Cunningham, who was parish priest of Clifden from 1940-1952, was a very powerful and positive influence on me during those years. I marvelled at his dedication and devotion. Every evening without fail he would visit the Blessed Sacrament in the darkness of the Church and then proceed to Clifden Hospital to visit the sick. Every Sunday evening at 7.30 p.m. he used to always give a talk on the life of a saint whose feast day would be coming up the following week. He had the gift of oratory and also of writing. He wrote a weekly book review for the *Irish Independent* under the initials CJC. When he died the editor of the *Irish Independent,* Frank Geary, paid tribute to him for his 'silent charity'.

I settled into life at Maynooth very quickly and very easily. I found the course of study very interesting and Pastoral Theology was my favourite subject area. The Moral Ttheology, Dogmatic Theology and Canon Law courses and examinations were conducted through Latin. Latin was very much the universal language of the priesthood at that time. Studying for examinations was probably the toughest aspect of life in Maynooth for me. There was a huge academic workload and we never seemed to get an adequate break from all the study. There was, without doubt, a lot of outstanding academic talent among the students and there was also an excellent quality of lecturing. At that time Maynooth could certainly hold its own with any other Irish University. There were a lot of rules and strictures. We were not allowed any daily newspapers or confectionery. Visitation to each other's private rooms was also forbidden. We were not allowed out of the College unless we had to go on urgent personal business. Permission had to be obtained from the Dean and the President if one needed to go to Dublin in this regard. I remember one particular student who was so fed up with life inside that he resolved to get away to Dublin for a day, just to preserve his sanity. He went to see Monsignor Dalton and informed him that he had to go to visit his father who was very sick in the Rotunda Hospital in Dublin. His choice of hospital was unfortunate as the Rotunda is a well-known Maternity Hospital! Needless to say his request was denied. We only had one social outing each year. This was on Easter Monday when we would dress up in priestly gear, including the black hats, and walk to Leixlip, two abreast. We would sit for a meal in Leixlip and then return promptly to Maynooth. We must have been the source of much curiosity and amusement among passing motorists during these outings.

However, we accepted all the restrictions and constraints as part of the necessary preparation for becoming a priest. We felt honoured and privileged to be in Maynooth. There was a great sense of camaraderie between us all. Socially there was a tendency for lads from the same diocese to hang around together. In fact each diocese had its own station so to speak, where the students would meet during breaks from classes. It was in this social context on campus that many lasting friendships were formed. There was great rivalry on the football field between the different classes. Maynooth had a very strong Gaelic football tradition. The inter-class leagues were always very tough and physical. Overall there was a great atmosphere of friendship and happiness in Maynooth.

Morning prayer was always at 6.30 a.m. and I can still recall my great sense of disappointment and sadness on finding a vacant seat, indicating another student had gone. Sixty-one men from my class were ordained and over the seven years, fifteen of the original seventy-six left. Every time a fellow student moved on, it used to unnerve me and bring on self-doubt. I always had great difficulty trying to rationalise why such a model student would suddenly just throw it all away. The fact that I always knew I had a business to fall back on did play a crucial role in easing any emotional insecurity I would feel at these times. There did eventually come a time however when I decided to leave, mainly because I considered myself to be so ordinary and unworthy compared to one especially brilliant student who had just left. That particular night, before going to sleep I decided to talk the whole thing through with Father Pat Travers, the Spiritual Director. During the course of our conversation he said the following words to me 'Go ahead and be a priest. I'll take full responsibility for you'. My interpretation of these words was that should I stray during my priesthood then Fr Travers would take responsibility for my actions or behaviour before God.

His words gave me great courage and all doubt immediately left me. I was never to seriously doubt again.

I was ordained as a priest on June 21st 1953 in Maynooth College by Archbishop John McQuaid who was the ordaining prelate. Due to the large numbers being ordained only my immediate family were allowed to attend. It was a day of overwhelming joy and happiness. I felt empowered to be in a position to do good for people and was totally without fear. The following day I presided over my first Mass and all I can remember is being very nervous. There was a Lithuanian graduate named Valentine Kamitis saying the Mass immediately before mine. He was from the diocese of Telfin in Lithuania and had been expelled from his homeland with two of his friends because of their clerical orientation. Fate decreed that they would train subsequently in Maynooth College. It saddened me to see that he had no family present to share in such a great occasion. Our first Masses were said through Latin and we had our back to the congregation. My daily office, or breviary as it is better known, was also in Latin. I never questioned any of these accepted practices or conventions at that time. We had a disposition of acceptance based mainly on the fact that all of these practices and conventions had gone on for centuries.

Clifden GAA had kindly arranged a reception to celebrate my ordination but I was unable to be present. Instead I celebrated by going to see the *Quiet Man* in Dublin with Fr Jim Lysaght who had been ordained two weeks before me. We missed our train subsequently and did not arrive into Galway City until 1 a.m. We were met by Billy Manning who drove us out to Clifden. We arrived in town around 3 a.m. to be met by Anthony Curran the Town Crier, John Conroy, Tommy Conneely and Sergeant Cassidy. I gave these men my blessing in the house and after Sergeant Cassidy fell asleep in the kitchen, I felt duty bound to pour the other men a quick drink in the bar as a token of my appreciation for all their kindness towards me. I was not given a permanent post straight away because I was actually surplus to requirements. I was called upon to do relief work instead and in my first year I served in Cloonfad, Corrandulla, Westport and Castlebar.

On Friday, 7th of October 1954, the Feast of the Holy Rosary, I was appointed as curate in Tullycross. Fr Michael Hanrahan was parish priest in Letterfrack and Fr Christopher Kilkelly was his curate. I was replacing Fr Michael Keane who had been a very popular priest with the people because he was young, energetic, enthusiastic and full of ideas. The first people I met on arrival were Mrs Anna Coyne and Mrs Rita Summerville who arranged to get Mass servers and a housekeeper for me. They made me feel very accepted and welcome straight away, My housekeeper, Mary Thornton, was a brilliant cook and Joseph Ruddy, who was my first server is now a priest in Venezuela with the Sacred Heart Fathers. The priest's house was not completed so I stayed initially in Mona and Annie Wallace's house in Tullycross. I was advised to get a car so I bought a three-month old Standard 8 for £350. I had no money but Hastings' Garage in Westport gave me the car on condition that I pay them back as soon as I could. They knew my father was in business and they were not worried about the impending repayments.

Coming from Clifden, I was no stranger to Tullycross, I was very familiar with the Ballinakill Parish socially and geographically. I had often played football for Clifden against Renvyle although from here on in I was not allowed to play publicly for a club anymore. Such were the rules of my chosen profession in the fifties. It was not uncommon for some priests to play for clubs under assumed names in those days. I was only allowed to train and practice with the Renvyle club. In June 1955 I moved into my new house. Rural electrification had not yet extended as far as Tullycross, in contrast to Clifden, and one of my earliest memories in relation to the

house was finding it so difficult to read with the old oil lamp. I took an instant liking to Tullycross Church. I liked its central location and its layout although it was a little strange trying to deal with certain tasks within the Church without the luxury of electricity.

Nappy Faherty dealt with the Church finances and I came to greatly admire her for her honesty and trustworthiness. Rural electrification finally arrived in Ballinakill parish in 1956 and I spent a lot ot time trying to persuade the elderly and people living alone to take it. Many of them were fearful of the possibility of fire and also of a rapid increase on the initial cost which would result in them not being able to afford it. It was difficult to allay these fears. I still have fond recollection of one woman in particular who informed me that she was getting it in because it would be "very handy for lighting the lamp!"

My first big task on arriving in Tullycross was to get to know all the people. It was relatively easy to get to know the children in school and I quickly got into the habit of visiting the schools on certain days every week. I always had some topic for discussion well prepared; otherwise, the visit would have been a waste of time. I always found the teachers in each of the schools to be very supportive and cooperative. House to house visitation in order to get to know all the people of the parish was a slow process and took me about one year to complete. I said Mass every morning and there were always two Masses every Sunday morning. I always marvelled at the people from Rossroe who used to walk nine miles in order to attend Mass after fasting since midnight. I remember saying to them on one particular Sunday "You know God does not expect you to do this every week." "Our parents did it and our grandparents, so why shouldn't we?" was the immediate reply. Funerals in those days were tough occasions for me. I found the funerals of young people particularly harrowing. There was no hearse and the coffin was usually carried on top of a car.

Sodalities were very much part of the Catholic faith throughout the 50s. There were usually three every month with the men, women and children having alternative weekends. People went to Confession on Saturday, either at midday or in the evening and then everyone received Communion on Sunday morning. All the seats at the front of the Church were reserved for whichever groups were having the sodality. On sodality day the group would display banners on the edge of the seats to indicate their respective townlands or villages. Each village or townland had a sodality promoter.

Opposite page: The official opening of Tullycross Community Sports Field, August 1957.

Tullycross Pioneers on tour in Achill, 1957.

The women used to wear special sodality medals on their day. The sodality was a type of regimentation, to facilitate the receiving of Confession and Holy Communion. However, all this was to change after the Second Vatican Council in 1966 when it was decided that it would be better for people to receive the sacraments and attend Mass as a family unit. Consequently the sodality was overtaken by the family but the modern day reality is that this has not really worked in the way that Vatican envisaged it would.

I always enjoyed the Station Masses. Theyhad the potential to bring neighbours together both in the practice of their faith and socially. Bishop Michael Browne wrote a dissertation on the Station Mass for the Vatican. At that time this type of Mass was unique to Ireland. Vatican II embraced the idea completely because it brought the Mass out to the people. They stipulated that it would be known henceforth as the Neighbourhood Mass and envisaged that its appeal would become universal in due course.

I also have very fond memories of all the processions which took place in Tullycross over the years. Many people used to paint their houses specially for the procession, and put up streamers and flower boxes to mark the occasion. I can especially remember the Children of Mary taking part in these processions. They were a group of young women who had taken a simple vow of chastity prior to marriage. They all wore blue capes and sodality medals. At the Corpus Christi procession in Clifden a special place was always reserved for the Children of Mary. To me, these processions were always symbolic of God moving among his people in the Eucharist.

The Parish Mission arrived in Tullycross every four or five years. My role was to select the missioners from the various orders and to advertise their coming well in advance, thereby creating a sense of anticipation, excitement and maybe even a little trepidation. The missioners, who were specially trained for their particular type of work, were famous for their loud voices and colourful oratory. They would attempt to rouse up the people who were becoming a little bit lax in their faith. They tried to preach positive sermons which would be of practical use to their congregation. However their style always tended to be very authoritarian and these 'Hellfire Sermons' as they came to be known often caused people to be frightened and upset because of their presentation. The Mission usually lasted two weeks with one week for the men and one for the women. It was common practice for the missioners to visit parishioners who were not attending Mass or receiving the sacraments. The missioners would try to persuade these people to go back to the outward practice of their faith. During the mission fortnight there were always stalls set up in the churchyard. Every family usually bought a new religious picture and a pair of rosary beads to mark the mission. There was also a tradition synonymous with the mission, of people exchanging religious gifts. There were many yarns and stories told at the Mission which caused great enjoyment when they were told and retold in later years.

Emigration was a scourge of western society throughout the 1950s. I felt that most of the young people who were emigrating for economic reasons needed some form of preparation for the future world outside and for this reason I decided to get involved in the emigrant question. For the emigrant, the priest's house was nearly always the last port of call on the way to England and the first port of call on the way back. I used to give talks in the house to potential emigrants, themain purpose of which was to teach young adults how to conform with society in America or England in order to avoid embarrassment and to help them gain acceptance. I decided also to meet the emigrants where they were and in 1959 the first ever Parish Reunion was held in Kilburn, London. Father Eamon Casey made all the arrangements in London. At our end I organised that each emigrant was sent two letters, one consisting of an invitation (venue, time, etc) and the other containing a list of all those invited. This strategy worked and the success of this first reunion prompted similar events in subsequent years. I also became involved in the Pioneer movement which was very strong in the parish at the time. We went on various outings each year. Young teenagers and women were rarely to be seen in public houses in those days. In any case people had not the money to spend on drink back then like they do today.

The idea for a community sportsfield had already been mooted prior to my arrival in Tullycross. My role was one of offering assistance in the organisation of the project. The whole project was based on voluntary labour and I helped to establish two working groups, one from Renvyle and one from Lettergesh, to work alternate weeks. The work began at the end of 1956 and the initial enthusiasm appeared to be waning over the winter until somebody came up with the idea of inviting the Galway All-

Ballinakill Parish Reunion, Kilburn, 1962.

Ireland winning team of 1956 to play in the opening match on the first Sunday in August 1957. This brought back all the enthusiasm and every man worked flat out to the best of his ability from there on in. I recall one man who seemed to be forever concentrating on the area around the forty yard line at either end. His preoccupation with these sections aroused my curiosity and I asked him why he was so taken up with these particular lines. He replied that it was "because Sean Purcell is going to stand here". The opening day of the field will always hold a special place in my memory. The people of the parish took a tremendous pride in their achievement and it gave them a great sense of belief and confidence in themselves.

It was no surprise that a meeting was convened soon after in Mona Wallace's house in Tullycross to discuss the building of a Community Hall. I was asked to chair the meeting. There were three main propositions for discussion. Was there really a need for a hall? If so, would people give support in the form of voluntary labour and would people also give financial support? The majority of those present were in favour of going for it, along the lines suggested above and a committee was duly formed. Paddy Coyne presented a site for a sum of £46. He wanted to give it for nothing but for the purpose of legal contract a donation had to be given. The work commenced in October 1958 and the hall was completed by August 1959 at a total cost of £1,100. The money was raised through raffles, sweeps and voluntary donations. That opening night I always remember the immense pride of the people in their great achievement. The women had everything prepared from the previous Friday night and on that Sunday night, the hall was thronged to capacity with the Blue Notes Band from Letterfrack providing the music. Fr Michael Hanrahan, parish priest, carried out the official opening and blessing.

The priests in the neighbouring parish at that time were very supportive

Clearing the site for the construction of Tullycross Hall.

to me. We established a custom of meeting every Tuesday night for a game of cards. This helped to cement the union between us. It was all very relaxed yet it was still a great learning experience for a young curate like myself starting off. Practical knowledge which came from dealing with people and problems were shared at these gatherings. It was on one of these occasions that I was first advised by my more experienced colleagues to always meet people more than halfway and to be always there to help people, not to dominate them. I was encouraged to try to always be available for people, to advise, not dictate and, above all, to be a good listener. As regards developmental issues within the parish I tried to have a policy of working with people in a non-judgmental way. I found that by not being authoritarian in my approach, it was easier to get certain things done.

In those years before the Second Vatican Council, people tended to put the priest up on a pedestal. I was acknowledged as being a very educated member of society and the fact that I presided over the Masses and sacraments in Latin and not the vernacular only served to create an extra aura of mystery about me. Now that the Mass is said in English or Irish it has lost some of its mystery and it would seem that the priest has lost some his mystery also. Having said that, there is no doubting the fact that people

Some of the men who developed Tullycross Sportsfield, 1957.

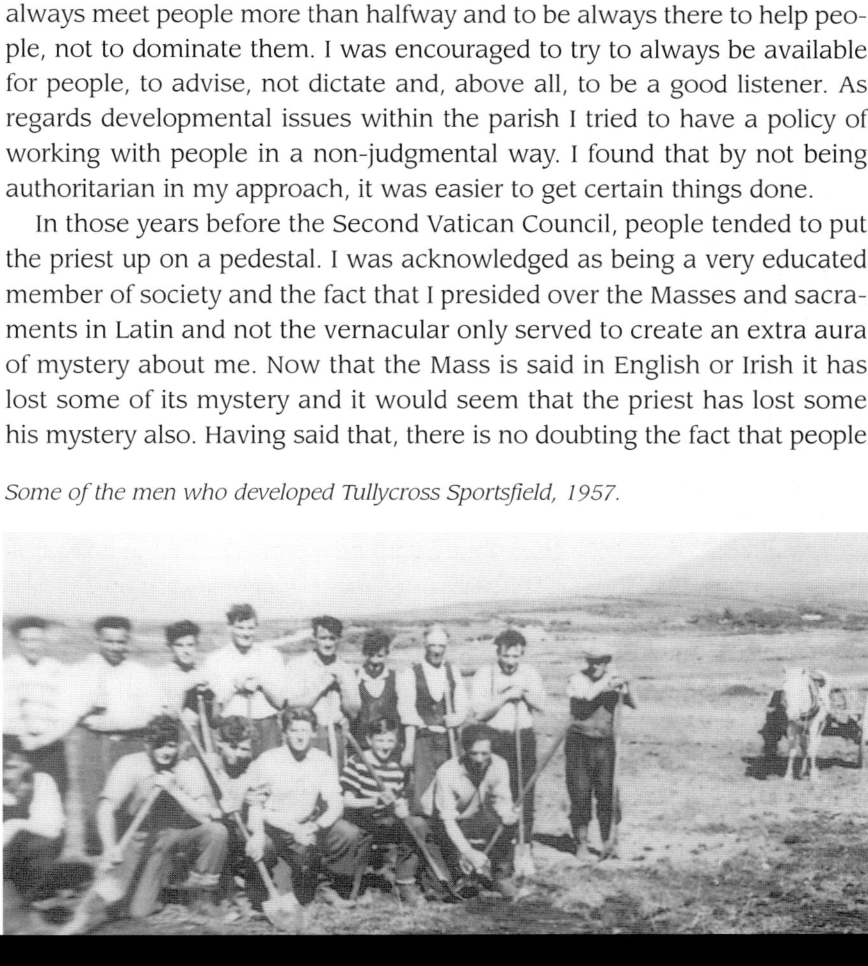

today are as good as they ever were. Years ago if a person attended Sunday Mass he or she was judged to be half way to Heaven. Nowadays I find people show great concern for each other in the wider context of the universal Church. Vatican II had to come because society was changing so rapidly the Church felt it had to keep in step. Pope John XXIII was the catalyst who saw the need for change. It was envisaged that the implementation of the Second Vatican Council directives would help to bring about a Church which might be leaner but ultimately would be more compassionate and better equipped to bear witness to Christ in the modern world.

In conclusion I would just like to say that I never felt lonely as a priest. I always felt part of the people. I lived among them and they were part of me. When I was first informed that I was to be transferred from Tullycross I became very upset at the prospect of leaving the people with whom I had shared my first ten years of priestly life. I still remember to this day the many kindnesses I received from the people of Ballinakill Parish. It was very easy that time to be part of the people, especially young people. Nowadays, in the light of recent revelations and events, priests are a lot more guarded in their contact with young people. This is a very sad development in the context of the priest's role in community life today.

Remembered by Fr Stephen Ludden and written by Paul Gannon

Manning the gate at the Opening Day of Tullycross Sportsfield. From left: Patrick Lydon, Stevie Salmon, Fr Stephen Ludden, Jim O'Neill, Michael Ruddy and John Wallace.

Among the People

I arrived in Cashel in October 1954 and left in the Autumn of 1961. I have very happy memories of Cashel and its friendly people. Every week there used to be a dance in the old school, christened by the comedian Paschal Spelman – 'The Riverside Ballroom'. That dance was always well attended. Coleman Nee used to man the box office. We had the top floor reinforced and furnished for showing movies once a week. We purchased a 16mm Bell & Howell projector for that purpose. The movies were very popular and well attended in the pre-TV era.

John Willie Joyce from Cloonacarton, Recess, provided the music for the dances. We had a good drama group at that time also. Johnny Nee, Martin Conneely, Monica Canavan, Peggy Cummins, Pakie McDonagh, Maire Conneely, Dan Kelly, Peter Veldon and Paddy Molloy were members of that group and gave sterling service. We staged such mortal classics as '*The Cobwebs Glory*', '*The Courting of Mary Doyle*' and '*A Man of Ideas*'.

On the economic front, I tried to put across the following scheme: there were about 90 families in Cashel in my time. If we could get every family interested in a project that would generate modest income of £10 more than the year before – then there would be nearly £1000 more in circulation than previously. If, in a few years, we could aim at every family making £100 more in income, then there would be an extra £9000 floating around Cashel annually.

Quite a lot of vegetables were being imported from Dublin into Clifden and Oughterard. I hoped that, in time, Cashel could supply both those markets. At that time, an acre of cabbage could generate a profit of £200.

I had in mind also bee-keeping and the production of honey. I had approached Kevin Stanley of Clifden who was interested, but pointed out that we would need a big range of products to supply his shop. The scheme was possible, but not as successful as I would have liked.

I tried to buy the sports field opposite Mag Keaney's from Mr Gahon, who was Guinness's Manager at the time. He was not prepared to sell but was prepared to rent it. I – foolishly, in hindsight – turned down his pepper-corn rent proposal.

I played a crucial role in persuading the Protestants to give us their church in Ballynahinch, in which Mass is now said. The local Protestants, especially Mr Gahon and Jack Milne (dentist) were very helpful.

Every year after our drama campaign, we used to organise an outing for the group. I remember on one occasion above the Cliffs of Moher, there was a herd of cattle grazing. I asked Paddy Crean who had an accordion, to walk around the field playing it. Before long, he was followed by every animal in the field. He looked like the Pied Piper of Hamelin!

Remembered and written by Fr Michael Keane

The Station Mass

Marty Conneely

During the mid-forties I remember the stations coming to our village. In those days, it caused great excitement and people would be getting the place ready for the great day for weeks before.
It was in the month of March when it came to Biddy's turn to have them, and she was contemplating for some time whether she should have them or not. The problem was that she had a hen hatching on a dozen eggs under the kitchen table, and what if she left the eggs due to all the extra noise on the day of the stations? That would be a disaster for poor Biddy.

Anyway, the neighbours said that they would all lend a helping hand for the occasion, and another table would have to be borrowed from the neighbourhood to use for the altar so as not to disturb Rosie the hen.

The house was white washed inside and out the day before the event. The door and half door and windows were all painted signal red. The big dresser was left till last: all the delph was taken down and washed, while Paddy Feeney and myself got the job of painting the dresser – yes, you guessed it – signal red again, and the panels white. We finished the job near midnight and were having tea when Tommy Green arrived, carrying the table on his back. Biddy was delighted and, in a flash, had a white linen table cloth, which she received from her sister in America, placed on the table, which was then erected on top of two chairs placed under the kitchen window. Later on, Tommy Guy and Dudley Folan arrived, and Dudley started telling us stories while Tommy got the altar ready for the morning.

Dudley said the dresser was a bit low down and should be lifted about a foot more off the floor while the delph was still off it, so Berty said he would find two wooden blocks. Sure enough, it looked much better in its new position, but someone asked whether it was steady enough, or would it topple over. Everybody in the kitchen had a look and the majority thought it was alright. Biddy was happy. Everybody left about 2 a.m. they would be back again at 9 a.m. for the Mass.

The next morning was lovely, with the sun shining, and the neighbours all heading for Biddy's house. I remember myself and the late Johnny Harte walking together across the fields and Jonny telling me about the day, many years before, when he went fishing in his currach, and after catching lots of fish, he thought he would pull some crannach. On the way home, he pulled into Mull-on-a-Cranny and forgot to tie up the boat. With the rising tide, it soon floated away, leaving him stranded on the rock which would soon be covered by ten feet of water. He started to shout for help, and luck was with him that day. Stephen Devane and Michael Mannion from Errislannan, as well as some people from Mannin, came to rescue him after hearing his cries for help.

When Johnny and I arrived at Biddy's house, the Mass was about to start. Some remained outside the door, looking in; others were inside, looking down to the kitchen. Johnny and I found a place in the kitchen. I spotted Biddy putting on the kettle. The fire was really hot, and she seemed very pleased that the place was looking great.

Then it was time for Communion, and as the people were receiving, some went outside. I think that the heat was too much for them. Just then, I noticed that one man, who had been leaning against the dresser from the start, waited to the very end to receive. The priest was about to put back the Host on the altar, and was taking one more look for latecomers, when your man made a dash forward to kneel down and, lo and behold, wasn't his jacket stuck to the paint! Missing the priest by inches, the dresser came crashing down in the middle of the kitchen floor, putting bits and pieces of delph flying all over the place. People were making for the door because they thought the roof had caved in. The clocking hen came flying from under the table and out the door. The kettle had collapsed on the fire, and there were ashes all over the house. When things quietened down, the priest told everyone to give thanks that no one was hurt.

People were looking for the man who caused the accident, but someone mentioned that they had seen him running across the fields. The funny thing was, Biddy was more upset about the clocking hen than all her lovely delph broken to smithereens on the floor, but she was much relieved when Paddy Feeney arrived, carrying Rosie under his arm. We all decided to buy Biddy more delph on the next fair day.

So a word of warning to you all: always paint your dressers well in advance of the stations...but perhaps I'm forgetting something here. That's right – sure, they don't make them anymore!

Remembered and written by Marty Conneely

Monuments of Faith and Sacrifice

In 1868, armed with a letter of commendation from Archbishop McHale, Reverend P. J. Lydon set out on a tour of the countryside to collect funds for a new church in the town of Clifden. While in Cork and Waterford he had this letter published in the respective local newspapers – *The Cork Examiner* and the *Waterford Citizen*, and he also added his own eloquent appeal for funds. The main theme of his letter can be summarised as follows:

"The people in Clifden and West Connemara have just come through a very trying period. A massive campaign has been launched to wean them from their allegiance to their Catholic heritage but in spite of many inducements they have remained loyal and steadfast. The practice of the faith is strong and vigorous."

Father Lydon continues "The public now have authentic certainty that it is not a big flock but a large church that is needed in the district. Anybody who has been in Clifden on a Sunday or a Holy day must have seen with pain a large portion of the pious flock compelled from want of even standing room within the old church to hear Mass as best they could outside as well in the cold and rain. It is not as a matter of choice but of necessity that we have to appeal to the public. We have taxed all our local resources. Charity which begins at home but does not end there, will not refuse the small assistance we ask to provide the faithful peasantry of Connemara with the house of worship where they may be able to return thanks to God for having safely brought them out of dreadful trials of the last quarter of a century."

It is not in any anti-ecumenical spirit that I have given this extract from a priest who lived in more difficult times – but rather to remind ourselves what people were prepared to do for their faith all those years ago.

To undertake the task of building such a magnificent church at that period of our history in a district so poor as Clifden was then, demanded exceptional courage and confidence. It is all the more surprising when we realise that the parish priest, Dean McManus, was well on in his seventies when he undertook the work. The first meeting of the committee took place on August 15th 1868; the foundation stone was laid four years later in August 1872 and the first Mass was celebrated on July 20th 1879.

Dean McManus died in 1882 and was succeeded by Canon Lynskey. It would seem that there were some defects in the building of the church because we find a record of a meeting held on March 16th 1884 and among the resolutions passed at that meeting we find the following:

Whereas the breakage and evident decay of our costly Church are becoming daily more sensibly serious, we deem it our bounden duty to make such efforts as will save and secure it from the immediate ruin which threatens it.

That as a means to this desired end we forthwith open a subscription list and form a committee from among respected parishioners for the purpose of devising means where with to meet the outlay necessitated by such expensive works. (1884)

The names of the committee are given: Chairman Canon Lynskey, Vice Chairman Joseph Gorham, Secretaries Fr McDermott CC and Daniel Cronin, Committee members William Casey, James Mullin, John M. Lydon, William Faherty, John M. Darcy, Bernard Bodkin, Bartholomew Malone, William Nee, William Gorham, Con King, Bernard Lee, John O'Connor, Patrick O'Hara, Brother Joseph, Brother Bernard.

At a later date we find the following resolution

"That the committee meet every Sunday at 12.30".

A special subscription list was opened in September 1881 (during the lifetime of Dean McManus) towards the cost of the high altar.

In 1896 an appeal was made for funds for the tower and spire and the spire itself was finished by Christmas 1898. Unfortunately a storm damaged the upper portion which had to be dismantled and rebuilt. It rises to a height of 200ft and at one period the large cross on top of it was illuminated by large electric bulbs. This fixture was later removed, in the interest of either economy or safety. The bell was erected in January 1889 and first rung on St Patrick's Day. The clock was installed at the same time and the organ was installed in 1900. The marble floor of the sanctuary, the gift of the brothers Tom and Andrew Lydon, was installed in 1922.

Monsignor McAlpine, parish priest of Clifden for 34 years (1898– 1932) had a great interest and pride in the church and did much in his lifetime to furnish and beautify it. His three successors Canon Patterson, Canon Cunningham and Chancellor Corcoran have each contributed their share in adorning and improving the church and its surroundings and all of them evoked a generous response from the people of the parish.

The list of subscribers to the church is still extant and makes interesting reading. All the familiar Clifden and West Connemara names are there

Clifden, 1870, prior to the construction of the Catholic Church. Clifden Workhouse can be seen in the background.

with amounts varying from £1500 (the bequest of Thomas Eyre) to one shilling (5 pence in new currency).

We read that John J. Eyre of Clifden Castle subscribed £200 – and we wonder what its equivalent would be in modern currency! Do any of the Eyre family survive anywhere today? A Sir Charles Clifford was a subscriber – so also was the Countess of Clare (£3), The Earl of Kenmare (£30), Lady Lothian (£3) and the Earl of Denbigh (amount not legible). On September 22nd the local branch of the Royal Irish Constabulary contributed £1.10.0 and the 'Railway men' subscribed £4.6.0. Lord O'Hagan of Dublin subscribed £2 on August 7th 1881. (It is also of interest to read that the Duke of Norfolk subscribed £5 towards Claddaghduff church in 1900). One wonders why these people were inspired to contribute towards the building fund. Was it as a result of the 'collecting excursions' of the two curates Father P. J. Lydon and Father Walter Conway. A tribute should also be paid to the trojan work in collecting funds accomplished by the Franciscan brothers. The old records mention sums of £20, £30, £40 and £50 received from Brother Francis Robinson and Brother Patrick from collections carried out by them in Cork, Dublin, Belfast, Liverpool and Manchester. At a later stage funds were collected by Brother Joseph Cafferty, Brother Fidelis Lynch, Brother Virgilius, Brother Pius Corcoran, Brother Joachim and Brother Paul McCabe.

St James' church forms the focal point of the village of Cashel. It is situated in the geographically largest parish in Ireland, namely the parish of Roundstone. Previous to the existence of the church, the people of the area attended Mass in McDonagh's house in Glenturkeen and there was also a time when the people would walk over the hills (barefoot) from Cashel to Ballinafad in order to get Mass there.

The church was built at the turn of the century and from what I have gathered, I imagine that the main influence behind getting it built, was the parish priest of Roundstone at that time – Revd Patrick Gleeson PP. A copy of the *Galway Observer* (dated Saturday 27th July, 1901), which came into my possession during my research contained an article about the church and in it the Revd Patrick Gleeson is described as "the esteemed and energetic parish priest of Roundstone". He was a much respected man as was reflected in a poem dedicated to him by a local poet – Patrick Kelly. The poem was called '*The Builder*'.

Work commenced on the church in the year 1899 and it was completed in two years. Due to a lack of funds at the time, the local people gave voluntary labour. This kept the costs to a minimum. The materials were bought at Hynes, Galway. Most of the stone was brought from Blue Island by boat to Creanes Quay and from there it was transported to the site by cart.

Morgan Folan brought forty-eight boat loads of stone from Blue Island and Canower. John O'Donnell cut the stone for the church at the site. Pat Mulkerrin carried the cement crosses on his back and put them in position on the church. Patrick Nee, Martin King and Josie King built the stone pillars for the gate and also the boundary wall. John Joyce was also involved. Pat and John Conneely roofed the tower and set the navigation wheel cross in position.

The barges and crosses were plastered by Tom Creane, he also did work on the arch over the altar. The marble altar was a gift from John J. O'Loughlin, JP, proprietor of the Zetland Arms Hotel – as it was known then. He also presented a set of vestments. The altar, with inlays of rich colouring, was designed by Dublin architect, Mr C. J. Taylor. There are twenty stained glass in the church, six of which are pictorial windows. The windows were all donated by local families.

The first person to be baptised in the new church was Colman Conroy and the first wedding was that of Martin Nee and May Faherty.

Written by Canon Michael Mooney and John Nee

THE BUILDER

He builded a church beside the road,
In the bushes above the sea,
For the poor plain folk o'the twisted lands,
An' poorer an' plainer he
than the poorest neighbour speaking his name,
With a blessin' night or day,
For all that he was, an' all that he die
In the Master's name an' way.

An' he who builded the grey-stone church,
In the bushes above the sea,
Is gone long years to the Master's land,
But somehow it seems to me
He's watchin' out an' over the stars
Thro' the length o' the earthly day,
An' helpin' the folk o' the twisted lands
Wherever they kneel to pray.

(The builder was Rev. Fr Gleeson PP of Roundstone)
and the church is that of St James, Cashel, in Connemara)

Written by Patrick Kelly 'Bard of Connemara'

The Procession

Corpus Christi procession, Cashel, c. 1960. In those days there was strict segregation, with the children leading, the women next and the men following.

In our youth; the Corpus Christi procession was a big occasion. My earliest recollection is, that it went from the church to O'Meara's (Cashel House) front lawn one year and the next year to the Zetland Arms Hotel. Altars were prepared at these venues for Benediction. Later the new school became the permanent venue. We would spend the day lining the route with flowers and bunting, and each gateway or gap along the way had a little altar with statues and flowers.

There was always a big crowd at the procession which was held in the late afternoon. Cross bearer, canopy bearers, and ushers were all appointed beforehand and did an excellent job for an orderly procession. We were lined up outside the church by the cross bearer: the children; the women; the men; the choir and the first Communion class, who threw petals to honour the Eucharist carried by the priest under a canopy.

The rosary was recited by the ushers and answered by the congregation along the route. Hymns were sung. There was always a good choir – mostly adult – I recall. I can remember people coming from Recess and Roundstone just for the procession.

Written by Barbara Joyce

The Corpus Christi Processions on Main Street, Clifden in 1919 (left) and 1957 (right).

Saved from the Brink

Sally Tierney was a poor Catholic woman, living alone in Ballinew in the 1890s. Evidently she had no family or close relatives. She was offered a weekly allowance by the Protestant community leaders in the area in return for agreeing to conform to the Protestant faith. Outwardly she had conformed but the story goes that she was very devoted to our Lady and always carried her rosary beads with her. When she realised that she was soon to die she sent a word to Pat Nee to get the parish priest. Pat Nee was very involved in the Land League at that time and was under the vigilant eye of the local RIC in Letterfrack. He knew he would arouse suspicion if he was seen going to Letterfrack early in the morning so he persuaded his wife, Mary, to go to Canon McAndrew instead. As Canon McAndrew was heading to Ballinew he met the Protestant carriage heading over to Moyard rectory with Sally Tierney on board. Not wishing to engage in public confrontation he told Mary Nee he could do no more and he returned home to Letterfrack. However, the local curate, Father Hannon, came to hear of these events and the following day he went to visit Sally Tierney, who was being kept in the old Protestant school house beside the rectory. He spoke to her in Irish and asked her if she wanted to be reconciled with the Catholic Church. She told him that this was her wish and he had her removed immediately and put into the care of Pat Canning of Moyard. She was given absolution by Father Hannon who also anointed her and administered the last rites when she passed away peacefully a few days later. She was buried in the Roman Catholic cemetery in Ballinakill.

The following poem, given to me by Kate Conneely, was written by her granduncle, Stephen Cosgrave. Pat and Mary Nee were Kate's grandparents.

THE SOUL OF SALLY TIERNEY

Come all ye friends and neighbours,
Pray listen to me awhile.
I'll sing to you a verse or two,
That will cause you all to smile.

It's about old Sally Tierney
Whom the 'jumpers' had long claimed.
When this long lost woman
Found her life was going to cease,
She begged and craved for mercy sake,
Some friend to bring the priest.

When Lutheran jumpers heard of it,
Like demons they flocked on guard,
They swore they would never part with her,
Till they'd bury her in Moyard

Long life to Father Hannon,
He did hisduty well,
He snatched the soul of Sally Tierney,
From the fiery gates of hell.

*Jumpers: A derogatory term referring to the Protestant proselytisers.

Devotion

Salruck is the area between Lough Muck and Killary Bay. Salruck means 'the Holy Ground'. St Ruckart built a church at Salruck, but it was later destroyed in the Penal Days. All that remains of the church apart from the rubble is the altar stone. Inside the gates of the cemetery there is a flagstone with the date 1167. Salruck was at one time widely known as a place of pilgrimage. Each year pilgrims travelled from all over Connemara to pray at St Roc's well. On the 15th August and 8th September, the people used to do a night vigil round the well and at dawn they would go to Mass at Tullycross church, nine miles away. The pilgrims held a lighted candle while they walked and prayed around the well. The custom was seven times around the well. By 1935 the pilgrimage had died away.

There are, in fact, three wells in the cemetery, and these wells are a reminder of the three holy men who once lived there. Their names were Sal Roc, Maol Roc and Bawn Roc. The story goes that the three, who were brothers, had a disagreement for which they were later sorry. To do penance for their misbehaviour they resolved to part, so that they could not see or hear each other. Sal Roc stayed in Salruck, Maol Roc moved to the Kylemore area and settled in Mweelin, to which he gave his name. The remains of a cemetery can be seen there today. Bawn Roc settled in Baunoges, which is called after him and which also has a cemetery.

The church in Ballinakill cemetery, dedicated to St Ceannanach, was built about the year 1600 by Edmund O'Flaherty. The remains suggest that it was a typical late parish church. To the east of the church is St Ceannanach's Well. This well was visited by local people on the 12th of March each year. St Ceannanach's Stone and Cross consist of a small heap of stones, the broken arms of a small stone cross and curious red stone. St Ceannanach, known familiarly as St Gregory, is the same Saint to whom is dedicated Cill Ceannanach on Inishmann, Aran Islands and after whom Gregory's Sound is called. He was one of the few legendary Irish martyrs. The story goes that, having been beheaded by pagans, he picked up his head to return to Aran. Passing this spot he felt tired and placed his head down to rest. His blood left its mark on the red stones.

It is said that on the eve of the Battle of Clontarf, Good Friday 1014, Brian Boru, High King of Ireland, visited his confessor, St Gormgall, on High Island. Brian was held in high esteem by the saint.

Before his departure the saint informed Brian that there was a holy well on the island. The saint said that he would watch the well on the following day, that a fly would come to rest on the water. If the king lost the battle the fly would drown in the well, but if successful it would fly away.

The battle started on the following day. The saint kept watch at the well, fasting and praying, all day. The fly rested on the waters of the well. At sunset it rose from the well and flew away. St Gormgall knew that Brian had been victorious at Clontarf.

Afterwards the well was called Brian Boru's Well. People worried about their sons, daughters and friends who have lost contact with their people at home, visit this well. The fly is always there before them. If all is well with their relatives and friends the fly rises into the air and flies way. If all is not well it remains swimming in the water.

The poet MacGoire, a contemporary of Brian Boru tells us that as a sign of Brian's death, Feithin's Frigid Bed – the Frigid waters in which the saint was accustomed to practice mortification – turned into blood. The words of the poet rendered into English read:

'There was found at Feithin's Frigid Bed,
Wells of overflowing blood,
The sign the Kingly Brian's death
In the Western Borderland of Erin'.

St Conal's well is situated in High Cashel, Cashel, Connemara. There was much devotion and belief in St Conal by the generation of people before us. Local lore says he may be a brother of Mac Dara, Cáillín and Ciaran.

There is no organised pilgrimage day for St Conal's well. Many believe his feast day is June 15th. In the early part of this century people travelled to the well, coming by boat from Carna, Kilkerrin and across the hill from Recess and further. Cures and favours were granted. One lady told me St Conal's water had a cure for eyes. Others maintain crutches were left here in the old days. I know a young lady who got rid of warts after washing her hand in the well.

To get to this holy well one has to go up the High Cashel road just beside St. James church in Cashel. The road goes to the graveyard, walk through the graveyard and out by the stile opposite the gate and just a few yards ahead is Tobar Conail. In the old graveyard there is a mound of stones called Conal's bed.

Even though one can drive to the graveyard it is well worthwhile to walk. The peace and tranquillity of this area is unique and the scenery on the return journey is breathtaking - a definite bonus for the trip. One person summed it up saying "If you have a problem or an ache and go in faith to St. Conal's well and pray, you get peace of mind."

The parish of Clifden is made up of the union of the two ancient parishes of Omey and Ballindoon. The Owenglin River upon which Clifden is built, separates these parishes. The name Ballindoon is from the Irish 'Baile na Dúin' which means the townland of the Fort, originally so called from the pagan fort which stood at the summit of Knockadoon and within the grounds of Bunowen Castle. At the foot of the hill and within the Bunowen Castle grounds was situated the original parish church. The walls of this ancient and venerable church still stand and are remarkably well preserved thanks to the skill of the builders and the quality of the stone used. St Feichin, St Flannan and St Cáillín all have strong associations with Clifden parish. St Flannan was a 7th century contemporary of St Feichin and laboured in the Ballindoon parish in and around the same time that Feichin ministered in Omey. Flannan came originally from Killaloe in Co Clare. His evangelical labours in the parish were chiefly confined to the northern end of Ballindoon. His church and monastery were established on the peninsula that still bears his name, Errislannan (Iorras Fhlannáin). There still remains some small traces of his monastic establishment within the present cemetery grounds near Errislannan Manor, and both it and his Holy Well are to the present day held in great veneration by the local people. St Cáillín holds the distinction of being the very first missionary and apostle of Connemara itself, having laboured among us in the fifth century. He was a disciple of St Benignus, the disciple and successor of St Patrick in the See of Armagh.

St Cáillín's memory is still perpetuated in the parish by two holy wells, one of which is on Duck Island (Oileán Lachán) where the saint erected his first chapel and the other is on the mainland in Keeraunmore. The latter, the well known as 'St Cáillín's Well', is a place of pilgrimage where pilgrims perform the 'station' on bended knees in order to implore his aid or to return him grateful thanks for favours received. What better friend could they have in Heaven that Cáillín who is described in the *Martyrology of Donegal* as 'a sea with ebbing in signs and miracles'

In olden days, a three-day Pattern was held in the village of Ballyconneely at the Feast of St Cáillín on November 13th. It is still observed as a local holiday. Devotion to St Cáillín extends along the coast to Cois Fharraige, and what is known as Iar-Chonnacht. The reason, it would appear, is that fishermen from these areas use Slyne Head and Tobar Cáillín as landmarks. Their devotion to him is without question – and why not? Cáillín has been good to them in the past and their sons and grandsons and future generations will continue to revere Cáillín Caiffeach (Stormy Cáillín) as he is known in the Gaelic.

Saint Cáillín's Bell is more romantically known in literature and folklore as Clog na Riogh (The Bell of the Kings). No fewer than nineteen Irish monarchs are said to have been baptised from it. These are reputed to have included Fergus and Dónall and Cónall. The bell, when inverted, could hold about one-and-a-half pints of water, which was then poured over them.

Today, Clog na Ríogh is preserved in the parochial house at Foxfield, Feenagh, Co Leitrim. The bell is alleged to have been given to St Cáillín by St Patrick. It was written about in the *Annals of the Four Masters* and in the *Book of Feenagh*, which dates from 1516. The original manuscript of the *Book of Feenagh* is in the Royal Irish Academy in Dublin and contains a poem of 268 lines dealing with St Cáillín's Bell. The poem says that when the bell is carried from place to place, it must be carried by a man in Holy Orders, who should be accompanied by twelve men. If a king saw the bell being carried towards him, he was bound to go to meet it. If it should be carried three times around the clan which possessed it the members would be protected from any threatened danger. The Revd John Hynes placed the year of origin as between 1050 and 1150 AD. He said the bell was very much revered.

We know that Cáillín himself founded a monastery at Feenagh, Co Leitrim, and was a man of great sanctity. We assume that he came to Connemara from Feenagh and built his church on Chapel Island near Slyne Head. The ruins of this oratory are to be seen today on their 14 acre island. In front of the church is a little well. There is no more beautiful or peaceful place on a summer day.

The local fishermen never leave the island without kneeling in prayer at the stone altar inside the little church. To witness this is to see and feel the great veneration of St Cáillín which exists in Errismore. Many miracles and prophesies were attributed to him in the *Book of Feenagh* which also states that he lived to be 500 years old.

Researched and written by Paul Gannon and Barbara Joyce

Climbing the Reek. Pilgrims on Croagh Patrick.
Photography by Kirstin Klein

ST CÁILLÍN'S HOLY WELL

There's many dates within the year
That most of us remember,
But there's one that's extra special
It's the 13th of November,
For that's the day that we all pray
As our parents did before,
When we go back to Cáillín's Well
In the Parish of Errismore.

From dawn till dusk the people came
As the rugged hill they climb,
And gaze around at scenery
And that countryside so fine,
They walk the old path further on
Through rocks and stones and dell,
And there it is down by your left
St Cáillín's Holy Well.

Barefoot you go as prayers you say
Around the little mound,
You pick up seven tiny stones
From off the holy ground,
With the Lord's Prayer and Hail Marys
And then the Glorias too,
And at each round you throw a stone
Until they are all threw.

Then down you go to the mound below
And repeat the same again,
You think about St Cáillín
And of when and why he came,
You look towards Chapel Island
Far out across the strand,
It's just out there past old Slyne Head
Where his little church still stands.

Now to complete you wash your feet
As you pray for fishermen,
Who sail and fish around Slyne Head
To come safely home again,

You meet your friends and neighbours
As they go there by the score,
To that old and holy blessed Well
In the parish of Errismore.

1990 was a special year
For all going to the Well,
It was the first time ever
We saw St Cáillín's Bell,
1000 years of age it is
From Longford it did come,
And we thank you John O'Malley
For the great thing that you've done.

The Mass it was at 12 o'clock
The people were all there,
The old, the young, the babies
Some grey, some golden haired,
It was such a saintly feeling
As we walked up the aisle,
To see the bell there standing
'Twas brought down by Fr Doyle.

All thoughts were on the altar
As our eyes with tears they stung,
When at the elevation
St Cáillín's Bell was rung.

Now to conclude my story,
As once more his feast day's o'er,
I hope our children's children
Will still go to Keerhaunmore,
That their faith will hold
Like the folks of old,
That they still will ring his Bell
As they make their way,
And barefoot they pray
Around St Cáillín's Holy Well.

Written by Penny O'Malley

THE PARISH OF ERRISMORE

(suggested air: *Can anybody tell me where the Blarney Roses grow?*)

This ballad, or comaile, was written by an unknown native of Roundstone about 75 years ago.

It was on a fine November's night, I mean to let you know,
The lads and lassies they did prepare for to St Cáillín's Well to go;
Myself and dear little Annie and a couple hundred more,
We made straight way for St Cáillín's Well in the Parish of Errismore.

When we arrived at Ballyconneely, there were refreshments all around;
The lads went to the public house and the girls went towards Bunowen;
For bottles of stout they did shout, something around three score;
Then they went straight way for Little's house in the Parish of Errismore.

When we arrived at Little's house, there was tea for every man,
Plenty of bread and butter and likewise lots of ham.
The house was fully crowded, and they danced from door to door;
There was always song and music in the Parish of Errismore.

When the dance it was all over, at the dawning of the day,
Every man and woman to the well they did make their way,
There they knelt on those holy stones, some both lame and sore,
Saying: 'May St Cáillín be our safeguard in the Parish of Errismore'.

Long life to Martin O'Malley – we met him on the way –
He brought us to his own house and entertained us there all day;
He gave us so much whiskey, it made us sleep and snore,
And we awoke in Roundstone town, far away from Errismore.

Goodbye to Kings and Darcys, to Connollys and Duanes;
Three cheers to Festeen Tameen – the King of Errismore –
May God Bless those who dwell back there in dear old Kerraunmore,
And bring you all back safe again to your home in Errismore.

Given to me by by Nra Burke

The Statue on the Mountain

For many years, thousands of tourists, and all the people of the area have looked up to the statue of the Sacred Heart half-way up the slopes of Altnagaighera as it rises behind Kylemore Abbey – for almost seventy years, in fact.

When the Benedictine nuns came to Kylemore in 1920, they erected a small plaster statue, which rapidly succumbed to the severe erosion that we experience in North Connemara. In the year of the Eucharistic Congress, 1932, the nuns decided to have a more durable statue erected. This proved expensive for the then struggling community, but the foresight of the community has been well rewarded by the uplift which this notable landmark has given to so many who 'lift up their eyes to the mountain.' The men, who worked at the Abbey at the time, with help from some others, achieved the great feat of bringing the statue up the mountain and erecting it on its platform. It weighs five-and-a-half hundredweight. Many people still ask how it was done! Mr Michael Fitzsimmons constructed a large stretcher with protruding shafts, and the entire statue was placed on this. Two men manned the shafts, and assisted by the chaplain, Father Morley, carried the statue up to the prepared site. Three of these men are still happily with us: Mr John Joyce of Currywongane, Mr John Lydon of Kylemore and Mr Francis Keane, now in the USA. Others involved were Tom Conroy, Lettergesh, Pat Nee, Kylemore, J. J. McLoughlin, Tullycross, Anthony McDonnell, Kylemore, Jack Joyce, Kylemore, John Coyne, Mullaghgloss, Tommie Kearney and Jack Cape.

The actual blessing of the statue took place on June 3rd, 1932. It was quite an occasion, locally. The parish priest, the Very Revd Fr Diskin, the curate, Fr Tiernan, and the Abbey Chaplain, Fr Morley, performed the blessing. The procession up the mountain was led by the Letterfrack School Brass Band, with the bandmaster, Mr Hickey, later to appear regularly at All-Ireland finals at Croke Park. The schoolmaster, Mr Heffernan looked after the children. Members of the Christian Brothers community and many local people took part, and of course the community at Kylemore, including Sr Martha, Sr Columba, Sr Brendan, Sr Dymphna, Sr Jarleth and Sr Frances.

Many of these nuns were able to take part in a 50th Anniversary pilgrimage to the statue on the feast of the Sacred Heart. They were led by the parish priest the Very Revd Fr Joseph McNamara, Fr J. Porter, CC, Ballinakill, and Dom Paul McDonnell, chaplain to the Abbey. A solemn Mass of the feast was concelebrated at which Father Porter preached. Mother Abbess was accompanied by the community, and a goodly gathering of parishioners. It was recalled that our forebears often had to attend Mass on the Irish hill-sides, in fear of their lives. It was right that we should remember the sacrifices they made to hand on the faith to us and repay them by our own fidelity to the Mass. The very fine weather greatly contributed to the sense of celebration, and all present were very happy to have taken part.

Written by Dom Paul McDonnell, OSB, Kylemore.

Consummatus in Brevi

It is only in the last twenty years that the rich tapestry of Connemara's archaeology has been explored and documented. Connemara has been densely populated for thousands of years and its people have left signs of their habitation, religious and burial sites behind them during all that time. These include field systems, cooking sites, monasteries, pilgrim sites both pagan and Christian and, of course – and maybe most importantly – burial sites. Some are thousands of years old; others are more recent.

The people of Connemara undoubtedly practised their own form of paganism and Celtic belief for thousands of years. When Christianity came they embraced it completely while, at the same time, not totally abandoning their old belief systems which were very closely linked to the elements and to the landscape that they knew intimately.

Often, ancient pagan sites were given a new Christian significance. Maméan (the gap of the birds) high up in the Maam Turk mountains was an important ancient pagan site. It later became a site of Christian pilgrimage and is celebrated as the place where St Patrick rested on his journey through Connemara after leaving Croagh Patrick. Fr Michael McGreal, priest and social historian, is the guardian of the Mamean pilgrimage. Every year on Good Friday he leads the congregation at the Mass Rock in Maméan, just above the little unmarked, overgrown and abandoned children's burial ground where, for centuries, the people buried their unbaptised dead without any Christian service or burial.

Children's burial grounds are so common in Connemara that a person walking the hills or shorelines of Connemara, once he or she begins to recognise the hillocks and dunes packed tightly with stones to mark the little graves, might think that they are spots picked at random or for convenience. This is not the case though. They are situated in places that are of great importance to people since they first came to Connemara. They are situated in places that bind people to their ancestors. There are about forty of these children's burial grounds marked out on Tim Robinson's map of Connemara. These are sites where the people of Connemara buried those outside the family of the Catholic Church, unbaptised children, stillborn children, unknown adults found dead during the famine and suicides. The local name for children's burial ground is *cillín* or *liosín*, both of which mean little graveyard. The local placenames of these graveyards, testify to the burial of infants there, *Liosín na bPáistí* (little graveyard of the children); *Liosín na leanaí* (little graveyard of the babies); *Trá na bPáistí* (beach of the children); *Cnocán na bPáistí* (hillock of the children); *Cnocán na leanbh* (hill of the babies); *Reilg na bPáistí Maru* (graveyard of the dead children); *Clochar na bPáistí* (stony ridge of the children); *Aill na bPáistí* (cliff of the children); *Gaire na bPáistí* (The sandbank of the children); *Creg na leanbh* (The crag of the babies); *Garraí na bPáistí* (The field of the children) and so on.

The foremost archaeologist to explore the Connemara landscape is Michael Gibbons of Clifden. He has visited almost all of the burial grounds in the region. "Wherever you look, you have them. Connemara has some of the most extraordinary ones. I remember first getting interested in children's burial grounds when I went to a site in Derryrush on the site of *Cnoc Mártán*, crawling up through the scrub in a beautiful little valley going into this very overgrown graveyard. It was hard to make out the graves because there was a lot of lichen, primroses and beautiful heather. I remember one grave in particular which stood out above all the rest because it had a rush cross with a red bow on it. I remember standing watching it and thinking there's some woman out there, an old woman now, climbing up here, probably on the anniversary of the death of her child, going to the trouble of scrambling up the hillside to mark this child's grave. This was not some anonymous death; she was still grieving. She was still acknowledging that this child existed and had a presence, no matter how short. She had put her marker to her child on this little grave in the landscape and this marker was such a powerful symbol".

Some of the graves are incredibly simple. There's one at *Poll na bPáistí* in Ballinew where there's just the faint outline of an enclosure and the interior of it is just peppered with little stones. There is a beautiful one in Mullaghgloss, Renvyle, in a hidden hollow where all the graves are lined with white quartz, the graves themselves having been on top of cultivation ridges. Here we have this little area, hidden out of view, an amazing little hidden valley with a whole series of graves. The quartz is symbolic of the innocence of children. Salerno beach has an extraordinary one where, again, you have the use of white quartz as a symbol of innocence or hope that these children who had nothing in life might have something in the afterlife. Their families put them on the edge of the tide in Salerno, on the edge of the mountainous sacred pilgrim route in Maméan, on the edge of a nice limestone ridge in the case of Mweelin mountain and also on the edge of more infertile schist and quartzite rock further down. The location was very important, very site specific. They were tiny, but packed with the simplest graves one has ever seen.

The Fountain Hill site, overlooking Omey Island, is probably the most stark in its bleakness, situated on a rounded knoll overlooking the ocean. At the same time it is very simple and well-preserved. It is a beautiful, spectacular spot on a fine summer's day with the sun beating down on the beach. Contrast this with a bleak January day with its howling Atlantic gales and one would have to wonder at how anyone could bury their children in such a raw, rough place. However, these type of locations were always selected for children's burial grounds. They were on the outside of the world, so to speak, out of the community. Those who were buried there were regarded as being on the edge of the world, temporally, physically and spiritually. These locations symbolised the state of the unbaptised and expressed the concept of 'limbo' – that in-between state, neither heaven nor hell.

Fr Enda Lyons, priest and theologian, elaborates further on the term: "The word 'limbo' means margin or border. The image was that people in limbo were in the border or marginal state. It was really a theological solution to a theological problem. In a way, theologians got trapped in their own logic. On the one hand they believed that without baptism you could not enter the fullness of God's eternal life yet, on the other hand, a child who died without baptism could not have been punished. They could not see how that child could be in heaven in the presence of God or in hell either, in any sort of punished state, so they devised this border situation where they saw such a child going. They did not really see the child as being punished, although actually, in the end, it turned out that it was punishment. They did not see the child as being in darkness. I know it might be hard to understand. They did not see the child as being unhappy, yet the child still would not have been as happy as a child who died having been baptised. That was the system at the time but it is largely dismantled now."

Whatever the system, it was of little comfort to the mothers of Connemara up to the 1950s. They had large families and losing babies was almost inevitable. Hospitals were rarely visited and doctors were thin on the ground. Infant mortality rates were very high. The greatest comfort most people had at that time was their Catholic faith. In some cases, where newborn babies were sick and there was little or no time to call a priest, people baptised those babies themselves to ensure a Christian burial. As Molly Fitzpatrick (now deceased) from Cashleen recalled: "They christened those sick babies themselves. Anybody could do it – father, mother, sister, brother or grandparent. They had their own way for christening the baby and that baby then, you see, could be buried in the consecrated ground of the graveyard. If the baby was not baptised they had to have a special place for them to be buried. There's a lot of these baby graves on the islands."

While most of the burial grounds are the reserves of the infants there are others buried in some of them. These are adults and the larger outlines of their graves contrast starkly with the tininess of the children's graves. These adults were buried with the children for strong reasons as Michael Gibbons explains: 'The adults tended to be people found dead on a hillside or washed ashore. People were not too sure what religion they were. It was a horrible thought of course that if you were a Protestant you would be buried in a Catholic graveyard or if you were a Catholic that you would end upbeing planted with the Protestants. So to be fair to all sides, an unclaimed body would be buried outside the graveyard wall or, to be even safer still, it could be buried in the children's burial grounds.

Those who committed suicide were also buried away from the graveyards. These places were often called 'Strangers' graveyards' because the adult people buried were regarded as having been strange. They may have been emotionally or mentally disturbed. Traditionally, suicide victims would not receive Catholic burial rites and would not be buried on consecrated ground.

As well as suicide victims there is little doubt that there were famine victims buried with the children. Such was the scale of death during the famine that funeral and burial rites became something of very little importance. People died on the side of the road and may not have been buried at all. There are unmarked graves in fields throughout Connemara. At one such site in Aughris it is refreshing to hear about the innocence of local children who knew the spot, prayed at it and marked it in their own way, throughout the generations, as described by Mary Margaret McDonnell from Aughrisbeg: "There are two big adult graves raised above the ground. They are there for as long as I can remember. My children used to mind cows up in that field and when they did, they prayed. They must have said seven rosaries there during the day. They kept putting flowers on the graves, just the wild flowers that they picked themselves and they kept the graves trimmed and clean. They thought it was a great thing to do."

The *cillíns* are just part of the history of the burial of unbaptised children in Connemara. Tragic as they are, secluded in the loneliest corners of Connemara, on the edge of a society that lived by a faith that denied these children burial with their families, and under threat of the sea and the elements, they are still at least recognised, commemorated with stones and respected even if only by way of being left alone. There is, for those who are part of the burial ground story, some comfort to be taken from the fact that their children are buried with hundreds of other children who were buried there over the generations.

The other part of the story is the burial of so many unbaptised babies in the sod fence, the maring wall or the maring drain. Why some children were buried in sod fences rather than in burial grounds is unknown. The significance of the sod fence though is the same: the physical expression of limbo, being not in one man's land nor in the other, being no one's responsibility. More often than not the drain was between two townlands, being then neither in one place nor the other. Feichin Mulkerrin of Claddaghduff remembers seeing one child being dug out of a maring drain between two townlands, Claddaghduff and Curragh, "I saw one being dug up out of it. I think it was the Board of Works who did the job. The workman working the spade came across the wooden box. They dug it up and afterwards they opened it and they found a lovely little baby. It had been preserved in the bog. The baby's face was perfect. It was brought in for a post-mortem and according to the post-mortem it could have been years in it."

The grief of the mother must have been so much more unbearable in these cases, where often she did not even know the whereabouts of the remains of the child. Although little is written by Irish writers on this subject there are some poignant descriptions of the lot of the woman who lost children. The finest modern Irish language writers in Connemara, Padraic O'Conaire and Máirtín O'Cadhain chose the women of Connemara and their fate as their subjects. Their finest writing concentrates on the women – the ones who suffered most in a society racked by poverty, emigration and the uncertainty of everything. The following piece has been translated from the Irish prose of Máirtín O'Cadhain.

If they could only have been born
If the five of them could only have been born
Not one of them was born alive
If she had seen them alive
Even if only for the blink of an eye
To hear one child cry under the covers
To feel a hungry mouth on her breast
To hold one child to her heart
Before his death
But she did not see
Did not hear
Did not feel
Did not hold
If they had lived

Lived a year, a week, a day
Even a moment
She'd have the comfort of grieving over them
She'd be able to speak their names
Without shame or embarrassment
She would not be ashamed to
say a prayer for their souls
She could talk about them with
the women and the neighbours
Was not it well for Kitty and Kate and Mairéad
Their children died but they saw them
They kissed their mouths
Their memories of their children's lives
Would be comforting sunshine
In their dark grief forever
Was not it well for Our Lady
Her son was crucified on the cross
But she could see him
And she would see him again
There was not a time that Kitty
spoke of her children who died
That she did not say that they
Would be before her at her death
Each a candle in his hand
Showing her the way to paradise
Every child of Kitty's would be
bright angels calling 'Mother' to her
at the gates of Heaven.

She was always reluctant to visit Brid
Brid had living family around her
But she only wanted to talk about the ones that died.
Nora could not call her offspring family
She could not speak of them
Too stained for saving
Too clean for damning
The lost souls of eternity
They were in a place
Neither God nor the devil wanted to possess
In a dark painless place
Where she would go
It would not be with them

She would not even lie in the clay with them
at the end of it all
She was to be buried in the
consecrated ground of the graveyard
They were buried in the sod fence
Buried in boxes
Buried in secret at night
With no witness to the burial but the stars
Uncaring stars that never shed a tear.

It is only in the last few decades that the church and adult society in general have caught up with the innocence and sensitivity of the unbaptised children who died. 'And where does life begin?' reflects Fr Michael McGreal. 'It begins in the womb. We see this very strongly brought out in the Visitation when Elizabeth told Our Lady that the child in her womb leapt with joy. My understanding then is that God destroys nothing that He gives and that once life begins, as far as God is concerned, that life is safe. Therefore, when an infant dies, that infant is *Consummatus in Brevi:* it is in a very short time brought to perfection. It is in an instant. In my opinion, therefore, all of these miscarriages, all these aborted babies, all those who die before birth, just like those who die after birth before being baptised, are *Consummatus in Brevi*. I think there can be some consolation for a mother in knowing that she has a person in eternity with God, particularly a woman who has been trying for a long time to have a child and may never have another child. In the past I do not think we really understood the grief involved or the bond that exists between the stillborn child and the parents, particularly the mother.'

Both society and the Catholic Church have progressed in the latter half of this century. The Church now recognises stillborn and unbaptised children through its funeral rites, as does society by recording their existence and naming them as the parents wish. The process of recognising the burial grounds has begun in Connemara. Some have been blessed and are now being tended to and maintained by the people around them. It is hoped that all of them will be brought into the proper care of their communities before the sea, the elements and the ongoing changes in the use of the landscape threaten them further. The burial grounds will always bear quiet, common and stark witness to the history of Connemara, both ancient and recent. Recognising them, blessing them, tending to and respecting them will be a comfort to the families linked to them.

Story based on 'The Children's Burial Grounds' a documentary by Michael Gannon for Connemara Community Radio.

SMÉARÓID

I lost four children. Patrick died at five months from pneumonia and Stephen died at five weeks from an obstruction of the bowel. They are both buried in Renvyle Cemetery along with my husband Stevie. The other two babies were stillborn. I lost the first of these in 1934 at the age of twenty. The baby was delivered at home by my mother-in-law, Mary Walsh, who was a midwife and delivered most of the local babies. After the birth I was not allowed to see the baby. It affected me very badly and I went weeks and weeks without eating. I hated everyone and everything on the face of the earth and most of all I hated my husband because I felt he should have stood up to the women and made sure I saw the baby but he was not strong enough to do this. He told me that the women stopped him and he promised to bring me to the grave as soon as possible. He told me that my baby had a lovely face with lovely hair. In later years he often said sorry to me for not being able to let me see my stillborn children. Maybe he thought at that time that the women were right to protect me but, like any man, he could not have understood how I was feeling. The whole thing badly affected our relationship for some time but Stevie was a loving husband to me and a great father to my eight children who lived. I remember one time when I was very sick I dreamt that Stevie came to me in a dream with one of my babies on the palm of his hand and he said to the baby 'That's Mam now'.

I hated God because I thought he should not have done such a thing to me, to take away four babies from me. I felt very let down by the Catholic Church also. I remember one priest saying to me "surely you did not cry for that baby", to which I replied "I did cry for that baby and I think there's no God in Heaven to take him away from me". I told him that my baby was not in purgatory or in limbo and that I did not believe in such places. I also told him that I would see my baby very soon. I had taken the baby's death so hard that I felt like dying. In those days it was customary for the local priest to bless a pregnant woman before giving birth and to consecrate her with oil two or three weeks after the birth. After I had the dead born babies the priests never came near me and because of this I stopped going to the church to be consecrated after giving birth to my other children. I was very bitter towards the clergy, because I believed at the time that they wanted to almost pretend that nothing had ever happened. I stopped attending Mass and it was only after Fr Keane visited me and pleaded with me to return to Mass that I eventually agreed to go again. In recent years I have had many visits from priests in America who know my sons over there. These priests have all talked to me about my loss and these conversations have brought me some consolation but they will never fully make up for the clergy's uncaring attitude back then.

Mary Walsh, who lived in the house with us, was a great help to me. She told me she was sorry that she could not do anything to let me see the babies. She also told me how lovely they were and she kept reassuring me that I would have lots of lovely babies. I was blessed with eight beautiful children in the end. This encouragement, reassurance and love that my mother-in-law gave me was the closest thing to counselling I ever received. I knew of some other women who had lost babies like me but we never got together to try to help each other. Bereavement support groups were unheard of in those days. I was difficult to deal with, often running off to my bedroom when Mary would try to talk to me about how I was feeling. My own mother was very considerate also but she did not know what to do for me.

As the years went by, I used often to visit the graves of my children. I would just sit in silence for ages. I remember on one such occasion my son Jackie saying to me, "Mammy why do you come down here so often?" When I replied that I had a reason for it he said, "Well, you come down here too often. I do see you crying sometimes. Is there anything belonging to you here?' I answered him "No, there's nothing for you here, there's nothing you can do for me." I was not able to communicate properly to my son about the whole thing and to this day I still find it hard to talk to my children about the babies I lost. Those babies I lost, I will never forget them. When my children come home from America on holidays they always visit the graves and they have also taken photographs back home with them.

It was in my head for many years to do something at the *Sméaróid* burial ground to make sure that all the unbaptised children there would be properly remembered. I never believed that an unborn child should be thrown into the clay, into an unmarked grave and then that there be nothing at all about them after that. I decided that the best way to honour their memory would be to erect a tombstone and have the ground consecrated if possible. When I asked Fr Pat O'Donoghue if he would help me he told me that he would assist me as much as he could and added that he thought it was great that I wanted to do such a thing. He went to Fr Patrick Mullins, the Parish Priest, to inform him of my wish and Fr Mullins was totally supportive. *Sméaróid* burial ground is on Anthony Heanue's land. I wanted to enclose the graves properly so I asked him for a piece of ground to make this possible. He told me to go ahead and do whatever I liked, adding that something should have been done long ago. He told me to take in as much of the land as I wanted. John Mongan in Derryinver made the tombstone and inscribed the words 'In memory of the Little Children' on it. My son Gerry got the stakes and wire and enclosed it for me. He also erected the tombstone in August 1994. Fr Mullins led a simple prayer service during which he consecrated the ground with holy water. I was surprised but delighted that such a big crowd came to witness the ceremony. It gave me great consolation after so many years. The event was covered by some of the newspapers and I was interviewed on the national news by RTE journalist Jim Fahy. I received some lovely letters from people in Ireland and England who read the various newspaper accounts and wanted to show their appreciation of what I had achieved.

My faith is still strong today. I do not believe in purgatory or limbo, but I believe in God and I do not believe that he would ever send someone to hell. I have great devotion to St Philomena whom I regard as the patron saint of expectant mothers. I keep a picture of her in the house. I have always had a special devotion to the Blessed Virgin and I never blamed her for my loss. All my life I have never gone to sleep before saying the Rosary and I often fall asleep with the beads in my hands. Maybe that is how they will find me when my time comes to be reunited with my husband Stevie and my four babies I never got to bring through this life.

Remembered by Mary Salmon and written by Paul Gannon.

THE IRISH TIMES (Wednesday 10th August, 1994)

A plot of land by the sea in Co Galway, which contains the graves of hundreds of unchristened babies, will become a formal graveyard for the first time when it is blessed by a Catholic Priest today.

Father Patrick Mullins of Letterfrack, the Ballinakill Parish Priest, will bless a new memorial on the site this afternoon. The first infant burials there were made around 150 years ago, during the Famine.

This memorial is a tribute not only to the babies, but also to the persistence of a local woman, 80-year-old Mrs Mary Salmon of Tullybeg, Renvyle. Twin babies born to her nearly 60 years ago are buried in the plot. 'They would not be let into consecrated ground because they had not been christened before they died', Mrs. Salmon said. "My husband Stephen, made two little boxes for them and carried them two miles from Derrylough to bury them there."

"My first reaction was that they should be buried in consecrated ground, but children were buried in sod fences. I organised the memorial because I knew that they should have gone into the consecrated ground and not be thrown into sod fences."

There are no records of the young children buried at the site, but Mrs Salmon said she knew that twins, cousins of her dead babies, were also buried there. "There are babies from all over the area in the grave," she said. "I always regretted and wondered why somebody did not come together and take them and bring them into consecrated ground and bury them all in one little grave." Three years ago, when she finally decided she would have to take matters into her own hands to have the ground sanctified. She went to the owner of the land, Mr Patrick Anthony Heanue. "He gave it to me immediately," she said. She contacted a stonemason from Derryinver, Mr John Mongan, and arranged to have a stone marker, inscribed 'To the memory of the little children', placed at the site.

Details of today's ceremony were announced from the altar of the local church in recent weeks. "The priest invited other people with babies to attend," Mrs Salmon said.

Mrs Salmon, whose youthful vigour belies her age, is the mother of twelve children – eight of them alive – and operates a guesthouse at her Beachview home. Her son, Gerry, has fenced off the graveyard, but it has been ravaged by time and tide. Mrs Salmon said some of the graves have been swept away by the sea. "There have not been any babies buried for some years," she said. "I do not think people would allow it."

By Paul Harman

THE IRISH TIMES (Thursday 11th August, 1994)

Gulls hung in the air, their mournful cries carried by the wind and mixed with the prayers, as a plot of land on scenic Connemara shore where hundreds of unbaptised babies had been buried over the last 150 years was blessed yesterday.

At the front of a crowd of more than 50 people who attended the ceremony, Mrs Mary Salmon (80), of Tullybeg, Co Galway, somehow looked all alone as Father Patrick Mullins, of Letterfrack, the Ballinakill parish priest, led the prayers on the little bluff overlooking the Atlantic.

Prayer answered...Mary Salmon by the memorial stone to her two children.

She had staged a one-woman campaign for recognition of the burial site – where two of her twelve children had been buried some 60 years ago – on Renvyle peninsula, a few hundred metres from the Renvyle House Hotel. "I was very lonely for a while," Mrs Salmon said of her feelings during the 25-minute rite in front of the gravestone she had paid to have put in place. "I was thinking that for years and years the children were there and nothing was done. I am happy about it now. The graveyard is blessed." The marker, placed at a location where the bluff forms a natural star, reads: 'In memory of the little children.'

At first glance the windswept bluff, looking out to Inishturk and Clare Islands to the north and overlooked by the Twelve Bens to the east, appears to be covered in a jumble of stones. But closer scrutiny shows the outlines of little graves where grieving parents had interred their children, who could not be buried in consecrated ground because they had not been christened before they died. The first child had been buried there 150 years ago at the time of the Famine. Time has stood still at *Sméaróid*, as the location is called. Countless tides have rolled in and out since the first baby was laid to rest. But for Mrs Salmon and the other mothers the memories are as fresh as today. Mrs Salmon remembered her husband, Stephen, who died twelve years ago, making two small boxes and carrying them two miles to the burial site. Even then she thought it was wrong. She believed they should have been laid to rest in consecrated land.

"We have prayed for all the dead including the children buried here," Father Mullins said after the reciting of the Rosary. "We remember the children buried in former times."

"Lord, we pray that the children will be with you," he concluded.

As the crowd walked back over soggy fields after the ceremony, Mrs Salmon stood with her family – many over from the US for her birthday celebrations last night – and watched them go.

"I was surprised by the number who attended," she said. "It was a nice ceremony. Now the babies are blessed."

By Alan Harman.

THE STAR (11th August 1994)

Pensioner Mary Salmon yesterday saw a lifetime's wish come true – on her 80th birthday. The Catholic Church finally blessed two of her children refused a Christian burial 60 years ago. The simple ceremony conducted by parish priest Father Patrick Mullins officially recognised Mary's children, and hundreds more in an unconsecrated burial plot, as innocents. Prior to that they were shunned by the Church. All were stillborn or died before they were baptised. Under church law at the time they could not be buried in consecrated ground. It meant torment for thousands of Irish parents. Yesterday's blessing at Letterfrack, County Galway, in the rural plot by the sea, was the first public sign that the cruel rule has been relaxed. Mary's heartache began six decades ago when as a 20-year-old Mum she watched her husband, Stephen, carry their still born son away to be buried. "I didn't even get to see the baby," said Mary yesterday. "My husband had the child in a little box and took it to the seashore two miles away. Then I lost another baby and it was buried there as well. Hundreds of babies are buried here. We were told they were in limbo and could not be let into consecrated ground." Throughout her life Mary has refused to accept the Church's position. She marked her children's grave with a stone. Recently she had a proper headstone made in memory of all the children buried in the plot. She asked her local priest to bless it. He agreed. Mary had eight other children who survived. Many of them and her grandchildren travelled from as far away as America to share her joy. She said: "I feel very happy. What was done to us all those years ago was terribly wrong. As far as I was concerned the children went to heaven. This is confirmation that the Church now recognises that." A Catholic Church spokesman in Dublin agreed that for centuries unbaptised children were banned from burial in consecrated ground. 'It was not just a whim,' he said. 'The whole thing was theologically based. If people were not baptised then they were beyond salvation.'

By Paddy Clancy

CITY TRIBUNE (Friday 12 August, 1994)

An old coastal graveyard where hundreds of unchristened babies were buried in the past in the parish of Ballinakill, near Clifden, was blessed by the Parish Priest on Wednesday afternoon. Babies who did not live long enough to be baptised were taken to be buried in this small patch of land by the sea – some of them had died within days of birth and others were stillbirths. Father Patrick Mullins, of Letterfrack, the Ballinakill Parish Priest, officially sanctified the ground, and after the ceremony a Mass was held in the house of 80 year-old Mary Salmon in Tullybeg.

Said Mary: 'Two of my children were buried in that patch of land almost 60 years ago. It was the custom then to send babies who had not been baptised to that graveyard, but I always regret that we did not bury our children in the back garden.

"I never believed that my children were in limbo, even though this is what the Catholic Church led us to believe. I knew that all those babies went straight to Heaven and I am very happy that this has now been recognised by the Church."

Mary can take all the credit for the Catholic Church's blessing of the new memorial on the old site. She contacted the owner of the plot Patrick Heanue, three years ago, and after he gave her the land she convinced the parish priest to aid her in the quest to sanctify the plot of land.

Despite her age Mary is a very active lady who runs a guesthouse in her Beachview home. It has been a lifelong aim of hers to get the old graveyard consecrated and she thinks many others will also appreciate knowing that souls of relatives – who were buried here – have finally been acknowledged by the Catholic Church.

By Shelley Horgan

26, Foxfield Road
Dublin 5
10th August 1994

Mrs. Mary Salmon
Tullybeg
Renvyle
Connemara

Dear Mrs. Salmon

I read with interest of your endeavours to have the children's graveyard consecrated.

The stone memorial you have had erected will stand as a memorial to your work on this project as well as all the little children buried there. A lot of what was accepted as correct in the past we now know to have been flawed judgement, however, as long as there are people like you around mistakes of the past will be corrected to benefit us all for the future. We will remember you, your children and all other children in our prayers.

Yours sincerely,

Brian and Geraldine Deane

Co Donegal
August 11th 1994

Dear Mrs Salmon
I saw an article about you in *The Irish Times* of August 10th and I had to write to you. Please forgive me if I choose to stay anonymous.

I applaud the work you have done to have the Babies' Cemetery blessed. You see, my wife and I lost our second child and first daughter 22 years ago when she was born dead. But in Northern Ireland, stillborn babies are registered. They are not here. Also, our baby was buried in consecrated ground after a simple service by a Catholic priest coincidentally called Mullen, who later became something of a rebel.

But I bless his name because he helped us in our hour of need and gave my lovely daughter a proper burial. Parents like us must fight for proper treatment for the stillborn and unbaptised babies both by the Church and by the State (stillborns must be registered)

Bless you for your work and bless Father Mullins and others who help you.

A friend.

26, Wilfield Road
Ballsbridge
Dublin 4
31st August 1994

Mrs Mary Salmon
Tullybeg
Co Galway

Dear Mrs Salmon
Many, many congratulations on your one-woman campaign for recognition of the burial site at *Sméaróid*.

I was so moved by the excellent reporting of it in *The Irish Times* by Mr Alan Harman that I wrote the attached poem, which I hope you will enjoy.

Yours sincerely,
Marge Aylward

Congratulations on your achievement in having the cemetery blessed after all these years. Your faith and persistence in your belief has brought about a wonderful result. What a tribute this is to you. The memorial will stand forever in memory of you.

Mary Zita King, Dublin

The Famine years from 1845–1848 represent a dark chapter in Ireland's turbulent history. One hundred and fifty years on, sad reminders of those times are still in evidence, particularly in some of the rural areas to the West of Ireland. Such remote communities, which relied mainly on farming and agriculture for their livelihood, were devastated by the potato crop failure over a successive four-year period. Ireland's population at that time was around 8 million; an estimated 1 million people died (many of them children) and a further 3 million emigrated. To this day Ireland's population has never recovered and presently stands at around 5 million – North and South.

Because the majority of the children who died had not been baptised they were buried in unconsecrated ground. Such mass graves became a common feature of the rural landscape. Today, many of the sites are no more but near the West Cork town of Skibbereen one such 'Children's Graveyard' is still intact, although few people know of its existence. Unmarked, undefiled and undisturbed down the years, it stands in the middle of a field, which successive generations of farmers have ploughed and sown around.

Because of ignorance and superstition, those innocents, who suffered cruelly in their short, sad lives, were ultimately denied the reward of a Christian burial. It was the tragic plight of those victims of Ireland's 'Great Hunger', allied to the high incidence of poverty and famine in our times, which promoted this tribute.

As you can see from the enclosed poem I too was disturbed by the treatment of the Famine children. Approaching the 150th Anniversary of that dark chapter in our history, I think it is about time that the Irish government and Roman Catholic Church set to right the wrongs of the past generations with regard to the status of the graves of those innocents. Notwithstanding the Christian principle, they are a part of our national heritage and as such should be remembered. May God reward you for your love and persistence. You are indeed blessed to have a sensitive and understanding man like Fr Patrick Mullins on your side; I salute you both!

THE SOULS OF THE FAMINE

The wild rose is fragrant, the fuchsia is red
and they grow in profusion around the last bed
of the souls of the famine, who went to their rest
in a grave on a hillside, somewhere in the west.

Disturb not the unholy ground where they sleep
but pray for their mothers who anguished, did weep
and pity the souls of their fathers that burned
as they sailed from the quayside and never returned.

The hillside once rang to their laughter 'tis said,
now only the echoes of silence instead
resound on the morning, where unquiet lay
the souls of the famine, in restless array.

Away on the hillside where vistas are fair,
forlorn, ruined homesteads in mute witness bear
to thriving communities gathered before
where rattle and tempest through dwellings no more.

The lobster-pots gay dancing out on the sea
and quietly meandering herds on the lea
tempt the eye of the traveller where who may comb,
a vision that lingers where'er he may roam.

The quayside that once served a multitude throng
of fishing fraternities clustered along
the road to the refuge, commanding on high,
juts idly, deserted there, under the sky.

The legends abounding about them are few
though keen was the suffering and hardship they knew;
yet one tale is spoken of which there's no doubt –
of a time when the souls in their torment cried out.

Grey mountains of water rushed in from the sea
to batter the shoreline and shatter the quay;
the souls of the famine, so fearful that night
howled long on the wind of their fate and their plight.

The country was stricken and grief lingered on
'twas all of the families were perished or gone
and left in their mis'ry to fret and to moan
the souls of the famine, forsaken, alone.

Disturb not the tranquil serenity there,
nor speak of that passage of history bare,
but pray for those lost souls which unquiet rest,
in a grave on a hillside, somewhere in the West.

Michael B. O'Brien
May 1994

THE BLESSING

For five score and fifty since our infant birth,
Our blanket worn friendly earth,
Our grab mantles of dark clay,
Covered by lines of stained stones grey.
Our friends raindrops, birds cry, sea sound,
Our home Sméaróig a bluff windbound,
Akin to an altar shape,
The Twelve Bens our family cape.
But now a gift of heavenly release,
Where we must arrive without a crease.
The friendly growth gives us moisture to bathe,
A gentle breeze our towel to swathe,
Hair styles of soft green ferns,
Clothes, large leaves some with upturns,
And temporary halos pecked by birds,
To be replaced afterwards.
'We're ready', we cry to new friend, Sun,
When our final shining by stars is done,
He then sends forth a golden ray,
For our golden chariot's highway.
A highway long to Moon's Theme Park,
Where planet rides are exciting, stark,
And his Moon beam slides are such a lark,
None of us want to disembark,
Cousin angels come from Heaven above,
To tie yellow ribbons to clouds of white dove,
Already for us wardrobes they built,
To house our starched white wings,
Our silver circles and maybe other things,
But now our journey's end is ending,
A hymn written for us, God on the air is sending,
For us no frightening big gate awaits,
But a golden rope, golden tassel fringed,
We lift, enter, unsinged.

DEAR PARENTS

We did not die young
We lived our span of life
within your body
and within your love.
There are many
Who have lived long lives
And not been loved as we.

If you would honour us,
Then speak our names
And number us among your kin.
If you would honour us
Then strive to live in love
For, in that love, we live.
Never, ever doubt
That we will meet again.

Until that happy day,
We will grow with God
And wait for you.

(For Cathal)
By Christy Kenneally
November 1993

Woody Allen urged us to think of death as a good way of cutting down on your expenses. Unlike the Christian churches' approach to 'The Big Sleep', Woody's viewpoint expresses an immutable truth no matter how you look at it. Death gets you out of debt and that's a fact.

This week we have seen how the Catholic and Protestant authorities approach the finer points of buying the farm, and how their pronouncements on the subject are not to be taken too seriously.

At a rocky field near Letterfrack, Co Galway, Mrs Mary Salmon, an 80-year-old mother of 12, finally achieved her wish to have the land consecrated. Two of her children were among hundreds of unbaptised babies buried in the plot beside the sea, excluded from the consecrated graveyard due to being in limbo.

For the younger Catholics among you, I could best describe limbo as a kind of ethereal version of the waiting room at Portarlington station, where the trains don't run. You waited and you waited and you waited in vain, and if there was any consolation to be found at all, it lay in the hope that you would be either too dead or too young to appreciate your predicament.

Limbo, we were led to believe, was as real as heaven, hell and purgatory. And then they just closed it down, rationalised it out of the celestial budget. 'You know all that stuff about limbo? Well, forget it', they seemed to be saying.

It was as though a new Vatican PR department decided that limbo was more trouble than it was worth. Which is all well and good, and a fine thing all around, as long as you realise that in this, as in many other matters, they are making it up as they go along.

This is not my opinion; it is an eternal truth. Limbo was merely their opinion dressed up as an eternal truth. And they changed their mind when it suited them. Making it up as they go along.

By Declan Lynch

Maggie's

When my aunt Maggie returned from America after seven years of hard saving she set about realising her dream of becoming a successful businesswoman, something which would have been quite unique in West Connemara in the early 1900s. She rented a premises in Tully village from a man named Pat Heanue who ran a co-operative store next door. Eventually in 1919 Pat agreed to sell her the house for £300, a considerable amount of money at that time. She had now realised her dream and a simple sign over the door bearing the words 'Margaret Flaherty' must have given her a great sense of pride and satisfaction.

It was easy enough to set up a shop in those days. One could purchase a huge barrel of groceries for £5. Maggies main suppliers, surprisingly enough, were Musgraves from Cork. The goods were usually transported by boat to Galway and transferred subsequently to the train. There were always carts travelling to Clifden and it was easy enough for Maggie to organise one to collect her supplies from the train station. O'Malleys in Westport also brought groceries to her. Along with Musgraves they would have sent travelling salesmen to take her order. Her shop was a topsy-turvy sort of place. She had everything and anything. People used to say that she had from a needle to an anchor in it. She had a great variety of things in small quantities. I remember she had special leather laces for strong boots called whangs. She also sold hemp, which was used for sewing and stitching shoes. People did that sort of thing in those days. She sold globes, bicycle lamps, batteries, candles,

Maggie with a tourist, outside her shop in Tully.

wax, Sunlight soap and a washing-up powder called Rinso. She sold washing soda, which her customers used to bleach flour bags in the making of sheets. I can also remember the big bags of sugar and Quaker oats on the floor at the back of the shop.

My favourite part of the shop was the sweet department. Maggie had so many varieties of sweets and I was totally fascinated with them all. She had every kind of a sweet, sugar sucks, penny bars, pennies legs, bulls eyes, mints, liquorice, can sweets, lozengers, M&Ms, a beautiful American sweet, the likes of which cannot be found nowadays. The M&Ms were my favourites. Maggie kept her sweets in glass jars and one could buy a half-penny's or a penny's worth.

Andrew Ferguson was the sweet supplier who arrived faithfully in Tully every Monday. He would always throw a fist of sweets to the children who would crowd in excitedly around the door. Maggie never weighed sweets when she was selling them. She always counted them out ten for a penny but if the good humour was on her she would just catch a fistful and throw them into the bag.

She also sold lemon soda and ginger ale. The man from Livingstone's usually came once a fortnight. She did not sell any milk as everyone had their own milk in those days.

She sold Sweet Afton, Players, Woodbines, Carrolls and Kerry Blues cigarettes. She sold Clarkes tobacco and she also had the common Walnut Plug, which came in a big round coil-like shape. She had a special knife for cutting off ounces for sale. I can remember a bit of controversy over cigarettes during the Emergency when tobacco rationing was commonplace. The guard in Letterfrack smoked Carrolls and he himself wrote off to the company instructing it to advance him five hundred cigarettes each month. However Maggie was the local agent for Carrolls so the company posted the cigarettes to her. Each day the guard would arrive down and buy ten cigarettes from her. Many of the locals became quite upset because they were unable to buy the same daily quantity and even though Maggie explained time and time again about the guard writing to the company, they did not give her a favourable ear. The whole arrangement created a lot of bad feeling at the time but Maggie felt powerless to do anything about it and I suppose it would not do to fall out with the guard either. Every six months she was duty bound to visit the station to have all her weights and measures checked. The constant use of the weights could result in them losing some of their weight. The guard or sergeant always had a man present to put lead into them if need be.

Every year Maggie used to buy two pigs from local farmers. I remember my father used to cut them up into pieces and salt them for her. She used to store these pieces in the huge barrel, which previously would have contained her grocery supplies. She also used to buy herrings from the O'Malley's during the winter and in summertime she would use the same barrel to store mackerel which she used to buy off a local fisherman called Martin Walsh from Gurteen. I often remember his sons delivering a hundred of them, all cleaned. Maggie would salt them herself out the back. She would layer them around the bottom of the barrel and throw in fists of salt to cure them. She would sell them, four for a shilling and there was always a great run on them. People were glad to get them in those days. She also sold ling, which was cured dry in boxes.

Maggie in America

There were a few different women from around the locality who supplied Maggie with fresh eggs. I remember we would have to wash the eggs and clean them off to make sure they were perfect for displaying. Sometimes Maggie would give the women a certain amount of groceries in exchange for the eggs. Nora Davin in Curragh used to sell homemade butter to Maggie. I can still vividly remember the mioscán of butter (two to three pounds weight) which used to be so clear we could see the pure water coming out of it. Nora would have it protected inside the paper with a few cabbage leaves. Maggie would put a cover over it and sell it off by the pound or half pound. Lydon-O'Neills bakery in Clifden delivered fresh bread to Maggie every day. The most popular loaf was the buillín, a small white batch. Sliced pan was unheard of in those days.

People could purchase paraffin oil in Maggie's. She had a sixty gallon tank in the shop, which she was careful to conceal as much as possible with cardboard boxes. She used to charge sixpence for a gallon of oil and nobody except herself would fill the oil for fear of wastage. Maggie was the first of the local shopkeepers to order newspapers. She always told me that she got her first ever *Irish Independent* for Mr Coyne, the principal teacher in Eagles Nest National School in Renvyle. He was the first customer who directed her to order a newspaper. She also used to get the *Irish Press*. The papers used to arrive in the postcar, an old Ford Lincoln, driven by Mickey Mullen. As far as I can recall it was only the well-off who bought papers in those days. The ordinary working man had not time for reading them.

Maggie always had a well stocked drapery section in her shop. She had worked, as a domestic in America and in the process had also become a very skilled seamstress. Hughes in Westport was her main supplier. Every two months a sales representative would visit her with all the new samples and Maggie would pick out whatever she wanted. A couple of parcels would duly arrive a few days later. Maggie used to make curtains for many different people. She often made beautiful lace curtains for station masses. She also made blouses for women. She would sell them the material first and them make the item. I remember she sold creton, a fabric for covering chairs. She also stocked a material called union, which was used for lining coffins. She ordered her towels and tea cloths by post from the Belfast Linen Company. She also sold underwear, shirts and beautiful homespun woollen socks for men. A Mrs Conway from Lettergesh supplied her with the homespun woollen socks. She always stocked tips for shoes, rubber heels, rivets and upper leather as well as leather for soling shoes. This leather was sold in twelve inch squares.

I first got to know Maggie during the 1930s when I was still attending primary school. I used to go to the shop after school to see if Maggie needed any help. I was never classed as a shop assistant. Maggie never advertised for an assistant. She was bright and alert and did everything herself and even though her shop had a somewhat disorganised look about it Maggie always knew exactly where everything was located.

She never paid me any formal wages but I could always have whatever I wanted out of the shop and in later years as long as I got a half-crown every now and then for the local dance I was quite happy and content. By the early 1940s we both ran the shop like equal partners. It was a very busy time during the Emergency on account of the rationing. The customers used to leave their ration books and coupon cards for the various items in the shop. There was a lot of administration involved and my main responsibility was to ensure fair distribution to each customer. Maggie was better stocked than most during those years. I remember she had three main tea suppliers Daly's in Cork, and Lyons and Owens in Dublin.

Maggie was very well respected within the local community. She was looked upon as someone who was prosperous yet very generous in her own way. I remember, every year without fail she would give out small Christmas boxes to almost seventy customers. They would usually contain half-a-pound of tea, two pounds of jam, currants, raisins, and a Christmas candle. She always gave a free comb to the young fellows when they would arrive in to buy brilliantine for their hair. To the young ladies she usually gave curlers and a handkerchief or maybe a box of powder or face cream. Maggie was very considerate and thoughtful in her own way. She was a comical kind of woman when I think of it. She loved children and would always let them play around on the floor. I have no recollection of her ever getting cross with children and ordering them out. Maggie was a very quiet and discreet woman. She never talked anybody's business to the next person. Many's the bits of gossip she heard at the counter but never related. Her customers appreciated this and thought a lot of her for it. One piece of advice she always gave me was to put whatever I had heard to the back of my mind and never reveal it.

People always felt free and easy talking about their situations in Maggie's because they knew she was very discreet and they trusted her.

Maggie had a relaxed enough attitude to life generally. She never rushed or worried about anything. She never took too much pride out of her achievements and she certainly was not the complaining type. Her shop was usually open from 9.30 a.m. to midnight. She nearly always sat inside the counter and beside the front window. She usually ate her meals there also. That is my outstanding memory of the shop, Maggie reading

Irish cobblers at work.

the newspapers from end to end when there were no customers about. Her shop was renowned as a meeting place. People came in regardless of whether they bought or not. If you wanted to come in you were made welcome and it did not matter how long you stayed for. Maggie never tried to entice anyone to buy and never told anyone to leave on account of not buying. She could never be accused of favouritism regarding her customers. There was hardly ever a person in those days who on coming to Tully, would pass up or down the street without coming in. That was the kind of shop it was. There were even certain people who used to come in specifically to read the daily paper. Maggie never minded. The shop would always be packed on dole day and it was also very common for people who were waiting to go in and see the doctor, to wait in Maggie's. People would debate the issues of the day and sometimes this could result in heated argument. Whenever this would occur she would always say to the people involved, "Well, ye better go out in the street to finish that!" Her wishes in these matters were always respected such was the high esteem she was held in by all her customers.

When it came to business, Maggie nearly always took her prices from the travelling salesmen. She was not afraid to fight her battles with them in order to get everything at a good price. She would bargain hard and often they would have to relent a little and come down in price yet they all had great time for her. She usually only ordered what she considered to be appropriate for the ordinary country person. She was very conscientious and never overcharged anybody. She could be very compassionate also. She probably gave too much credit. She often lent money to people and never got it back. She was definitely a little bit naive in the sense that she thought nobody would wrong her. She was always inclined to see the good side of people and sometimes this resulted in her being somewhat led astray by people who would take advantage of her good nature. She was not a feminist in the modern sense of the word, yet I always considered her to be very much the equal of men. She took care never to interfere with a man's work or in whatever men had to do. She believed that a man's place was out working and that a woman's place was in the home. Knowing all this, I often wondered why Maggie never got married. Maybe she was having too good of a time being on her own. Perhaps she considered the whole business to be too risky and was fearful of her hard earned money being wasted by a husband. It is possible that a fear of heavy drinking was a major factor as she was often pestered by men looking for money for drink. Often times it was these men's wives who repaid her the money subsequently. I sometimes wonder did she meet someone special during her years in America and did it not work out, or was she a victim of unrequited love and was that the main reason she decided to come home and go it alone thereafter. The shop was her home and her customers were very much her family. After she died in 1963 I continued to run the business for a number of years but eventually closed the shop permanently in 1978. At that stage I felt I was not really able to manage the business on my own any longer and all of my children were away pursuing their own careers.

Remembered by Kathleen Faherty and written by Paul Gannon

SOME OF MAGGIE'S PRICES 1935

½lb tea	£0.1.6	1 Milk Crock	£0.5.0
Loaf of bread	£0.0.5	1 Cup	£0.0.3
Pot of Jam	£0.0.9	1 Jug	£0.0.8
1 lb Sugar	£0.0.4	1 Roll of Wallpaper	£0.0.9
1 lb Butter	£0.1.10	1 Table Clock	£0.1.6
1 lb Tomatoes	£0.1.4	3 yards of elastic	£0.0.6
2½lb Beef	£2.0.3	1 Yard of flannel	£0.2.0
1 lb Bacon	£1.0.3	Lace Curtains	£0.3.0
2 lb Mutton	£0.2.0	1 Piece of Leather	£0.0.3
1 lb Currants	£0.0.8	Braces	£0.1.0
1 ounce of tobacco	£0.0.8½	1 Mans Trousers	£0.5.6
1 Plug of tobacco	£0.1.5	1 Cardigan	£0.4.3
1 lb Soap	£0.0.6	1 Lady's overall	£0.2.6
Aspirin Tablets	£0.0.6	Child's shoes	£0.2.0
1 large Magnesia	£2.0.6	Clogs	£0.7.6
2 gallons of Oil	£2.0.8	Lady's Shoes	£0.10.6
2 lb Nails	£0.0.8	1 Pair of sandals	£0.3.4

TJ's

I remember all the toys were kept in the far counter and one could spend ages looking at them wondering what to buy with your half-crown. Most times I would settle for a large Christmas stocking full to the brim with all sorts of games and toys. Then in later years I can recall the big weighing scale that used to be positioned outside the shop entrance, a great attraction to all. Some would not get up on it if they thought anybody was looking and would wait until the coast was clear.

I remember one fair day, myself and Sean King from Errislannan, were looking at the window display when this couple came along. He said to herself "Get up on it Mary and weigh yourself" and she looked at him and said "Think would it be safe Tom?" And he said back "I will go first and chance it. Mary give me a penny, will you?' After a search in a well-worn handbag a penny was found and he said to her "What will we do next?" "I don't know Tom," came the reply.

Then we were called over to drop in the penny, which she handed over looking me in the eyes looking innocent like nothing happened. Sean said, "It did not drop down, give it a bang". Your man, at that, gave it one almighty bang of his big fist. I thought the glass was broken. Still nothing happened.

"Now you have it broken" she said.

"Blast you!" he said, "Sure, I did not hit it hard at all."

He was now springing up and down on the scale and banging it at the same time. The penny dropped at last, the big hand moved up the scales, stopped at 13 stone and then suddenly moved up again 14, 15, 16, and stopped at 17 stone, we all looked and said nothing.

"Well?" he said "what does it say lads?"

We both said together "You are over 17 stone!"

"There's something wrong there!" he exclaimed, looking very cross at us. Then the wife said "I told you Tom you're eating too many spuds."

"Stop it, woman!" he roared. "You're out of your mind!" And with that he sprang off the scales went down the street and into Mannion's pub, leaving her standing there.

She turned to Sean and myself and said, "Don't mind him, astór, he'll come round after having a half one." She then opened the bag again and after a search inside came up with another penny.

"Ye might weigh me astór," looking Sean in the eyes this time, she handed him the penny. She was very nervous getting up on the scales and after doing so was holding on with all her might. We had to tell her it would not work properly if she was holding it and said we would not let her fall. One of us would stand on either side. She seemed more relaxed now. Sean dropped in the penny, Click! Click! She jumped off the scales and ran off down the street.

We shouted, "It's okay! It's only the penny falling down the tube". She slowly came back again, had another search in the bag and this time handed me the penny, blessed herself and got up on the scales once more. With Sean and myself on guard on either side I dropped in the penny. Click! Click! She jumped. We both held on to her this time. The hand started moving up, stopped at nine stone and suddenly took off again 10-11-12-13 and stopped at 14 stone.

She looked at us and said "What does it say astór?"

I looked at Sean. He nodded. I said, "You're 14 stone dear".

"Jesus, Mary and Joseph! I am not that heavy!" she roared. "Who do ye think yer foolin' this time!" and jumped off the scales, making a swipe with her bag at us and missing by inches! I looked around and, lo and behold, her husband was coming running towards us shouting.

"What happened Mary? Is it those two jokers again?"

With that, Sean and myself took off like two March hares across the street and down Jail Hill. Later, when things got quiet, we stole back to get our bikes which were parked outside the late Packy King's shop. That was one fair day we shall always remember in Clifden.

But getting back to T. J. Mullens' shop, they first started trading there in 1946. The best stocked shop in town where one could buy from the needle to the anchor. I always found Tom and Mrs Mullen ever so helpful to the customer; nothing was too much trouble to them. They would go out of their way to help others.

Remembered and written by Marty Conneely

End of a Weighbridge

Clifden weighbridge in 1910. In the background is the site of the present premises of the Allied Irish Bank.

It was a long time with us, on, if not adorning, our landscape. We had seen it, known it, passed it, rounded it, cursed it, leant upon it and used it for a vast and surprising variety of purposes. In its last days we had even painted it . . . .

Still, we knew that earth had many things to show more fair than it, and in our unsentimental way we shed no tear at its going. Just two days it took to level and clear it, after all its hundred years of stubborn stand, and all we wonder now is – how many days will it take before we see the demise of its still unknocked, unbeautiful neighbour, and the arrival of its long awaited, brand-new, suitably subterranean, more commodious and much more convenient substitute...

For the record, it was erected in the 1870s for an English firm, for whom the auctioneering firm of Joyce, Mackey and Lockheed of Galway were agents. It was purchased from them, in 1953, by Mr Festy King of Main Street, who in turn sold it to the County Council, its eventual demolishers, two years ago. For many years it provided a useful and essential service, weighing cattle, oats, potatoes, seeds and goods of all kinds, until time, and the more universal distribution of the weighing-scale rendered it obsolete.

Scenes change, landmarks go, time marches on . . . .

Author unknown

The Village Hall

From the moment of his arrival at Ballyconneely in the summer of 1955, it was obvious that Fr Malachy Stephens had it on his mind to make a worth-while contribution during his term as curate in the parish. He had a theory that without a base or centre of operation it would be difficult to make any progress towards uplifting the social, cultural and economic lives of the parishioners, and when he mooted the possibility of having a parochial hall, he had willing supporters, aiders and abettors in the local community.

Fr Stephens consulted with his new parishioners over the first couple of years and a number of meetings were held locally where endorsement for the building of a hall was earnestly forthcoming but, of course, the question of funding such a large undertaking at that time was a matter that deserved and received a great deal of consideration and planning. The usual fund-raising projects were suggested and agreed but a plan that would raise substantial funds in a short time was put forward by Fr Stephens himself – marquee dancing, which was taking hold successfully throughout other parts of the country.

Many people had some doubt about the matter as Ballyconneely was

Dancing at the crossroads

situated on a periphery and we would have to look only in one direction for patrons to support the marquee dancing.

In the meantime, crossroads dancing and dances in the local schools became sufficiently popular in the parish that it was decided to take a chance on the marquee proposition, and so the first marquee ever in Connemara was brought to Ballyconneely over two summer seasons. With top class bands making their Connemara début, the idea took off with magnificent support and success, and through this fund-raising idea the basis of the finance needed for building of the hall had a substantial launch.

Alongside the marquee project, other fund-raising ideas were getting enormous support and the building of the new hall proceeded with great energy and enthusiasm under the direction of Jimmy O'Malley and James O'Donnell, with the men of the parish providing voluntary labour. The former Church of Ireland at Ballyconneely was acquired and demolished and roofing and other timber from it was used in the erection of the hall.

This was about the time that rural electrification was being extended to remote areas and so the ESB was installed and became a great source of power for the building operation.

The building work was carried out at a fast pace and so we were able to hold public dancing in the hall before the end of 1958 and this helped immensely towards paying off any debt due.

The official opening and blessing did not happen until 1959 when the hall was blessed by the Most Revd Joseph Walsh, Archbishop of Tuam, and officially opened by Gerald Bartley, TD and Minister for Defence.

Some of the leading bands of the showband era played at very successful dances in Ballyconneely Hall over the next number of years and, of course, the hall became the parish centre for many activities benefitting the community.

Written by Tom Connolly

A Proud and Unique Achievement

(A newspaper extract from 1958)

A fine parish hall, built entirely by local labour, was formally blessed and opened by His Grace, Dr Walsh, Archbishop of Tuam, in the village of Ballyconneely, Connemara, on Sunday last. The hall, named the Lourdes Centenary Hall, and erected at a cost of £3,500, took two years to build and the completed structure is an outstanding achievement when compared with the relatively low cost of construction.

Under the guidance of Revd M. Stephens, CC, Ballyconneely, 125 men from the district gave their free labour and time towards erecting the hall. The work was supervised by Mr James O'Malley, Aillebrack, and Mr James O'Donnell, Ballyconneely. With accommodation for over 400 people it contains a stage, dance hall and balcony, which is an innovation in halls in Connemara, and rooms which may be used for vocational education classes and other cultural activities.

The attendance at the ceremonies included the Minister for the Gaeltacht, Mr Gerald Bartley, and Lieut. Col. F. C. Mac Leagha, OC, Cead Cath.

Speaking after the ceremony, His Grace, Most Revd Dr Walsh said a parochial hall was a necessity in every parish, and should be the centre of parochial life, the centre from which education and instruction and culture would radiate and influence the lives of all for good. Indeed the utility of a parochial hall could not be exaggerated. Here for instance would meet the various societies belonging to the parish, and their meeting would be of great benefit to the people. And if the occasion demanded, representatives of the whole parish could come together for an exchange of views or to make an important decision on matters of common interest.

AGRICULTURE

Continuing, His Grace said: "But it is not merely for the expression of public opinion or the deliberations of picked bodies that a parochial hall provides a meeting place. Such a hall as this ought to be a centre of popular education. People of all ages and conditions ought to have an opportunity of hearing lectures, for instance, on music and all the fine arts, lectures

His Grace, the Most Revd Dr Walsh, Archbishop of Tuam with some of the parishioners of Ballyconneely at the blessing of the Lourdes Centenary Hall. Also in the picture are: Very Revd Chancellor D. Corcoran, PP, VF, Clifden; Revd M. Stephens CC, Ballyconneely, who was responsible for the building of the hall; and Revd M. Walsh, Diocesan Secretary.

in vocational subjects, lectures on the ordinary arts and crafts that will help the people to foster small industries and to give employment? Above all, I say, why not have special lectures on agricultural subjects? In spite of what many people affirm, agriculture is our chief, our staple industry: and you will pardon me if I say in passing that I fear the education and outlook of the people have been given a wrong bias. If the farmer is the backbone of the community, as I think must be admitted, I venture to say both our public men and our young people through the country must revise their outlook and get a new sense of relative values.

"Finally a parochial hall ought to be a centre of cultured amusement. You all know the old adage about 'all work and no play'. Every man is entitled to have legitimate recreation.

"What an advance then to have a parochial hall which provides a meeting place for all to get pleasure and relaxation without allowing liberty to degenerate into licence and wrong-doing.

TRIBUTES

"With all my heart I congratulate Fr Stephens on undertaking this important work of providing a parochial hall. He is a man of intellect, a man of many parts. Some of you may not know that he actually planned the hall himself. His work will stand as a splendid achievement. In your name and my own I offer him our deep gratitude.

"But of course I do not forget the fact that Fr Stephens could not have achieved much, if he had not received the valuable assistance and fullest co-operation of the people who have given willing and generous help in every way – by your subscriptions, by free labour, by a willingness to share the burden all round. Everyone gave his best. There has been a wonderful spirit of co-operation and charity and good citizenship which reflects the highest credit on the people of this district.

"In one respect I think this Community Centre is quite unique. The people have built it without getting any grant or any help from outside.

"So in every sense the Centre is yours, and you can be very proud of it. You can see for yourselves that it is a solid, substantial building which will stand for years and years as a memorial to the splendid workmanship of the two builders, Messrs. O'Malley and O'Donnell and their helpers."

The Minister for the Gaeltacht, Gerald Bartley, speaking at the opening of the Lourdes Centenary Hall. Also in the picture are, from left: the Very Revd D. Corcoran, PP, Clifden; His Grace, Most Revd Dr Walsh, Archbishop of Tuam, and the Revd M. Stephens, CC, Ballyconneely.

The Minister for the Gaeltacht, speaking in Irish and English, said that the people of the district might be justly proud of their achievement which was carried out without any outside help. The new hall would serve as a recreation centre and would also play a major role in the cultural activities of the district. The task of disseminating information and getting it seeped into the minds of people was at no time an easy task. Prejudices and predictions had to be contended with and while conversation was to be recommended people might go a little too far with old ideas. The hall should be a centre for discussion groups and a rallying point in which good neighbourliness could be established and differences discussed reasonably.

"SPEAK LANGUAGE"

Continuing, Mr Bartley appealed to the people to show a livelier interest in the language. They did not wish to ram it down anybody's throat, but the people of the Gaeltacht should lead in the language revival. A sound knowledge of language was no handicap and was indeed a great advantage even abroad. Very Revd Chancellor D. Corcoran PP, VF, Clifden, also congratulated people of the district and expressed hope that the new hall would provide a major force in combating the heavy flow of emigration from the district.

In the past two years eighty people from the parish had married in England. This was a tremendous strain on the area and he appealed to the people to remain at home.

Revd M. Stephens, CC, thanked His Grace, the Minister and representatives of the first Battalion for attending the ceremonies. Formerly, the people had no place to go to enjoy themselves but now, as from having a recreation centre, they have facilities for domestic science, woodwork and metalwork classes. 125 men from the parish had given their labour free so as to erect the centre and the entire responsibility was shouldered by two men, James O'Malley and James O'Donnell.

Many people believed that they could do very little by themselves but the new hall was a shining example what local people could do if they wished without the slightest assistance from any outside quarter.

He appealed to the County Vocational Education Committee to send teachers from time to time and classes could be held in the hall. Before the ceremony His Grace inspected a guard of honour drawn from D. Company, first Battalion, under P. Barrett. Also present were Commandant Guy; Capt. L. Clancy, First battalion; and Lieut. J. Kissane, Area Organising Officer. Other clergy present were Revd Jennings, CC, Cleggan; Revd M. Eaton CC. Clifden; and Revd M, Walsh, the Archbishop's secretary.

In The Line Of Duty

Sergeant Sean Kelly

After leaving school I went to work in a grocery and hardware business in Ballingeary, West Cork, a little village about the size of Leenane, where hundreds of children came from all parts of the country during the summer months to learn Irish.

There happened to be a young sergeant called Paddy Keane, a native of Clare, stationed there. He cut a fine figure and was highly thought of in the locality as being very efficient and upright. I thought I would like to emulate him, so the idea of applying to join the gardai was born. When my application in 1953 was successful, the news came as a disappointment to some of my relatives as there was an expectation that if I had remained where I was, I would become a successful businessman like two of my uncles.

However, I never regretted the move as fate decreed that I go for a brief period as sergeant to Burtonport, Co Donegal, in 1960, where I met my wife, Maureen. (Incidentally, my role model Sergeant Paddy Keane progressed through the ranks in the Garda Siochana and he retired as Assistant Commissioner.)

I spent six months as a training recruit in the Phoenix Park Depot in Dublin. It was a regimental set-up. Breakfast at 8 a.m. was followed by parade at 8.45 a.m. Roll call was taken at parade. Then we had morning classes, followed by one hour's drill before lunch. We had further classes in the afternoon followed by a second hour's drill. We had to learn a lot of laws that specifically concerned gardai. I enjoyed the drill a lot because it gave us a welcome break from the classroom and it was also very good physical exercise. Boxing was compulsory for self-defence purposes but it did not appeal to me and I do not think I ever really mastered the art. Every Sunday morning 240 of us were marched, four abreast, to Aughrim Street Church for Mass, dressed in full uniform. There was always an inspection beforehand to ensure that everyone was properly attired, including gloves. I can remember certain lads opting to change their socks from feet to hands hoping to avoid detection. We were allowed out of the depot to socialise but we had to be in by 11 p.m. for roll call. There

During training at the Depot in Phoenix Park, Dublin, 19th December, 1953. The open neck tunic was introduced a few months later.

was no such thing as going home to our families during the training period, so Christmas 1953 was also spent in the Phoenix Park.

In April 1954, three young gardai travelled from the Garda Depot, Dublin, to their first station in Galway City. I was one of them, the others being Pat Campbell and John Buckley, both now deceased.

We were very happy and full of enthusiasm for the challenges ahead. Our pay in the Depot was £5-10-1 per week, but on allocation to our first station it was increased to £5-11-2. We were accommodated in the station where our meals were provided at a cost of £2 per week.

Our duties were performed on foot or pedal bicycle. Only one official garda car was provided to the station and that was for the use of Detective Branch members. I bought a new 3-speed Raleigh bicycle for £20. The population of Galway City then was about 30,000.My first duty was to walk the streets of Galway and try to get evidence of begging against well-known operators in the trade who were a nuisance to the general public. I had some success at first but it was short-lived once my identity became known!

Burglary and stealing were the most common crimes commited. "Travelling criminals", as they were referred to, very often travelled on foot. An investigation was often commenced by visiting the local convent or priest's house to enquire if anybody had recently visited them looking for a meal or shelter.

There was a roll call each night at 11 p.m. and all gardai and sergeants in the station had to be present unless they were out on duty. Otherwise, it was necessary to have permission from the Superintendent to be absent after 11 p.m. This ridiculous rule was abolished about 1960 when it was being honoured more in the breach than in the observance.

Traffic lights were unheard of in the 1950s so the gardai had to ensure that traffic flowed as freely as possible. There were few restrictions on parking but not few enough to be observed by all.

In September 1958 I travelled by bus, with my bicycle on top, on transfer to Lettermore station in south Connemara. The station is situated a quarter mile off the bus route. Dutifully the sergeant, Tony O'Doherty, and garda John McCullough met me at the bus to help with my luggage. It seems strange now to reflect on the transport they used: two wheelbarrows!

The sergeant and three gardai lived in the station and we did our own cooking, each for a week in turn. This experience of cooking and learning from each other stood us in good stead afterwards! The facilities in the station were spartan or non-existent. As those were pre-electricity days, our means of light was an oil lamp and globe. We had running water in the station, but for some reason nobody thought of installing toilet facilities there. These were provided in a shed 50 yards away and were of the dry variety. Central heating was something else we hadn't dreamed of at the time and we kept ourselves comfortable with an open fire.

The cost of fuel had to be strictly accounted for and any excess over the previous year's expenditure had to be explained. No fuel expenditure was allowed for the period April to September inclusive as the weather during this period was deemed to be such that heating was unnecessary.

It is only when measured against these standards that the improvements in working conditons which have taken place in the intervening years can be fully appreciated. Nobody in the public service would be asked to work under those conditions nowadays, nor would they be prepared to do so.

Our official duties were conducted almost entirely through the medium of Irish, which I enjoyed. Although the Connemara "blas" is different to that of my native Coolea in West Cork, it didn't create any great difficulties.

Our work was varied which gave us an opportunity to meet and get to know the people in our area. A garda visited each school in his area at least once a month to give a talk on road safety and to ensure that no pupil was absent without a reasonable excuse.

Every garda in the station was fully occupied one day per week certifying Unemployment Assistance forms at the station and at outlying areas.

Carna Garda Station, 1958

"Poitín duty", as it was known, took up a lot of garda time in south Connemara, especially approaching Christmas. There was no stigma was attached to a conviction for making, supplying or possessing poitín but I witnessed a lot of unfortunate results from consumption of illicit spirits. Ironically, some poitín makers welcomed garda activity in relation to poitín as it

On poitín duty at Inishterk, Lettermullen, with other gardai in February, 1961.

limited the number of producers, and consequently the value of the product increased!

Collecting Agricultural Statistics was another job gardai had to perform for a month or so each year. This entailed visiting each household and taking particulars of the number of milk cows, calves under one year old and all other animals owned by the householders. Information on fowl was also asked for, even down to the question of the number of eggs laid yesterday. I remember one occasion, having recorded all the details from a conscientious wife, her husband came along and enquired what information she had given under each heading. He told her in unparliamentary language that she had overstated the number, so I had to drastically downgrade his standard of living. No doubt he didn't want officialdom to get the wrong idea about his wealth. I found myself apologising for causing so much trouble!

I introduced road bowling with a 28 ounce iron ball to Connemara but it never caught on. I remember purchasing twenty bowls in a hardware store in West Cork and playing them with my colleagues in Lettermore. We realised that the bowls could have proved dangerous to people using the public road and unfamiliar with the game. So when all twenty bowls were lost in the course of play, we discontinued that hobby.

I came to Clifden in 1961 as a young sergeant and assumed that my stay here would be as brief as in other stations. In the event it lasted 25 years. The station was located in the premises now occupied by J. B. Joyce Solicitors. There were a number of senior gardai here at that time whose experience proved very helpful to me. The strength of the station party was one sergeant and eight gardai. At each of the other stations of the district – Letterfrack, Leenane, Maam, Recess, Carna and Roundstone – there was a sergeant and two gardai. The total strength of the district force is more or less the same concentration of numbers that is now in Clifden, where the force has doubled, while the other stations in the district have been correspondingly reduced.

Before 1970, gardai had to work split tours of duty each day: 4 hours in the morning and 4 hours at night. Overtime work was performed whenever the exigencies of the service demanded but there was no provision for overtime pay. All that ended in 1970 when the Conroy Commission provided for a 40-hour week and payment at rate-and-a-half for overtime whenever necessary. Now all gardai are rostered for a straight 8-hour tour of duty.

During my time in Clifden, there was one policewoman in the station. Her name was Mary Doherty and she came from Donegal. She was a bit of a novelty at first, but she wasn't long assimilating, and after a while there was no distinction made. The attitude of the men was one of wanting to help in any way possible to make her time that bit easier. Her presence in the station brought a sense of refinement to the station party and that was very positive. Policewomen are now accepted as equals in every respect, so much so that the term bangarda is no longer in official use.

The busiest day of the year for gardai at Clifden in the 1960s and 1970s was Christmas Eve. On that day, about three bus-loads of emigrants would return home for the festive season. The last port of call for many of them before reaching home was an extended visit to one of the pubs in town. At closing time and into the wee hours, gardai found themselves fully extended dealing with people who had over-indulged and all the problems that arise from that.

There was very little development in Clifden in the 1960s and 1970s. Several years elapsed when not a single house was built.

Traffic in the '60s was light compared with the '90s. The gardai introduced the one-way system in Clifden on Show Day each year, but their proposal to introduce it on a permanent basis in the early 1980s was defeated at a public meeting. It took a further twelve years before it became a reality.

In the '50s, '60s and '70s, dances were held in parish halls in Connemara. It was a great form of entertainment for the young people and provided an ideal opportunity to make new friends. I regret the passing of this era.

I feel very privileged to have had a career as a garda and to have been promoted later to the rank of sergeant. I looked on my work as being more than just a job. I gave all my interest to it with no regard for the extra hours worked. Overtime was done on a voluntary basis only. I wasn't influenced by money and I didn't ever compare my rate of pay with those of other professions. I got great fulfilment from solving problems for people. Being a pioneer was probably the greatest single thing that helped me throughout my career since it enabled me to be more independent in the performance of my duty and allowed me to avoid compromising situations. I will never know what I have missed by staying a pioneer but I don't regret it. I still

At the official opening of the new Garda Station at Clifden in June 1972 by the Minister for Justice, Mr Des O'Malley, TD.

enjoy myself very much at weddings and other social functions. Indeed, I've seen so much evidence of the abuse of drink that it reinforces my view that I have not missed anything. When I reflect on my time in the force and compare my days as a young garda with the new recruits nowadays, I must say that I have no regrets about being a policeman in a bygone era. In my time, very few members had cars and because of this we nearly all lived locally. I think we were better known and understood by the community we served than the gardai are today. I don't believe they have the same degree of local knowledge today. When people get to know and trust a guard they are more likely to be of assistance in the course of investigating a serious crime. I feel also that we may have had a greater sense of camaraderie in my time than gardai have today. Mainly because, as young men, we were obliged to live in the station. I don't think the job is looked upon as a vocation to the same degree as it was in our time. I suspect that the introduction of paid overtime has contributed significantly to bringing about a different mindset and attitude within the force.

Undoubtedly policing is a much more difficult and complex profession today, than it was when I graduated. The problems today are much greater, particularly in relation to drugs. There is less respect in today's society and it is no different for members of the Garda Siochana. Having said that, however, gardai today have many advanced technological and scientific procedures at their disposal which significantly enhance their capacity to solve serious crimes. I never would have thought that we could have reached such high levels of sophistication in this regard as we approach the Millennium. When we left the depot in 1954, we felt well prepared for what lay ahead, but the new Garda College takes a much more enlightened approach to training than we experienced. It represents a big improvement and is playing an important role in making a career in policing more attractive.

Remembered and written by Sean Kelly

Out To Tender

Eamonn Guy

I grew up in Letterfrack. My mother's aunt, Nellie Walsh, left her the pub but I had very little interest in the pub business as a child. My father worked as a linesman for Marconi's company on the Greenmount wireless scheme. After the IRA burnt down the main station at Derrygimla in 1921, the company moved to Cornwall and my father went with them. He was to return home later and in 1926 he was taken into employment by the Christian brothers in Letterfrack School. They got him to wire the whole school, which he was well qualified to do after his years with Marconi's. My father became very good friends with Brother Keegan, the school manager, and by virtue of that friendship I was to become the first of the outsiders to serve my time in the school as an apprentice.

In 1932, at the age of fourteen, I finished in Letterfrack Primary School. I could have gone to St. Mary's College in Galway, like my older brother Tommy, but the prospect of learning the carpentry trade through an apprenticeship was much more appealing to me. I always had a great interest in, and love of wood, from a very young age and was always in the habit of calling into Mickey Conneely's carpentry shop to watch him at work. I served a three-year apprenticeship with Mickey Conneely and in 1935, at the age of seventeen, I decided to go out on my own, making doors and windows, roofing and such like.

My first job was a small cottage for John Conneely in Letterfrack. The house is still there today, beside Letterfrack Post Office. There were no concrete blocks at that time so we built the walls with mass concrete. We had to put casing all the way up and fill it in with the concrete. Each wall was completed in about three stages. The concrete had to be mixed by hand. We could only get a limited supply of bags of cement at the time from McDonagh's in Galway. I remember a bag of cement cost half-a-crown and Patrick James Salmon, who drove for Diamond's at the time, used to drive to Galway to get our supplies. There were very few men around at that time who were capable of roofing or making doors and windows. I remember us ordering special door boards and using nearly all white deal timber. I put in all the panes of glass myself. The panes at that time were all single glass, of course. There was no such thing as double-glazing. There were no plasterers then in the whole of west Connemara and the two of us eventually had to take on the plastering ourselves. We put on an ordinary pitched roof and slated it. The roofing cost about £400 and the overall cost of building the house was something in the region of £1000. There was no plumbing or electrical work involved. I was supposed to be paid every week but money was scarce and there were weeks when I couldn't be paid. I was averaging about £4.10s a week for the duration of the job which took about five months.

I felt a great sense of achievement on the completion of my first house, but I knew in my heart and soul that I should have been on much better money, considering the range of skills I had. I decided to go to work for Stuart's Construction Company in Galway City as an improver and became fully qualified. Stuart was a registered building contractor and I knew that working for his company would also give me valuable insights into how the contracting business worked. I was on £5 a week and it was guaranteed pay. I was building all the time and by 1940 I was a much more accomplished tradesman than I ever could have been had I stayed out on my own in west Connemara. Stuart's taught me a different, more effective and, most importantly, a quicker way of getting work completed. It was my first introduction to pricework and a lot of the ideas and systems I incorporated,into my own contracting business in subsequent years were learned from Stuart's.

On the 10th of June 1940, I joined the army. Like many other young men at that time, I felt a responsibility to sign up and be there for my country if it ever needed me. I was based in Galway, Athlone and Dublin. I started off as a private on 13s 2d a week. There was food and board laid on but it was still a big come-down from Stuart's. I was promoted to Training Sergeant after two years and my wages were increased to 36 shillings a week. I didn't really like the army, but Ireland was very economically depressed during World War II and I knew that steady work in construction with good wages would have been nearly impossible to find. The army was definitely one of the best jobs a man could have had in those years. When I was released from the army in 1946 and I returned home to Letterfrack. I didn't totally sever my relationship with the army however. In 1947, I joined the FCA and later that year I was commissioned by the Minister of Defence to the position of 2nd Lieutenant in 1948, and became a Captain in 1950. I was very honoured to be appointed a Commandant in 1955 and I eventually retired from the FCA in 1975.

When I came home to Letterfrack in 1946, I wasn't sure initially what I would do because times were so bad after the war. I thought about emigrating, but had no desire to leave west Connemara again, so I decided to base myself in Clifden and to try to get back into the building again. I decided that I would be my own boss, relying on all the skills and experience I had gained at Stuart's.

I also made a decision to get into pricework. I was fortunate in that I did have a reputable name as a tradesman at the time. My first clients were Mrs O'Toole and Mrs Donaldson who lived side by side on Main Street. Both women wanted their premises refurbished. Mrs O'Toole wanted to convert a private house into a shop and Mrs Donaldson needed renovations carried out on her hairdressing salon. The job involved stripping the roofs, re-roofing and putting in new doors and windows. John Joyce from Clifden and Paul Conneely from Streamstown were my first employees. Concrete blocks were just about in by the mid-1940s and they were a great help in speeding up the work. I remember the price for Mrs O'Toole's job was £300. As we worked on these projects, more work started to come in around the town, and from then on until I retired from building construction in 1973, I was never without work. In 1950, I sold the public house in Letterfrack to Molly Freeney, a first cousin of my own, who had just returned from America. The £3000 I received from the sale was a big help to my business at that early stage.

There was no such thing as a workers' union in those days. The wages were controlled by the County Council and during my years as an employer I had to pay the same rate as the Council. In the 1940s the standard wage would have been £1.4s.6d increasing to about £8 a week by the 1960s. There was no direct taxation until the early 1970s so I used to put up a stamp for my employees. It was a card comprising fifty-two spaces for the fifty-two weeks of the year. Every week I would buy stamps and every month inspectors from the labour exchange would check all my cards to see how many employees I had. At the end of each year I had to return to the labour exchange for new cards. I still have one Cárta Arachaís from 1972. It amounted to £2.0s.3d a week. I, being the employer, paid £1.0s.1d and my employees paid £1.0s.2d. There was also another book called a Wet Time book, for men who were out sick and unable to work. I used to pay them a special wet time rate at the end of the week. Then every quarter, I used to fill out a claim form, which I sent in to the

Department of Social Welfare. It would be something similar to business people claiming back VAT today.

Throughout the '40s and '50s, I had accounts with McDonagh's and Higgins' in Galway who delivered the various types of building and plumbing materials out to me. As the years went by, the quality of building materials was to improve dramatically. In 1963, I employed Chip Conneely as a full-time driver. During the 1960s I was contracted by the Board of Works to build a few schools in west Connemara. These included Claddaghduff, Kingstown and Tully, which I built for £12000 in 1966. I also had a substantial contract in the Convent School in Clifden where we built on science laboratories and a kitchen.The Board of Works was very slow to release money and this caused me a lot of stress on these projects. In 1963, I did a big refurbishing job on Ballinakill Roman Catholic church for £5000. I also worked on the Protestant church in Errislannan. I was the only registered building contractor in west Connemara at this time. I had no competition and had things very much my own way. By the late 1960s I was so busy I had thirty-three men working for me. About half of these were skilled tradesmen, the other half being labourers. Getting skilled tradesmen at the time was a huge problem; I nearly always had to go outside the west Connemara region especially for plumbers, carpenters and plasterers. This cost me a lot of money in wages. Indeed, a lot of these tradesmen wouldn't come out to Connemara anyway, because they were getting handier work around Galway City. The last big job I did was the Celtic Hotel in 1968. It was a ten-bedroom luxury hotel incorporating a spacious restaurant. The proprietors were Mr and Mrs Graeme Allen, who owned the rectory at Errislannan. They were hoping to eventually enlarge the hotel to forty-bedroom capacity. My contract price for this project was £12,000. Looking back, this project was the one that nearly broke me because of the difficulty in getting tradesmen. I was forced to go as far as Athlone for them and this pushed up my cost substantially. All of this is in stark contrast to the west Connemara of today, where there is no shortage of highly qualified tradesmen, and contractors are spoiled for choice. I was never afforded that same luxury in my time.

In 1969, I bought a site in Kylemore, comprising twenty acres of land, with a view to opening a quarry, in order to have my own source of sand and gravel for building projects. I set up a company called the Connemara Sand and Gravel Company. There was a very heavy financial investment to get things up and running. I had to buy a grader, a washer, a loading shovel and a truck. It was a big decision at the time but thankfully, a good one and the company is still thriving today under the management of my daughter, Mary. The advent of direct taxation in the early 1970s was one of the main reasons for me finally getting out of the building contracting business in 1973. Looking back on those twenty-seven years, I would have to say that, overall, I had a good run of it. There was great satisfaction in a good day's work. Some of the jobs were quite difficult but we always managed to overcome any new challenges. I loved working on the jobs with the men, and although a lot of the jobs tested us, I was privileged to work with so many men of great calibre down through the years. We enjoyed the crack and the banter, and I suppose it was this that kept us all going really. Mondays traditionally were the worst days in terms of productivity because some of the men might not turn up after the weekend's activities. I did have to let some men go over the years because of their continued absenteeism, which delayed other men and held up jobs for too long. I never took any holidays because I was always too constrained by my work, trying to meet deadlines particularly with the Board of Works. On the bigger jobs, I usually went in on time and material, where I would charge the client so much for time and so much for material. I usually took 25% commission on the material. Throughout the '50s and '60s the Bank of Ireland in Clifden afforded me an overdraft facility. I found the bank managers accommodating enough (especially Jimmy Faulkner), as long as they considered one to be honest. It was difficult to meet their demands at times, particularly if I, in turn, was waiting for money to come through from a client. There were many stressful days in relation to money.

My work prevented me from spending as much time with my family as I would have liked and I will always have regrets about this. My wife, who ran her own grocery and bar business in Clifden during all this time, was a tower of strength to me. She did most of the bookwork and always kept herself well informed and up to date on whatever construction projects I had on hand. My son Pat runs the bar business today and has expanded and modernised the public house in recent years to meet the ever increasing demands of the tourist industry as well as our young population. Another son of mine, Peter, is a tradesman who does a lot of contract work of his own. We talk a lot about building and he keeps me well informed of any new developments in the construction industry within the region. The industry seems to have grown at an enormous rate and present day prices seem colossal compared to my time.

The contractor's outlay today is so huge compared with my experience. In my time I was able to get the biggest jobs that were going, but that doesn't appear to be the case today for any of the locally based contractors, who seem to be unable to compete with companies like Rhatigan's from Galway City, who recently completed the Station House development in Clifden. Property prices have gone through the roof and it seems to be almost impossible any more for a young married couple starting off in life to be able to purchase their own house. Obtaining planning permission in my time was nearly as difficult as it is now, and many was the returned emigrant I knew, who had acquired a fine site on his parents' land, but couldn't get permission to build on it. The County Council were every bit as powerful back then as they are today.

In conclusion I would just like to add that, for the most part, the general public were very good to me throughout all my contracting years. I never had to go to Law to extricate money from any of my clients and although I did have a good few bad debts by 1973, there was never anything too substantial. By that stage, I had accepted that this problem always was and always will be an occupational hazard for building contractors.

Remembered by Eamonn Guy and written by Paul Gannon

The Fruits of My Labour

The Australian foreman seemed to be a bit stressed out as he addressed me in a somewhat agitated manner: "Mr Bartley, I am after asking fourteen countrymen of yours to make me a mould for a sill and they've all told me they've never done it. Would you be able to give it a shot?"

"Yes", I replied, "I'll be able to do it if you get me the right materials." I made the mould and concreted it in an artistic way. Some time later the architect arrived back, delighted with my efforts.

"Lovely job," he said, "real class. We do not get it that good out of the factory." Three weeks later the foreman offered me the position of section foreman on a big hospital job that the company were undertaking in Bristol but by that stage I was tired of England and had it in my head to return home and go into the contracting business. The mould I had created was a regular feature in Jack Feehan's workshop in Leenane in the 1950s, the place where I served my apprenticeship and learnt my trade.

It was always my ambition from a very young age to be a carpenter. I was always of the opinion that it would be a far more interesting occupation than office work or one of the professions. I always figured I would have some end product to satisfy me after a day's work. I would know exactly what had been achieved, unlike so many other types of work where it must be so frustrating not really being able to measure one's progress.

Gerard Bartley, 1975

My Uncle Gerald once said to me "If I could start life out again, I'd be a tradesman too. I was in academics but being a tradesman is a great life because at the end of each day you can see the fruits of your labour. Jack Feehan was an old colleague of Gerald's from the Anglo Irish War and when Gerald asked him if he would take me on as an apprentice in his workshop he was happy to oblige.

He gave Gerald an extensive list of the general tools required in carpentry and Gerald bought these for me in McDonagh's in Galway. It cost him £6 altogether, a substantial amount of money in 1952, and a very generous gesture to a sixteen year old boy who was determined to prove to himself and his sponsor that it was money well invested. My apprenticeship was to last four years. I received £1 a week the first year, 30 shillings the second year, £2 the third and 50 shillings in my final year. Room and board were free of charge. I stayed in Jack's house for the duration of the apprenticeship. There was the usual strictness on tidiness. I was expected to be in at a regular time each night and any laziness about getting up early in the morning was not tolerated. I was up every morning at 7 a.m. to be on the job by 8 a.m.

During my time in Leenane there was not much in the way of social life. I played a bit of football at the weekends and enjoyed a game of cards in the local pub. I liked listening to the wireless as I always had a very enquiring mind. Jack and I also spent many an hour talking about his days in the IRA and I always looked forward to my Uncle Gerald's visits. I very rarely got home during the four years.

Jack Feehan's two sons were qualified carpenters who had trained in Kelly's in Westport. It was one of these sons, Joe, who was to become my teacher. I was confined to the workshop for the first two years where Joe taught me a range of carpentry and joinery skills. He was exceptionally good at setting out work and making templates. He was very technically minded, a complete perfectionist and a tough taskmaster. He was not interested in lame excuses when things went wrong and mistakes were made. I got fed up a number of times and seriously contemplated packing it all in. I did not like being chastised in a humiliating manner, but the work was so varied and challenging and Joe was so gifted that it was impossible not to maintain a high level of interest, and as I started to get better the abuse started to disappear. I discovered that I, too, was technically minded and that if I really put my mind to it, I could be very neat and accurate. I loved the way the work kept my brain very active. Measuring and setting out work was very mathematical and this suited me, as I had always loved maths in Primary school.

Slowly but surely, I became more accomplished and confident in my work and Joe was to reward my endeavours by giving me extra responsibility in the whole area of furniture production. We produced a wide range of furniture. A staircase cost £18; an old fashioned dresser £14; a kitchen table £9; a bed with timber head and bottom £4; a wardrobe £3; six chairs £22; and a fitted kitchen £45. We also made coffins on request for £9 and picture frames at £3 each. The only available windows of the day were pulley style. It would still be some years before the casement windows with hinges would come on the market. McDonagh's of Galway and Kelly's of Westport were our main timber suppliers and the only timber available was red or white deal.

During the final two years of my apprenticeship I spent a lot of time working out on the buildings with Jack Feehan whose building contracting business brought him all over Connemara. My work mainly consisted of roofing, doorhanging and shuttering. I enjoyed being out on site a lot more than being in the workshop and as time went on, the more complicated the work became the more I enjoyed it. It cost in the region of £1400 to build a standard house in the 1950s, rising to about £2,000 in the 1960's and increasing threefold to £7,000 by the mid 1970s. A house built in the 1970s would be near enough to present day standards, in my opinion, but houses built back in the 1950s were way off modern standards. There was no proper insulation in cavities or ceilings, no damp proof course, no heating and only the most basic of plumbing. We also built a number of schools including Moyard school at a cost of £6,000. In the 1960s the cost of building a school rose to about £8,000.

A carpenter's wages were about £4 a week. In the final year of my apprenticeship I was not satisfied with my weekly wage. I asked for a pay rise, but it was not forthcoming, and this was one of the main reasons I decided to leave after having completed my apprenticeship. There was no such thing as ANCO or FÁS in those days. I went to night classes twice a week in the technical school in Westport and received my indentures, or qualification papers, on completing the course. When the four years were up and I was finally a fully qualified carpenter, Jack Feehan wanted me to stay on. He was of the opinion that I was qualified, that I was quite good and that I should give him a few years of service in return for all the training and instruction which he had afforded me. However, I felt that the wages being offered were well below what they should have been, considering the range of skills I had now acquired. I was grateful to Jack for everything he had done for me but I knew I was now ready to go it alone and determine my own destiny.

I returned home to Ballinaboy. Qualified tradesmen were in short supply. The only other qualified carpenters in the whole of West Connemara at the time were Jackie Lydon from Kylemore, John Addeley from Cleggan, Val King and Eamonn Guy from Clifden. I was confident of getting plenty of work considering my qualifications, but Ireland was very economically depressed throughout the 1950s and I was very quickly dealt a lesson in harsh reality. There was very little carpentry work going, a few small jobs here and there, but nothing to suggest that there was any future in it. I was forced to look for some alternative way of making money.

I invested in a hand machine for making concrete blocks and set up in Errislannan beside a sheltered cove where there was an unlimited supply of gravel coming in from the sea. I employed one person with a tractor to transport the gravel on to level ground and two other lads to manufacture the blocks using the machine and timber pallets measuring 18 inches by 9. I spent three years in this business, and supplied all the blocks for the building of Ballyconneely hall and Ballyconneely seaweed factory. In 1960 legislation was introduced forbidding anyone to take gravel from the sea and I was officially notified to close down my operation. I was back to square one and now resigned myself to the fact that, in order to make a decent living for myself, I would have to either migrate or emigrate.

I joined the Woodworkers' Amalgamated Union in Galway to improve my chances of gaining secure employment. I decided to go to Limerick to work on McInerney's housing scheme. They had advertised in the national newspaper and were offering £9 a week plus 30 shillings counting money to pay for lodgings. I left for Limerick with one suitcase and my toolbox but I never got there. A brother of mine had just emigrated to England and had informed me that carpenters were able to earn £22 a week over there. It was on my journey to Limerick that I decided that my destiny lay in England. The following morning I arrived at my brother's lodgings in Gloucester city, hoping that my impulsive decision had been the correct one.

I was to spend the next ten years in England, spending 1960 in Gloucester city and moving to Bristol with a fellow called Simon Carr in 1961 where we worked on a chemical works. It was a huge project. Every morning fifty-five coach loads of men used to make the three-quarters of an hour journey from Bristol out to the construction site. We were on £30 a week. In 1962 I moved down to London, where I remained for the rest of my time in England. I worked on a lot of shuttering jobs and did a lot of piecework. By 1964 I was earning £35 a week, and by the time I left London in 1970 to return home, I was on about £50 a week. The money was great in England. I was well rewarded for the work I did. English bosses were fine to work for but one was still "Paddy" to the core in their estimation.

I could never understand how they were so incapable of remembering our Christian names. It used to irritate me greatly and I was forever reminding them of my proper name. There is no way such practice would be tolerated nowadays in the workplace, but I suppose the English did not realise or appreciate how much offence they were causing us. In 1965, I decided to attend night classes in the London Technical College. I spent three years taking classes in Civil Engineering and felt a great sense of achievement on receiving my diploma. The classes cost £20 a month. I found the Civil Engineering course very helpful after I returned to Ireland. I never had to hire an engineer or a draughtsman or anyone to price my work. I spent many nights in London drawing out plans with the help of Joe Gibbons from Clifden, who was a great tradesman and a foreman over there. When I went into the building contracting business in the early 1970s the combination of night school and these long hours of practising really stood to me in that I was able to submit full planning applications without assistance for all my clients. I had a good quality of social life in England and enjoyed many a dance at the Galteemore, the Buffalo and the Gresham. I also liked going to the pictures. However, by 1970 I had had enough of what England had to offer and I decided to return to West Connemara and set up my own building contracting business.

I spent the next fifteen years in the contracting business, but being a councillor for eleven of those years did have an adverse effect on the quality of service I was able to give. In 1976, I was offered a once-in-a-lifetime opportunity by a married couple from Sweden to build a unique type of house. When they approached me initially I told them I would draw the plans of the house myself provided they gave me a rough sketch first. They agreed to my request, I submitted the plans to the council and obtained planning permission. I gave them the contract price of £7,000 and went ahead and designed everything myself. I got my brother, Padraig, along with Patrick Kerrigan and his son, Martin, from Lettergesh, to scallop thatch the roof. I made the old style teak windows myself in my workshop in Clifden. The panes of glass were 9 by 7 inches. I also made the kitchen table and the old fashioned dresser

Outside the cottage in Dereen, 1976. From left, M. Corbett, J. O'Malley, P. Bartley, J. J. Corbett, G. Bartley, J. Wallace, Pia Hellburg.

from red deal as well as all the beds. All the rooms had ceiling boards and floorboards. The front door was sheeted with a half door on the outside and all the walls inside and outside were done in crooked plaster. The kitchen floor was made from Ballinakill flagstone and the polished marble worktop in the kitchen was one of my favourite features of the whole house. This marble was cut in Streamstown quarry and polished there also.

My clients gave me details of a one hundred year old Swedish heating system which they wanted me to install, involving a smokeless chamber at the back of the fire. The chamber was smokeproof and built allround with firebrick. A pipe, placed in the centre of the wall, was run from the chamber through to the partition wall. There were two vents fitted on either side of the wall for each of the two bedrooms. When the fire was on the heat went through the vents and circulated around the bedrooms, thereby ensuring a low degree of constant heat. This project was the most satisfying and fulfilling of my career and I was offered a lot of contracts subsequently because of it. I would estimate that the same house today would probably cost in the region of £100,000 to build. It was my showpiece, the culmination of all my knowledge and experience gained over the preceding twenty four years, and I will always be very thankful to the owners for affording me such scope and freedom in the construction and design of their house. I hope Jack Feehan would have been satisfied with my efforts.

Remembered by Gerard Bartley and written by Paul Gannon

O Holy Night

Mary Kane

The boys had to go a day or two before Christmas to gather the greenery, the holly and the ivy and bring home cartloads of it. We lived in Tullycross and because of this, our Christmas preparations always involved the decorating of the chapel. We used the greenery to make chain or rope ornaments. It all had to do with making us realise that is was Christmas day and that we were preparing to make the little stable and Christ's place of birth, more attractive for our Lord. My mother and Aunt Julia used to make these decorations during Christmas Eve. It took a long time. We would be watching them and we used to hand them the branches and collect the waste bits as they went along. They made thick ropes for in front of and over the altar and thinner ropes for decorating the little altars. This work in the chapel took up a good part of Christmas morning.

We loved watching the people coming home from the shops. It was lovely to see them passing with their beautifully washed white flour bags full of the Christmas box. The few different coloured candles would be sticking up as they went along and that to me was good fun and great delight. Then when my parents brought home their own Christmas box it was great to see what would come out of it. There was tea, sugar and the buillín. The buillín was a little white loaf, which was a great treat in those days because it was all homemade bread and to get some loaf bread and jam was a big thing. After that you had currants and raisins, treacle and golden syrup, the candles, spice, ginger and mixed peel. The Christmas box was something we really loved. It was part of the Christmas spirit and was in memory of when the wise men brought the gifts to our Lord. It was also a type of discount from the shops for being such a good customer during the year. I remember the shops sometimes vied with each other about who would give the best Christmas box and the mothers used to be asking each other what they got. We used to hear them comparing when they would meet each other as they went along and we used to love to watch and listen in.

I cannot remember at what time the confessions started but the older ones would always be sent out first, so that they in turn could come home and tell our parents when there would not be too many waiting at the box. There was only the one box in our small chapel. It was not as it is now. It was not renovated until 1928 and these memories of mine go back to about 1920. People fasted during Lent and Advent in those days. People from the age of seven to twenty-one as well as people over sixty were only expected to abstain but anyone between the age of twenty-one and sixty was expected to fast and abstain unless they had special permission not do to so from the priest for health reasons. The fast was very severe. There was a collation in the morning. I cannot remember the weight of the bread but it usually amounted to what would be two slices of homemade cake. There were three days a week of fasting and abstinence. On the days of abstinence we were not allowed to eat meat so we either had fish or eggs. It was not always that easy to get fish, although we often got shellfish when the strand was good. Christmas Eve was the last fasting day. We usually had ling for dinner. Ling was the easiest fish to get for people like us who were not fisher people or who had not salted fish in the house. Ling was sold in the shops. It was a very dry hard fish. We soaked it overnight before cooking and it was served with a cream sauce along with potatoes. That was the last meal before midnight. All of us who were going to receive Holy Communion on Christmas morning had to fast from midnight.

I never saw an iced cake in those days. My mother used to make a very good ginger cake and she used to also make the ordinary treacle cake, baked in the pot oven. There was something special about the bread that came out of the pot oven in the way that the flavour would stay in on account of the lid being left on. The making of the plum pudding was a big event. The younger ones used to take seeds out of the raisins and I remember my mother used to allow us one raisin for every ten we'd open. She used to have the beef suet bought from the butchers in advance and she'd have it peeled and prepared for chopping. The boys used to chop it but Mam always had to finish it off herself of course, to make it finer before using it in the making of the pudding. The plum pudding resembled a big cake. It was put into a cloth, covered in flour and boiled and after it was finally cooked in the three-legged pot it was emptied into a great big enamel dish.

People came long distances on Christmas morning to get to Mass and many had to walk, not having a horse and trap or a sidecar. Many walked from Letter, Cashleen and Salruck to the chapel in Tullycross. There were Masses in Tullycross as well as one in Creeragh. After Mass, people often called into houses in the village for tea before the long walk home. Some form of refreshment was badly needed because they would have been fasting since midnight. Apart from this visitation after the Masses, there was no such thing as visiting on Christmas day. Each family stayed in their own home celebrating Christmas with Jesus in the crib. For breakfast we had some of the black pudding and sometimes we'd dive into the plum pudding too. We usually had goose for dinner although I do also remember chicken being roasted in the pot oven. We had potatoes with this and we'd be well full after the dinner. Later on in the evening we might have some more of the plum pudding. Also on Christmas evening the boys would always go out to catch the wren. I remember them coming to our house on St Stephen's Day. They would dance or sing or play music in the hope of getting some money. I remember my mother always insisted on them doing something before she would give them anything. Then, of course, they would have a bit of the plum pudding or Christmas cake. The older ones had a musical band. They would be all dressed up and they used to play in the gathering houses. You would not know them but some people used to recognise them through their music. In some places I think they were known as the Mummers.

We looked forward to Santa at Christmas. It was a sort of a prize for being good. It was all about the Baby Jesus in those days. Now it's all about Santa, all about what you'll get and everyone vying with the other, trying to keep up with the Jones's. There was none of that when I was young. You hung up your stocking. If you found a stick or a turnip in it, in the morning, then you had been a bold child. I remember my first gift from Santa was a little sandwich of bread and jam and a comic. A lady had been home from America and after she went back she used to send on comics. My mother used to hide them away and she would put them in the Christmas stocking for us. I remember another Christmas getting an apple and an orange. I remember my younger sister getting the same in later years.

We were just as happy with the little bit of the buillín and jam in those days as children are nowadays who get so many things. I think they get so much now that they have no real appreciation of anything and I think modern society is in danger of losing the true meaning of Christmas. We had very little of the material things but it did not matter because we had no expectations. It did not stop Christmas from being a time of great joy and happiness. We were filled with a great love of the Baby Jesus and there was nothing to compare with the magic of the lighted candles in all the village windows on that holiest of nights.

Remembered by Mary Kane and written by Paul Gannon

A Memorable Trip

Yes, even though it was the Christmas of 1948, I can remember as if it were yesterday, getting up that morning at the crack of dawn and mother getting the breakfast ready. In those days everything was cooked over the open turf fire. While waiting for breakfast, I would go out and feed Neddy the donkey in the barn next door. There would be no school for me that day as I would be driving Mother to town in the ass and cart to do the Christmas shopping. Dad would be working on the road, my mother would be at school and Granny would be minding the house.

At about 9.30 a.m. I would put the tackle on Neddy, put some hay in the cart and at 10 o'clock we would be ready to hit the road. Mom would warn me to be extra careful today as there would be lots of other traffic heading for town. Mostly common carts, side cars, traps, people riding on horses, donkeys and, at that time, even bullocks. I remember one man used to always ride a big bullock to town.

That morning when we reached the main road it was chockablock at the Marconi Cross. I spotted Brigid who was putting on her shoes by the side of the road. She used to always walk across the Marconi Bog in her bare feet rather than get her shoes and socks wet. She always said it was good for her feet; perhaps she was right. Anyway, we stopped and gave her a lift and with Mom and her chatting away in the back very soon we were rounding the corner at Millar's old mill which was situated at the waterfall in those days.

I guess when Neddy heard all the noise of the machinery from the mill he suddenly stopped and cocked his ears and he then took off like the hammers of hell. Mom and Brigid started shouting: "Jesus, Mary and Joseph! Stop him or we will all be killed!" I was pulling hard on the reins but he seemed to go faster and after going round Lee's corner (now Vaughans) I saw this man riding on an ass with baskets right in our path. We went flying past, and as we did I pulled the reins right, but our left wheel hit the outside basket which was put spinning across towards Stanley's shop window. As I glanced round I could see the man shaking his stick at me as he went to recover his basket.

We raced on up Market Street – they were praying in the back by now and someone must have heard because as we drew near the Square two men rushed across the street. One took off his jacket and threw it over Neddy's head and we finally came to a halt at the weigh house. They helped Brigid and Mom out of the cart, who were delighted to get their feet on solid ground once more.

After thanking the men for coming to our rescue, I left them all chatting there and guided Neddy round the corner, unhitched him from the cart and tied him to it. I fed him some hay outside of Casey's shop in Main Street and I then headed down to do shopping at the Market Square which was thronged with people selling and buying for Christmas. That day I had the large sum of five shillings to spend so I headed for T. J. Mullens' toy shop where I looked at many toys and settled for a clockwork train set costing half-a-crown.

Later I met up with Mom outside Mannion's and we both went across to Annie Heffernan's Tea Shop, now Fogerty's Restaurant, where we had tea, bread and butter and sweet cake – all for three-and-sixpence. At the next table was our friend Brigid, looking more relaxed now. We chatted there for a while before heading up town again. Brigid was carrying a heavy load of groceries in a white flour bag on her back. I remember saying to her outside of Flanagans shop, "the cart is parked outside of Casey's, Brigid. Leave your bag in it and have a lift home with us". I had forgotten all about the morning episode, but not Brigid, for she stopped in her tracks and looked at me and said "ah no thanks, astór. It's a fine day and the walk will do me good. But may God bless ye and guide ye safely home". We all said, "Happy Christmas".

Mom and I went towards the Square where she bought some cured fish, crannach and carraigín moss. Then we went back and hitched Neddy to the cart. It was getting dark now as we headed off up Main Street. Mom went ahead to O'Toole's to get the shopping ready. I stopped outside Durkins. I remember all the candles were lighting in the shops by then. There was a lovely spirit. There were horses and carts, traps, side cars parked all along Main Street. The shops were thronged with people, all in the festive mood, doing their shopping.

I can still see Ms Durkin packing the big poke of sweets for me, while she chatted of Christmas long ago and as I paid my sixpence she handed me a big Christmas brack to take home to Granny. I had one more stop at Mrs. Payne's across the street, where I had a big glass of lemonade for sixpence for the road home.

Then it was on to O'Toole's to collect Mom and the shopping. The big red Christmas candle sticking out of the box was a familiar sight in those days as, indeed, was the big sack of flour and, of course, the Christmas Box. As we were packing them in the cart I remember a man from Errismore came up to me holding a large bottle of stout and said to me, "will you have a drop of the bottle sonny?" I said, "ah no thank you sir, but a Merry Christmas to you anyway." Across the street I could hear the Lydon brothers working in the forge as they were striking the anvil. Later, as we passed on our way home, you could smell the smoke and almost feel the heat from the big coal fire that was used to heat the iron for the horse shoes. Mom said to walk past the mill this time but as we drew near everything was quiet. I guess they had closed the place down for Christmas. All you could hear was the noise from the waterfall as it wound its way to the sea.

At the top of Pat Nee's hill we hopped in the cart and lit the candle in the jam jar and Neddy trotted home. On reaching the old oak tree across from Duffy's hotel (now the Community School) Neddy stopped suddenly and a familiar voice said, "who have we here?" "Help me I am lost." It was our good friend, Dudley, sitting on the wall by the spring well holding a bag of groceries, less his cap, which he told me had blown over the wall. With the help of the candle in the jar I found it beside the well. I helped him into the cart. He was telling us fairy stories for the rest of the way home. At the Marconi crossroads we went to bid him good night and as we went up the hill we could hear the noise of his hob-nailed boots as he wound his way home. From around the bend we could see the lights of Slyne Head lighthouse and in the distance the light from our cottage. Then Neddy turned left down the boreen. I could feel the wheels grinding into the fresh coral sand Dad had put down for Christmas. You could smell the fresh whitewash, and as we drew near, one could see the red berried holly at the back of each picture and the big turf fire with the kettle boiling on the crook. I will always remember the welcome home. There was a big parcel waiting for us from America. Granny had the supper ready, after which the table was cleared, Dad put Neddy in the barn, gave him a drink and hay for the night. The parcel was opened – presents for everybody. We all sat around the fire (even the cat). We were discussing the day's events. Mom said we were lucky to be alive, I was laughing. Suddenly there was a knock on the door and on answering it, lo and behold, who was standing there but our good friend Dudley, saying, "where am I, begories, I am lost!"

We sat him down by the fire. After a while there was another tap on the door. It slowly opened and a voice said over the half door "God save all in" and we all replied "God save you kindly". It was our good friend and neighbour, Tommy Green, and when he saw Dudley he said, "oh good

Christmas Market Day in Clifden, c. 1910

God, is that you Dudley? What harm, but didn't I meet you going home an hour ago?" We all laughed and Dudley started telling stories about getting lost and turning the jacket inside out to find his way home.

Then we all had tea and home made treacle bread. Later the old gramophone was taken down from the dresser and cranked. The old 78 was playing with Michael Coleman on the fiddle playing the *Bucks of Oranmore*. Dudley started telling stories again. Tommy added that he was better than any gramophone. At about midnight, Tommy said he would leave Dudley home with the lantern light.

That night I would dream about fairies and Dudley getting lost. Then I would awake to the sound of Neddy calling from the barn next door and another day. Oh yes, it was time to clean the chimney now as Santa Claus would be coming soon.

This was Christmas 1948. Sadly most of those lovely people have now departed this life, but for me they are not forgotten, for every Christmas when I pass by the old mill site by the waterfall, fond memories come flooding back of that day near Christmas all those years past when mother, Brigid and I went galloping for our lives up the old Market Street in the ass and cart.

Written by Marty Conneely

Over Yonder

Amongst my most vivid memories of the summer of 1955 was meeting three Letterfrack men, all of whom were back home on holidays from the north of England, at a dance in Ulick's dancehall. Martin Coyne, John Conneely and Dominic Hastings worked with my uncle Paddy Nee in Burnley.

"The uncle is wondering," said one of them "if you have any notion of going over?" Going over or emigrating was the done thing. No preparation, or educational qualifications required, not even the travel money, as this was available by way of loan, to be repaid when the big money started to roll in 'Over Yonder' – as England was often referred to. I thought about what they had said and packed a suitcase, the contents of which were soon to be discarded in favour of the British version. That was it; a week later I was on my way.

My recollections in the following pages are about ordinary people most of whom, once they started out to work abroad, never looked back or let doubt overwhelm them. It is also very much a part of the social history of that era, and the major role played by our emigrants in the development of our Irish economy, but never credited to them. Central in my recollections are issues concerning the exiles' sense of belonging in a new and unfamiliar community and how this was expressed in the daily discourse of work and social pastimes. It is about relationships formed, about coping with loneliness, and above all trying to come to terms with indifferent attitudes, to the loss of life in the workplace, the total absence of safety precautions for workers and to the spiritual needs of the predominately Catholic Irish workforce.

To a lesser extent I will recall some of the symbolic aspects of the medium-sized Lancashire town where I settled first and I will attempt to focus on how we Irish, perceived as being backward, understood and used our Irish ideology based on our heritage and culture in our strange and new surroundings. Trying to cram eight years of history into a few pages is not an easy task, obviously. Naming the hundreds of people with whom I shared those years with, in the work place, and in the social sphere would be impossible. The model and the structure, which I am adopting, is what I saw and remember of the actions of people in the course of events. I trust that I can express meaning connected to locality and the lifestyle of an Irish rural people thrust of necessity into a modern day society.

I arrived at 28, Belvedere Road on a Wednesday in mid-August 1955, having completed the last stage of my journey by train from Liverpool to Manchester, free of charge, courtesy of British Rail personnel unable to cope adequately with the hordes of Irish immigrants returning from holidays, plus the first timers like myself, who were being lured across the sea with promises of rich pickings, and a better way of life. 28, Belvedere Road – the digs or lodgings as they were referred to in those days, were like most of them, rough and ready, ideally suited for six rough and ready Irishmen. The massive corrugated roofed building directly across the street looked totally out of place. I was later to learn that it was in fact Turf Moor the home of Burnley FC, where the silken skills of Jimmy McIlroy, himself an Irishman, dominated for many seasons to follow.

I had come here to take up an appointment as a labourer on an open-cast coal site. I am joking of course, most of the men including the bosses on coal sites would not know the meaning of the word. In reality, I was here to slave for twelve hours each day, including Sunday, if I were required to work it. That was to be my way of life for the next four and a half years. Our landlady was a kindly sort, middle aged. She appeared tired and worn-out looking. One suspected that she had long since fallen out of love with a good-for-nothing husband who rarely, if ever, made any contact with us. Coarse porridge, thin slivers of bacon, two large sausages and a few thin slices of poor quality bread – that was breakfast A neatly packed lunch consisted of banana sandwiches which by mid-day, in the boiling sun of mid-August were reduced to mush. The evening meal served at 8 p.m. very often had horsemeat for the main course. It was quite common to have horsemeat served in digs in those days. Self-catering and room rental was unheard of then.

I liked that kind middle-aged lady, who like numerous other landladies that I came to know took upon themselves a motherly responsibility for many of us young Irish lads and girls. I appreciated her best for safeguarding the first £40 I had ever saved. "Do not ever," she said, "leave your money underneath your mattress again, because if my husband were to find it, he'd be off to the bookies."

Burnley was a town which would not have attracted too many Irish men or women, were it not for the fact that it was a rich source of coal, large seams of which were relatively close to the earth's surface. The process employed to extract these seams was known as opencast strip mining. Virtually all worthwhile Civil Engineering firms in England, Scotland and Wales, McGregor's, Wimpy's, McAlpine's, Tarmac's, being the largest, worked around the clock, seven days a week, stripping, extracting and restoring the lands to their original state after the coal was removed. The process was identical to that operating on the huge Ohio coalfields in the USA and to that which operates in the rich oil sands of Fort McMurray in the northern regions of Alberta, Canada, at the present time.

The town was not prepared for what was about to hit it. Big time money-earners, and big-spenders with all kinds of strange accents now had to be accommodated in many ways. The pubs became the main focal points and names such as the 'Footballers', the 'Peeks Arms' and the 'Red and White Lions' suddenly became famous landmarks for those of us looking for directions, but the 'Dog and Duck' with its one toilet serving the two sexes was the most acclaimed of all. Many old customs and behaviour patterns which had survived the test of time were still very much in fashion in Burnley in the mid-1950s. Perhaps the most striking old custom of all, and one which I had not encountered anywhere before or since, was the custom of arousing workers in the early morning by tapping on their bedroom window panes with a long pole which reached from street level to the second storey bedroom window. I often wondered how the guy employed to do that job managed to get out himself. Another custom, which was most irritating, was the continuous ringing of the church bells. However I did ultimately come to appreciate the significance of this particular custom when I found out that it had its origins in the persecution of the Catholic clergy throughout the turbulent period of the reformation and the role played by the people of Burnley in providing safe refuge for Catholic priests whose lives were under threat. The custom of wearing clogs – a leather shoe fitted with wooden soles to which irons were attached – was still very much in vogue. The clattering of the irons on the streets, the constant ringing of church bells, and the persistent knocking on the window panes of people deep in slumber were sounds which still ring in my ears occasionally.

"I worked", he said, "with lots of Connemara men, and I'll tell you one thing, you're not a Connemara man". That first working day in a field in Lancashire, stands out as vivid today as though it were only yesterday. The two old boys, both approaching their seventies, had commenced digging a trench on what we always referred to as the access road on Monday morning. Pick and shovel work in sweltering hot weather, I joined them Thursday at 7 a.m. Not much banter, I had to make an impression if I were to survive beyond the Friday week, Friday being sacking or thinning out day. No advance warnings issued, just a curt message relayed from the top via the gombeen-man who acted as a ganger "Your cards are ready in the office".

Shortly after first tea break, which was at 10 a.m. sharp, the tallest and most talkative of the two ventured forward to where I had advanced in the trench and even at that early stage of the day my progress was quite considerable.

"Slow down, young fella", he said, "we're here since Monday and we have not much more than that done".

I made some rather silly comment about having to impress the bosses.

"Where do you come from", he asked.

"Galway, " I said.

"What part of Galway"?

"From Connemara if you ever heard of it".

"Wherever you came from, I'd say you left a young girl crying back home, but not in Connemara."

" I am from a place called Renvyle," I said, "but you would not have heard of that place".

"Do you know Mark Coyne?" he said.

"I danced many a night in his home. He's a neighbour of mine", I told him.

"Hey, Johnny," he called, "This fella is here to stay. He comes from across the bay and knows the Mark Coynes well. We're both from Louisburg, Co Mayo; the gangerman, Austie Burke, is from Louisburg; the slasher, Paddy Gibbons, is from Louisburg; the general foreman Joe Walsh is from Kiltimagh". He said about the only one who was not from Mayo or Galway was the night watchman. "You do not have to kill yourself in that trench. We'll see you ok."

The Mayomen may very well have had some influence in the way things worked out for me from that Thursday on, but one man, a full-blooded Orangeman, called Sam Martin played a major role in my progression from being a £13 per week navvy – the term used to describe a pick and shovel labourer – to becoming a highly paid excavator driver taking home a £40 pay cheque seven months from the day I commenced work.

Sam was a Belfast man, he was a slasher, one step above the ganger and one step below the general foreman. I got to work on Sam's night shift, after I had spent many weeks studiously observing the co-ordinated hands and feet movements of Paddy Long, a Tipperary man, regarded as the best drag-line driver in all of Lancashire. I had been assigned to Paddy's machine, my first promotional step. There I was, entrusted with the responsibility of ensuring that the machine was thoroughly serviced, and that the immediate vicinity of the machine was kept clear of traffic, a very necessary precaution, as serious (some fatal) accidents involving heavy earth-moving machinery occurred quite frequently on all coal-sites. Two such fatal accidents did occur during my five year stint with Tarmac, and I myself came within the proverbial whisker of being the third victim.

Paddy Long was a man you just had to like. There was always a very positive conviction about the manner in which he approached life and work. When he spoke to me about his family, I realised that the man was asking for some practical assistance to see him through the inevitable trauma of losing his wife who was seriously ill with cancer, and not expected to live beyond four weeks.

"I have six children to care for," he said, "three still at primary school level, the other three at second level. You have replaced Joe Dunleavy. He was with me for three years. I made him into a good drag-line driver. Too good maybe. He has now gone to Wimpey's, earning big bucks. I am going to miss him. He relieved me for many hours throughout the night shift, which meant I could catch up on lost sleep, I do not sleep much at home nowadays." He was not looking for sympathy, or a shoulder to cry on. He was being very practical. If I was not prepared to learn to drive that huge complicated looking man of steel, powered by a 400 h.p diesel electric engine, and known as the Marian, I had no business being there on the machine. I assured him that I had only one thing in mind and that was making money fast, and the faster one moved those machine levers the faster the money accrued.

Sunday 7 p.m when most normal young lads were preparing to socialise in some form or other, I was about to start my first week on night shift. My first ever experience of working through the night. That shift and every other subsequent one was to carry through until 7 a.m. next day. I came fully prepared, with a notebook and biro. With these strange tools, seldom if ever carried on to a coal site, I planned to note down, at every given opportunity, the hands and leg movements employed by Paddy Long, to get that machine in motion, and strip bare the layers of coal which lay beneath the surface – some layers at a depth of two hundred feet. From these notes I hoped to be able to co-ordinate his movements, memorise them, and have the level of concentration required to put them into practice when Paddy would offer me a chance to do so.

This method I had used many years previously when learning to play the accordion. Co-ordinating the ins and outs of the bellows and the depressing of the keys as given to me by my uncle John Gannon was an exercise very similar to that which I was now toiling with, in the hope that I would come to terms with the controls of the Marian sooner rather then later.

I remember getting into the driver's seat. I was petrified, wondering would my plan work, or would all the hours spent memorising what I had to do be of no avail as I was about to be confronted with the real thing. Paddy Long, himself, was uneasy, I had assured him that I had learned how to handle it. In his lifetime he had come across many young lads, full of ambition, all of them urging him to train them, but never before had he had to cope with someone who professed to know how to drive an excavator without ever having touched a control. The sweat had started to run down between my shoulder blades right down to my waistline, a river of it, and I was not ever a person to sweat much. Forty-five minutes later Paddy called a halt. I could see that he was impressed. Never a man to say too much, his only comment was, "Dunleavy was with me six months before he could do what you've just done. I feel much better now", and so did I. Paddy's wife died within four weeks. He sought a transfer to a site nearer home, which he got. Word had got out that I had learned to drive and it was then that Sam Martin began to show an interest in my progression.

Lest anybody get the false impression from what I have already written, that progressing through the ranks was all above board and nice and easy, I must tell you that nothing could be farther from the truth. Working at any level on an opencast coalsite was an endurance test, for which I had been adequately prepared, having worked at hard manual labour from the age of sixteen.

Many failed to survive the conditions and the long hours of outdoor toil, beyond the first week. Being adequately prepared had many connotations. Apart from being able to work, one had to experience the wrath of gangermen and a certain level of bias and/or prejudice. The coal sites were renowned as places where square pegs fitted perfectly into round holes. Our general foreman was as square as you could get. I had several close encounters with him, as he attempted to prevent my advancement, and protect his beautiful Marian. Were it not for the fact that we shared one thing in common, he might well have sacked me for getting beyond his control ahead of my time. We were both members of the Pioneer Total Abstinence Association. But Sam, that staunch Orangeman who, with his nephew Sammy Fry, never missed the 12th of July back home, he was a right good one, as they would say. His main concern was for the workers, not for the machines.

"There is a machine here, on the site that nobody wants to drive, a 33RB no power-assisted control, it will pull your arms from their sockets, but if you want to take it over she's all yours," he said. (Machines were always referred to as 'she' which sounded rather odd.) Even if it meant having to have my arms replaced at some future point in time, I was to accept his offer and so my career as a machine operator was launched. Sam stayed close through the first week, occasionally putting Paddy Collins, a Roscommon man, in beside me with his 22EB to help create the impression that the 33RB was shifting a sizeable amount of muck. The ploy worked. The general foreman was very impressed, and I was on big money. Much easier now to afford the remittance home in the registered letter, which was the first real outlay from the weekly pay packet.

Tarmacs Civil Engineering firm was one of the elite group of companies working the coal-sites of Lancashire. They looked far and found a degree of over-achievement, which was viewed by many machine operatives as a mild form of lunacy. We had Mad Kelly from Mayo; responsible supervisors would take an extremely dim view of his antics on a machine until one looked at the results of his day's work. It soon became evident that all that mattered were results, not how they were achieved. I graduated quite rapidly from one machine to a better one. Pearse Guy from Letterfrack was assigned to the maintenance of my machine. He was the best, he became an all-rounder and in his spare time he would fill me in on all the news of the previous day which he read without fail in three different editions of the days tabloids. Our association and my association with Burnley was to end quite unexpectedly when I was offered a transfer to Wigan and the opportunity to learn to handle the much bigger earth-movers operating there.

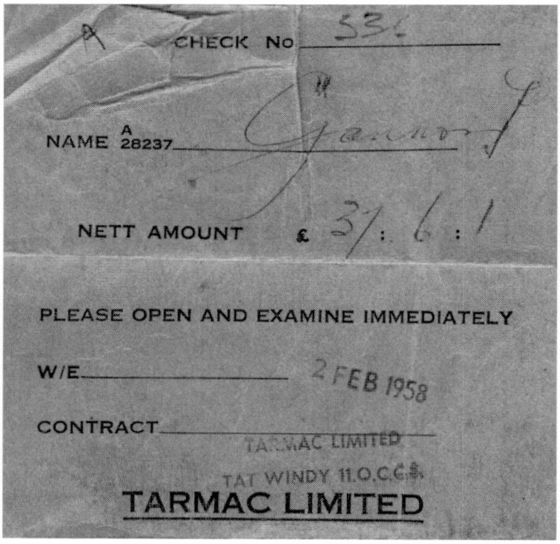
CHECK No
NAME A 28237 Gannon
NETT AMOUNT £ 37 : 6 : 1
PLEASE OPEN AND EXAMINE IMMEDIATELY
W/E 2 FEB 1958
CONTRACT TARMAC LIMITED
TAT WINDY 11.O.C.C.S.
TARMAC LIMITED

Paddy Gannon's Tarmac payslip

The social scene differed somewhat from home. The cinema was a big attraction for me. At home I rarely missed going to the films which were shown in the Letterfrack Industrial School. Here now was an opportunity to visit a number of properly designed cinemas. Few, if any, of my workmates visited the cinema. They preferred having a pint or two on the odd occasion that they did go out, so I found myself going there alone and late, never being able to make it before 8.30 p.m. The young usherette employed to see patrons to their seats with the aid of a torch, quickly realised that I was a new boy on the block. She gave me preferential treatment, reserving the end seat of the back row for me and the seat next to that for herself. She was Protestant, but a good church going one.

"I play the Church organ at St Thomas's" she told me. "My parents divorced last year; it has been a traumatic time for me, You Irish are not allowed divorce. If I ever marry I want it to be for keeps. The Irish make good husbands, they work hard and earn good money".

"Am I being seduced in a very direct way", I asked myself. She was the first English girl I had got to know, and her directness and frank admissions regarding her home life was a conversational line new to me, and one which, quite frankly, I was not prepared to handle. Later Blondie Burke was to advise me to be careful lest I would find myself stranded in Burnley for longer than I had intended.

The Irish did not frequent the English ballrooms, and I appreciated why after I attended one dance, and one only, in one of them. Their dance hall behaviour patterns were totally at variance with ours. One was expected to dance all night to continuous non-stop music with one's partner. No going back to the seats, girls to one side, lads to the other, or to the back door. Their style of dancing was not structured in any way, they simply shuffled about the floor locked in each others arms, occasionally looking into each others eyes. Body-language was very much in evidence, vocabulary quite sparse. Certainly it was no place for an Irishman accustomed to picking and choosing his dance partners and getting his kicks from the *Set*, the *Siege of Ennis* and the *Old Time Waltz*.

The Irish did have their own dancing scene, every Saturday night in a spacious upper room of a semi-derilect building. I still remember, about ninety per cent all of the Irish lads and girls who went there were pure Irish, and the other ten per cent would have been of Irish extraction. Johnny Grady, the eldest of a family of twenty-two from Louisburg; Blondie Burke, a Galway lad; Michael Coyne, again from Louisburg and his mate John Prendergest. We got to know each other quite easily without any formal introductions. Prendergast was one of those fellas who would come and go from Ireland to England on a seasonal basis. He helped looking after the farm through the spring and early summer months and spent the rest of the year in England. Many Mayo lads seemed to operate that system.

"You're from Galway", he said. It was his first ever time to address me,

"Tell me something," he said, and this was a direct follow-up to his first question, "Have you much money saved ?"

" I drew my first wage packet on Thursday last," I told him, What I did not tell him was that it contained £9-9-0, the amount of my earnings for the three days worked in the previous week.

"Johnny Grady has a lot of money saved," he added, and that was the end of that conversation with Mr Prendergast

We had good nights there. Moylan, a native of Glenamaddy and Fagan, from across the border in Roscommon, ensured that curious English teddy-boys did not disrupt our party.

Paddy Gannon with friends in the Sharrocks Dance Hall in Manchester, 1955.

The beautifully manicured playing-field was the quietest place on God's earth on that early Sunday afternoon, as I sat looking from my bedroom window. My mind was pre-occupied with thoughts of home as I prepared my first letter, which I was to address to my mother. Why, I asked myself, to her rather than to my father, who was still alive and well at that time. I guess I figured that she would be the one doing the correspondence back. What the lads down on Sailor's Beach would not give for a playing pitch like that. It certainly would not be lying idle on a summer Sunday afternoon. No jumping into the tide or adjoining lakes to retrieve the football here I thought.

Sunday was the day I most dreaded, at first. I was not required to work it in my early days with Tarmacs. I tried not to think too much of home, of family, of Sunday football, the girl I had chosen to marry and the dances in Ulick's or Clifden Town Hall. But there were reminders – the sight of young couples strolling together arm-in-arm, and obviously very much in love, was heart-rending in the extreme. But I realised that that kind of pain had to be endured and, in any event, Christmas was but four-and-a-half months away. My mind was already made up; I would be going home for Christmas come hell or high water.

Sunday night in Burnley had nothing to offer us Irish lads and girls. So it was off to Manchester to one or other of the two Irish dance halls there

– the Sharrocks or the Astoria. It was always a matter of choice. Each had its own special attraction. Manchester at that time had a huge Irish population, many from home. Over the years they had worked hard to promote their Irish culture and independence. The Irish clubs flourished and numerous GAA football and hurling clubs had been established. Many of the pubs which they frequented, were Irish owned, yet everyone seemed to want to get into Auntie's Bar. Belle Vue was a major attraction with the Zoo, its famous Wall of Death, motorcycle escapades, and professional wrestling contests the star attractions. It was of course also the home of Matt Busby and his Babes.

Old Trafford attracted ninety per cent of the Manchester and surrounding towns' Irish support. I was later to become very much acquainted with the game of soccer, and with Old Trafford, Turf Moor and numerous other venues both in the North and Midlands of England.

The attitudes of the Irish I found interesting in comparison with the English. The Irish community could be described as fairly simple structurally – with few strata, and no extended family. Simple things like keeping to a time schedule was a headache for most, as the countryside farmers of that era would have been almost totally unaffected by time back home. The English invariably perceived us as being rural or being linked to the rural countryside. There was a strong sense of collectivity which helped us immigrants function better away from home. The vast majority grasped change quickly and soon came to terms with new things and new inventions, much better than our English counterparts. But the old ways of life began to die out fast, and certain values were being disregarded, and looked down upon. In our overriding preoccupation with work and getting rich quick many of us failed, or at the very least had problems with, grasping or identifying the new attitudes which were emerging. There were those who, in their efforts to scale the British social ladder, consciously suppressed their Irishness, adopting new customs, contrived English accents, and, in some instances, name changes. Paddy was changed to Peter. Paddy would always be an Irishman regardless of social standing, or locality. Paddy would remain synonymous with a more primitive lifestyle, and with the labour hiring houses, which existed in Britain at that time. "Clitheroe House" and the "Paddy House" were two of the better known houses where English squires (wealthy landowners) hired Irish Labour to harvest their crops at a pay rate of £40 per month plus full board, and a daily ration of two pints of alcohol served from a barrel purchased for that reason.

The change of accent was brought on primarily to facilitate better communication with the English. That the English did not endorse this practice, or reciprocate it, except on stage when entertaining audiences with Paddy jokes seemed to matter little to the social climbers. My own personal problem was an enviromental one, being very conscious at first of the fact that my voice did not carry well in the highly industrialised and noisy atmosphere of my new surroundings. In making these observations I hope I am not being misunderstood. Adopting new habits and dropping the brogue did not constitute wrong doing. Huge divides did exist within the Irish community in Britain, and a sociological study of the Irish at the time, if one were undertaken, would have painted a bleak picture of those whose social pastimes centred around the activities of the ale houses and houses of prostitution. Tom, a young lad from Co Laois, was a good friend and workmate of mine. His inability to cope with, or grasp, the full meaning of change and new attitudes to life resulted in his death at the early age of forty-two. We worked together and from our earnings we supported our families back home, and safeguarded what we did not need in our post office accounts. But our social lives differed. Tom began to frequent the pubs more and more. The young female post office assistant enquired of his whereabouts, "I have not seen your friend Tom for some weeks now. He has stopped saving money here," she said. I did not have the heart to tell her that Tom had been seduced by a city street prostitute. He was now supporting her and a two-year-old daughter. She destroyed his quality of life, and was to a very large extent responsible for his early death.

The English nation prospered as never before in the 1950s and 60s. Public services there were the envy of the world. Medical and dental services were free, communications were second to none, rail travel existed in every town and village and London had its underground network. The wealthy or better-off enjoyed at least one sun holiday annually abroad. They would also be the leading owners of holiday homes in Europe at that time. Sport stadiums, soccer pavilions, greyhound and horse-racing tracks had been developed, to the acceptable standard of the times, providing ample entertainment for the pleasure seekers at home, and for the punters who gambled on the result of soccer games and greyhound and horse races on a daily basis. Yet the newspapers constantly reported a daily litany of industrial unrest and strikes. Successive governments always seemed to be loitering on the brink of collapse.

I soon began to realise that there were two faces to England, that it was a divided country. There was the official England, sluggish and rigid, and on the other hand, the human England agile and enterprising. One was the government which, in order to get anything moving, required a mountain of seemingly useless forms to be filled in. My first personal experience of this was when I applied for my first insurance card there. I was advised to write requesting that a card be issued to me. I was taught well in the art of letter writing by a man who himself loved to write, Malachy Conboy. The letter went something like this:

A Chara,
Please forward etc, etc.
Mise le meas etc.

I received a letter back requesting that I attend the office, and explain the contents of the letter. A very stern faced senior civil servant demanded an explanation. Needless to say there was a verbal blow-up.

"I do not suppose, like the rest of ye, you know your Irish insurance number," he said,

"1217210," I replied without batting an eyelid. Grudgingly he conceded that I might not be all that stupid after all. Filing and filling forms for tax relief and ensuring that all registered letter receipts were forwarded was an onerous task. It was a new experience for us as direct taxation had not as yet been introduced in Ireland. Tax officials also demanded verification from either the Garda or the clergy back home of claims being made by the Irish in respect of family dependants. Officialdom moved sluggishly but rigidly. They had to be satisfied at all times that their laws were not being sidestepped, or their systems beaten.

The England of the worker housed in rows upon rows of terraced houses, and in the new suburbs that were constantly springing up, I would feel without any planning permission at that time, was an enterprising and productive one. Within the cities, factories, some barely visible, others with great chimney stacks reaching into the sky produced millions of pounds worth of produce daily. I was later to work in two such factories, one in the North of England producing baked beans and fifty-six other varieties of Heinz foods and one in the Midlands producing Dunlop tyres. By that time the post war industrialisation had prompted an exodus from the country to the city, and farming was being transformed, industrialised, and becoming less labour intensive. The average English working man did not engage himself in the hard manual labour which characterised us Irish. He was nevertheless lively, agile and very productive when engaged in what one might term repetitive piecework where the objective was to achieve the financial incentives offered by the employers. There was also the unreported second job or 'nixers' as they called it. The English worker, basically in rebellion against the government's waste of their hard earned tax money, began to engage more and more in second jobbing. Plumbers, electricians, carpenters and bricklayers succeeded in beating the tax system and side-stepping the law. Selling goods, and selling football pool coupons on commission was a popular sideline and a very profitable one. The back street and black economy had been launched by the Irish with the introduction of the "Subbie" system, a system which worked very effectively, but which created enormous headaches for the other half: the government. Despite the best legislative efforts of Barbara Castle, Minister for Labour, in a Labour government, the predominantly uneducated Irish workforce continued on their merry way, evading taxation and making a mockery of the laws designed to prevent it. And now we were about to see our English counterparts adapt themselves to the same system. The black economy was to become an open secret and government officials were beginning to look foolish in trying to clamp down on it. Many officials would subscribe to the notion that it was a real pillar of the economy and would undoubtedly be engaged in it themselves.

An alien setting down on the earth's surface for the first time on that day would have asked "Why is everyone crying?" The whole world would have answered in unison "The Busby Babes have been killed in a plane crash". On the streets of Wigan on that fateful evening, adults and children alike were unable to control their emotions, tears were shed uncontrollably, few words were spoken, and Wigan was not even a soccer town. Wigan prided itself on its ability to produce some of the best exponents in the world of another code – Rugby League football, and their big star of that era was Billy Boston. I had arrived in Wigan in 1957 and commenced work where I had left off in Burnley on an open-cast coal-site called 'Fat Windy'. The year 1957 was to bring about many changes, the most notable being the exceptional experience of marriage. In November of that year I married Tessie, the young girl that the old man from Louisburg correctly surmised I had left behind over two years ago. Tessie had joined me in England, we were married in Birmingham where she lived and worked. With the onset of marriage I began to experience change in the form of a new identity. I had to prepare for a transition in life, and for getting away from some old ties and memories. Finding a home is the second biggest step in the life cycle. I selected a house in a place called Standish, some miles from Wigan. I liked what I saw, the price was right and I had one third of the purchase price saved. Saturday being a free day after a night-shift, I was set to close the deal through the good office of my solicitor. At work it was no secret that I was house hunting.

An engineer enquired if I had had the property I was about to purchase surveyed. "I would strongly advise that you do so," he said. He recommended that I go to see a friend of his a Mr Fizakarley. For the princely sum of two guineas Mr Fizakarley surveyed the property and advised against purchasing it.

"It has been iron-banded by the National Coal Board to prevent structural damage, which could result from subsidence sometime in the future," he told me.

He also advised that a value had been put on the property at the time of iron banding to safeguard the insurance companies. "But I do have a good house for sale in Woodhouse Lane, a little more expensive but structurally sound," he added.

I began to have grave doubts and declined his offer, and it was because of that experience that I got to know Helen Murray, the most Christian person I ever had the privilege of knowing, and through Helen I got to know Mary who must otherwise remain anonymous. Mary was a Galway girl who endured years of heartbreak and utter rejection at the hands of her Irish boyfriend. She moved to London then, an unmarried mother. Helen travelled to London every weekend to assist with caring for Mary's baby and to help console and comfort Mary herself. Mary died as a direct result of her boyfriend's rejection of her. Cases such as Mary's were an all too frequent occurrence in Britain. Carers like Helen were few.

It was Thursday evening, Helen met me on arrival home from work. She had leased Tessie and I the best part of her home, which doubled as a millinery shop, from which she derived her total means of support up to then.

"Congratulations", she said "You have a son. I knew it would be a boy, I said so all along". She was deliriously happy and utterly pleased at being the first with the good news. She had been phoning Billenge hospital on the hour for three whole days.

"I know, I've just come from there," I answered. It was the first evening I had visited the hospital before getting home first and sprucing up. I had stolen Helen's thunder. I regretted having said I already knew. It was September 1958, an English son had been born to Irish parents and an English Protestant lady, approaching her seventies and unmarried was overcome with joy.

As I said, marriage is an exceptional experience, a form of rebirth, which requires one to become disconnected in many ways with old ties and habits. The Church, in its wisdom had recognised this, hence the sacrament or ceremony of marriage. In the initation period of the new stage of living, I was having serious doubts about my role and attitude to work, long hours, sometimes seven days a week, every other week working through the night. Was I to continue indefinitely in that vein, to the exclusion of all other considerations, including my health which I knew would suffer as I had observed in others who had stayed on too long? Did the big pay packet justify taking high risks with one's general welfare? The answer was simple: no it did not,

I had my first ever serious medical examination, I remember being tapped on the elbows and knee joints with a little wooden hammer, that was to test my reflex action. I was passed fit to take up employment with Heinz Foods. My medical condition, coupled with the fact that I had an impeccable time-keeping record stretching over four years with my previous employer, were the two key factors in my gaining entry to the Heinz workforce of approximately 1,400 employees. I was only the second ever Irishman to be taken on by Heinz in their Wigan factory up to that time.

We were to leave Wigan within the year. We were to leave behind friends and acquaintances very dear to us. The McAllister family, Paddy from Co Leitrim, and Kathleen from Co Sligo, recently married back home, they began their lives afresh in Wigan. We assisted them in every way possible to settle in in their strange new environment. Paddy and Kathleen were to stay on in Wigan, where Paddy was to spend thirty-seven years in the job he commenced in 1958 and where Kathleen somehow managed to combine motherhood, child-rearing, and education. She graduated from Liverpool University as a schoolteacher. Both are now retired. We left Helen and her shop front windows where she displayed our son Pat sitting amongst her hats and silk scarves, and being admired by passers-by. She loved that. I was to meet Helen on two occasions in subsequent years long after I had returned home.

"Who could ever forget an Irishman" was the answer she made me, twenty-five years later when I called to see her on a rare visit back to Wigan. She had aged beyond recognition. " I still go to Church every Sunday", she said. "St John's was for the rich, St Mary's catered for the poor" she added. She was referring to the two Catholic churches in the heart of Wigan. Helen was Church of England but she also attended the Masses in St John's and St Mary's every Sunday without fail.

I tendered my resignation at the Heinz Food Plant. They were reluctant to accept it and offered me promotion if I were to reconsider. Heinz was an excellent place to work. Management looked for and rewarded excellence. They seemed to draw their power from the rank and file of the shop floor workers, which was in complete contrast to the attitude of many of the management teams employed on the coal-sites. They allowed scope for creativity and permitted a certain level of chaos in return for a little experimentation. I learned many valuable lessons there from my close contact with a predominantly English workforce who in general worked hard to keep life simple and basic, and I never regretted having worked for a company who treated its workers as adults.

I left behind Billy Boston and his amazing exploits in Rugby League Football and I was also having to leave behind Old Trafford. I was an ardent United fan then. Later I was to become an even more fervent Aston Villa supporter and have continued to remain so to the present time. Finally, to the English midlands, to Birmingham, to working at Fort Dunlop making tyres for motor cars, the most physically demanding job I ever worked at. Our second son Stephen was born there. He was the only one to be born at home with the assistance of a midwife. Mothers were only hospitalised for the birth of their first child under the existing medical system operating in England at that time.

The vast majority of Irish immigrants kept in touch with home. Ireland was changing, government policies were moving towards more industrialisation. The Irish at home were moving into a new existence with hope and confidence.

Many of us began to see our futures and that of our families, not in England but back home where we really felt we belonged. But there were unwanted memories of home, and, in a strange way, remembering them seemed to help us forget them. We trusted our judgement, and spent very little time on questioning. We had made the necessary preparation for living and working at home. There was, however, a sense of disquiet at severing old ties, and departing from friends and neighbours was an occasion of sadness.

Not all memories of England are good. I have discovered in the course of my life that dragging up bad memories takes more time and energy that they are worth. However there are tormenting memories that still remain. The telegram received at 10 p.m. one Saturday night read very simply "Stephen accidentally drowned". I had to accept its meaning, two days later, as I looked down on the face of my nineteen year old brother, laid out beautifully, but now lifeless, in the front room of our home at Tullycross. That was September 1959. A year previously I had come home to attend the burial of my father who died at the early age of forty-six. He had not been in good health on my previous visit and had asked if I might leave him a gaberdine coat, which he said he would wear if he decided to go to Cork for heart surgery. Gaberdine coats, charcoal grey suits, white shirts, red or brown shoes, that was the fashion trend in those days particularly amongst the Irish in Britain. He never did get to Cork or to wearing the coat. Sadness too on being told of the deaths of my two remaining grandparents, with whom I had a splendid relationship throughout all of my young life. Pat and Mary Gannon both lived into their eighties. The sadness stemmed mainly from the fact that I was not permitted time off from work to attend their funerals.

I recall the accidental death of a Co Mayo man on a coal-site. He was married, the father of six children, forced to emigrate because of a large fine imposed on him by the courts for making poitín. His workmates were granted two hours leave with full pay to attend the removal of his remains to the church. They were also advised that should they wish to attend his funeral the following day, they would forfeit a day's wages. Contrast that with the attitude of a man I knew well. He was not a workmate, but I enjoyed playing the game of *Twenty-five* with him and his friends. His name was Danny Sullivan and he came from Cork. He was a gentle giant of a man who rarely raised his voice except when debating politics with Pearse Guy. He visited the Regan home with the intention of sympathising with the family. Words never came easy to Danny but in his extended right hand he held £100, which he felt, would be much more appreciated. It is a memory, which I never laid to rest.

My only other close encounter with death in England and the resultant grief and sorrow was when my landlord died. I was offered the privilege of being a pallbearer which I accepted with not a little trepidation. Irish Catholics were asked to refrain from attending Protestant services, and from entering their churches. I enjoyed the service and felt that my prayers for the deceased man were fully acknowledged up above. I had only once before entered a Protestant church. That was in Westport after climbing the reek.

There are memories, which I have recalled on numerous occasions, because of their humorous content. They are of happenings and instances, which because of the construction put on them, have remained with me through life. The Irish 'dosser', the term used to describe a down-and-out, was going about town begging a few shillings here and there, casually swinging his "billy-can" backwards and forward. The 'billy-can' contained the few bob he had collected. Suddenly, a loud crash and the biggest window in Woolworth's store collapsed. The dosser's billy-can had gone straight through to the shop floor. He had caused the handle to become detached from the can because of his swinging it to attract attention. He attracted attention all right. He was charged in the local police station with 'spurious begging and not having control over a billy-can'.

The young seventeen year old from the Cornamona Gaeltacht, when asked, "What the hell are you standing there looking at" replied, "Well if it isn't the birdeen cat". He had spotted a weathercock on a church spire some distance away from his place of work. That remark of his became the catch phrase of his workmates for sometime to come.

Then there was the Connemara Gaeltacht lad, who on being asked, "Where is Cáillín to-day" replied "He is gone down town on the leathb-hus", that being the single decker.

To get a letter from loved ones back home was one of life's incomparable joys. I still remember the tremor of anticipation I felt on getting home expecting to be reassured by letter that all was well there. There were those who were unable to read, but who had in their life experience developed a talent for insulating themselves against taunts and jibes directed against them because of their lack of basic education. A Galway man whose wife lived back home had a problem with his reading glasses. They would be either mislaid or broken, so he had his letters read to him. His room-mates, at least one of whom was from his home place, suspected that he was unable to read. They devised a plan to find out. His next letter was purported to contain the news of the death of a neighbour. Later that night he was observed reading the contents of the letter. He had obviously found his reading glasses. "Be Jesus, he's dead alright", he announced. They had their answer. Their suspicions were fully confirmed.

Then there was the Corkman who insisted on saying "Hello" to everyone he met on his arrival in Liverpool and who returned home to farm his land five or six months later because nobody had sympathised with him over his injured hand. He had injured it at work and subsequently jacked in his job. "Nobody has any interest in me here", he said.

I remember the almost overwhelming feeling of disquiet and confusion I felt on having to miss Mass for the first time in my life when first required to work on Sunday. I attended Rosary and Benediction, which was some consolation, and I still vividly remember the seat I occupied in the church that evening. But another more vivid memory has stayed with me through my whole life, from that Rosary and Benediction service so many years ago. I learned for the first time how to express the true meaning and petition contained in the Hail Mary. An unusual feature of that service was that a collection was held. I put £1 on the plate.

It would be altogether impossible for me in the limited context of this – my contribution – to a social history to attempt to define the Irish experience in the communities in which they lived in England. It would be safe to say that the different models of communities which did exist there did have some meaning for all of us, even if they meant different things to different people. But one had to experience feeling for a place. Many of us tried to bring that about. The sense of belonging was never more than a good expression. I do not think any of us accepted that we belonged there. We attempted to create communities where there never was one, and whilst those efforts met with some success their structures never really provided the sense of togetherness which we had experienced back home. I have attempted to fit together memories, by drawing pictures in my mind of places and faces and recalling sounds like snatches of music and the jingle of Church bells, which can really jog the mind, and at the same time I have attempted to clear away the rubbish and find some pattern to it all.

Hidden within the numerous incidents which make up life or even part of it for us all there must lay a plot. Our difficulty with that is in distinguishing the plot, so we are left with little more than a recording of memories. It has been just great for me to have had been given this opportunity to record my experiences pertaining to emigration after all these years. My effort, I trust, will not be wasted if it helps to affirm our Irish identities in another country. At the very least, I have recalled the fact that I was there and so were countless other Irish men and women. I still count many of those people both Irish and English as being amongst the best friends and Christian neighbours I have ever known, friends like Paddy and Kathleen McAllister who came to visit a few short weeks ago. Forty years and a lifetime of change had elapsed since we met and spoke last, but it seemed like only the day before. And who could ever forget an English woman named Helen.

Remembered and Written by Paddy Gannon.

MY MOTHER'S LAST GOODBYE

When I was but a youngster bold,
I thought I'd like to roam;
Like many another foolish lad,
I had no thoughts for home.
My father asked me for to stay,
Saying, "My lad where ere you roam,
Let no false bride make you forget
The loving ones at home."

My mother, too, could hardly speak,
The day I went away,
She threw her arms around my neck
And this to me did say,
"Goodbye, God bless you, darling son;
No matter where you roam,
Let no false bride make you forget
The loving ones at home."

At length I started o'er the sea
To the lands far, far away,
And toiled beneath the burning sun
For many a dreary day,
Until I gained a wish for gold.
The thoughts rang in my ears
The last kind words I heard from home
Were from my mother dear:

"Goodbye, God bless, my darling son;
No matter where you roam,
Let no false bride make you forget
The loving ones at home.
Goodbye, God bless you, darling son,"
So sadly she did say,
But while I have life, I'll not forget
My mother's last goodbye.

Written by Festy Mortimer

Prodigal Son

It is Friday evening. As usual the men were beginning to filter back from around the site to the hut to pick up 'the few bob'.

But this was not just another weekend. The lads' usual Friday pay-day high spirits were cooled only by a heavy fall of crisp white snow which made the place almost picturesque for this Friday was the beginning of the Christmas holidays; it was the day before Christmas Eve.

As the ganger handed out the wages and holiday money, the men standing around the blazing tar barrel, rubbing their hands together, eagerly made their plans for a riotous Christmas, starting immediately with a few pints 'down at the Spotted Dog'.

Mickey Quinn, the ganger, held out a brown wage envelope to one of the men, who was gazing into the flames of the fire, and seemed to be miles away. Looking up with a start, Mick took the wage packet and slipped it into his back pocket absent-mindedly.

"Are you coming down for a quick one, Mick?" asked one of the lads giving Mick a nudge and smiling. "Ah, I won't tonight, Frank. I was thinking of heading off home for the Christmas."' Mick replied vaguely, still gazing into the fire.

"You'd better make a start if you're going tonight, the boat train leaves at 7 o'clock," advised the ganger.

Mick took off his overalls, and tossed them into his locker. "Right lads. Merry Christmas! Not too merry mind!" Mick grinned at his workmates, picked up his coat and after a few friendly taunts, he bounded out briskly and made his way through the ploughed up site to the bus stop.

Seated in the dimly lit carriage on the train, later that evening, as it shuddered towards Holyhead, he began to reflect.

After fifteen years in London, he was going home. Home? How would it be? What had changed? He had hardly exchanged a real letter with his parents since he left the farm one angry day after an argument with the old man. Of course, he sent the odd Christmas card with a few pounds, but no real news had passed either way. He tried to think back to the place, to imagine how it used to be when, as a seventeen year-old, he had taken that well-trodden path to London.

He thought of the good days, the long warm summer evenings, saving hay, lying back on the reek of hay in the sun or tired after a hard day on the bog, followed by an evening 'cutting turf' in Keane's with the neighbours! Good days. But in London it was different. He had enjoyed it at first, the novelty of it all, he supposed, but it had now become pretty routine even tedious. "Am I better? Or wiser?" he wondered as he gazed through the carriage window, and wondered.

It was a smooth crossing. The ferry was packed with passengers. There was a bit of a sing-song in the lounge, and he had not minded the crossing much. Everyone was in high spirits – a very different atmosphere to that day he had first crossed over to England. The memory of that dismal departure and the cheerless faces of the passengers on that occasion were still a vivid memory to him so many years later.

He disembarked, and as the long train journey began, a feeling of exhilaration and excitement overtook him. A heavy fall of snow and clear blue cloudless skies made the countryside startlingly beautiful. He gazed at the landscape as he sipped his plastic cupful of Guinness. It had been a long time since he had been out of the city, and anyway the countryside was not the same 'over there' somehow.

"Things have certainly changed here," he thought. New houses replaced old; the train, to his delight and surprise, arrived in Galway after just 3 hours. Whilst he waited for the bus he decided he'd take a look around the town, pick up a few presents or something. He had not given any warning to his family of his arrival. He wondered whether he should have.

"No," he thought, "I'll surprise them! Just a bunch of flowers and some tobacco for the 'ole fella'."

The length of the bus journey had not changed much or the state of the roads! Two-and-a-half hours of head banging, knee bumping travel, and he was at last there. Home. Connemara.

The night had long since closed in but a full moon bathed the snow-covered mountains in light. A little snow was falling. Mick, grabbing his bunch of flowers and buttoning up his overcoat, hit off towards the farm. Soon, the snow was falling heavily and a strong wind drove the snow into his face and bent the flowers back. In the distance behind him, he heard a car, then headlights caught the outline of the bushes in from of him. The car stopped and the door swung open in front of him.

An old friend turned out to be the driver of the car. Mick and the friend after much shaking of hands heartily agreed to meet later and discuss 'old times' over a pint. Mick jumped out of the car at the farm, and a little apprehensively walked towards the house. His mind was filled with all kinds of excitement and apprehension about the meeting. He knocked loudly on the door and a moment later his mother opened it. She peered at the snow-covered man on the doorstep. Amazed and overwhelmed she pulled her son into the kitchen, shouting "John, John, come and see who's here!"

In a second, Mick was face to face with his father. Tears filled the old man's eyes as he embraced his son enthusiastically. A moment passed before any of them spoke; then, as if there was no time to lose, an excited babble filled the kitchen. Such a welcome home – everything was forgiven. How they had missed him! How had he been? It had been so long! And many tears from the old lady as she bustled around the kitchen making tea, and pulling out a large plate of mince pies from the oven. What had he been doing in London, the old man asked? And then of course, the question Mick had feared most – "How long can you stay?" The reply "only a few days" silenced the old lady instantly, and a look of disappointment flashed across the old man's face, before conversation resumed on a different topic.

After tea, Mick looked at his surroundings. The place had certainly changed very much for the better. The kitchen was decked with different colours, a Christmas tree in the corner, and the sweet aroma of fresh baking, completed a perfect festive scene. Mick's father, hearing his son's enthusiastic comments about the improvements, explained that he and Mick's cousin had worked hard to bring it about, it had not been easy, but times had improved recently.

After all the excitement of his arrival and his third cup of tea, Mick sat back and with an overwhelming feeling of contentment turned to his father and said "It's good to be home!"

But the welcome was not over yet. By the time the three arrived at Keane's bar that night, the news of Mick's return was out, and being well liked as a young man, a great gathering of his friends and neighbours had arrived. The festive spirit flowed freely, and a couple of lads played a few tunes in the corner. Mick did not have a chance to as much as put his hand in his pocket!

Christmas Day came and passed and such a Christmas! In fifteen years Mick had not felt so contented or so well fed! What had he been missing? He wondered as he took a stroll down to the bar on Stephen's night. Already in the bar a number of neighbours had gathered in search of 'the crack'. But Mick felt strangely depressed and edgy. He realised that soon all this must end for him because he had to go home. No, not home. Go back to London.

His departure on the bus, a few days later, left him in very low spirits, and as he turned his back on his weeping mother, his old father feebly lifted his stick in farewell. Mick was overcome with sorrow, but as the bus tumbled along he tried to put it out of his mind. "I have to go back. I have a job," he thought. He gazed through the window for a last look, as the mountains gradually became part of the background. He picked up his book and fingered through it in a daze. "Sleep," he thought, "Yes, sleep would help."

Mick dozed off, and arrived in Galway, awakened by the abrupt braking of the bus. He boarded the train after a short delay at the crowded station. He wanted to be alone with his unhappiness, but other people intruded. He looked around him at the long faces of the other passengers and the stark memory of that first ferry passage to England flashed before him and left him, for a moment, horrified by such a prospect again.

The journey to Dublin seemed endless. A picture of his old parents, that morning, on the steps of the cottage, came into his mind. He tried to ignore it: then he thought of his old mother's pathetic attempts to try to persuade him to stay. He asked himself again "Why am I going back if I want to stay on the farm? Was it the job? The money? Friends?" He could not think of a good enough reason, but he felt he should go back and that was it.

Mick walked jerkily, almost running to the taxi rank outside the station. "Dun Laoghaire ferry, please." For a few minutes the driver exchanged pleasantries with his passenger as he drove through the heavy Dublin traffic. The streets of Dublin were ugly now with slush, noise and traffic. They reminded Mick of London. He felt horribly miserable and continued to wonder why. Why? He felt tormented. Suddenly, it was all too much.

He turned to the driver and said "Turn back please, I've forgotten..." He did not finish.

"You forgotten something?" asked the driver.

"Yes!" Mick smiled, "I've forgotten something. Can you take me back to the station?" The driver glanced sideways at Mick and turned around. Mick anxiously eyed his watch and muttered something about "just make it back in time".

Mick edged through the crowds to the ticket box and, panting loudly, asked for a ticket to Galway.

"Single or return?" asked the ticket girl.

"Eh, single..." Mick replied hesitantly.

"Pardon me, sir, single or return?" the girl repeated.

"Single, please," Mick replied. Clutching his case and ticket, Mick sprinted up the platform to the Galway train. It was just pulling out of the station. He jumped aboard and sank heavily into a seat facing an old lady who greeted him with a pleasant smile. As the afternoon sun glinted on the railway lines, Mick turned to his travelling companion with a feeling of massive relief, and beamed a broad smile.

Author unknown

THE SHORES OF MY OWN NATIVE LAND

When I left Ireland long ago my age it was scarcely eighteen,
And many a time I often thought of going back again,
But the years rolled on and I grew old now and feeble now I stand,
For I am dying here in America far away from my native land.

When I told my parents I should go it would grieve your heart to see,
They looked at one another and then they looked at me,
Saying son we reared you from your youth and now you are a man,
Don't leave us here to pine and fear and go off to a foreign land.

At Queenstown Quay when I sailed away it nearly broke my heart,
To hoist my sails so far away and from loved ones to part,
Saying fare thee well dear Éireann far away across the foam,
And fare thee well dear Éireann to your shores I ne'er may roam.

How I long to see the little cot I was born in long ago,
And I yearn to meet the dear old friends who kissed me leaving the shore,
I long for things I never had and my mother's parting prayers,
Oh I long to see the old place once more and the green grass over her grave.

My father died and my mother too when I was far from home,
And in dreams it seemed I heard them say our boy we'll never see no more",
They are both moldering in the clay while in America I stand,
But there is room for me between them both on the shores of my native land.

Author unknown
Given to me by Michael Lavery

MY HOME IN CONNEMARA

While I toil and moil in London town,
I think of days gone by.
When happy and free, we roamed by the sea,
Or played in the meadow green.
Then, in laughter and fun,
The day's work done,
We sat around the big turf fire.
Then, the Rosary said, we all went to bed,
In my home in Connemara.

How oft on a summer's eve,
We sat and watched the fishermen come home from sea.
When they rowed their boats,
And landed their catch,
On dear old Gurteen Quay.
And my prayer ascends to God on high,
That soon I may return
To that lovely place by the western sea,
And my home in Connemara.

Written by Kate Conneely

Homecoming

"You've come to the right place," said smiling Packy Coyne, tossing another hunk of peat on the turf fire.

"These hills are full of Heanues – and that's what you are. Never mind the Heaney, You're a Heanue."

"But we met a butcher down in Galway this morning whose name was Heaney."

"I know who you mean," said Packy. "He's a Heanue, too. You are all Heanues. I do not know where you got the Heaney. But there will be plenty of time to talk about that after we get the fire going good – and after we have a drink to warm us."

It was a misty grey day in Connemara. There was a chill in the air and you could smell the salt water. And if it meant changing your name from Heaney to Heanue for a warm fire and a drink of whiskey – it was worth it.

Packy Coyne's cottage faces the rocky, wind-swept ocean shore of this wild and beautiful area called Renvyle near the village of Tully. It is a place where cattle, sheep and the famous Connemara ponies are so frequently on the highways it might as well be open range.

Mrs O'Toole, a storekeeper in the next village, had sent us to Peter Nee in Tully, and it was the obliging Nee who led us to Packy Coyne with repeated assurances: "If you are Heaneys or Heanues, Packy Coyne is your man."

Coyne is a cheerful, middle-aged bachelor with a rosy complexion, who lives with his sister, Nora. Their mother was Bridget Heanue. She married Martin Coyne and before her death at 96 became the Heanue-Heaney genealogist for the area. Packy and Nora produced some of their mother's records showing that the Heaneys of Arlington Heights, Belmont, Lexington, Mt Vernon, NH and other global points were truly the Heanues of Renvyle.

And then the fun began.

My 80-year-old father was with me. He was trying to get a lead on his father, a stone mason named Pat Heaney, who left Renvyle almost a century ago to seek his fortune in the States. Grandpa used to say he never saw a stone he could not move with the right crowbar.

"A lot of the Yanks like Guinness," said Packy Coyne, sliding a wooden case of the famous beer from under the kitchen table. "But there is Powers' whiskey, too. You can have one, the other or both. You are welcome here. You are in the right place now, if it's Heanues or Heaneys you are"

Packy said he would have filled the house with Heanues if he had known we were coming, but, even so, before the night was out the cottage shook with song and laughter of Heanues, Heaneys, Salmons and Kanes.

"I cannot sing," said Packy, when it was his turn for a song. "But I've made some songs and poems for the public house where you have to do your best and the only prize I ever won was a pint of whiskey in Willie Diamond's Pub." (I was to learn later that Mrs Willie Diamond, co-proprietor of Diamond's Singing Lounge in Tully, was a Heanue before she met Willie Diamond.)

Packy let loose with a few poems and then urged Mrs Maisie Kane to favour us with a song. Maisie held back, but Packy urged: "I know you cannot sing, but you'll do the best you can." Moments later, Maisie delivered a fine rendition of '*Renvyle by the Sea*'.

And then her daughter-in-law, Mrs Mamie Kane, came through with the sweet words of '*Doonerie*'. Then somebody sang the '*Wild Colonial Boy*', and the songs and stories and laughter continued into the morning.

Dad recited '*The Face of the Bar Room Floor*', '*The Cremation of Sam McGee*', plus a medley of songs and dances of the great Scottish comedian Harry Lauder.

"Any man with song and verses like that, could give us a lot more," said Packy Coyne and 80-year-old Pat Heaney, hard as the Connemara mountains that produced him, filled his glass and offered an encore.

Then, somehow the talk turned to keening, the mournful crying and wailing that used to be customary at Irish wakes. A keening contest began, and Packy Coyne and Pat Heaney emerged the finalists. And when the sobbing was over, Coyne had edged Heaney, aided by a skilful use of the handkerchief to catch the mock tears.

"That prize I won in Willie Diamond's pub was for crying," Packy confessed.

Another round, or two and it was time to go.

"If you could stay for a while, I'd show you every Heanue in Connemara," said Packy Coyne. "But you came to the right place anyway, and you'll be back some day."

Written by Joe Heaney

OLD ERRISMORE

O'er the green mountains the grey dawn is breaking
And wild flowers are blooming along the lake's shore
The song of the skylark high o'er the moorland
Brings back to memory my childhood astór.

Often I strolled at the foot of the mountain
As the evening sun was sinking to rest
Its golden rays cast shadows around me
As I silently gazed on that old rugged crest.

Oh how I long to be back in the homeland
And roam once more in that place I adore
To see the grey clouds floating high in the heavens
O'er the majestic summit of Old Errismore.

When I'll return to those scenes of my childhood
And places I loved in dear days of yore
Nevermore will I roam from the valleys and wild woods
And the kind hearted neighbours neath Old Errismore

Written by P. J. Conroy

CONNEMARA

Connemara, gaunt, noble beauty of the west,
Whose children left thee for a warmer breast,
In distant lands unguided, oft we roam
And fondly think of thee, our only home.

We long for Connemara in the early spring,
When nature in her glory doth always bring
Wild flowers content only to bloom
In shaded glades and silence of the tomb.

We long for Connemara when summer's glory
Whispers to mankind a hasty story
Of passion hot that must soon grow cold,
And we, who are so young, too soon so old.

We long for Connemara when falling leaves
Dance merrily, happily in the autumn breeze,
And mankind, too, finds happiness in strife
While journeying onward to another life.

We long for Connemara when winter doth roar,
And breakers wither on the rugged shore,
And worn man a spirit doth release,
To seek other shores and everlasting peace.

Written by Pete Lee

Casadh an tSugáin

Barbara Flaherty

In January the men would take the water off the land. They would clear up all the old drains. It used to take about a week. We all used to love to see the drains running again, as the land would dry up. Of course, it is all done with machines nowadays. The dung had to be cleared out of the sheds and piled into heaps. It would be needed later in the making of ridges.

I remember that in February the men and women would go to the shore to cut seaweed. They would use a sharp knife or maybe a reaping hook. I recall having to wait in the cold on a rock for my mother because there was nobody at home. This is one of my earliest childhood memories. It was February 1916 and I was seven years old. The weed that was drawn up was also used in the making of ridges. I lived on a fourteen-acre farm in Errislannan in West Connemara and farming became my life's work, second only to my vocation to marriage and motherhood.

There was a lot of skill in the making of a ridge. In order to keep the ridge straight the man would lay out a line. A súgán was usually used as a line. The line was the edge of the ridge so to speak. Every ridge had to be four feet wide to leave enough room for the potatoes to grow and there had to be a one-and-a-half foot ditch between each ridge. The weed was laid out first by hand, to a height of two inches. When this was done four inches of stable manure would be spread over the weed with a fork. The ditch would then be split down the middle and one half turned in onto the ridge. The loose clay would then be scooped up and spread out on top. Each ridge would look like a soft bed of clay when finished.

There were two ways of putting in seed. One method was to put the seed right down on the stable manure before the ditch sod would be turned in. The other method was to finish the ridge first and then spread out the seed on top. After this the man would get a long stick with which he would bore holes into the ridge before shoving the seeds down. He

Gathering seaweed

would leave about ten inches between each seed. The seed was taken from the previous crop of potatoes. On every big potato there were buds which were called 'eyes'. These were cut out leaving a good bit of potato with each. We called them splits. It was these splits that the sower put into the ridges. People said that the second method of sowing involving the long stick was preferable to the first method because the potatoes would be up about two weeks earlier. This was because the seed would not have to work its way up through the scraw and the loose clay. We used both methods. There was more work to do if you used a stick but I liked it better because the potatoes would be up quicker.

We always had the potato ridge sown by St Patrick's Day. In May, the men would dig up the ditches again loosening the clay. They would then give all the ridges a second coat of clay in order to help the potatoes to grow more quickly. This process was known as 'moulding the potatoes'. I remember the potatoes would put up a lovely white and pink blossom in June. People could look for new potatoes then but we did not like to use up many of them because we knew they could still get bigger if left for a few more weeks into the summer.

In July, all the potato ridges had to be sprayed to protect the new crop against blight. The July heat used to draw the blight up out of the ground. This blight used to blacken the soft potato leaves. We bought bluestone in Clifden, which we then mixed with lime and water, making up the mix in a barrel. It was left to soak overnight. When the mix was ready it was poured into a spraying machine. I remember a time when the government gave free spraying machines to the small farmers – usually one between every two farmers. These machines were made from copper and the man would strap it onto his back. If the year was a particularly fine one weatherwise, the men would have to give the potato ridges two or three coats of spray. After this, the ridges were checked every fortnight for weeds. I remember harvested potatoes being stored in big pits out on the land because of the lack of shed space. These pits were covered with rushes and the rushes in turn were covered with clay. We used to sell potatoes for seed to some families in the Ballyconneely area. They considered our potatoes to be of a high quality.

We sowed turnips every year in May, having bought the seed in Wards in Clifden. Two-inch deep furrows were cut across the ridges. These furrows were one to one and a half feet apart. We sowed the seeds in small clumps inside these furrows. The clumps were kept about two inches apart. We then closed them up well to keep the air out. Too much air would dry them up and they would die. When the turnips had grown to a height of about four inches we would come along and pinch out some of the seeds in order to leave enough space and nourishment for the remaining seeds. Often the seeds that were pinched out would be sowed again. The turnips would be ready to eat in August but the longer they were left in the ground, the better they tasted. We also sowed carrots and parsnips like this. Sometimes in May, the weather could be very dry and the seed would fail on account of there not being enough moisture. When this happened reseeding had to take place.

We used to buy cabbage plants at the open market in Clifden. We just stuck the plants down into the ridge keeping them about one and a half feet apart. There were two types of cabbage, a summer cabbage and a winter cabbage. The summer cabbage was sown in March and had to be used up by early July or it would rot. The winter cabbage did not have to be sown until July and it could be used all year round.

We tilled some of our land every year in order to grow rye and oats. The potato ridges from the previous year were dug out in April and the fertile soil was spread out evenly over the field. We had a four-year crop rotation system in order to get the best yield out of our fields. The seed, which was bought in Clifden, was shook into the soil and the field could then be left until September when we would harvest the crop. My husband, Michael, would lead, cutting down the crop with a reaping hook. I would follow behind gathering the dornáns or sheaves and standing them up in clumps of twenty-five. These clumps were known as stooks. Eventually the field would be covered in these stooks. They would be left out for a week before being brought into the shed where they would be threshed off a big stone on a plank. The seed would fall to the floor. We would gather it up in bags for feeding the hens. The heavy grain would also be bagged. On a windy day these bags of grain could be winded in order to separate the chaff. The only year I ever remember us sowing wheat was in 1942 during the World War II. There was very little flour to be got that year. I remember bringing the grain to the mill in Clifden where the miller would charge us a small fee for grinding the wheat. He had a machine for turning grain into flour. It made a coarse wheaten flour, which was not as good as the flour we would buy in Clifden. Palmer's Mill in Galway city had another machine for turning this coarse flour into fine white flour but Galway city was too far away for us. The procedure for sowing wheat was the same as that for rye or oats but the problem with wheat was that it needed really fertile soil and this was in short supply in West Connemara. Every year in September when the oats and the rye were being harvested, straw from the dornáns would be used for the purpose of making home-made ropes called súgáns. I remember my brother, Stevie, making them with my daughter Sadie. Stevie sat on a stool holding the dornán upright as Sadie unravelled it with a reaping hook walking backwards. As she walked, she kept twisting the hook until all the straw was finally unravelled, twisted and woven into a ten-foot rope. Stevie and herself then tied up their own end of the rope to secure it. It was slow tedious work, requiring great patience and concentration but súgáns were needed to tie down thatch hay stacks and hayreeks. Straw, which was stored in the shed, was used for bedding for animals and also for thatching. I remember Michael thatching our house along with three other men. They had four ladders altogether two on each side of the house, one to get up to the roof and one for on the roof. The two roof ladders were tied together at the top. On each side, one thatched while the other man carried up sheaves of straw to him. I remember it was a beautiful summer's day, without a puff of wind.

Michael would always cut the hay in June with the scythe. It was very tough work. The rest of us would come after him shaking it out. I remember the hay used to have such a beautiful smell. When it was all shook out we would leave it for three days. On the fourth day we would rake it up into windrows and then that same evening we would make little lapcocks of it all. It would then be left like this for another two days. At the end of the week we would make big cocks out of the lapcocks. The field would be well raked making sure that nothing went to waste. These cocks would be covered, tied down with súgáns and left for a fortnight to season. The final part of the process was to transport the hay in cartloads into the sheltered haggarth where the reek would be constructed. If the weather was kind and I remember in those days it seemed to be consistently fine, the hay would all be harvested in about one month. I remember we used to sell some of our hay to people in Goulane who kept a lot of horses.

In the 1940s we acquired a bog on Marconi's mountain in Derrygimla. I used to love to spend a day footing turf. You would see a lot after your day's work. The bog was hard work, not a place where you would go for fun. Michael had to cut all the turf himself by hand using a sleán. We used to always light a fire and I remember the tea used to taste delicious along with the homemade bread and cheese we used to have. The day the turf was being brought home was always an exciting day. In the days leading up to it our donkey would have brought the turf off the bog in two cleaves which were attached to his back. It was a slow process, but one had to persevere. When the big day finally arrived there were usually about six men to fill Guy's lorry. I remember we used to sell turf to two families in Clifden and it was because of money made solely from the sale of turf that Michael was able to start the construction of our house in 1950.

We usually had nine cattle altogether each year: three cows, three two-year olds and three calves. I milked cows regularly from the age of fifteen until I was thirty-one. I gave it up when I got married in 1940. The calves would usually feed for themselves after four or five months. We would wean them off at that stage because the milk was not really of any great nutritional value to them. We fed our cattle on hay or crushed oats. Silage was unheard of in those times. We would sell the three two-year olds at the April fair in Clifden. We often got up to £9 for each of them. There were usually fairs every month. I can still remember some of the dates – 21st April, 24th May, 23rd June (St John's Fair), and 13th November (St Cáillín's Fair), which was also a big horse fair. The first thing Michael always did after selling the two-year olds was to go to Casey's shop to settle up what he owed. Mr Casey always allowed us credit because he knew we would eventually be able to pay him on an April or May fair day. I had a great love for the cattle. I was always with them and feeding them gave me a great sense of satisfaction, inner peace and happiness. I cried many times over the deaths of baby calves. I remember them getting sick in February and no matter what we did they would die. There was no cure for liverfluke in those days.

We always had two pigs every year when I was growing up. We used to buy them as banbhs in March at the big fair in Clifden. They would usually be about six weeks old and cost five shillings each. They were lovely and cute at that age but they used to let out awful loud screams on account of being taken from their mother. We would initially have to keep them inside in a box in the kitchen and nobody would get much sleep for the first few nights because of all their squealing. We had to keep them very warm and feed them with light food usually well mashed potato with plenty of milk. Eventually we'd move them out of the house and into a shed where they had to have a very warm clean bed of straw. The pig would never dirty his bed. I remember how our pigs used to love to get out into the open air during the daytime. The first thing the banbhs would do then they'd get outside was to turn up the scraw with their noses. Such was their nature. We used to have to buy rings and the ring would be put on the banbh's nose with a pincer. After that they could only eat grass and run around. We fed them twice a day, on potatoes, meal and milk. They were well able to scream for their food. We would sell them in November. They could realise a good profit provided they were well fed. The pig was very highly valued by the old people who used to call it 'The Gentleman who paid the Rent'. A well fed pig would mature quickly and earn fast money for his owner. I remember us getting £4.10.0 for each pig and using this money to pay rent, rates and debts to shopkeepers. In my mother's time, when the pig was being brought to the market in Clifden, she would have to rise as early as four o'clock in the morning and prepare a big feed of potatoes and pollard for the pig. Pollard was the last thing which was taken off flour in order to make flour white. The woman always fed the pig and because of this the pig always followed the woman and would not do much for the man. The pig had to be coaxed, not driven but generally he was easy enough to coax. My parents would head off for the market at about 5 a.m. to walk the four miles into Clifden. A rope would be tied to one of the pig's legs. My father walked behind the pig and had a hold on the rope while my mother walked ahead. The pig would instinctively follow my mother unaware of the rope. If he got stubborn along the way my mother would turn back and pet him in order to coax him along again. It would be 7 a.m. before my parents would reach Clifden. There were two local men from Clifden who used to buy the pigs and sell them on at a profit to the pig factory in Castlebar. I remember we had no cart until the year 1926. From then on, my father brought the pigs into town in the cart. My last memory of a pig fair in Clifden is in 1940. After that, the local pig jobbers started buying up the pigs off the land. As more and more young people either acquired jobs or took the boat to England, there was less and less tillage farming and this contributed to the decline of the pig population because there was not enough food being produced to sustain him.

The donkey was often referred to as the beast of burden because he carried everything on his back. He belonged to a warm climate by right and did not like the harsh Irish winter weather. We took great care of the donkey because he was such an important means of transport. It was very common that time to hear a chorus of donkeys braying in our village where one donkey braying at the end of the village would spark off a chain reaction from the rest. They often kept it up for over an hour. I remember my sister Mary coming home from Boston in 1957. By this time the donkey had almost disappeared from our locality. Mary told me that she had this great longing to hear a donkey braying. One day as we were walking over the Errislannan road, we suddenly heard a donkey braying across on the other side of Mannin Bay in Derrygimla. Mary was so delighted and I remember she turned to me and said 'You know, Barbara he did that for me'. We fed our donkey on oats and hay and we always kept him in, in wintertime. Once a year, we brought him to John Lydon the blacksmith for new shoes. The donkey was quiet and co-operative if treated with kindness. However, if he was treated in a rough manner he could become very awkward and stubborn. He could be intelligent enough in his own way, for example, he'd a habit of smelling the ground and if the ground was too soft he'd refuse to move. The donkey did everything in those days – carrying weed from the shore, dung from the sheds, hay from the meadows and turf from the bogs. Michael used to make the cleaves from sallyrods in wintertime. Nearly all the farmers grew sallyrods in those days. We used to use sallyrod baskets for storing onions. They'd prevent against the onions rotting because they were dry and airy. I've a childhood memory from 1923 of a neighbour coming to our house to cut some of our sallyrods so he could bring them back and sow them on his land.

Michael bought our first mare in November 1942 at the horse fair in Clifden, two years after we got married. She would feed off the hill for part of the year and off the land for the rest of the year. One horse on the land was as bad as three cows. She would leave the land awful bare so we never left her on the land for too long. She nearly always foaled in May. There was no looking after the foal only to let it go with its mother. We used to sell the foal in November. Michael often rode into Clifden on the mare to get the shopping. He used to park her at the forge at the top of Peeler's Row. The mare was also used to transport turf, seaweed and stable manure. Michael made his own cart but he had to go to Cummins' forge in Letterfrack to buy the wheels which he would transport back to Errislannan in another cart, borrowed from a neighbour.

All the farms in Errislannan had hens, geese and ducks when I was a teenager growing up in the 1920's. Most families had twenty hens but I remember us having twenty-five to thirty. I often sold three score of eggs of a Friday or a Saturday. I used to pack them in three rows in a special tin box, each row being separated by newspaper. Then I would transfer the box into a heavy plastic bag before heading off on foot in the direction of Clifden. I remember selling eggs to Duffy's Hotel in Ardagh (Clifden Community School is now located on the same site) and later to Lydon's Hotel on Main Street, Clifden (where Millar's Tweed Shop is today). I used to get a halfpenny an egg. I often remember all our hens perched on the roost in the outhouse, clutched together in a straight line guggling away among themselves until they would eventually fall off asleep. They would stay that way until the morning. When they would see the daylight they would be glad to get outside again.

Foxes were always a problem but that time nearly all the men had guns. There was a man in Clifden who used to buy the foxskins. I often saw the fox lying quietly in a field all day long waiting to snatch a straying hen. We used to feed the hens twice a day on oats or rye. Their outhouse had to be cleaned out every day also. 1924 is the only year I ever remember us having geese. We had four of them. Geese were very difficult to rear. The goslings were so weak that one heavy shower of rain could kill them. They would faint from the exposure, lying down flat on the ground. In order to be saved they had to be gathered up, brought inside and dried off by the fire. The ducks were much hardier creatures. They fed the same as the hens but wanted a lot of water, which they used to get for themselves in the lake beside our house. When they were big enough and strong enough they'd fly off to the lake and never come back. The fox used to often get them at night when they'd come in off the lake to sleep on the lakes edge. We did not have any ducks after 1926. We always had a cock and he was a great timekeeper. He always crowed around 3 a.m. and again at 6 or 7 a.m. Many's the night we cursed him as he woke us from our slumber.

I used to make my own butter. I remember a man called Harte who used to make churns for the people in 1939. He was a gifted carpenter who trained in Letterfrack. We already had a churn, passed down through two generations. We eventually bought a machine churn in 1944. After milking the cow in the morning the milk would be strained and set in big dishes. The cream would rise to the top throughout the duration of the day. This

A quiet moment in front of the hearth. There was a peaceful serenity about life on the farm which came mainly from the satisfaction of a good day's work done and a happy family life.

cream was then skimmed off into a big crock and the remaining milk would be fed to the calves. This work was done for four consecutive days after which time there would be enough cream to fill the churn. When the churn was full we would dash a wooden board up and down through the cream for about thirty minutes until the butter would begin to show in lovely big lumps. The butter had to be put into wooden dishes, otherwise it would stick. The next stage involved the pouring of spring water, about three quarts in total, on to the butter in the wooden dish. The function of the water was to take the buttermilk out of the butter, otherwise it would only rot the butter. Two butterhands were used to doing this job. This had to be kept up until the water would come up clear. The pure butter could then be shaped whatever way we wanted, using the butterhands. It was also very important not to put too much salt into the butter.

There was always plenty of housework to be done. Washing the clothes was probably the most physically demanding aspect of housework. we would fill the bath with water and put in the washboard. The clothes would have to be rubbed up and down the board, using red carbolic soap. We were luckier than most in that we lived beside a lake and could rinse out the clothes in it. I had to bake a lot of bread also although my daughters were quick to learn from me and liked to bake themselves. The Sunday dinner was always the highlight of the week because it was the only day of the week we could eat meat. I suppose it was our little treat after the week's labours.

We had to work extremely hard to make our small farm economically viable. The State provided no financial assistance in those days like it does now. Still we were self-sufficient for the most part. I had no great ambitions or expectations throughout my life but there was a peaceful serenity about life on the farm which came mainly from the satisfaction of a good day's work done and a happy family life. Our health was our wealth and we had the gift of contentment, which came from a great atmosphere of love and stability in our home. I always had the house homely and warm for my children when they'd come home from school and I remember they'd always share their daily school experiences with Michael and I. When I was a child myself, I often remember my mother reassuring me about school matters and giving me the courage to go in again the following day. We had a great quality of family life. I think that the focus, definition and set pattern of family life gave me and my children in turn a great emotional stability. There may have been a measure of economic poverty in our lives but certainly no emotional poverty. I worked all my life alongside my husband and as we would take a rest from our labours in the fields, we used to openly discuss everything that needed to be discussed. There was great equality between us. I always felt very close to God because I was so close to nature and the changing seasons. As well as this, God's name was so often mentioned by people in ordinary passing conversation and we often said the Rosary together at night. When I look out my kitchen window today, it saddens me not to see any fields of oats or hay. So much of the land has gone into rushes and so many of the old farming practices have died forever. Still, it is not for me to be critical. Time moves on and things change forever. I am glad that I have lived long enough to witness so many of these changes but I will be happy to be reunited with my husband Michael when my God calls on me to leave this Earth.

Remembered by Barbara Flaherty and written by Paul Gannon

THOSE DAYS OF SUMMER

Kate Conneely

The haymaking season is with us once more and with tractors fitted with devices for cutting and saving the hay, the work is done in four days if the weather is good. The bales are stacked, ready to be moved into the hayshed, a vast contrast of the haymaking we, the older generatin, remembered.

How we looked forward to the summer holidays when we saw the men moving the hay with the scythes. The swarths were left for a day to season. Then our day came to help our parents shake the hay. My mother used to make rush hats to protect our heads from the sun while we worked. The gráinneogs were made the first day and after a few days larger cocks were made. Step by step the mowing and saving went on until all the day was gathered and drawn into the haggarth by back loads or donkey cart in readiness for the big day, when the reek would be constructed.

All the men in the neighbourhood helped each other in turn. It was sheer joy to be allowed up to tramp the reek before it got too high. There was no more pleasing sight that a well built reek, trimmed and neatly tied with handmade súgán ropes. Life is much easier today. The drudgery has gone out of haymaking but the children of today will have none of the pleasant memories, which we have of our childhood years playing and working the meadows. The scent of new mown hay could not be equalled by any perfume.

I was interested to read lately about turf ash being put in a barrel of water to soften it for washing clothes. As one who grew up in the bogs I recall that as children we worked at saving the turf in our feet which we always washed in the bog using the moss as a sponge. The water from the spring well was used for drinking, cooking, washing, clothes and personal hygiene. In summertime we used to make a fire near the river. We would bring the iron pot and bath and do a really big wash. Blankets would be put out to dry afterwards and sheets made of flour bags were spread on the grass to bleach for several days. The dew and the sun did the bleaching, as there was no bleach or detergents in those days, only Sunlight soap and plenty of water.

It was a pleasure to walk or cycle along the country roads here in the west and view the neat patches of tillage, side by side with plots of vegetables. Farms were small consisting of a few acres of arable land and a strip of mountain on which the cows grazed during the summer. Every sod of ground was treasured and cared for. The land was cleared of rushes which were cut and used for bedding for the livestock in winter. The farmyard manure was used to fertilise the crops. What a contrast today when one can travel for miles without seeing a single plot of tillage while cattle can be seen grazing often on rush infested fields.

Tilling the land.

Gone indeed are the days of hard slaving with the spade and the shovel. Gone also is the love of the little patch of ground which was treasured long before the Brussels agricats laid down the law for the farmers of Ireland, big and small. Life was more leisurely in those days and people had more time for people. Nowadays, we are always finding people having to rush.

Remembered and written by Kate Conneely

Cattle Driving

Towards the end of the last century there was great agitation for the land in Curragh, Renvyle, then owned by the Blakes. At this time, the Blakes put the land for lease and it was rented, not by the people who lived beside the estate but by others in the area who could afford the rent. Mr. Robinson collected rent in Tully and the day of its collection was known as 'Gale Day'. There was great bitterness as the land was then the only means of survival for the vast majority of the people. This bitterness led to what was known as 'Cattle Driving'. Cattle were driven off the land at night by local men and women, aided and abetted by sympathisers from outlying villages. The cattle were driven as far as Clifden. Arrests followed and jail sentences were served. The following is a fragment of a song, written by Peter Conneely of Ardnagreevagh to commemorate a cattle drive.

Pat Heanue from Leitir, that mighty big man
He came to assist us to clear out the land
When the peelers arrived they looked at his frame
And what could they do but to take down his name
Then Tony McDonnell, that hero so bold
He went through the fields like a warrior of old
The police they pursued him but 'twas of no avail
When he came to the gate, he did clear at the rail
I thought of Clontarf and Tara's old halls
And the battle of Aughrim where heroes did fall.

THE CATTLE DRIVE

Come all you pretty fair maids who love your liberty,
Who love to stand with sword in hand to set old Ireland free;
Come raise your voice in chorus with a glass in every hand
In praise of those fair maidens who have cleared the grazing lands

On the 16th of November as the moon was in the sky
Those maids set out together the law for to defy;
They handled their shillelaghs, their hearts were brave and true,
And swore they would clear the grazing lands which the men had failed to do

When Mike Davis saw the crowd, along the road he ran
To try and find the drivers, of course it was his plan.
To his surprise what met his eyes, a lot of cailíns fair
Where he swore the men wore petticoats and diamonds in their hair

The police, they soon were on the scene and searched each inch of ground
To try and find the drivers, they searched the country round,
Their rifles on their shoulders and their bayonets flashing fire
When these maids were cleaning up their boots, at home beside the fire

In Cashleen and Cloonluane, some of these maids do dwell
But for fear of Dublin Castle their names to you I'd tell;
A few also from Tullaroe, who sailed across the main,
Saying three cheers for Pittsburgh City and we'll have the lands again

Those maids whom I have mentioned are cailíns fair and grand
Who were forced to go some years ago unto a foreign land
But now they have returned again to their old Renvyle shore
To drive those herds of bullocks from the fields in Curraghmór

Author unknown
Given to me by Teresa Bradley

The Old Horse

He came to work in the garden in 1895 at the age of twelve. He decided to finally call it a day in 1970 after seventy years in that same garden, having been awarded an RDS medal for long service some thirty years before his retirement. He worked for a man who fought in the Crimea and lived to see a man land on the moon, in a lifetime that spanned a long and crucial period in Irish history. At a time when most of his contemporaries were either Free Staters or Republicans, he shunned both ideologies, remaining to the end a dedicated Royalist, with a lifelong hatred of De Valera, whom he rather unfairly labelled as a communist

He worked through generations of the same family and by the time it came to the third generation, his employers had virtually handed the garden over to him. He would brook no interference from anyone in any matter concerning the growing of fruit and vegetables. Machines, sprays and other useful growing aids were banned, and even in his eighties he was using a spade when anyone half his age would have used a rotovator, if not a JCB. Attempts to persuade him that modern technology would make his life a lot easier proved fruitless; contrary old devil that he was, he did not want his life made easier; he was contented the way he was.

For contentment was the keynote of his life, and probably the reason for his longevity. By the standards of the affluent society he had very little; he did not even own the small garden he looked after. But it was his garden, and out of it he created his own Eden, where intruding serpents were dealt with in the spirit of the Old Testament.

Written by Jerry Lidwell

A Noble Art

First you choose a nice looking sheep for a fleece, clean, of good texture and not torn by brambles. To clean it you soak it in urine. Then you take the fleece to the river and wash it with a bar of soap. Peg it down with stones on the grass to dry. Curiously as long as it is a complete fleece it will not blow away.

When dry it is carded. Carding is teasing the wool to make it suitable for spinning. It is done by hand between what looks like two butter pats. These minute teeth on the fronts are used to comb the wool free of tangles. The wool is combed and rolled into rolls of Roiléirí – a soft ball or handful of wool. The rolls are now ready for the spinner.

The wool is tied onto the spinning wheel and by swift movement of hand and foot, it is spun into a thread and wound into a ball. Each ball will weigh 1lb approx. If you wanted to colour it without dyeing you bought an oz. of coloured wool at the shop and snipped into pieces. Then as you spun your own thread you would add a twist of the new colour and you'd be ready for warping. The warp is the length of the material. So you

add all the lengths together – 2 six-foot lengths for blankets – 8 yards dark for a man's suit – a coloured bit for a child's coat. That came to eleven yards – you would add a bit for shrinkage and start warping.

You set up your own warping frame, like the more familiar quilting frame, it must be adjustable in length. You walked around and around it until you had all the wool laid out ready for weavers. At one corner of the frame was a very important twist or 'chomairle cleasach'. This meant that when the weaver lifted it on to the loom, he used this twist or space as the spot where he could put his weft or cross thread. Then you tied your long hanks at intervals to prevent snailing and took it to the weaver. But you need a coloured weaving thread to vary the different weavings. To colour the weft thread they used: - furze = golden brown; stonescraw or lichen = yellow; healthy flowers & tops = bright brown; fern = green (if you wanted to shade the green you used old and new fern); blackberries & brambles = black (which was inclined to shade towards purple after repeated washings). Of course dye could and was bought in packets called Diamond's or Drummer's. Salt was used to set the colours.

When you called to collect your materials you paid the weaver and he gave you the blanket, your bréidín for the 'Fear a Ti' suit and the little coloured bit for the cailín óg.

Then all you had to do was to sit down and sew them and knit the socks.

Remembered by Mollie Fitzpatrick and Maggie O'Malley
and written by Frances Nugent

The Days of the Thatcher

Nowadays one could travel for miles through the countryside before seeing a thatched cottage. But not so forty or fifty years ago when there were lots of them dotting the landscape...which reminds me that my first job after leaving school was attending the thatcher.

During that time each district would have their own man for the job. The man in our place was Dudley, a wonderful character and a great storyteller too. Working with him was a pleasure and the day would fly listening to him telling tales of long ago.

One day that I will never forget was when Dudley went to thatch the roof of Biddy's house who lived alone in the next village. We arrived there at about 9.30 a.m. and were greeted with a nice cup of tea. We all sat down to have a chat about the job, and listening to Biddy we could tell she was very particular about her little house and wanted a neat job done. We assured her that we would do our very best. She then said she would have to walk into Clifden to do some shopping, a distance of over three miles, and said she should be home about 1 o'clock and to have the kettle boiled for her. We said fine and bid her safe journey as she went on her way with the shopping bag.

Dudley and I started preparing the roof for the day's thatching. First we had to cut away all the old Indian weed, then arrange the ladder on the roof. We would start on the sunny side, throw a rope across the roof which was tied to a big stone at the other end and the ladder on this end. Dudley then climbed up on the roof and we were ready to start. It was my job to tie up bundles of straw which were already stacked with the help of a two pronged fork. At intervals I would have to go to the back of the house to change the big stone, while the thatcher shifted the ladder.

Everything was going lovely for us and coming up towards 1 o'clock Dudley shouted down that he had seen Biddy coming in the distance and to put on the kettle. I went to the kitchen, put more turf on the fire, filled up the big iron kettle and was about to hang it on the crook when suddenly I heard an almighty crash in the bedroom. I dropped the kettle and went to investigate, and what a sight met my eyes. There was Dudley sprawled smack in the centre of the bed covered in dust and straw, and right above him a big gaping hole in the roof. After checking that he was all right I stood there in fits of laughter. He looked across at me and muttered something. I was unable to speak and on turning round, who was standing there in the middle of the room door, still holding the bag of groceries, but the lady of the house. I felt weak at the knees. She looked at Dudley still sprawled on her bed covered in dust and straw, looked at me and finally the big hole in the roof and she started to scream and shout.

She dropped the bag of groceries, ran to the fireplace and grabbed the tongs. With that Dudley sprang from the bed and out the door. I followed and we both took to our heels down the boreen with Biddy in hot pursuit still shouting and waving the tongs at us. We ran for our lives and did not turn around until we got to the main road and well out of her reach. We walked home the rest of the way without one word being spoken and I made sure to keep well in the distance.

Anyway, next morning Dudley called for me again and said we would go and finish the job. I looked at him in amazement and was relieved when he said that Biddy had called on him that evening after getting over the shock and asked us to come back to finish the thatching. She had also sent word to the local carpenter, Michael Joyce, to repair the rafters. When we arrived there that morning Michael was already on the roof hammering away and almost finished. We were again greeted by a cup of tea, this time joined by Michael the carpenter who had already finished and done a good job on the roof. Biddy was in good mood going around the kitchen singing. We knew everything that had happened the day before was forgotten.

Later, as Michael bid us goodbye and hopped on his bike, Dudley and I continued where we had left off the previous day and this time Biddy helped by tying the bundles of straw. We had the roof all covered by 1 o'clock and retired for dinner. Then it was time to tie it all down and make it secure for the winter. Biddy had all the balls of Indian weed ready for us. She then got up on the roof to help throw down the ball to Dudley and me who were on a ladder either side tying. Sometimes I would throw up the ball and Biddy would miss and it would go right down past Dudley and I could hear his swearing. Anyway, we had it all finished around 6 o'clock and had our tea. She then paid us for the job and asked us to wait on as she was having a bit of a hooley to celebrate the thatching and had asked the local musicians to come later. She had also hired Paddy Feeney with his ass and cart to fetch half a barrel of porter from Clifden. In the meantime we sat down at a lovely turf fire while Dudley told us stories of days gone by.

Soon the musicians began to arrive. There was Tom Lee on melodeon, Joe Dishell on the fiddle, Tom Flaherty on the banjo and Bernie Keaney on the spoons. The night being so calm the music could be heard drifting throughout the valley and people began to head for Biddy's house. Very soon we had enough for a half set and it was "round the house and mind the dresser". I can still remember the sparks flying from Dudley's hob-nailed boots as he swung Biddy round and round the concrete floor to the music of *The Swallows Tail*. After we had the tea and some of Biddy's home-made currant cake, our good friend Gerald arrived and knocked more sparks out of the floor as he danced *The Stack of Barley*. Then John Feeney danced *The Haymakers Jig*.

At about 9 o'clock Paddy and Bernie arrived with the half-barrel of porter on the ass and cart. Dudley got the job of tapping the barrel. As he was doing this some of the porter went right up to the rafters but there was plenty left for everybody. There were mugs of porter handed round to all the lads and wine for the ladies. People were asked to sing a song and Dudley was first with *The Little Old Thatched Cabin on the Hill*. Tom Lee followed with *Paddy McGinty's Goat*. Gerald sang *The Bogs of Shanaheever*; John Feeney sang *Sitting on the Bridge of Below The Town*; Biddy sang *The Old Plaid Shawl*; and I sang *Down the Old Bog Road*, after which Dudley and I said goodnight to all and headed home in the dark.

We found our way to the bridge where we rested while Dudley lit his pipe. We could hear the corncrake in the field by the river, and the trout jumping on the lake with the music still drifting across the valley from Biddy's house in our ears. We headed off again and at the next crossroads we met Packy who was visiting Frank's across the bogs. We chatted there for a while and then said good-bye. We could still hear the sound of Dudley's hob-nailed boots on the road below. As we got round the bend we could see the light of Slyne Head lighthouse as it flashed its warning beam across the rocky shore and headland. Suddenly we were stopped in our tracks by the sound of the sharpening of a scythe up amongst the rocks at Darby's place. Then we saw the lantern light coming towards us and we were about to take to our heels when we heard the friendly, familiar voice of our good friend and neighbour, Tommy Green. He told us he was cutting a bed of rushes for the cow, which was after calving that night.

After chatting to Tommy for a while we continued on our way home. Near the old schoolhouse Packy and I said goodnight and parted company. As I opened the old wooden gate leading to our cottage, I could see mother had left the light burning in the window to guide me home.

Sadly now most of those lovely people have departed this life and their little houses have disappeared also. Whenever I see a thatched cottage I always remember that day over forty years ago when Dudley and I ran for our lives down the old boreen.

Remembered and written by Marty Conneely

MAN OF IRON

John Walsh

I could tell that Mattie was feeling a little bit awkward and embarrassed as he entered the forge.

"I don't blame you if you don't do what I want", he said.

"What's wrong with Mattie"? I asked.

"They failed in Letterfrack to put shoes on her and I have a lot of work to do for myself and the neighbours", he replied.

I set about the task, luckily the horse never moved and I shod her without any bother. Mattie was very grateful and I could tell he was feeling guilty about not giving me the business in the first place. I was never one to get upset about that kind of thing, however, because I knew that my forge in Ardnagreevagh was a little bit off the beaten track and it had probably been more convenient and attractive for Mattie to go to Letterfrack. Mattie was one of a small number of people during those years who came to me for service after failing to get satisfaction in Letterfrack or Clifden. I was very much a last resort and their last hope but thankfully no job ever failed me and I was always able to see them right. John Moran managed the forge in Letterfrack on behalf of the monks. He was already well established by the time I arrived in Renvyle in 1930 along with my parents at the age of seventeen. Over the years we developed a great friendship based on mutual co-operation and he never saw me stuck anytime I was short of bolts in the making of carts.

My people had always been blacksmiths and I was the fifth generation. I spent nearly all my free time, as a child in my father's forge in Cornamona and it was there that I developed my love of iron and horses as well as learning my trade. The iron was delivered by cart from Westport and Ballinrobe in eighteen-foot lengths. My mother was from Ardnagreevagh in Renvyle and her father was very anxious for her to return at some stage. After he left her the home place in 1930 we decided to move to Renvyle and build a new forge. We drew all the stone from the seashore by horse and cart and it took the best part of a year to build. The local people were very happy to see the new development in the area and everybody wished

Blacksmith at work, 1920.

us well. I shoed a lot of horses before the forge was ready and I recall my first customer was Patrick Heanue from Cashleen who wanted me to put a set of slippers on his horse for going to the Clifden Pony Show. Slippers were old horseshoes that had been worn some time previously. When we finally opened for business Austin O'Malley from Ardnagreevagh was the first man to arrive in the door.

Diamonds delivered all the iron and coal to the forge and over the years Mrs Diamond never let me down in the line of anything I needed. During World War II when there were great coal shortages I used to prepare the fire in a particular way in order to create charcoal, which was almost as effective as coal. The process entailed selecting a few big sods of quality turf and breaking them up into clods. These clods were piled together set alight and allowed to burn until they resembled red-hot coals. More turf was then added and the enlarged fire was subsequently covered over with scraws and plastered all around with gutter. A hole was then sunk down through the middle with the handle of a spade. The reward for persisting with such an elaborate process was that I'd end up with big black lumps of coke, which gave off the type of heat required for my work. I often made this type of fire several times a day during the war years.

I always had a great love of horses and learnt how to ride a horse at the age of seven. I always felt relaxed and confident around horses and over the years my understanding and knowledge of horses improved greatly through practice and experience. There were occasions when people brought horses to me after having already brought them to the vet. On one such occasion the horse had been diagnosed as suffering from rheumatism. On observing the horse I noticed that he appeared to be lame when walking on gravel yet he walked perfectly on grass, I concluded that the horse had neither rheumatism nor arthritis but merely sore hooves. Accordingly I made him a special set of shoes and he walked fine. On another occasion on being asked to examine a lame horse I discovered that the animal was on the verge of blood poisoning and this necessitated me splitting the hoof in order to let out the matter. I did this on a Tuesday evening and the following Thursday the same horse brought home a cart of turf. I had no special gift but in all my years at the forge things nearly always seemed to go right for me.

The main service I provided was making horseshoes and shoeing horses. The standard shoe size required a twelve-inch length. Ponies shoes were usually made from an eight-inch length and at the other end of the scale a 5 year old Clydesdale or Draught horse required a 16 inch length. Having cut the length of iron required, the next step was to hold it inside the fire with a tongs in order to redden it in the middle. It could then be turned into the horseshoe shape. The next task was to cut a track all around the shoe and countersink the nails. The average horseshoe usually took eight nails. Indeed I was always of the opinion that eight nails were enough to sink in any shoe no matter how big the horse. The final part of the job was to put on the toeclip. I shod my first ever horse in my father's forge at the age of twelve. It was always difficult to shoe a horse that had been spoiled by its owner. The easiest horses were those that were brought in raw off the mountain before they could be spoiled in any way. It usually took half an hour to shoe a quiet horse. I was never badly injured by any horse and can only recall one occasion when I was kicked. The owner went to great lengths to inform me that the horse was quiet and that I would have no bother shoeing her on my own. He had some business to attend to and had deceived me in order to be able to attend to his business. This was the one

Blacksmith James O'Malley at work in his forge in Aillebrack.

Seamus Breathnach, Seán Breathnach, Tomás Ó Corcáin. Cearta Seán Breathnach, Rinn Mhaoile. 'John Smith's' Forge, Renvyle. Circa 1930.

and only time I was ever let down by a customer in this manner. I always felt a great sense of pride and satisfaction on sending both horse and owner home happy and I usually stayed a few sets of horseshoes ahead in case of a rush. My busiest day ever was a day I shod eight horses. All of those horseshoes with the exception of one set had already been made the day before. When I started off in 1930 I charged five shillings to make and put on a set of horseshoes. By 1950 the cost had gone up to twelve shillings.

My work, however, was not totally confined to the making of horseshoes and the shoeing of horses. Throughout the '30s and '40s I made a range of iron products. A firegrate cost from fifteen to eighteen shillings, tongs were sold for four shillings, pot hooks for two and sixpence, cranes for £4 10s, gates for £5, penknives for one shilling and spades, sleáns and scythes for a half-a-crown each. The introduction of tubular gates in the late 1940s put me out of making gates. I pointed hand drills for the County Council. There were three drills in a set, a two-foot, a three-foot, and a four-foot and I charged one shilling per point. I also made branding irons for sheep known as hornbrands, which I sold for seven shillings. This was probably one of the most technically demanding products I used to make. During the forties I made asscarts for £5 and horsecarts for £12. There were often jobs from time to time where I left it up to the customer to pay whatever he or she deemed appropriate. I suppose I was happy to help out my neighbours and didn't want to be coming down too hard on them. These jobs included the building of bicycle wheels, the making of gaffs (these were special hooks for killing salmon) and also the construction of iron rims for cartwheels. There were unusual requests from time to time like the time I spent nearly two days making eight uprights and rivets for a man who needed them to enable him to raise the roof of his mobile van. His plan was to sell takeaway food from the van at fairs and markets around Connemara. He paid me £10 for my trouble a substantial amount of money for a couple of days work in the forties. I worked long hours, often right through until 3 a.m. in order to get things finished and I can never remember taking any days off except for Sundays. Even on Sundays I often shod horses for people who were stuck.

I really loved my work and I can honestly say there was no aspect of my trade that I did not enjoy. Like the garages of today, the forge was a great meeting place, a focal point in local neighbourhood especially on wet days. I always seemed to have company as I worked and I always enjoyed having people in. My neighbours always gave me the impression that they appreciated my endeavours and they always had great faith in my ability to deliver. It was their faith in me, which gave me the greatest happiness during the twenty good years I had in my forge. I was often inundated by tourists also. They liked to come in and view the place. They used to be fascinated by the bellows blowing and by the way I would take the horses feet without showing any fear. I was always a bit nervous that a horse would kick them but thankfully this never happened. A lot of them took photographs, which I didn't mind unless they were taken without asking my permission first. I was never able to afford to take anyone on as my assistant because there was never enough steady work but having said that I was never short. The way it was, I might have empty pockets in the morning but as much as £5 before nightfall. It was a very unpredictable business and I just went from day to day and hoped for the best. I am glad to day I never had any problems with people paying and never experienced any bad debts.

In 1953 I took up employment with the Forestry. I was on £7 10s a week starting off and the work involved manuring, drainage and planting. By that stage, there was very little demand for my services as a blacksmith and there was no way I could earn a living from it any longer. The Forestry was a secure job with a steady wage but it saddened me greatly at the time that my own trade could no longer sustain me. I still did a few bits and pieces over the years, spades, sleans, scythes, and teeth for mowing machines as well as the odd pair of horseshoes. It does sadden me that there are no blacksmiths anymore. I would like to meet a blacksmith any day of the week because we were always a crowd that got on well together. I also miss not having horses around the neighbourhood but having said that I would not like to return to the economic hardship of the thirties and forties and I am delighted to see the people of West Connemara doing so well for themselves in this, the age of the Celtic Tiger. There can be no going back as we all look forward to the start of a new millennium.

Remembered by John Walsh and written by Paul Gannon.

Mind the Dresser

Teresa Bradley

It was as traditional scene as one could ever wish to see. The kitchen was the heart of the house and the dance was always held in the kitchen. Whatever sparse amount of furniture there was was removed into one of the two bedrooms and planks, rested on big stones, were laid out around the perimeter of the kitchen to enable one group of dancers to take a breather while another group were out on the floor. My parents sat, one on either side of the big open fire, keeping an eye on proceedings as well as playing music. The kettle would be hanging on the crook and I often remember eels and smoked fish hanging over the fire. The cailleach was in the corner next to the fireplace but the curtain would always be drawn across it during a dance. Bags of onions would usually lie hanging from the rafters. Apart from the light of the fire, the only other light was the paraffin lamp on the wall above the fireplace. It was always my job to buy the paraffin oil and clean the globe of the lamp with newspaper. My father always reminded me to make sure there was enough paraffin oil for the night of a dance. The only picture that adorned the whitewashed stone walls was the Sacred Heart with itís little light. The fire cast shadows on the flagstone floor and the sparks would fly from the hobnailed boots as the dancers flew around the floor in a frenzy of excitement. "Mind the dresser and give the oul cailleach in the bed more porter" they'd shout as the dance would rise to fever pitch. "Up Ballaghdereen" was another favourite.

It cost sixpence to gain entry to the dance. The coats were usually thrown in one of the bedrooms but before we'd get halfway up to the room a hand would be grabbing us for a dance. The floor would be packed to capacity and there was hardly ever any time for a good long breather between dances. There was no agonising over who one would ask out for a dance; the participants were carried along in the welter of excitement. The love of dancing was the great common denominator and no girl ever refused a dance. Even the shyest of people never had a problem at the country house dances that were held in my father's house nearly every Sunday night of the year. Everybody danced with such great gusto. They put their whole heart and soul into it and the livelier the tune, the livelier the dancers became and the more they got carried away. It was all good clean fun, just a group of boys and girls enjoying themselves under the vigilant eye of the man and the woman of the house. There was never anything out of place; everybody was always sober and well behaved. If a man did come in under the influence and started getting a bit rowdy there was always someone there to put him in his place and persuade him to leave quietly without causing any trouble. It was unheard of for girls to take a drink and there would have been no respect for any girl who did. A girl might sit on her boyfriend's knee if the room was really crowded but there was never any misconduct and the lads were always very mannerly and often very shy in this regard. It was strictly all fun and it was very dignified.

The dresser would be full of dishes yet not a single item would be damaged even though the lads would swing hard and try to lift the girls. Everybody would be perspiring so much that the big bucket of spring water on the dresser would not be long going down. When the dance was over the lads would walk the girls home to their doors. They always showed us the height of respect, we felt safe with them and looked up to them as our protectors. We all knew each other; we were at the dance together. If a lad asked one of us out and we politely declined, he accepted and respected our wishes and never tried to force himself on us. I can truthfully say that not one lad ever used any bad language towards us or disrespected us in any way when we were teenagers growing up in West Connemara during the 1940s.

I attended my first ever country house dance in our house at the age of eleven and Peter Faherty from Mullaghgloss was the first ever lad to ask me out for a dance. I was very shy towards, and a little fearful of, my father and I made sure to keep well back near the door with Peter so that my father would not see us dancing. Somehow I felt he would not approve. I had learned to dance very soon after learning to walk. Indeed it was as natural to dance in our house as it was to walk. My mother Helena was a great traditional step dancer and I picked up the steps through imitation and practice without even being conscious of it.

Traditional music was played in our house every day of the week and we always seem to be inundated with visitors, many of whom were holidaying in West Connemara and anxious to experience some traditional Irish culture. My father was very well-versed, friendly, outgoing and hospitable. He was always a warm welcoming host who loved to see people coming into the dances especially those who had travelled long distances. He really appreciated all the trouble they had gone to in order to attend the dance, and he always insisted on them staying for a cup of tea afterwards before embarking on their long journey home. People came from all over the parish as well as from Louisburg, Tullabawn and Inis Turk. The islanders were often obliged to stay on as our guests for a few days after dances on account of being weather-bound. My parents and two of my brothers usually played the music at the dances. My father and mother both played the accordion, my twin brother Michael played the flute and tin whistle and Johnny played the fiddle. They always played a great selection of waltzes, reels and jigs. The most popular dances of the day were *The Siege of Ennis, The Stack of Barley, The Tommio*, (this was a highland fling), *Shoe the Donkey, The Waves of Toria, The Bridge of Athlone* and of course *The Old Time Waltz*.

During breaks in the dancing different people would be called up to "put a step on it". These were the solo step dancers, the cream of the crop so to speak. The real traditional step dance was very well defined and a joy to behold. The performer danced from the hips down in straight up fashion. The feet remained very much on the ground and there was actually very little movement involved. Martin Connolly and Austin O'Malley from Ardnagreevagh, Mick Fitzpatrick from Cashleen and Jim Kane from Gleanntan were all exceptionally good stepdancers. It was also quite normal for people to sing songs during intervals. My mother's favourite was *Moonlight in Mayo*, Michael Laffey from Culfin always gave a stirring rendition of *Lovely Old Finn Town* and rebel songs like *Kevin Barry, The Boys of Wexford, Tipperary So Far Away*, and *The Wearing of the Green* were also popular. My personal favourite was *Old Ireland Free Again*. Recitations weren't that popular at country houses but I do recall Denis Kane from Culfin making a great job of *Sam McGee*, on one occasion.

The Dancehall Act signalled the beginning of the end for the country house dances. The guards often arrived during dances and fined my father £1.00 for holding them in his house. He always received a warning not to organise any more dances but he paid little heed to these warnings. However the dawn of a new era was fast approaching and traditional music and dancing were about to enter their darkest hour. The clergy were also anxious to put an end to the country house dances because they were against large congregations of people gathering in country houses and felt that public halls and marquees were a better social alternative. The priest often denounced the country house dances as "dens of iniquity" from the pulpit when in reality nothing could be further from the truth. It was very common during the '40s and 50s for both the guard and the priest to be out patrolling the roads on the night of a country house dance. The guard was always easy to identify because of the big dynamo on his bicycle. Many of the dancers would travel by bicycle often without any light and they would have to hide in ditches or behind hedges or walls until the guard would cycle by. The priest had a different agenda, namely to catch courting couples. However the shuffle of his cassock and the tapping of his stick both made very distinct sounds which usually gave the young lovers enough time to make their getaway. I will never accept that the legal and clerical establishments of the day had any justifiable basis for putting an end to country house dances.

In my opinion the country house dance was the great social institution of rural Ireland up to the end of the 1950s. It was a very close knit thing. People were very happy and there was a togetherness and an intimacy that could never be rekindled in the dancehall. The parish hall was undoubtedly a great development in the life of any community but it did carry a lot of social baggage. Dances in public dancehalls were plagued by excessive drinking, vandalism, fighting, and sexual immorality, phenomena that were completely alien to the country house dance scene.

The dancehalls were never able to match the country house dances for atmosphere. I could never understand how a lad in a public hall could be looking across at a girl half the night, like a sheep before he would finally venture to ask her for a dance. Contrast that kind of behaviour with the spontaneity that epitomised the country house dance. The transition didn't suit a lot of people, myself included. Being a creature of habit it took us a long time to get used to the changeover. The termination of the country house dance was in my opinion a tragic social loss of catastrophic proportions and the social life of many people I knew, died a death, at the prospect of having to face the parish hall.

As the parish halls and showbands enjoyed a honeymoon period from the mid-fifties to the mid-seventies traditional music seemed to die a death. In 1977 the Teach Ceoil in Tully was officially opened and my first visit there to see Seisiún was a very joyful experience for me because it brought back so many memories of the dances that used to take place in our house at one time. I remember sitting there thinking, "If only the parish halls could be like this". People like Michael O'Neill and Labhras O'Murchú deserve great credit for all the trojan work they put in at that time on behalf of our traditional culture which was in danger of disappearing altogether in this part of Connemara. We all owe them a deep debt of gratitude for bringing about a renaissance in traditional music and dancing and recapturing the spirit of the country house dance.

Remembered by Teresa Bradley and written by Paul Gannon

Recitation To Explain What Love Is

You know, my dear friends, that LOVE is a most peculiar sort of thing. May God help us, it makes some poor devils do queer things. I knew a fellow and before he fell in love, he could do nothing, but since then he could coax any man's daughter over a ditch of furze. I spoke about love the other day to a lazy class of a fellow who badly wanted something to shake himself up a bit.

"Tell me," said I "did you ever fall in love?"

"Oh! no" said he "but I once fell into a bog hole"

"Ah," said I, "falling into LOVE and falling into a bog hole aren't a bit in the world alike."

"And what is it like?" said he.

"Love," said I "isn't like anything. It is a sort of something more like nothing. You can't touch it, hear it or see it, and yet you are positively sure that you have got it and that you have fallen into it – and still you can't tell where it is."

"How in the name of God," said he "could you fall into Love if it is a thing you can't see?"

Said I: "It is the thing you can't see you are always bound to fall into – just the same as you fell into the bog hole."

"Oh then," said he "if I was as wet and as libernach and as cold coming out of love as I was coming out of the bog hole, I wouldn't ask to fall into it for anyone."

Now, my friends, I know you will agree with me that talking about love to that class of an amadán is only a waste of time – pure waste of time – because...why? He has got no imagination, and imagination is chiefly what love is made from. Let me give you a simple example. Supposing you looked at a good looking girl and if you caught the girl looking at you ...well then, wouldn't you be expecting that she was expecting what yourself was expecting? Love makes a poor devil get up early, stay up all hours of the night, it lowers his pocket money but it wipes his expectations. And above all – and this is what you would be most surprised about – it gives a man an insane desire to support another man's daughter. The old people used to tell me that love has nothing at all do with marriage but my opinion is different.

For when you go courting a young and dainty lass,
Don't be too shy or ready to faint for her.
Ah! Little she'll care about your placeless philandering,
Soon my poor boy she would send you a rambling,
Just let her see that your love you would like to grant,
And politely explain to her that yourself is the boy she wants.
Tip her a wink, get hold of the fist of her,
And kiss her before she'll have time to say, "Stop it, sir",
Give her another and then half a score of them,
Talk to her, laugh to her, be saucy and stylish, sir,
That is the way to make love like an Irishman,
Sing to her, smile to her, sit down near the side of her,
And I will go bail that you'll soon make your bride of her.

Sean Kelly

BY THE CASHLEEN RIVERSIDE

One sunny summer's evening in the very month of June
Down by the Curragh farms, the meadows were in bloom
I heard a couple talking as they sat down below
Down by a hedge of bushes by Cashleen's riverside

The man that sat beside the maid, he pressed her to his heart
Saying "darling won't you be my bride, till death do us part
My life I swore for you before and if you'll be my bride
We'll save the hay together by the Cashleen Riverside".

The maid she pondered deeply before she did decide
Saying "Would your father let me in if I became your bride
What would the neighbours call me they'd call me the cuckoo
Who lays her eggs in small birds' nests as her customs are to do"

"Oh never mind the cuckoo, love, or what the people say
My father's nest it's empty now, the birds have flown away
And when we will be married, love, and you will be my bride
We'll save the hay together by the Cashleen riverside".

"There's one thing about our farm, which oftimes gives me bane
Because we are divided by the lands of Mikey Kane
If only he'd exchange with me t'would be my greatest pride
We'd save the hay together by the Cashleen riverside".

Written by Martin Conneely and Pakie Coyne
Given to me by Festy Mortimer

Rocky Mountain Traveller

Showbands first came to prominence in Ireland in the mid-'50s and for the following twenty years they reigned supreme in dancehalls and marquees all over Ireland. They were very much influenced by the emergence of rock-and-roll in America and they tried to emulate the music of artists like Elvis Presley, Fats Domino, Buddy Holly and Chuck Berry. While they may have sometimes struggled vocally in this regard, they were usually well able to reproduce the instrumental sound.

Prior to the advent of the showbands it was quite common for a lot of sets and half-sets to be played in rural dancehalls. It was also the era of what I could only describe as 'big band music'. Artists such as Des Fretwell and Stephen Garvey and their bands remained seated on stage as they played an arranged instrumental medley of music in orchestral fashion.

However, the arrival of the showbands heralded a major upheaval in the whole dancehall scene which seemed to be transformed almost overnight. The showbands all stood up while they played and they were somewhat more adventurous, outgoing and spontaneous in their presentation than the bands which preceded them.

In the late '50s new dancehalls seemed to spring up all over the country and they were packed out night after night as people came to enjoy the popular showbands of the day. The showbands' defining characteristic was their versatility and this really set them apart. They could play the type of instrumental music which had dominated the scene before their arrival, but they could also play ballads, traditional music and country music as well as the popular rock-and-roll music of the day. They could play such a wide range of music because they were all top class musicians who were very professional in their approach and who were always well rehearsed.

Throughout the 1960s the Royal Showband was the most famous showband in Ireland. They had a rhythm section and a brass section as well as a drummer. The rhythm section was a combination of lead bass and rhythm guitar and the brass section comprised trombone, trumpet and tenor saxophone.

During those years I was also privileged to see many other great showbands, especially during my student days in Dublin from 1959 to 1961. These included Joe Dolan and the Drifters, whose first-ever performance I saw in Dublin in 1960; the Capital, who were the second biggest act in the country; and the Royal Blues from Claremorris who could reproduce the music of the Beatles so brilliantly. I also danced to the sound of the Black Aces, the Miami, The Blue Aces, the Clipper Carlton, the Swingtime Aces and Pat McGuigan and the Big Four. Then there was Maurice Mulcahy and his fifteen-piece band and Mick Delahunty and his band, who were originally orchestral-type bands, but later adopted the showband style.

The social scene in Dublin at that time was very exciting and we enjoyed many great nights in the National Ballroom, the Ierne, the Crystal Ballroom and the Four Provinces.

In Galway city, the Seapoint Ballroom in Salthill was a real Mecca for followers of showbands, as was the Hanger which was located where Leisureland is today. I rarely missed a dance in the Hanger between 1962 and 1965, when I was doing my BA and HDip in UCG.

My outstanding memory of Seapoint will always be the hundreds of bicycles thrown outside along the street for as far as the eye could see. While the bicycles were usually left unlocked, the owners usually brought the pump into the dance with them because it was much more likely that the pump would be stolen that the actual bicycle. I heard a humorous story once of a young man in Seapoint, who on being asked what he had concealed inside his trousers, whilst waltzing with a young lady, replied "Oh that! That's my pump", upon which the young lady took grave offence and slapped him across the face before walking off indignantly.

In 1970 I realised a lifetime ambition when I went to see the legendary Buck Owens and the Buckaroos in the National Stadium in Dublin. On the night in question some of the cream of Ireland's showbands were also on the bill as support acts but all paled into insignificance when Buck Owens eventually took the stage. The control he had over the crowd was unbelievable and for the first time in my life I realised what star quality was and what it meant to be a star.

I bought my first guitar in Walton's in Dublin in 1959 for £12. It was an ordinary acoustic guitar and during my time in Dublin I managed to teach myself the necessary basics. Soon after I began my teaching career in Renvyle in 1961, I bought my second guitar in Raftery's in Galway for £28 – about three week's wages at the time. It was an electric guitar. In 1966, I bought a top of the range Fender for £129 which I still have to this day and which is presently worth something in the region of £2,500.

One of the problems in those years was that when one bought a guitar, one had to buy an amplifier as well and the amplifier usually cost as much as the guitar. I used various amplifiers in my time. For rhythm and lead guitars the amplifier and speaker were in the one unit, but in the case of a bass guitar a separate speaker was required because of the bass guitar sound, and this speaker usually had an amplifier placed on top of it. These speakers and amplifiers were much bigger and more cumbersome than what is available today and consequently there was a lot of time and energy spent on hauling gear around and setting it up when we were on the road.

In 1962 I was approached by Bunny Joyce who asked me to join his band, The Emerald. The band, which had been on the road since 1955, were short of a bass player so I agreed to give it a go and Bunny was able to procure a bass guitar for me. In 1963 we renamed the band The Mystic Aces and later in 1968 the name was changed again to The Rocky Mountain Travellers in an attempt to give it more of a country kind of flavour.

I played in the band until 1970 and we had many great times. We played all the local dancehalls in West Connemara on a regular basis, Tullycross, Letterfrack, Clifden, Ballyconneely, Roundstone, Recess and Leenane. We were usually playing three times a week but his could increase to four or five nights during the summer season. The two biggest nights of the week were always Friday and Sunday and, of course, there were never any dances held on a Saturday night on account of the Sabbath. We were usually paid about £25 between the five of us.

The Rocky Mountain Travellers (left to right): Tom Mullen, Bunny Joyce, Frank King, Ulick Joyce, Michael O'Neill and Tommy Sullivan

There were many other small bands like ourselves from the west of Ireland who travelled around playing to small crowds in small dancehalls. These included Quicksilver from Galway; Pat Friel and his band from Westport; Basil Moran and The Beat Minstrels from Louisburg; Mick Cummins and the Blue Notes from Letterfrack; and the Kingstown band.

It is very difficult to say which venue gave me the greatest satisfaction but at that time Ulick's Hall in Letterfrack was generally regarded as being the best hall in West Connemara for a dance. It was probably the right size and there was always a lovely atmosphere because the lighting was just right and there was always a good crowd. There was usually a good mix also with people coming from Clifden, Ballyconneely, Roundstone, Cleggan, Letterfrack and Renvyle. There was very rarely if ever a bad dance in Ulick's. Rows were common enough especially around Christmas. One never stopped playing when a row started. Indeed, that was when one played for all one was worth in order to keep attention off the row and stop everybody from converging on it.

We travelled all over the west of Ireland throughout the 1960s playing in different dancehalls as well as marquees. In fact we played at so many different venues that I cannot recall them all. We played all over Mayo, including Louisburg, Achill, Aughagower, Mulranny, Bonniconlon, Ballycastle and Glenamoy. We often played in Oughterard as well as in Tubbercurry in Sligo. Clare was a very popular destination and I remember playing in Kilrush, Kilkee, Cooraclare and Mullagh. We also played a number of dancehalls in Tipperary including Bansha and Borrisoleigh. The money was not much better than what we received in West Connemara. I remember us playing in Kilkee in 1965 for £35. However it was not about money. We found it very refreshing to play outside West Connemara from time to time. We always enjoyed the novelty of a new place, a new crowd and of course meeting new people. It was a completely different scene to home and we had great fun, which compensated for all the long distance travel.

Most of us did not drink and there were never any problems because of drink. A trip to North Mayo or West Clare usually entailed leaving at 2 p.m. on a Sunday afternoon and not getting home to Renvyle until about 6 a.m. the following morning. I had youth on my side in those years and the travelling never bothered me. Unlike some of the band members I could never sleep while on the road and usually chatted away to whoever was on driving duty. The conversation always helped to shorten the journey home.

Looking back on those times, I was indeed very privileged to play with such talented and versatile musicians. I never considered myself to be a true musician because I never had the discipline to get really serious about it and to practise, as one should. Once I changed over to bass guitar, I had no real problems following the rest of the band. It was easy enough to get into the swing of it and I usually sang nine or ten songs during each performance. Being part of the band on stage was always a very uplifting experience and there was always a great buzz attached to it.

There were nights when we regretted that we had not practised longer and prepared better beforehand, but as a band we generally did as much as we could afford to, considering that everyone had work responsibilities to attend to during the day. It was really a hobby and indeed it was a lovely hobby, which brought us all great happiness. The kind of level we were operating at, there was only a certain quality we could achieve. Having said that, we derived great satisfaction from the bond that developed between all the band members. We also developed a great ability to read a crowd and understand how they were going to react. Eventually we could tell, just by looking at them, what we should play next. There was great fulfilment in playing music and it was wonderful to experience and be part of the whole showband scene. Back in the sixties, people were very different to what they are today, in the sense that it was very easy to satisfy their demands and their tastes. People are much more demanding nowadays because they have so many forms of entertainment at their fingertips. In the sixties people were much more easily pleased. There was such tremendous enjoyment experienced by the dancers. It was so obvious, we could feel the vibes coming up to us on stage and that was a great feeling for us as performers.

I am sure that if we re-formed and tried to reproduce the same phenomenon today we would find it extremely difficult, if not impossible, because today's generation would be far more demanding and if we were not good enough we would probably be booed off the stage. Such a reaction would never happen during the '60s. There were possibly many people who privately considered us to be of a poor standard but if they did, they would never have considered coming up to us and saying it to our faces or showing it in any way.

In 1970, the Rocky Mountain Travellers played their final gig in Clifden House Hotel. The decision to pack it in and go our separate ways was a mutual one. Like everything else in life, I suppose when one is long enough at something, it can all become a bit stale. The thrill or the buzz, which was there in the early days, can fizzle out and it becomes more of a chore trying to do it. By 1970, performing had become tedious and harder to do for all the band members. In my own case, it was starting to impinge too greatly on my family life and when this happened I knew I had to call it a day.

It had been a wonderful eight years and I would not change anything. I have always believed that it is wrong for people to pin themselves to one particular thing. Everyone should have outlets and variety in their lives in order to be more rounded and fruitful in their endeavours. I believe that diversity of interest keeps the mind in good working order and in this respect the music was great, in that it allowed me to turn away completely from more mundane affairs for a time, in order to do something totally different. I have always maintained that no matter what one does in life, it is invaluable because of the experience gained from it and, of course, experience is something which cannot be bought. The greater the variety of experiences, the more one's life is enriched. When we are young we usually think we know everything, but I think as we go through life and look back we discover that we have learned so much along the way and thereafter a natural maturity takes over. Down through the years, music has always been an integral part of my life and all the wonderful experiences I had in those years have helped me greatly ever since. I would always be the first to acknowledge that music has played no small part in moulding me into the type of person I am today and that is something I will always be thankful for.

Remembered by Michael O' Neill and written by Paul Gannon.

On the Air

It was early Spring and the year was 1936. King Edward VIII was planning to abdicate in England and in March Hitler marched his troops into the Rhineland which, by treaty, had been demilitarised. The countries of Europe did nothing to stop him, so Hitler decided that in future he could risk anything.

Austin O'Malley and Martin Conneely had just finished cutting their turf and their minds were on matters other than the troubled state of Europe. With other members of the Renvyle Ceili Band they were booked to play for a dance in Clifden organised by the late P. K. Joyce. Little did they realise how close to stardom they were to come as a result of that dance. Present in Clifden were two representatives from Radio Eireann who, when they heard the band, invited the members to take part in a Ceili Band competition being run by Radio Eireann. After some initial hesitation they decided to enter.

Reinforcements were summoned and the countryside was scoured for a flute player but none could be found. Five musicians – two accordions and three fiddles went into rehearsal. The accordion players were Michael Canavan and Michael Ruddy, and on fiddles were Austin O'Malley, Phil Kane, and Martin Conneely. Mrs Curley organised a dance in Tullycross to raise funds for the momentous trip and another was held in Clifden. Rehearsals were held in Austin's, and Martin Conneely's, with one or two in Tommy O'Malley's of the Castle. By all accounts they were stormy affairs with heated arguments developing about triplets and rolls. However, everything came along nicely and just when the finishing touches had been put to the programme disaster struck.

Everybody felt that Paddy Coyne who lived in Letterfrack at the time would be in charge of transport and act as a general road manager for the group. Paddy , however, had other ideas. Apparently at that time, he used to go to bed very early each night and on one or two occasions he had driven the band to dances and did not get back till daylight the following day. The idea of being caught in Dublin maybe for a couple of days, with those lads did not altogether appeal to him.

Cars being scarce at that time, the trip was about to be abandoned when someone remembered that Jack McDonnell in Ballinakill had a car. It was felt that Jack, who was not noted for his dare-devil driving, might need some convincing to undertake such an adventure. Austin, being the most persuasive of the group was despatched to Ballinakill on his bike, and he met with success in convincing Jack to go. The price for the round trip was £14.

On the eventful day, Jack arrived in Ardnagreevagh shortly after 8 a.m. He was driving a Austin Seven and he had to get four of the band into the back. Martin Conneely had an unusually long pair of legs, and one of the other members had to help Jack to get Martin's legs in. The doors were closed and whatever music the four in the back seat had on leaving Ardnagreevagh it was well squeezed out of them by the time they were in Oughterard, not to mention Dublin. Around Ballinasloe the temperature in the back of the car was in the nineties and Jack's driving was not helping to calm already frayed tempers. When they were passed by a lorry load of potatoes, Austin demanded that the car be stopped so that he could get out and walk. A few miles farther on an argument developed between the accordion players and in the ensuing battle of words, Martin Conneely was almost smothered.

Finally, the GPO was reached at 10.30 p.m., exactly 14 hours after they had left Renvyle. While they were unloading the instruments three Dubliners who were standing at the corner of the GPO remarked:

"Here come the culchies. Can ye play '*The Geese in the Bog*' lad?"

"We can indeed," says Austin, "and we can play '*The Bums on the Corner*."

They emerged from the Radio Eireann Studio in the GPO at about two in the morning exhausted and hungry. They had something to eat and drink and after a few hours set out on the long journey home. They had the wind on their backs on the return journey, and it only took about ten hours. They did not accept any more invitations to play on Radio Eireann and Martin Conneely still blames the trip in the back of Jack McDonnell's car for the arthritis he developed in later years!

Remembered by Martin Conneely and Margaret O'Malley,
and written by Michael O'Neill.

Seisiún

In September 1973, while holidaying with May and my family in the quiet village of Murroe in Co Limerick, we chanced a night out in a small cottage not far from our lodgings. We were told there would be a good night's musical entertainment. It was our first time ever in a Teach Ceoil. The cottage had a big open fireplace up at one end, around which all the musicians were gathered. There was a little ardán or stage in front of these for the dancers. We were later to learn that the musicians and dancers were nearly all from Limerick city.

It was easy enough to fill the cottage and that night the place was particularly full. The atmosphere was unbelievable. I had never experienced anything quite like it before and that night was a watershed in my musical experience because I returned to Connemara not converted as such from modern or pop music but, nevertheless, very hooked on traditional music. I said to myself, "If we could create something like that in Renvyle it would be absolutely wonderful".

Seisiún group in rehearsal for London tour, 1989. Back row from left: Charlie Malley, Ray Stewart (dancer), Louis Curran (dancer), Patricia Conneely (dancer), Pam Conroy (singer), Evelyn Laffey (dancer), Mary Aspell (dancer), Michael O'Neill (dancer) and Johnny Coyne. Front row, l to r: Jim O'Neill, Phil Coyne, Elizabeth Kane, Mary Finn and Frank Coyne.

Later that year I made contact with both Bord Fáilte and Comhalthas. They agreed to send a delegation to Tullycross to meet our organising committee and we, for our part, organised all the local musical talent to play a session together in one of the Tullycross cottages for the benefit of this delegation. Unfortunately there was a mix-up on the day. We had organised the musicians to arrive in the evening and the delegation arrived in the afternoon to meet us and were unable to stay on. Nevertheless we went ahead with the session in the cottage, which I recorded. After that night I was convinced that we had the talent locally to make the concept a reality.

I pushed ahead with the idea and eventually we were given the go-ahead by Bord Fáilte to establish a group. That first group, set up during the Christmas of 1974 included Charlie O'Malley, Johnny Mark Coyne, Phil Coyne, John Gerard Walsh, Jarlath Hession and myself, along with Chrissie O'Malley, Mary Quinn, Nora Hynes and Mary McDonnell, who were the dancers. We had nowhere to put on the show, only Tullycross Hall, so we had to get a stage specially built to put in the middle of the hall, to enable us to get the right kind of intimate atmosphere that this kind of show required. That opening night the hall was jammed to capacity. There were also representatives from Bord Fáilte and Comhaltas present and the whole group was really on tenterhooks, because we were very anxious to impress our financial backers.

Towards the end of the first half of the show the stage suddenly started to wobble and just as were finishing our last tune, didn't it collapse in the middle. I can still see Johnny Mark Coyne sinking into the abyss and him holding the fiddle above his head for fear it would get broken.

During the break I headed down with Dan O'Neill, Assistant Manager of Bord Fáilte, to the cottages in Tullycross where there was still some construction work to be completed. We piled as many building blocks as we could into the back of my Volkswagen Variant, returned hastily to the hall, and put them under the stage to hold it up. It was a classic case of "the show must go on". When the show was over, everybody said that the stage collapsing was probably the best thing that could have happened, because it got rid of all the nerves and the tension and we played the second half of the show with joyful abandonment. The show was a great success and Seisiún had arrived in Renvyle.

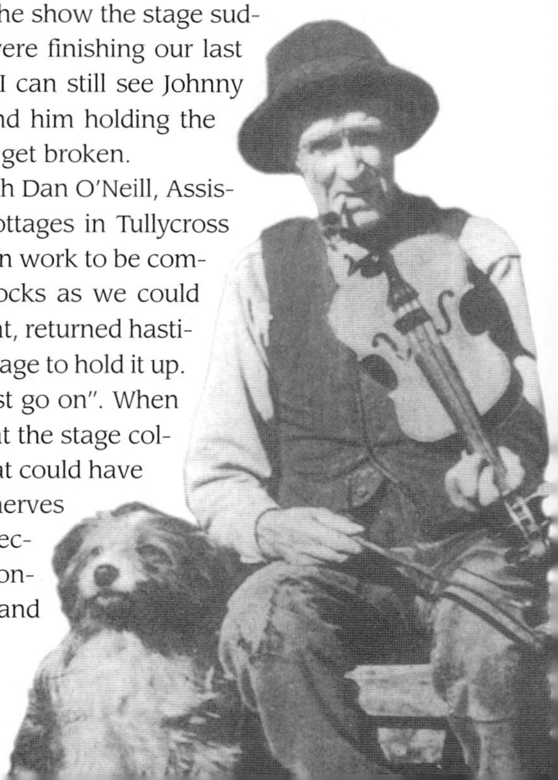

Mary Flaherty (RIP) performing on the opening night of the Galway County Fleadh in 1985, along with the Renvyle Seisiún Group. Seated in the background are Labhras Ó Murchú, Director of Comhaltas and Michael Cunningham, Chairman of Galway County Board Comhaltas.

We continued in Tullycross Hall for the following three years. Every week, without fail, Paul Aspell and myself would set up the stage, blocks and all, and take it down again, when the show was finished. I will always remember Paul had a special pair of thick gloves to keep his hands from getting skinned by the big six-inch blocks. The hall was always packed for every show in those years.

It is quite amazing, really, how much the whole scene has changed over the years. I remember a clash one Tuesday night with Diamond's in Tully. They used to have big bands in on a regular basis and on this particular night Margo was the attraction. We felt we had to go ahead with our show, however, or we could be badly affected subsequently. Both venues were packed out. The two shows happened to finish around the same time and I remember the traffic between Tully and Tullycross being at a total standstill. It is hard to imagine a similar scenario today.

Throughout the 1970s, Bord Fáilte covered 75 per cent of the cost, which was a great help because it was costing about £300 a night to put on the show. I decided that the musicians would have to be paid the equivalent of what they would normally get in a public house. I felt that people should be paid and that the only way to ensure the continued success of Seisiún was to adopt a totally professional approach. I feared I would not be able to rely on the musicians if the whole thing was being run on a voluntary basis. It was a very tightly controlled programme and even the costumes had to be done beforehand. The advertising was all done in Dublin and we always had beautifully-designed posters every year. I used to attend a special two-day conference in Dublin for all the producers of Seisiún around the country.

In 1977 the show moved to the Teach Ceoil in Tully, which had been specially designed for putting on that kind of show. That first performance in the Teach Ceoil was probably one of the most emotional nights of my life, and it was a great privilege to be one of the performers.

Every October Bank Holiday weekend, all the Seisiún groups in the country used to come together for Seisiún na Samhna. I remember us going to Thurles, Dingle, Lisdoonvarna and Dungarvan. There was nothing competitive about the weekend. Each group would put on a half-an -hour show at night time and then we would all get together during the day for sessions. These were wonderful weekends where lasting friendships were made. I still keep in regular contact today with people I first met on such occasions.

Over the years our group was fortunate to embark on two wonderful tours. Out first tape was launched on a three-week tour of France in 1987 and we released our second tape on the 1990 tour of America. The Board Fáilte subsidy was removed during the 1980s and this hit us very hard. The increase in other forms of entertainment along with falling tourist numbers, often due to bad weather, eventually resulted in Seisiún coming to an end in 1994, twenty years after that very first, unforgettable night in Tullycross Hall.

Remembered by Michael O'Neill and written by Paul Gannon

Renvyle Comhaltas Group, Gannot, Auvergne, France in July, 1987. Back row, from left: Elizabeth Kane, John Nee, Maeve O'Neill (dancer) and Pat Lydon. Front row, l to r: Mary Garrett, Veronica Murray, Margaret McBride (dancer), Mary Finn, Maria O'Connell and Michael O'Neill.

Entertaining Memories

Way back in the '20s and '30s, the 8th of December, apart from being a Church holyday, was a very special day in the local calendar for the whole parish. Many older people will have nostalgic memories of the evening's entertainment provided by the Brothers and boys of St. Joseph's School at Letterfrack for that particular evening. Entertainment usually took the form of a play which was produced by the Brothers and acted by the boys, whose talents exceeded the expectations of many.

It must have been a painstaking task to coach and train young boys under sixteen to act and play their parts so well, and great credit was due to the Brothers for their fervour and perseverance. Not only did they teach acting, but singing and dancing as well. There was also a brass band in the school whose members consisted of some of the boys.

Everybody looked forward to the big night and people came from the four corners of the parish and beyond. Many walked, others travelled on side-cars or bicycles and some lucky people had the luxury of a model 'T' to travel in. The spacious hall in the school grounds was usually crammed with young and old long before the programme started. The stage would be artistically set and before the play began, the audience would be treated to a selection of airs by the band, which received a resounding ovation. Then came the play. The scenery was a credit to the artist, who usually was one of the brothers, and the background for the various scenes left nothing to be desired. The boys filled their roles as if they were professionals and the audience showed their appreciation after each scene in no uncertain manner. Between the scenes, a boy would sing or give an exhibition of Irish dancing which was always well received. And so the entertainment went on until the final curtain, which always brought down the house. The people went their various ways home, exulting over the night's entertainment. Everybody had enjoyed the programme and for weeks afterwards it was a feature of discussion. As evidence of the success of the effort, the Brothers were often requested to travel to other venues in Galway and Mayo with their production. Alas, these wonderful nights are only memories now but it goes to show that a good eveningís entertainment was obtainable in the days before films and television became commonplace.

Author unknown.

Marian Players

My first introduction to drama was in St Patrick's Teacher Training College in Drumcondra, which I attended from 1959 to 1961. Myself and a fellow called Brendan Murphy had written a sketch, which was a sort of send up of all the different goings-on in the college. When the Dean heard about it, he called us to the office on day and asked us to develop it into a stage play of about forty-five minutes duration. We felt we had no option but to adhere to his wishes.

We got a group together and set about our task and eventually came up with a final product. We performed the play on the night of the annual college concert and fortunately it went down well with the audience. One of the actors, Michael Campion, was so taken by the whole experience that he approached me afterwards with a view to producing a full-length play for the benefit of the students and staff alike. The play he had in mind was *'Journey's End'*, a World War I play. The group agreed to give it a go. We put

Clifden Dramatic Society 1940, "Professor Tim" by George Shiels. Back row: Olive Harley, Fursey Clancy, Liam Clancy, Petie Gough, John Gough; front row: Mickey O'Toole, Veronica Savage, Gabriel Bourke, Kathleen Daly, Thomas McInerney.

in many long hours of rehearsal and I remember an army fellow called O'Keefe brought in all the army paraphernalia, including props. We performed it in front of a packed house in the college theatre and I suppose the whole experience left me with a great love of drama thereafter.

Shortly after returning to Renvyle in 1962 to begin my teaching career, I was recruited by Fr Ludden to get involved in the local drama group. Plays were put on during Lent at that time as dances were forbidden. We would all receive a copy of whatever play was to be performed and meet for a few readings initially, before the serious business of rehearsals would begin.

The opening night of a play was always a huge event in the social life of the people at that time. I can remember years before that, when I was attending primary school, there was always a Christmas concert and play in the Monks' hall in Letterfrack. We used to be six months looking forward to it and when it was all over we would be another six months talking about it.

People nowadays could not possibly grasp the importance of it at the time and how much it meant to the whole community. Nowadays it is very hard to entertain people because they are so exposed to entertainment and they don't really wonder at anything. However, entertainment was so scarce when I was young that people had a great sense of occasion whenever the opportunity presented itself.

Back in the early 1960s, the only type of drama that people wanted was comedy. Even if we attempted a serious play, the audience would still start laughing, almost as soon as the curtain would be raised. It only took a few people to set everyone else off. Rehearsing was always hard work and difficult, yet we had so much fun and it was always really worth it in the end.

In 1964 we performed a play called '*Marriage is a Lottery*' and the opening night in the Marian Hall, Tullycross, was one I will never forget. The hall was packed and the atmosphere was electric. We brought the play to Inishbofin. I remember I was a tailor and in one particular part of the play I was sitting down at a table and not really making much headway with a particular suit. The fellow I was making the suit for would throw a big roll of tweed in through the window. I would be sitting at the table having my dinner and normally it would hit me and I would fall. However, the stage in Inishbofin was very small and whatever way I was situated, I could actually see the roll of tweed coming for me. There were people sitting right under the stage and whatever way I pulled back my head, the roll of tweed missed me, landed on the table and knocked the contents down on the people in the front row. I will always remember one young lad in a minor state of shock, wiping milk off his face.

We also brought the play to Kylemore Abbey, where we performed for

Marian Players 1964, "Marriage is a Lottery". Pictured l to r: Fr Stephen Ludden, Michael O'Neill, Joey Ribbon, Maureen O'Neill, Vincent Little, Kevin McDonald, Chrissie O'Malley, Mikey Gannon and John Mark Coyne.

the Benedictine nuns. Even though the play was a comedy we were not getting much in the way of laughs. Again, I found myself sitting down at a table having my dinner. Whatever way I mixed up my lines, I suddenly found myself into the third act of the play when I still should have been in act two. The line I had to say will always be indelibly imprinted on my mind because I sweated blood with embarrassment over it. The line was, "I stand here, erect, free and independent". I remember saying to myself; "I can't say that sitting, down". I was forced to improvise, as can often be the case in drama, so I grabbed a knife, stuck it into a half-pound of butter which was on a plate, put the plate over my head, stood up and said "I stand here erect, free and..." It failed me four times to finish the line because I was not able to contain myself and had burst out laughing. Laughing is infectious and the rest of the cast on stage with me followed suit. I can still remember Fr Ludden, who was prompting us from side stage scratching the leg of his trousers with embarrassment. He had been very anxious for us to put on an impressive performance for the nuns.

Stage acting is so unpredictable. Despite all the rehearsing, and the striving for the perfect performance, there is still just as much potential,for things to go wrong as to go right, but we never worried too much if there was the odd hiccup here and there. A lot of the time mistakes actually added to the fun and the enjoyment and gave the audience more to talk about and laugh about afterwards.

In 1966, our drama group, the Marian Players, came up with the idea of organising a drama festival in the Marian Hall, Tullycross. The festival was a great success and in 1967 we decided to enter the festival ourselves with a play called '*The Country Boy*'. The festival ran for a week with a different play being performed each night. We were quite pleased with our own performance and were hopeful of doing well. However, to our dismay, we were lambasted by the adjudicators – a very humiliating experience considering all the hard work we had put in. Obviously we had done everything wrong and everybody was gutted.

I was determined that we would not lose heart and give up, so I organised a meeting with Joe O'Donnell who was the head of the adjudicating panel. We talked for about two hours, especially about production, because I was the producer of the play and felt most responsible for our poor showing. He gave me a list of books which he recommended I read, and I wrote away to Dublin for them without delay. I tried to glean as much knowledge as possible from these books during the following months.

Early in 1968 we got the cast together again and resolved to make one huge effort for the upcoming festival. We chose a play by John B. Keane called '*Sive*'. We built a very fine set. We also built a model of the stage for rehearsals to ensure that we got the stage patterns and groupings worked out in order that every actor would know where they were supposed to be at any given time.

We put in a tremendous amount of work in the two months leading up to the festival. We had great fun and a lot of laughs, particularly during rehearsals and especially when things were going wrong. A great bond developed among all the members of the cast during that time. Tom Hickey was head of the adjudicating panel in 1968 and there was a very high standard of entry that year. There were groups from Clifden, Belcare and also from different parts of Mayo. To our great surprise we were declared the winners. We had come full circle in one year, and I suppose drama is no different to anything else one does in life, in the sense that if enough dedication and commitment is put in, there is no reason why one should not experience success at the end of it all.

The 1968 Drama festival was the last such festival held in Tullycross. I was beginning to get involved in a wide range of community development issues at the time and was unable to devote the time to it anymore. The drama festivals resulted in the audiences becoming much more critical and by the end of the third festival most of the audience felt qualified to adjudicate themselves. The beautiful innocence of the earlier years had been lost.

I have often thought about reviving a drama group in the parish but constraints of time have always prevented me from doing so. Drama involves a lot of hard work, if it is to be done right. There is tremendous acting talent within our community and drama is now given greater priority in the primary schools than ever before. However, young people have so much going on in their lives today, compared to forty years ago, that it is difficult to see them giving the same type of commitment which we were happy to give because we had the time and the interest. It would be a very joyful experience for me to return to a packed Tullycross Hall some night to watch a play by a local drama group. This scenario does not appear very likely to occur as we approach the Millennium, but I live in hope that a once proud drama tradition will enjoy a renaissance at some stage in the next century.

Remembered by Michael O'Neill and written by Paul Gannon

Women of Substance

In October 1959, the Tullycross Guild of the ICA was formed. Pauline Frawley, County Organiser at that time, helped us during our formative years, and being such an outstanding craft worker herself, she encouraged us all to get going at the crafts from the word go. Her tweed pictures and putty jars of that night were our first efforts at doing such things.

Words of advice given that night proved so helpful and so true. "Always read and reply to correspondence", "have a proper minutes book", "have a treasurer's statement", "never say 'I cannot do that job,' always say 'I'll try", "do a little Guild competition", "have a cup of tea and a social half-hour", and "remember that there is always something new to learn". For twenty-five years we have adhered to that advice, hence the success of our Guild.

Down the years many and varied have been our activities: we have shared our talents and skills; we have worked together as a team; we have helped each other in time of sorrow; and we have enjoyed many, many laughs and happy moments.

Our first team effort was a sale-of-work in aid of the Marian Hall which, although complete, was £800.00 in debt. We cadged, gathered, made and sold, and achieved our goal: the debt was no more! We held our first birthday party in the hall which was a 'free-for-all'. (Where did we get the money?)

At this time Cleggan Guild were very helpful to us, and our sincere thanks go to Delia O'Toole, Eileen O'Malley and others whom we remember in our prayers, who gave us so many demonstrations, and invited us to what must have been our first outing – a garden party on Cleggan Beach. There were so many goodies, so many party games, such warmth and friendliness, that from that day on a special love and dedication for our great association was fostered.

Now we were ready to move out to group meetings and federation meetings. There are pleasant memories of our first federation meeting in Loughrea on a June evening, a cup of tea and a warm welcome when we got there, but no idea of what went on at the meeting. Many introductions and sharing of ideas set up a special friendship with Loughrea which exists to this day.

We soon began to enter national competitions, our first venture being verse speaking, which was held in Oughterard. If the ground could have swallowed us up that night, it would have been grand; we were just hopeless! Our first production of a one-act play staged in Headford was a fiasco. The comments of the judge, "I've never seen a worse production!" earned for us a week-long drama course at An Grianon!

On the craft side, however, we were getting places. Our first national entry – a child's smocked dress was highly commended. Later we had a first prize for a pair of men's hand-knitted socks. The winner had never knitted a pair of socks before! Then we won a prize for Báinin table mats.

Down the years we have entered all kinds of competitions:– cookery, crafts, essays, drama, set dancing, public speaking and debating. We have spent many hours making up themes for Eleanor Gibbon competitions. We composed our own play, *'Bubbles'*, which was highly praised. We composed songs:– *Over the Village The Wild Wind is Blowing* and *In the Green Tree Tops the Songbirds Sing*. We wrote poems:– 'This Asian Flu is a terrible curse; I am certainly hoping it won't get the nurse.' We have paintings:– *'A doorway'*; *'A street scene'*. There were springtime stories and ghost stories, *'If I ruled Ireland'; 'The Cave of Dona Mor'*.

We have been involved in many issues at local level, and have delegates on the Community Council, Connemara West, Legion of Mary and Country Markets and have always been actively involved in community affairs.

One of our members was Federation Secretary, Federation President and Voluntary County Organiser, and got support from the guild members in promoting ICA throughout the country.

Now, as we have embarked on our twenty-fifth year in the ICA, we can look back with pride on our achievements, our hard work and the satisfaction derived from every little effort. 'Our Heritage' being the theme of last year's programmes, must have made it one of our most interesting years. We have learned that nothing is impossible provided we have the desire to do it, and that it is up to us to foster and promote all that is worthwhile in our Irish heritage.

For the past twenty-five years we were fortunate to have so many idealistic members in our guild, women of talent, vision and ability who have encouraged us, who have worked for us and with us. Some gave of their talents, imparting knowledge and skills; others helped in administration; some made the tea and the buns, while entertainment on our annual outings was equally important.

We thank and honour each and every person who has ever been a member of our guild. It is sad to think we have only a few founder members left, and for all those members who have passed from us, we say – Lord, grant them eternal rest.

By kind permission of Tullycross ICA Guild (Written in 1984)

TOWN COMMEMORATES FLIGHT OF 40 YEARS AGO

Airlines of the world will pay tribute to pioneers

June 7, 1959, from Clifden
Reuter and Associated Press

The town of Clifden in Connemara is alive with excitement to-day. To-morrow week it will commemorate the flight of forty years ago.

The people of Clifden were excited and proud that wet, grey Sunday morning as they rushed to help and greet the two heroes.

This year, on June 15, the little town will again be excited as they celebrate their greatest link with history.

For on that day a memorial in Carlow limestone, shaped like an aircraft fin, will be unveiled to commemorate the great event.

Not only the people of Clifden will gather round the memorial, to be erected on high ground overlooking the spot in the desolate marshland where the plane sank up to its axles and toppled forward burying its nose in the mud.

As Ireland's Minister for Industry and Commerce, Mr Sean Lemass, performs the unveiling ceremony, 100 special guests from Ireland, America and Canada as well as the UK. – including relatives of the two flyers – will remember that triumphant moment 40 years ago.

This week Aer Lingus officials in Dublin, led by Captain J.C Kelly-Rodgers, Sir Winston Churchill's wartime pilot, are making arrangements for the reception of the overseas visitors. Commandant Eamon Guy of the Irish Army is in charge of operations at Ballinaboy.

Mr. A.G Alcock and Captain E.S. Alcock, brothers of the pioneering pilot, will attend.

With them will be representatives of every airline in the world. Colonel James Fitzmaurice has been invited.

At 8.25 a.m. on June 15, a special train will take the party of VIPs from Dublin to Galway, over 100 miles away. Then coaches will take them the 48 miles to Clifden.

Hotelier Matt O'Connor, a member of the 10-man memorial committee, said, "This is going to be Clifden's greatest day.

"The only pity is that it does not fall on a Sunday but on a Monday this year. We have been trying to erect a fitting memorial for the past 40 years but something always held it up. Now the dream comes true. I hope it does for Marconi too. A cairn of stones is being erected on the edge of the bog a few hundred yards from the spot where the plane landed."

A Dublin firm of monumental sculptors is chipping the memorial fin into shape. The design was chosen after consultations with the Cork sculptor, Seamus Murphy, a member of the Royal Hibernian Society.

One of the people who saw the bi-plane landing is 80-year-old publican Mr Eddie King.

He jumped out of bed as the aircraft zoomed over his 100-year-old inn at the corner of Main Street and Market Street.

Yesterday as he cast his mind back he told me:

"Everybody in the town dashed towards the bogland to see the two young fliers. I remember congratulating them. They were tired and worn, but all smiles. Like ants, Connemara men and people from Marconi Radio Station crawled all over the plane hunting for souvenirs.

"We tried to erect a memorial while Brown was still alive, but he would not agree to it. At last the town is getting it."

Mr Winston Churchill, as Secretary of State for War, said of the flight:

"Think of the broad Atlantic, that terrible waste of desolate waters, tossing in tumult, and across that water two human beings hurtling through the air, piercing the clouds and darkness, finding their unerring path – and at any moment liable to destruction from a drop of water in the carburettor, a spot of oil on the plugs, or a tiny grain of dirt in their feed pipe."

His words vividly describe the flight of which answered one of man's greatest challenges.

Moments in history and their subsequent impact on our impending lives can occur at a moment's notice. Since the transatlantic flight of Alcock & Brown in June 1919, countless numbers of people from all corners of the globe have sought to stand on the landing site in Derrygimla Bog, or take in the panoramic view beside the monument erected to their memory on the High Road at Errislannan. In this letter, Michael John King reflects on the memory interacting with current events of that first flight and the 75th anniversary celebrations, which occurred in 1994.

I WAS THERE

Errislannan,
Clifden,
Co Galway.

Dear Bríd,

Trusting that I find you in fine fettle and good spirits as you prepare to take yet another holiday from your beloved teaching career. You know, when I think of it, teaching has its just rewards for all those moments of stress and provocation that we read so much about in the media today.

Have not seen you since Confirmation Day in Clifden. That's over two weeks ago, but it does seem much longer. The good news is the photos came back and lucky enough I got two good ones of yourself and Caroline – separately, of course. To look at one beautiful girl is fine but to have the two of you together, well that is kind of unfair.

I have been intending to drop down to Lakeside but Christopher has some photos of the walking group, which I had better, bring with me. Your good friends will be asking and it would not do to appear with the sole reason of seeing you, dear.

Michael John King

Last night, and what a beautiful one it was, the thought struck me that if you were here at Errislannan looking out on a silent bay with the pale shadow of the moon reflecting on the crystal waters, what would your topic of conversation be. I recall some time ago promising you an account of last year's *'Adventure to Clifden'* celebrations, and in particular the commemoration of June 15th at the monument to Alcock and Brown in its scenic splendour on the crest of the High Road.

We both share a special interest in aviation and

you've told me so often that I should pursue it and the dream could become reality. This is as good a time as any to share my thoughts and reflections on that historic occasion at Clifden on June 15th 1994 when we celebrated the 75th Anniversary of Alcock & Brown's historic Transatlantic crossing.

Awareness of the occasion was not remote from any mind in the proceeding few months. I told you then that when the 50th anniversary was being commemorated I was beginning national school at Ballinaboy in the summer of 1969. The first time we realised something was up was when scaffolding was erected by the monument to give it a face lift for the approaching Sunday the 15th. That day in 1969 was misty and foggy. Faint memories return of aero-engines throughout the day and model aircraft kits being dropped by mini-parachute around the area, although I was disappointed none came my way. The events passed into history but I was most grateful indeed to have been lucky enough to be present this time around. For us in Errislannan, guardians in a geographical sense of that most photographed of monuments, it would be an opportunity to pay our tribute to a remarkable event which ensured that Clifden and Derrygimla Bog would be forever associated with this big step in the history of aviation.

Unlike that day in 1969, this was summer at its best. The dawn of the 15th, a Wednesday, was bright, a little chill from a gentle breeze blowing from the northwest. It was 7.00 a.m. and the first event of the day was about to take place. A flight re-enacted by a bi-plane from Galway Flying Club which would travel the same flight path as Alcock and Brown by coming in over Turbot Island, heading east over Clifden Bay up over the town, circling the church as on that day in 1919, and proceeding south, sweeping by the tail fin at Errislannan, on the cairn in the bog which marked the spot where they landed, immediately afterwards setting course for Galway.

While most people went to the church in Clifden and waited for the plane to come in, others headed for the bog. For those who wished to have a grandstand view they chose Errislannan with its panoramic sights as far as the eye is capable of. Bríd, I had to be different and went by bike to Boatharbour, that most westerly tip of the peninsula with a clear sight out to sea with Inishturbot and the approaches to Clifden Bay visible in the distance. Sure enough, at 8.35 a.m a dot appeared in the sky over the island and the drone of the engines grew progressively louder as the speck became bigger and even closer. This was a moment to treasure. What must it have been like 75 years ago on that Sunday morning? My grand uncles, God rest them, owned land around here. Perhaps they were milking cows and witnessed just what I was seeing now. The mind starts to play tricks then...what if I was there? The camera is out, a shot for the archives. A gentle tear rolls down the cheek – the excitement or thanksgiving for just being able to be present, perhaps a bit of both.

I know you felt basically the same degree of awe and wonder at watching the plane sweep over the church at Clifden while on your way to school. I love to hear you describe how you felt when you travelled back in time to that fateful Sunday, only the schools were minus the children. They were probably in church anyway. I was delighted for you for when growing up on that easter seaboard, little did you realise that you would be there when history was being repeated and commemorated in such a fashion and with such enthusiasm.

While you proceeded to the classroom, I together with most of the people of Errislannan and all the family headed for the monument for the unveiling of the plaque as a memento of such an historic day. This was performed by direct descendants of the two aviators. Some items of clothing and equipment as worn by the men all those years ago had been brought from London to be part of the display. The car park was thronged at twelve o'clock, the sun high in a cloudless sky when Anne Alcock, a niece of the pilot, and Anthony Kilminister, a nephew of Whitten-Brown unveiled the limestone tablet. Following some introductory remarks by the members of the festival committee, Anne Alcock spoke of her pride on behalf of Anthony and herself at being in Clifden to celebrate a unique achievement. As the speech was drawing to a conclusion, an Air Corps officer was gesturing with his outstretched arm to the south, and from the distant Errisbeg, dots in the blue sky grew larger by the second. Two jets

Alcock and Brown on the way to Marconi. The locomotive was made from a motor car and was specially designed to fit the narrow railway gauge.

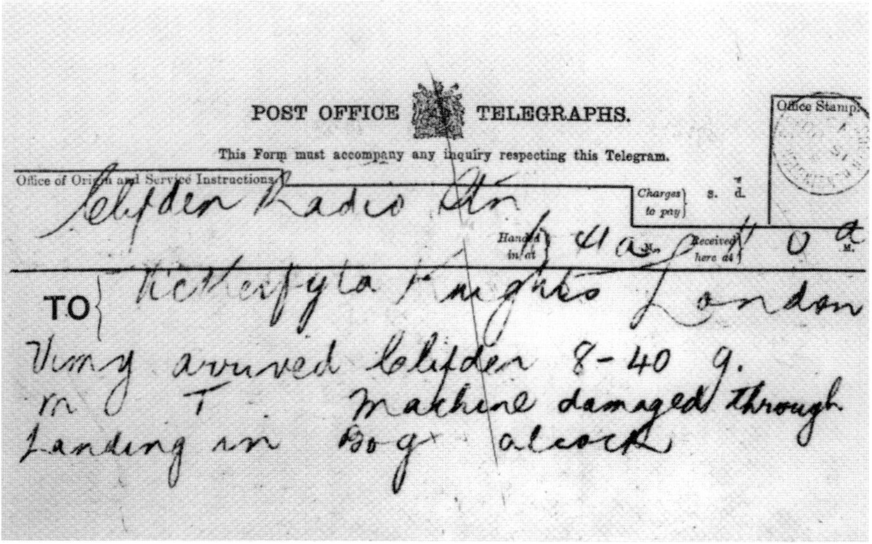

POST OFFICE TELEGRAPHS.

This Form must accompany any inquiry respecting this Telegram.

Office of Origin and Service Instructions. Clifden Radio Stn

Charges to pay s. d.

Handed in at

Received here at

TO

Vimy arrived Clifden 8-40 G. M. T. Machine damaged through landing in Bog. Alcock

Office Stamp

Telegram sent by Alcock and Brown announcing their landing near Clifden.

of the Irish Air Corps swept in over the white cairn in the bog.

Albert Millar, a boy of ten when the original event occurred watched in delight at the wonder of the speeding jets as they performed breathtaking aerobatics above the tail fin erected in 1959 and unveiled by Seán Lamass. A fitting salute to these brave pioneers from a younger generation of pilots flying jet age machines, acknowledging the debt owed to flyers the world over to John Alcock and Arthur Whitten-Brown.

With a two o'clock approach from the west and a low sweep, one final pass heading for the Twelve Bens and home. The air filled once again by the conversation of the people who were then treated by a phone call direct from the mayor of Newfoundland in Canada, where the original flight had departed from. It was a moment to savour, Bríd. I wonder when the 100th anniversary comes around what type of phone will make the call then. The flags of Canada, Great Britain and Ireland flew gently in the afternoon breeze as we headed down the hill on Wednesday afternoon.

We had paid a fitting tribute to the men who had captured the imagination of all, and for which we in Errislannan hold a special place. Should you wish to have me read this on top of some stage, you've only got to say the word and your request will be granted.

I know that June is not far away now and the notion of your departure from Clifden is something I've put off thinking about for as long as possible. Those years have flown and still there is so much of Connemara that I should like you to see. The old saying of when you're enjoying yourself, time flies, is so very true in my opinion.

The community at large acknowledges the contribution made by this generation of teachers, to the educational standards for which the young people are so very lucky to enjoy the fruits of your labour. You know that your part in this success story will without doubt be remembered. The senior citizens group was instrumental in being introduced to one another. I had hoped that you would have had the opportunity to take part in the forthcoming musical. Alas, that may now not be possible. Your co-operation and helping hand were always readily available. It shall not be forgotten.

I am concluding this letter on an inspiring evening when the signs of an awakening are so earnestly approaching. Let's take advantage of the time remaining to discover all that is best in a lifestyle that is so enriching. The sound of the helicopter heading to Slyne Head can be heard in the distance. Even today flying is still very much to the fore. Now is not that another way for an alternative view of this place and its people that you have grown to cherish?

Take care.

With warmest wishes,

Michael John

MEMORIES OF MARCONI

My very first memory of the Marconi station was looking across the bogs as a child and wondering what it was all about. I used to hear Mom and Dad chatting about the old days and the Marconi station and the people who used to work there.

Later, as I grew older, I often asked Dad about the station and it was joy unbounded for me when one Sunday afternoon he suggested we go and see the place. We headed off after Sunday Mass in the old schoolhouse beside the Alcock & Brown Memorial. Leaving the main Clifden/Ballyconneely Road, the old mission school was on our left where people were given food and sustenance during the difficult famine times. Sadly, the old building has now gone and with it a chapter of history.

Further up the lane lived a man called Frank who always had a friendly word for the passer-by. In his time he must have answered many queries

Last train out of Clifden, 1935.

Recess Station, July 1934.

about the Marconi station. He has long since departed this life and the little house which was his home has also disappeared from the landscape.

Two hundred yards up the lane was the starting point of the Marconi railway. Dad told me that the little 8hp engine was called 'The Marconi Express'. Each item was taken to the station by that little engine.

"Who was the driver?" I asked Dad.

"A man by the name of Peter Feeney," he said.

We continued our walk along the line for about a mile until we came to a lake which Dad named as Loch An Eilion. There we stood watching the water hen and her chicks swimming amongst the water lilies. The young lambs were playing in the heather and in the distance I could hear the cuckoo calling.

"We are about halfway there," said Dad when I enquired how much more we had to travel. When we came to a fork in the road we turned right. Bogs of turf were everywhere and another lake was looming in the distance.

"This is Marconi Lake," said Dad – an appropriate name because of its proximity to the station, I thought as we crossed the stepping-stones up the hill. On the right we saw a red brick building, our first port of call, and we headed straight for it.

"This was the operators' bungalow," said Dad, which prompted my question, "What did they do?"

"The operators were the people who sent and received messages from around the world by morse code, the dots and dashes system."

We rested for a while, drinking in the vista of a magnificent landscape that stretches for miles on all sides. Climbing to the top of the hill, we inspected the old water tank to which the water was piped from the lake and from there by gravity feed to buildings on site.

A series of concrete slabs half-a-mile further on showed where the main station building was – "the hub of all activity," said Dad. Part of the old flywheel weighing ten tonnes or more was in evidence and he told me how it came to Clifden by train and how seventy men were employed for two weeks getting it out to the site.

The foundation of the mast was clearly visible, along with chains used to keep it in position, each link weighing about two stone. The further interrogations of a youthful mind elicited the information from Dad that the mast was over 300 ft high and the big steam-driven wheel was used to generate electricity. Nine boilers were in turn used to generate the steam which turned the flywheel. Native peat along with some coal was used to heat the boilers – "so there was no shortage of power in those days," he said.

For local people, one of the station's great attractions was to see it lit up against the skyline at night at a time when households had to do with oil lamps and candles.

Dad also told me about the canteen building, the place where workers would gather for a few drinks on a Friday evening after they had been paid, before heading home across the bogs to their families. On Saturday it was into Clifden for some shopping, then Mass on Sunday and a quiet day with families before heading off on Monday again for another week's work.

The information poured freely from my father's lips and before we knew it, it was time to return home for the tea. It was a memorable day in my life, the day when I learned about Marconi, the inventor of wireless telegraphy, the station named after him at Clifden, and the workers associated with it who gave it life for so many years.

"Marconi was a genius, son," said Dad, as he picked our way home along the bog roads. He was indeed, and that night as I slept I dreamt about the famous inventor and days gone by.

Written by Marty Conneely

Maam Cross Station, July 1934.

Active Service

West Connemara Brigade, April 23, 1921

Galway and Mayo did not come actively into the fight for freedom until the spring of 1921. That they had not been in it earlier was by no means due to reluctance on the part of the men to fight but mainly because GHQ had delayed the formation of independent brigades in these areas until late in 1920. Prior to that battalion officers were not permitted to carry out operations which did not have the approval of their brigade authorities. As a result, opportunities for action were lost whilst detailed plans were being examined at brigade level, and the enemy was able to concentrate his strength against IRA forces who were active in other areas.

Richard Mulcahy, Chief-of-Staff of the IRA, came to Connemara, under an assumed name, in September 1920, to convalesce following an illness. While in the west he was the guest of the late Thomas O'Malley, Kilmilkin, Maam, who was a brother of the surgeon, Michael O'Malley, Galway. Mulcahy told me that GHQ had considered the Army organisation in Galway too unwieldly to be effective, and that it had been decided to break it down into independent brigades, each responsible to GHQ only. Connemara was to constitute one such brigade. A meeting of the principal Volunteer Officers of the area was immediately called and the new developments were explained and discussed. In order to be in readiness for the change-over four battalions were formed and their officers appointed. The commanding officers were: No 1 Battalion (Leenane), Thomas O'Malley, No 2 Battalion (Rosmuck), Colm O'Gaora; No. 3 Battalion (Roundstone), Jim King; No. 4 Battalion (Clifden), Gerald Bartley. The battalion commanders were instructed to proceed at once with the organisation of their areas and to collect money for the purchase of arms. By the end of October I had received the sum of £120 from the battalion officers, which was a very good return considering the poverty of the area and the fact that neither the members of the IRA nor its supporters were amongst the wealthy.

About the first week of November 1920, I received a despatch from GHQ confirming my appointment as Commanding Officer of the newly-founded West Connemara Brigade, and instructing me to report at GHQ on November 12th. (Michael O'Droighnean, Furbo was appointed OC.East

Connemara Brigade). When I attended there the members of the Staff wanted to know when we could go out on active service and I replied that we were ready and would go when we had sufficient arms. I handed over the £120 which I had brought with me, and was given assurance that the necessary arms would be sent to us with the least possible delay. Following several visits to Dublin by Brigade Quartermaster, J. Feehan, we had acquired eleven rifles by the end of February, 1921. Five of these rifles were magazine type, five Martini single-shot carbines and one Howth rifle. In addition we had about a dozen revolvers and automatic pistols, and a similar number of shotguns. We had approximately sixty rounds of ammunition for each rifle and about a dozen for each revolver and shotgun. The Brigade Council decided that an active service unit should be mobilised at once, and on March 10th the men assembled for that purpose at a previously arranged rendezvous in the Twelve Pins, within easy reach of the Clifden/Galway road, and about seven miles from Clifden, across country.

For the four days following, we manned an ambush position on the Clifden/Galway road, as a result of information we had received that a lorry or a couple of lorries of RIC used that road daily. We had no luck, and, considering our armament, we might, in fact, have had all the luck that was going. At all events, the enemy did not appear there, so we decided to go into Clifden to make contact with him. On the night of March 16th the Column entered the town, six of the men carrying side arms, to engage a party of four RIC and Black and Tans, who comprised the usual nightly patrol of Clifden, while the remainder of the IRA force occupied positions to keep the barrack covered and prevent reinforcements going to the assistance of the patrol. Only two of the enemy went out on patrol that night, and they were duly eliminated. When their arms and ammunition had been collected the six IRA men linked up with the main body again, and the Column then moved out. On April 6th we collected a Lee Enfield rifle and two Webley revolvers with ammunition, after a partly successful ambush at Screebe, Rosmuck.

In our headquarters in Padraic O'Maille's house at Mounterowen, we received information from a source that we considered to be reliable, to the effect that the enemy had planned to carry out an extensive round-up of the Maam valley, from Cornamona to Leenane, with both regular military and RIC employed for the purpose. We decided to await their coming to Mounterowen and to give a good account of ourselves against them. Mounterowen House was set on the side of a hill, and faced north, about two hundred and fifty yards from the Maam/Leenane road. Between it and the main road flowed the Maam river, about fifty yards in from, and almost parallel to, the road. The river is about twenty yards in breadth at that point, and was crossed there by stepping-stones, with a shallow ford for horse-drawn traffic. The stepping-stones have since been done away with, and the river is now spanned by a bridge, about a hundred yards west of where they had been. Immediately behind the house the land rises steeply to a height of about three hundred feet, beyond which the broad Leagh Valley stretches south to the Maamturk mountains. To the west Mount Roighne rises to about fourteen hundred feet.

In preparation for the expected raid, every rifleman had been allotted a fixed position on the face of the hill to the rear of Mounterowen House, to both sides of the house itself. Every man knew the position he was to occupy when the enemy arrived. We assumed the enemy would set out from Cornamona at daybreak and arrive at our positions about noon. Constant watch was maintained for him, but day followed day without his forces being sighted, and we had begun to think that it might have been the RIC who started the rumour, with the intention of scaring us out of the area. There was no fear that the Column would withdraw to avoid contact with the enemy, for we were anxious for a good fight to justify our existence as a fighting unit. As our headquarters was less than three miles from Maam RIC barrack, sentries were posted on the lookout during daylight, and at night regular guard was mounted with an officer in charge, who changed the sentries every two hours. This was done to prevent our being taken by surprise during the night.

On the night of April 22nd the guard was mounted as usual, and the sentries had instruction that anything suspicious should be reported immediately to the officer of the guard. Before daylight I was awakened by someone shaking my shoulder. I opened my eyes and saw the officer of the guard standing by my bed. In response to an urgent question by me, he replied

Members of the West Connemara Brigade with supporters outside Mulranney Hotel.

that there were dark objects approaching over the road from Maam but, that because of the darkness, he had been unable to determine whether they were men or cattle. I jumped out of bed immediately and told him to rouse the rest of the men and get them outside, while I was going down to have a look. I just pulled on my breeches, jacket and boots which remained unlaced, grabbed my rifle, bandolier and haversack, rushed downstairs and out to the front of the house. It was then about three o'clock and starting to get bright, so that I had no difficulty about identifying the objects as police. They were clustered in a group, about a hundred yards from the stepping-stones, and it looked as though they were then being given last minute instructions for a raid on Mounterowen House.

The men of the Column were all ready when I rejoined them. I then gave them instructions to man the fences that extended from both sides of the house, and not to fire a shot until the RIC at the end of the stepping-stones would be in a cluster on the bank. We were then to fire as fast as we could before the enemy broke for cover. The range was 200 yards. My men quickly spread out to occupy their positions, and while they were doing so the police began to mount their bicycles and to cycle towards the stepping-stones. Three of them had already entered the by-path when a revolver shot was accidentally discharged by a policeman amongst the group still on the main road. Almost immediately an answering rifle shot rang out, fired by one of my own men from the right of the position, despite orders that fire should be withheld until the police had come to the river. The element of surprise, on which we had counted, was thus destroyed, for the police immediately scattered without attempting to advance against the house. Some of them dashed to the north side of the road and took cover in a depression made there by a mountain stream that flows beneath the road and into the Maam river. Others got down behind low banks near the road. They were already down by the river when the rifle shot was fired. I had one of them in my sights, from my position beside the pillar of a wicket gate to the left front of the house. He was standing at the far end of the stepping-stones, apparently making up his mind whether to cross the river or not. I squeezed the trigger. There was a faint click. The cartridge had misfired. I quickly ejected the dud cartridge and shoved up another, but found that I could not get the bolt quite home. Apparently the bullet from the faulty cartridge had remained in the breach, so I took a stone off the top of the wall and used it to hammer the bolt home. The extra seconds required to do this had probably saved the policeman's life, as before I was ready to fire, he had taken cover behind a big block of bog oak which had been left on the river bank following a flood.

When I fired my double-bullet shot I was extraordinarily lucky to get away with nothing worse than a severe 'kick' on the shoulder, in return for the doubtful satisfaction of lifting a sod in front of the policeman's position.

Early in the engagement some of our men were inclined to waste ammunition in their excitement, but the officers quickly got them under control, reserving their fire for visible targets. As the enemy kept well under cover, our fire was eventually reduced to what was sufficient to keep him engaged. Most of his fire seemed to be controlled and in volleys that were to a great extent concentrated on the house, which was then empty of men. All through that day Mrs Eamonn O'Malley with her two young children and her sister-in-law remained in the kitchen at the rear of the house, and managed to send out to us some welcome hot tea with bread and butter. Although we were only 250 yards from the police positions, it was impossible to see a target to fire at, and we concentrated on keeping them pinned down.

When the fight had been in progress for some time, it occurred to me that the force of police, which I estimated to number no more than twenty-five, could hardly expect to capture us unaided, and that its purpose must be to hold us there while another enemy party was crossing the mountain and coming through Leagh Valley to take us in the rear. Accordingly, I decided to send a man to the shoulder of the hill from which he would have a view of the valley, and be able to give us timely warning of an enemy advance from that direction. The man I picked for the task was John Dundass, Adjutant of the Roundstone Battalion, whom I knew to be a fearless soldier. I told him what I wanted done. It was a dangerous mission, as it entailed running up the bare face of the hill, carrying his shotgun and haversack, with twenty or twenty-five RIC firing at him from 250 yards range. I told him to wait until the police had fired one of their volleys and then to run for it. Behind the fence, he was on his toes like a sprinter waiting for the starter's gun, and as soon as the next volley had cracked out, he was way up the hill. The police fire lifted immediately as they tried to get him, and I held my breadth as their bullets kicked up sods at his heels and all about him. To my intense relief, he arrived safely at the crest of the hill, and then, instead of diving to safety, he deliberately turned round to thumb his nose at the police and give them the 'international phrase' which was, however, drowned in rifle fire.

Around noon the fine weather which had prevailed gave way to heavy showers and these, at times, reduced visibility to about thirty yards. I decided to avail of the cover thus created to withdraw my entire force to the shoulder of the hill, where we would have greater freedom of movement should enemy reinforcements arrive. To get there we had to work our way along towards the right under cover of the fence we had manned, until we reached a sheep path which leads into the valley. About thirty yards of the steepest part of the path had been is plain view of the police, with no cover, but the shortening of visibility enabled us to negotiate that exposed stretch in relative safety. Once behind the shoulder of the hill we were able to take stock of the situation and to see whether anything could be done to dislodge the police from the positions they were holding. As there was no cover between them and the house that would enable us to close on them. It was decided to send G. Bartley and R. Joyce to the right, and J. Feehan and J. King to the left to work behind the police in order to encircle them. Because of the nature of the ground, these four men had to make wide detours to get round unobserved by the police. When they had succeeded in doing so, they found that, though within 150 yards of the police and directly above and behind them on the mountain, such was the conformation of the ground that they could get no sight of them. They saw only one of the enemy lying near a bank and had fired a few shots at him before they realised that he was already dead.

Three men, armed with shotguns only, were sent towards Leenane to demolish or barricade a bridge about a half-mile distant on the Leenane road in order to hold up lorries of reinforcements that might come from Clifden. While they were procuring some tools in a house near the bridge, Thomas F. Joyce of Leenane, drove by in a Ford car, and had passed before they had time to get back to stop him. There was a workman in the car with him, and they had some stakes and wire to repair fences on grazing land of Joyce's at Kilmilkin. Apparently there was a lull in the firing at the time and Joyce, unsuspectingly, had driven into the middle of the ambush when an RIC man suddenly appeared and leapt on the running board of the car and ordered him to drive through, at revolver point. Gerald Bartley and Dick Joyce fired on the policeman immediately that they saw him on the car, but they had to be sparing of ammunition, as they had less than fifty rounds apiece when the engagement began. The RIC man was hit on the arm but managed to hold on until the car reached Maam. There he got a police driver to take a lorry to Maam Cross and phone for reinforcements. Soon afterwards a beggarman sauntered along the road from Maam, going towards Leenane, and apparently the police must have given him a message to take with him, for about an hour and a half later a Ford car arrived from Leenane. A tall man dressed in black got out of it. About that time we were spread out along the shoulder of the mountain, roughly about 700 yards from the police position and through the haze

West Connemara Brigade Flying Column pictured during the truce, 1921.

caused by the showers, the newcomer looked very like one of the R.I.C. Some of the boys loosed off a few shots at him and a number must have passed too close to be comfortable for he made a dive for cover. Not until that night did we learn that he was not a policeman, but the Revd Father Cunningham PP, who had got word through the tramp to go out to the scene of the ambush to attend to some wounded policemen. He was annoyed by what had happened when he arrived there, as he thought we should have recognised him and not interfered while he was ministering to the wounded. When he had got out of his car he threw his travelling rug over one of the doors. Due to the distance and the bad visibility, the rug looked, to Christy Breen, one of the boys, like an RIC man taking things easy and, as Christy so far had had the opportunity to fire but a few shots, this seemed a heaven-sent target. When he had fired four shots at it without apparent effect, Christy decided that he was either a rotten shot or that he had been mistaken in his surmise that the object was one of the enemy. It was learned next day that three of his bullets had struck the rug and car panel, which was remarkable shooting, considering the visibility and range. At that time we were firing very few shots, just one now and again to show that we were still about.

Ammunition was running low, and we had nothing to show for it. From our elevated positions it was then possible for us to look down on the enemy positions. Following the most careful search with my glasses, the only movement discernible was that made by a few policemen under cover at the end of the culvert on the far side of the road with the river between them and our positions. With the aid of the glasses, I could make out their rifle barrels sticking up over the edge of the bank, but here was no sign of any heads behind them. I got the idea that if two more men could work their way down and get close enough to the river without being seen, then, with the assistance of the four men already behind the enemy, it might be possible to rush his positions. I decided to try to go down myself, and took with me, Volunteer Tommy Coyne, a member of my old company, and a man in whom I had plenty of confidence. We set out on our trek downwards, carrying only side arms, as rifles would be a hindrance having in mind the nature of the ground. We alternated between crawling on our stomachs and rushing from cover to cover. We did not get by unobserved. Our progress was spotted by a lone rifleman who tried out his markmanship on us. Sometimes a bullet of his would smack off a stone and there would be a sound as though an angry hornet were buzzing past. We kept on and, following what had appeared to be an age, we reached the shelter of a good mound, where we sat up and stretched ourselves. When we had rested we looked about to size up the possibilities of the situation and were disappointed to find that these offered no hope for the successful carrying out of our idea of rushing the enemy. We were still more that 150 yards from the river, between us and which there was not a scrap of cover. I decided that it would be foolhardy to try further. We could make a detour towards Maam, and cross the river but we would still be too far from the culvert in which most of the enemy force lay. There was also the fact that some hours had elapsed since the RIC man had got away in Joyce's car, so that enemy reinforcements might be expected at any time. If they caught us in the positions we then occupied, we would be dead men. Nothing remained but to withdraw up the mountain, and we got safely back without the unknown marksman having succeeded in registering a hit. That we had returned unscathed could not be attributed to his concern for our personal safety, as several of his shots had come very close to us.

Immediately that we had regained cover behind the shoulder of the mountain, I searched the Maam road with the glasses for movement that would indicate the approach of enemy reinforcements. Sure enough, I spotted a line of lorries coming down from Maam Cross to the Maam bridge. We had barely returned to our mountain position in time. I decided to move the Column further up the mountain, for in the position held behind the shoulder of the hill, we would be in plain sight of anybody coming along the road from Maam. It was then 4.30 in the afternoon, and we had been engaged for thirteen hours.

From the cover of a boundary fence, higher up on the mountain, we watched with interest the arrival and disposal of the reinforcements. An armoured car was first on the scene, and it was followed by thirteen lorries loaded with military and police. Some of the lorries had halted half-a-mile away from the place where the police had been held to the ground, and the soldiers who had come out in them were then spread in extended order and were advancing over river and bog towards Mounterown House. The place was black with men running and firing their rifles and Lewis guns. Had we ammunition to spare we would have inflicted casualties, even though the range was about 800 yards. I had only five rounds left myself, and practically all the others were similarly circumstanced.

Apparently the enemy had a healthy respect for those he considered to be inside the house. To our amusement, his forces spend three-quarters of an hour getting to grenade-throwing distance of it, advancing in rushes that were covered by rifle and machine-gun fire. When they had worked in close they bombed it by throwing grenades through the windows. Finally they captured the place, empty except for Mrs Eamonn O'Maille, her two young children, and Miss Jane O'Maille, who were found at the back, in an outoffice in which they had taken shelter before the arrival of the reinforcements. When the house was found to be empty the police moved in and started to remove clothes, bedclothes and anything that took their fancy. They then set fire to the house and outoffices. The women and children were made prisoners and taken as far as Leenane, where they were released. There Michael B. King took them in for a time.

We then pushed on to Cuilleaghbeg, a village of a few houses, on the Leenane side of the scene of the fight, and about a mile away from it. We sent messages to Leenane for food and I can tell you that we were well and truly hungry by that time. We did justice to the food when it arrived, and having posted sentries, we rested a few hours. While in Cuilleaghbeg we learned that the police had one man killed and two wounded, and that when the reinforcements had turned up, the police who had been engaged in the fight were immediately sent in two lorries to Maam barrack. Nearly all of them had to be lifted into the lorries, they were so badly cramped through having been pinned down all day in positions that had permitted of no movement. Some of the police had to kneel in the stream without moving from the time they were driven into the culvert. It was the good fortune of the police that they had been able to get one of their number away to summon reinforcements. They had been on the point of surrender prior to that, as after the first half-hour, they saw no hope of extracting themselves from the position in which they were pinned. Most of them had come from Oughterard in two lorries in which they also brought bicycles. At Maam RIC barracks they picked up the sergeant and some more men, all with bicycles, and then the entire force pushed on, in their two lorries. The Maam sergeant, it seems, had reported that the police would have no difficulty about capturing the IRA men in Mounterowen House. It was his belief that, once the police had fired a few shots, we would bolt up the face of the mountain and they could then pick us off whilst we were running. They had left their lorries and two drivers about a mile short of Mounterowen House, and had cycled the remaining distance in order to take us unawares, by the silence of their approach. When the firing had broken out and continued without any sign of the police returning, the drivers moved up to investigate. We permitted them to approach as far as the culvert, and then forced them to take cover in it with those of their comrades already sheltering there. None of the men sheltering in this difficult position was able to move out of it until the arrival of the reinforcements, the RIC elements amongst which were under the personal command of Chief Commissioner Cruise.

The driver of the car which had brought Father Cunningham out to the two wounded RIC men, was the Vice O/C of the Brigade, J. J Connolly, who was employed as a driver mechanic at Leenane Hotel which is situated on the south shore of Killary bay. Though most anxious to come out on active service with us, he was ordered to remain in his employment at the hotel, for the contacts he made there provided us with useful information. He had spent some time with the British Army transport during the 1914-1918 war and, as he had never been openly identified with us, he was able to mix around with the police and military who patronised the hotel. When he had brought Father Cunningham to the ambush site, he found that it was not healthy to remain in the car, so he went down to the stream where the police were under cover, and heard their conversation.

When we had rested a few hours at Cuilleaghbeg, we retraced our steps and passed the scene of the recent fighting. The enemy had then withdrawn from the place. We turned north across the mountains to the village of Touwnaleen, where we remained for two days. At the end of that period we crossed the mountains to Killary Harbour which we crossed by boat to the north shore, and went to the house of Michael Wallace, father of two members of the Column. Whilst in Wallace's, we had refreshments drawn from supplies that had been sent there for us by Mrs. Cuffe of Leenane. We also found there a small marquee which J. J. Connolly had obtained for us from Mr McKeown. Having packed our supplies and the marquee, we continued across the shoulder of Ben Gorm mountain and entered the deep, bowl-like valley of Luggacorry, where we had cover on every side. We pitched our camp and decided to remain in the valley for some days, or until we had obtained more arms and ammunition from GHQ. Our attempts to collect armaments from the enemy had been attended by little luck.

Our headquarters had been set up in the valley for some days when J. J. Connolly arrived one night with a case that contained four Lee Enfield rifles, two .45 calibre revolvers, 103 rounds of .303 ammunition, 120 rounds of .45 ammunition and ten hand grenades. He had crossed from the south shore by boat, for there was difficulty about having a motor car on the road after dark, and besides, it was easier to bring us the case of arms by boat. Connolly laughed heartily and gave us reason to laugh, too, when he told us that soon after he had taken delivery of the case from Mr Kelly, the stationmaster at Maam Cross railway station, the car he was driving was held up by the sergeant and two constables from Maam RIC barrack, who wanted a lift to Maam. "Yes, of course," he replied, but added that the two constable's would have to sit on a crate of china, he had in the back of the car, for Leenane Hotel. One of them talked all the way to Maam about the fight at Mounterowen, and wondered where we had got the up-to-date rifles with which we had pinned them to ground. He would have been greatly surprised to know that he was sitting on a box of the best weapons that had come our way so far.

Because of our limited armament and the terrain over which we had to operate, it was impossible for us to engage the enemy patrols that were sent out after we had fired the first shots of the campaign in the west, in Clifden, on the night of March 16th. After that it was seldom that patrols comprised as few as two lorries. More often that not they were composed of four lorries, well spaced out. The bleak Connemara countryside, bare as the Twelve Pins, offered no approach cover to roads which, themselves, were not even bordered by fences. Bearing these factors in mind, and the meagre armament at our disposal, it will be realised that in such circumstances we would have no chance to survive against strong enemy forces. Kylemore Pass, the one place in the entire area where we could engage them with reasonable hope of success, they avoided like a plague. British convoys from Leenane to Clifden went round by Recess in order to avoid passing through Kylemore.

During the fortnight which comprised the last week of June and the first week of July, a huge round-up was carried out, over the country from Ballina to the Killary, through Castlebar, Newport, Westport and Louisburg. We were on the Mayo side of the Killary on the 29th of June, and about midnight information reached us that troops were being landed from destroyers to join in this great enemy operation. The men of the Column were immediately roused and we marched to Bundorragha where we obtained two boats and crossed to the Galway side just before daylight. We had barely disembarked and moved up the mountain when we saw two enemy observation planes circling the island at the mouth of the Killary, and along the Mayo coast. Soon afterwards two destroyers arrived off the coast and hundreds of men were put ashore from them on the Mayo coast to the north of the Killary. One of the destroyers came into the bay and landed about a hundred men on the north shore, at the foot of the Mweelrea mountain. All boats and currachs were collected by the enemy and taken in tow to where the destroyer had anchored near Leenane. The operation continued until July 10th, on which day there were nine lorries of Auxiliaries drawn up at Leenane when an IRA courier arrived from Dublin and contacted J. J. Connolly who brought him to me. The courier was the bearer of the Truce notice. Michael Kilroy of the West Mayo Column, and three of his officers were with me at the time. They had almost been encircled in the huge round-up, but had managed to keep outside the enemy ring. As happened in the case of the round-up which followed the Mounterowen fight, not a single IRA man was captured.

One good result of our entry into the fight, late though it was in coming about, was the upset of enemy plans and calculations caused by the extension of the general campaign to our area which he had hitherto considered to be quiet and safe. Our activities drew upon West Connemara military and police which had previously formed part of forces that had been pressing the IRA columns in other places west of the Shannon, and the diversion thus created accorded more breathing space to the columns concerned. Soon after the Mounterowen fight, the British launched a great round-up in our area and employed more that a thousand troops and police on the operation, with planes to guide them. All males between the ages of sixteen and sixty were brought to Maam RIC barrack, to be identified. Not a single IRA man was caught in the net, though we had barely crossed over to the north of the Killary before all the mountains to the south were combed by the enemy.

Here is the list of names of the men who participated in the fight at Mounterowen, without ranks except in the cases of the Brigade and Battalion officers:– P J McDonnell, Brigade OC J. Feehan, Brigade QM Martin Conneely, Brigade Adjutant: Colm O'Gaora OC No 2 Battalion (Rosmuck): Jim King, OC No 3 Battalion (Roundstone); Gerald Bartley, OC No 4 Battalion (Clifden): Thomas Coyne, John C. King, Richard Joyce, Peter Wallace, Patrick Wallace, William King, Padraic O'Maille and E. O'Maille, all of the No. 1 Battalion. John Dundass, Michael Conroy, John King, John Conneely, Denis Keane, Stephen Mannion, all of No 3 Battalion. Thomas Madden, Paul Bartley, Christy Breen, William Conneely, Laurence O'Toole all of No 4 Battalion. These men are now scattered. Many have found a livelihood in foreign lands, and some are already in their graves. The cause for which they fought and were willing to give their lives, lives on, and it may be that those of us who still remain will yet witness its fulfilment and share in the complete freedom of all our country from foreign rule. If that privilege is not to be ours, we can but hand down the traditional love of freedom that has ever animated our race, to those who come after us, and pass on to join our departed comrades, thanking God to have lived in a generation that succeeded at least in driving the British invader out of twenty-six of our thirty-two counties.

Written by Peter J. McDonnell
(Formerly O/C West Connemara Brigade I.R.A
and Commander West Connemara Brigade Flying Column)
From 'I.R.A in the Fight for Freedom', by kind permission of Anvil Books

Gerald's Republic

Sir Henry Lawson, a Lieutenant General in the British Army during the Anglo-Irish war, assessed the type of man who formed the nucleus of the IRA in the countryside as follows.

Gerald Bartley O.C. 4th Battalion. IRA West Connemara Brigade

"The Captains of volunteers appear to almost all have been quite young men, farmers' sons for the most part, some of them schoolmasters, most with what for their class, must be considered a good deal of education, ignorant however of the world and many things, but as a class transparently sincere and single minded idealists, highly religious for the most part and often with an almost mythical sense of duty to their homeland. These men gave to the task of organising their volunteers their best in mind and spirit. They fought against drunkenness and self-indulgence and it is no exaggeration to say that as a class, they represented all that was best in the countryside. They and their volunteers were trained to discipline, they embibed the military spirit, the sense of military honour etc. and then as now, they looked upon their army as one in the very real sense, an organisation demanding implicit obedience and self abnegation from rank to rank. The Irish Republican Army seems to be particularly free of ruffians of the professional type and the killings of police and others sometimes under circumstances which evoke our horror, were almost certainly done by members of the IRA acting under military orders, young men imbued with no personal feelings against their victims, with no crimes to their record and probably then, shedding blood for the first time in their lives. Behind their organisation lies the spirit of a nation".

My uncle Gerald became a member of the local IRA unit in his area at the tender age of seventeen. During the first half of the War of Independence, from January 1919 to July 1920 his main operational area was South Mayo where he assisted local IRA units along with Jack 'the Brigadier' Conneely from Clifden and Pete McDonnell and Jack Feehan from Leenane. Some of these operations were led by Ernie O'Malley. There was little or no activity in West Connemara at this time. Gerald understood that if a concerted effective military campaign was to be launched against Crown forces and police in the region, then there was a need to train a select bunch of men in the art of soldiering with particular emphasis on guerilla warfare. When GHQ reorganised the West Connemara Brigade into four battalions in late 1920, Gerald was appointed OC of the 4th battalion. Gerald was a natural leader. He was a very intelligent self-educated man, forever reading when he got the chance. He was totally dedicated to the cause and was all the time organising. He was extremely disciplined. While other lads would use time off to go for a drink, Gerald would be studying books. He drank only the odd bottle of Guinness. After the Civil War he achieved a degree as a solicitor and later as a barrister of law. He became a fluent Irish speaker after spending some time on the Aran Islands. He had great regard for the men under his command. In order to prepare these men mentally and physically for the hard days ahead, he set up an outdoor training camp in an isolated mountain valley near Recess, called Lissoughter. It was a very safe place to train because British Forces would never risk venturing into remote mountainous areas during the war. To this day, Lissoughter is still referred to as "General Bartley's Republic" by the people who live there. It was from this base that the West Connemara Flying Column operated a lot into South Mayo. Gerald once told me that the Mayo people stood by them everywhere they ventured, but that Clifden was not a safe place for them, because there were too many people living there who were pro-Establishment and anti-IRA. I remember asking him once "Why did you spend so much time in Mayo, particularly after the burning of Clifden which included your own mother's house?" I continued, "There were two bridges either side of Clifden which you could have blown up, and then you could have fired at the Crown forces from the surrounding hills on all sides, yet you chose not to take this course of action". He replied as follows "I'll explain that to you now. We knew of the Black and Tans coming to Clifden but we got very little support in Clifden. In fact it was dangerous for us to be around Clifden. We didn't have the co-operation of the ordinary people so we decided, we'd stay employed in Mayo where the local people were behind us. We had an awful lot of people in the surrounding countryside interested in us and all for us, but there was awful small participation. We couldn't get them to go with the gun".

General Headquarters in Dublin supplied nearly all the arms and ammunition. Guns and grenades were procured in Galway City on a regular basis. The column also had an armoured vehicle for transport which was usually driven by Jack the Brig. The 4th Battalion were given a certain amount of money by GHQ to cover expenses. Most of the men were on social welfare, some used days off for making a few bob although this wasn't really an option for the men in the column who were very much leading the lives of professional soldiers. Most of their time was spent in mountainous regions where they slept rough. A lot of houses in South Mayo and West Connemara were ransacked in searches for Flying Column members. In one such raid on a house in Clifden, Gerald was concealed under the blankets in a bed with two women of the house. When the women were called upon to get out of the bed, they refused and luckily the soldiers didn't push the issue any further. He was captured at one stage along with a few others just outside Clifden on the Sky Road and immediately transferred to Belfast jail. Terence McSwiney, Lord Mayor of Cork, was interred there at the same time. It wasn't long before Gerald had orchestrated a mini-riot resulting in a lot of damage being done to the jail. This precipitated his transferral to Mountjoy jail in Dublin. He subsequently escaped from Mountjoy and made his was back to West Connemara.

Gerald was a participant in the Mounterown ambush under the overall command of Peter McDonnell. The Column had received information that a convoy of British soldiers would be passing through there, in the direction of Leenane. The convoy would, as was usually the case, be accompanied by an RIC man. One of the men who was positioned on a particular vantage point was given the responsibility of firing a shot when the convoy would pass through a particular stretch of road. This would be the signal to initiate the ambush. However, in his enthusiasm or possibly an error in judgement, he fired the shot a bit too soon and this enabled nearly all of the convoy to escape unhurt. One RIC man was killed and two others were injured without any casualties on the IRA side. However the arrival of reinforcements from Galway city forced the column to retreat to the hills. Gerald told me that some column members started to argue among themselves subsequently. The man who fired too soon was accused of being with the British and Tommy Madden wanted to shoot him. Gerald was forced to intervene and he calmed the situation with the following words, "Lads, everyone sit down first and I'll talk then after ten minutes". There was silence for the next ten minutes. Gerald then proceeded as follows. "We were in Mayo last night. We're all tired. If we shoot one another here on the hills, this morning, you'll have it written right across the daily papers in London, tomorrow morning. "IRA men shoot one another on the hills of Connemara". This would be a terrible situation to be in and I've no doubt in my mind that the man who fired the shot made a genuine mistake. He's as good a soldier as any of us here, as dedicated as any one of us. I'm advising you all to drop the matter now and try and get some sleep".

At Gerald's funeral in March 1975, I met a man down in the house in Salthill where Gerald was laid out. I noticed he was wearing a republican badge on his jacket and that he was crying. I offered a few words of consolation, namely that it must be so lonely and difficult for men of his and Gerald's calibre to be parting. He told me he was from Headford and that he was with the West Connemara Flying Column on the morning of the Mounterown ambush. He maintained that only for Gerald the men would all have shot one another. He told me that Gerald had such a great command, that he was so sensible and strong in his words and that he controlled the whole affair in a few minutes. Gerald was also involved in the Carrowkennedy ambush near Westport. He was helping out the local Flying Column and had no leadership role.Things went disastrously wrong and the column lost twelve men. Gerald told me later he was lucky to get out of it alive. In later years when I asked Gerald how many men he had killed, he refused to satisfy my curiousity. I remember his reply, "I'd prefer not to speak about those things, it's best forgotten about".

He was involved in the burning of the Marconi Station which many people locally never forgave him for. The men of the 4th Battalion took the petrol up to the station in relays before eventually setting it alight when they had sufficient quantities. Gerald explained to me later that he had no choice in this matter because the 4th Battalion had received a direct order from GHQ in Dublin. GHQ was anxious for the station to be destroyed because they saw it as a valuable line of communication for British Intelligence in the region. The 4th Battalion got a terrible knocking over the affair, because there had been seventy local men employed there. Gerald was sorry that all these people were now out of work in such hard times, but he was a soldier carrying out orders in a war of liberation and I suppose he believed that the means would ultimately justify the end. Marconi never rebuilt the station in Derrygimla moving instead to Cornwall.

Gerald was opposed to the signing of the Treaty in December 1921. He was a republican through and through and as far as he was concerned nothing less than a thirty-two county Irish republic could ever justify the hardship and the horror of the Anglo-Irish War. He was very loyal to De Valera and never felt that De Valera shirked his responsibilities as President of Sinn Fein by sending Michael Collins to London instead of going himself. He was a reluctant participant in the Civil War, but because of his strong beliefs he felt duty bound to fight on the republican side. He was involved in the Ballinaboy ambush in which a Free State soldier was killed on the Bog Road to Roundstone. This caused a lot of friction and military exercise in the area. Some time later, two IRA men from Kiltimagh in Mayo, James and Morrisson were sent on a reconnaissance mission to West Connemara. They were told to report their findings directly to Gerald Bartley. One Sunday morning they were having their lunch in an elevated area close to the site of the old Ballinaboy school. Mass was celebrated in the school every Sunday morning. On this particular Sunday morning a Free State supporter from the Errismore area hid behind the school when Mass was on and when everyone had left, he proceeded to ambush the two IRA men who were unarmed. The two men were taken initially to Lowry's in Ballinaboy and subsequently to Clifden where they were given medical attention on the street outside the old barracks. It was in such circumstances that they breathed their last. The attack which resulted in their deaths was a reprisal for the Ballinaboy ambush.

During the Civil War, Gerald was based a lot in Lissoughter. There were a lot of sporadic shootings in the region but no major ambushes. Gerald had a Thompson gun and somebody wrote a song called "Gerald Bartley and the Thompson Gun". On one occasion during the war, Gerald was in a house in Goulane, just outside Clifden, with a few other IRA men when the house was surrounded by about forty Free State soldiers. Gerald, who had the Thompson gun, was the only one armed. At one stage Tommy Madden, who could be quite outspoken at times, said to Gerald, "Bartley is there nothing up the breach of that gun you've got" to which Gerald replied, "Tommy, if I was to fire a shot from that gun, we would all be executed here. It wouldn't be a wise thing at all for me to fire a shot". The IRA men were arrested without a struggle and interned in Galway jail. At that time it was common knowledge that republican soldiers were being executed from time to time. It seemed that the West Connemara men were about to face the same fate. One Sunday night, one of the prison officers informed them that they were going to be executed the following morning at 7 a.m. in Tuam. Gerald wrote a letter to Jack 'the Brigadier' Conneely. He managed to scale the wall of the jail and flag down a passing female cyclist who fortunately for him was also on the republican side. He instructed her to get the letter to Jack the Brig that night. She didn't let Gerald down and that night the letter found its way to Jack. It instructed Jack to inform the strong Free State men in the area that if Gerald Bartley or any of his men were executed the following morning in Tuam, then there would be four Free State men taken out for every one of his men. Dick Joyce who was ex-4th Battalion, quickly sent word into Galway jail to release Gerald and his men to avoid fatalities on the Free State side. Gerald and his men were subsequently released.

During the Troubles, Gerald and the men under his command were notified in writing by the Archbishop of Tuam, that they were to be excommunicated from the Catholic Church. The same applied to women like Maggie Dundas, Maggie Joyce, Peig Clotherty and her sister Anna who were in Cumann na mBan. Gerald believed that it was certain people in Clifden who had given their names to the Archbishop. Some of the men, like Jack the Brig, took it very hard and consequently never returned to the practice of their faith. Gerald believed that the Archbishop acted wrongly but Gerald was always a man of strong faith and he never believed the Archbishop's course of action could ever justify him turning his back on God. When the troubles were over, the Archbishop announced that all those people who had been excommunicated were now welcome back to the Church. His sister Anna, an extremely religious woman, dedicated her whole life afterwards to the local church.

Remembered by Gerald Bartley and written by Paul Gannon

Another Era – Same Place

When the Anglo-Irish War ended in July 1921, many had hoped that the bloodshed of those traumatic years would be replaced by a period of calm progression bringing the new independent Irish state to take its rightful place among the nations of Europe.

Alas it was not to be, and even before the ink was dry on the Anglo-Irish Treaty of 1921, differences had already emerged which would lead to non-political means being employed to achieve a democratic goal. When the treaty was announced that fateful winter of '21, it gave the 26 counties the freedom to conduct normal day-to-day affairs with no outside interference. However, written together with this was a clause which contributed in an indirect fashion to armed conflict on the streets. Members of the elected Irish parliament were required to take an oath of allegiance to the British empire which effectively meant that the area of southern Ireland comprising the 26 counties was a dominion and not a republic as originally requested. Although the document was ratified by Dáil Éireann, it was totally unacceptable to its opponents. During the War of Independence, the weapons of war were all firing in the same direction, but a deep split was rapidly emerging. The national government in Dublin lost no time in establishing the normal functions of state which included the formation of the national army which would be known as the Free State Army. It drew into it, ranks of men who had fought with the volunteers, but equally so there were many who aligned themselves with the anti-Treaty side known during the course of the war as the irregulars. In Connemara as in much of Connacht, a majority of people took the anti-Treaty side, and while there was deep reluctance to start a shooting war, particularly against former comrades, it finally came to a head in June 1922. Clifden found itself in the hands of the Republican forces at this time as was true of most of Connemara. However, in army headquarters in Galway, a plan was devised to capture the town and its environs, for it was a strategic communications centre. With the advance of Free State troops from Mayo heading south, the plan was to make a pincer movement with forces from Galway. Although obstructions of many kinds were prepared, the element of surprise was an ace card in the hands of army intelligence in Galway.

On Monday 14 August, ships entered Mannin Bay carrying a large body of government forces who proceeded to secure positions at Ballinaboy, before heading to capture Clifden. The situation was not to last too long, for in October, Republican forces from Co Mayo came south and secured Clifden after heavy fighting in the streets. Following this rather amiable standard of war activity and resulting low casualty rates, the situation took a turn for the worse in November 1922 when executions and reprisals increased. The government in Dublin had begun to get tough with anti-Treaty forces and the death penalty was introduced to prohibit the carrying of weapons by anyone other than government forces. Many actions took place in the local area as military activity on all sides became the order of the day. With the national situation growing increasingly desperate for the anti-Treaty side, it was unsurprising that when winter arrived in January 1923, the fight was effectively over. With the capture for the second time of the capital of Connemara in December '22, anti-Treaty forces began to retreat to the hills, particularly the Twelve Bens and mountain terrain in South Mayo. Realising the war was lost, a campaign got underway throughout Connemara, and the coastguard station at Bunowen was among those destroyed. During the early spring months of 1923, the Free State Army was in control of most of the newly independent Irish state. A final push was declared on the Ballyconneely/Clifden area which resulted in the arrest of large numbers of irregulars, including their commanding officer, who displayed textbook leadership against the odds. The war had ended in West Connemara. As May 1923 approached, the cause of the anti-Treaty side was effectively over. A painful memory was about to be born. The divisions which had occurred would take many generations to overcome. In many cases, the people who had fought against friend and neighbour, maintained that silence was the only way to put that part of their lives behind them.

Perhaps it was the looming of another war that brought such a rapid and hastily-arranged erosion of bitter memories, for in September 1939, with the future of our small coutnry once more in a precarious position, people from what were two opposing sides joined together to serve their country above all else. This was to be the testing moment. The silence had returned to the tranquil countryside. A new era had begun to dawn.

Written by Michael John King

The Burning

Many stories have been written about the burning of Clifden by the Black and Tans on the 17th March, 1921. The history of my family would not be complete without a reference to it. I can only relate what was told to my by my sister Mary and other family members. My mother seldom spoke of it. Anytime I asked her to share her memories of that night with me she changed the subject. I suppose the memories were too painful to recall.

On the 14th March 1921, Tommy Whelan, a local boy from outside Clifden, was executed in Kilmainham Jail in Dublin. Tommy was hanged for an alleged shooting at a bakery in Dublin. On the night of the 16th March 1921 two policemen, named Reynolds and Sweeney, were detailed for duty on the square in Clifden. Reynolds was a native of Rooskey, Co Leitrim, and Sweeney was from Donegal.

Before going on duty they visited my home. One of them asked my sister Mary who was then a young girl of twelve years for some shamrock. She proudly pinned a sprig on each of their uniforms to honour our patron St Patrick, whose feast was the following day. They left my home for duty on the square. Shortly after 9 p.m. my family heard two shots. Reynolds and Sweeney were both shot dead. No one was charged with this shooting. It was alleged that the deed was carried out by a maverick group of the IRA. It was a reprisal for the hanging of Tommy Whelan. The shamrock on their uniforms was saturated with their blood. The local people were shocked and terrified.

My father, Willie Clancy (known as Boston), had just been released from Galway Jail (the site where the present Galway cathedral stands). My mother told me he was sent to jail because he was minding some ammunition for the boys on the run. My father was not a member of the local flying column but he was a contact person for the Republicans. He gained information for them about the movements of the British soldiers and the Black and Tans. He also stored their ammunition. He dug a hole in the garden at the back of our home and kept the ammunition there. In the month of February the weather was quite wet. He was afraid the ammunition would get wet in the garden so he transferred it to a safe hiding place in the house. Shortly after that the house was raided and Daddy was sent to jail. He spent some weeks there. As a result of dampness and malnutrition he developed pneumonia. Many pleas were made to the authorities to release him. It was all of no avail until Canon McAlpine, PP, Clifden, travelled to Galway where he met the Governor of the jail. He pleaded with him to release my father and added that he had left a wife and young family in Clifden. Later my father was released. He had many stories to tell of his time in prison. One was that nightly he heard the rattle of chains going up and down the corridor outside his prison cell. It was believed that it was the ghost of Ulick Joyce who was hanged in innocence for the Maam Treasna murders.

My father had just returned from jail when the policemen were shot so he was a very sick man the night the Black and Tans came to Clifden. The Black and Tans were sent over to Ireland from England to chastise the Irish. They were supposed to be the scum of English prisons who were sent to help the British Army. They were nicknamed Black and Tans by the Irish because they wore black tunics, tan pants and black caps. The Black and Tans were a noted pack of foxhounds in Tipperary – hence the name Black and Tans.

On the morning of the 17th March around 3.30 a.m., my mother was awakened from her sleep by a banging at the hall door. When she awoke she saw eight men rushing at the hall door. They wore balaclavas and carried guns. They asked for the whereabouts of my father. Dad was a man of ready wit. When he heard the noise downstairs he disappeared from the bed and hid in a press in the wall. The men searched around the room but they were so drunk they did not notice the press. They left the room and went downstairs. A member of the RIC who was a friend of my father came into the bedroom and told my mother to leave the house immediately as the Black and Tans were about to set it on fire.

She immediately left with her children. Mary the eldest was about twelve years; Tom the third eldest was six years and Padraic was just a baby of thirteen months. The second eldest James was not in Clifden that night. He was in Co Meath with his maternal grandparents – Thomas and Maria Mongey of Mullagha, Stackallen, Navan. When they came down the stairs the house was already on fire. They had no time to get any clothing. They were turned out on Main Street in their night attire.

My mother kept lodgers then. One was a railway porter called Mc Keanealy. He worked at the Clifden Railway Station. My father borrowed his uniform and escaped from the house as a railway porter. He joined my mother on the street. He winked at her and said, 'Will I carry the child for you Mam?'. Mary and Tom were the last to leave the house. Mary recalls seeing all the Tans gathered on the landing on the stairs. They were all carrying guns and drinking whiskey that they had stolen from our bar.

The Station Master in Clifden at that time was a man called O'Rourke. His wife was a native of Co Meath. Being strangers in Connemara and coming from the same county, my mother and Mrs. O'Rourke became close friends. So when her home went up in flames she went straight to her friend at the Railway Station. Many other Clifden people whose homes were burned went to the Convent of Mercy where the Sisters gave them shelter and clothing.

I will now include a detailed report I received from Brigid A. O'Rourke (Mrs Reid, Salthill, Galway). Brigid is a daughter of Station Master O'Rourke and was an eyewitness on that fatal night.

At 10 p.m. on St Patrick's Eve, March 16th 1921, my father Peter J. O'Rourke, then Station Master at Clifden Railway Station got a phone message to say a special train was leaving Galway for Clifden with a troop of Black and Tans to take over the town and to arrest IRA suspects. At that hour of the night all his men were off duty, so he had to set off down the railway line to make the points for the train coming in. The train had to be stopped some distance away from the Railway Station. It could not be let into the Railway Station (the platform) because a train was already there ready to leave for Galway the following morning at 10 a.m.

He had his lamp and when he saw the oncoming train he turned on the red light so the driver stopped. Immediately the Captain in charge who was on the engine plate with the driver stepped down. He confronted my father with a gun, and questioned him. 'Was this a set up for them being ambushed'. My father then explained to him the reason why they had to get off there on the line and march into town. He treated him to a few blows of the butts of his rifle.

In our house that night two women were visiting – a Mrs. Canning (RIC man's wife) and a Mrs. O'Connell who had a shop near the station. They asked my father if he would leave them home, so again taking his lamp he left them as far as the railway gates. He was halted there and asked to help carry a shutter to Eddie King's Shop where a wounded policeman named Sweeney lay dying. They took him to the Cottage Hospital on the Galway road. He was also told that Charlie Reynolds another policeman was shot dead; both men were on duty outside Eddie King's shop. All this time bullets were whizzing by from the Dooneen hills. This all happened sometime previous to the coming of the trainloads of Black and Tans.

After his ordeal my father returned to the Station House. Mrs Canning and Mrs O'Connell had returned there and told my mother what happened. All of us children got out of bed. Next thing a bullet came into the bedroom where my father and mother slept. We were put under beds in our own room for fear of any more bullets coming in.

After some hours, my Dad heard a woman crying outside the door. She was saying, 'Peter, for God's sake let us in, our house is on fire'. The woman was my mother's friend, Mrs Willie Clancy. They were looking for Willie to shoot him, as he was an IRA suspect. In Clancys' house there were a number of railwaymen lodging including the crew of the morning train due out at 10 a.m. As the soldiers interrogated each one as they let them out the front door all kept answering 'I work at the Station'. Willie Clancy was the last one out. He was lame and very sick. One of them said to him: 'Are you a railway man too with a bad leg?' Willie answered: 'I hurt myself yesterday at the turntable in the engine shed at the station'. The soldier gave him a kick in the backside and said 'All you good for nothing railway men, clear out'. Then up goes the house in flames. Willie ran down to our house with only his trousers, a jacket and no shoes. My mother put him lying on the sofa, as he was a very sick man and all got tea.

Next morning, a Mrs Grennan came to our house with her son Dan, who was also a railway porter. They came in for the Mass (St Patrick's Day) and discovered there was no Mass, and the town was all burned down.

At 10 a.m. a knock came to our front door. When my father opened it, who was there but a platoon of soldiers with a sergeant-in-charge. They demanded the keys of the engine shed, the store, office, etc., They were looking for anyone who might be hiding there. He gave them the keys. While they were gone Dad was terrified they would raid our house and find Willie Clancy there. My father and Willie put our piano crossways in the corner. Willie hid behind it. My mother put an old tablecloth across it. The women all said the Rosary. When they came back with the keys after inspecting all the outhouses the sergeant-in-charge said to my father: "No need to inspect your house I am sure". I remember well my Dad having me by the hand. He said: "All that's around are a few people who were disappointed that there was no Mass, and a few railwaymen having to go on duty on the next train out". The sergeant then handed my father the keys and told his men who were standing at the front gate to march on. My father breathed a sigh of relief. He knew that if Willie Clancy was found in our house, Dad would be shot dead for harbouring him and the Clancy family.

The next train that was to leave at 10 a.m. did not leave until 3 p.m. The Clancy family had to be fed and clothed. The children got all our clothes, our cloaks, shoes etc., Mrs. Clancy got Mammy's clothes, and a suit of Dad's for Willie. They all got on the 3 p.m. train. Mrs. Willie and the children got tickets. They had no money as all was lost in the fire, but Dad gave them tickets for Oughterard. Willie was a native of Glann, Oughterard. Willie was put into what was called a fish van with the air able to get in for him. It was arranged with the driver and guard of the train that when they came to Oughterard he was to be let off and hide until someone he knew came for him.

The town was a wreck after the burning. Many shops were burned. A young man named Joe McDonnell was also killed. He was a cousin of Willie Clancy's. Willie's brother Pete Clancy, an ex RIC man was also shot.

The Black and Tans took their train back to Galway at 8 p.m. They took any amount of cigarettes and whiskey with them that they found by looting. I always heard my father say that these men were really ruthless. They were all ex-convicts out of English jails. All the men on the train that night known as the Black and Tans will never be forgotten by the people of Clifden who lived there at that time.

Brigid A. O'Rourke Reid

My sister Mary confirms Brigid's report, but adds that my father who was pretty ill then was taken from the Oughterard Railway Station to the hospital in Oughterard. Andy Darcy (father of Mrs. Jones Ferris) met every train with his pony and side-car. He brought Daddy to the hospital where he spent many weeks after that. Andy then drove Mammy, Mary, Tom and Padraic to Rath Hill in Gleann where they were looked after by my father's brother Matthias Clancy and his wife Maggie.

One month after that my mother's father Thomas Mongey died in Mullagha, Stackallen, Navan, Co Meath. My Uncle Matthias brought herself and the children to the train in Oughterard on the first leg of their journey to attend the funeral. From there they travelled to Galway and from Galway by train to the Broadstone Station in Dublin.

There was no transport from Dublin to Navan as the lines were blocked by the Black and Tans. However, my mother eventually got a lift from the man who drove the mail van to Navan. At first he did not want to take her as he had been searched every day en route by the Black and Tans. My mother pleaded with him. She was a very prayerful woman and assured him that Our Lady and the Sacred Heart would take care of them. He consented to bringing them. For the first time in weeks the mail van was not stopped even once. When they reached Navan all doors were closed to them. The daily papers carried stories of the burning of Clifden. People were afraid to let them in, as the papers also carried the story of the shooting of Pete Clancy, my father's brother. The Navan people thought it was my father who was shot.

Eventually, a friend of my mother called Mrs. Carpenter took them in. She had a small house but she gave them their own beds for the night. Next day my uncle Paddy Mongey came in his pony and trap to collect them. The Sacred Heart and Our Lady brought her home in time for her father's funeral. They remained in Mullagha for some weeks after that. During all this time my father was in the hospital in Oughterard.

When they returned to Clifden the family home was in ruins. My father rented a house from Bodkins in Market Street where Walsh's coffee shop is at present. It was known locally as 'Bostons'. It later became 'The Sinn Fein Club'. My brother Liam was born in that house on the 15th July 1922. My father got very little compensation to rebuild the house in Main Street. Kathleen Villiers Tuttle in her book '*Beyond the Twelve Pins*' stated that he got £2,000. That figure is not correct.

At the rebuilding of the house in Main Street an extra storey was added to the original structure. The family lived there until it was sold in the '70s about eight years after my mother's death.

My father's cousin, John Joe McDonnell, owned the Central Hotel in Clifden. He was related to my father through my grandmother Mary Geogheghan. John Joe was a Sergeant Major in the British Army during the 1914-1918 War (World War 1). He returned to Clifden after the war and ran a thriving business in his hotel in Main Street. He was there on St Patrick's morning 1921.

The Tans called him out and threatened to kill him. He told them he was loyal to the Crown and that he served in the 1914-1918 War. They would not listen to him. They accused him of being a member of the IRA. He denied this. They took him outside his hotel and fired a hand grenade at him. They blew his head off. His brains were scattered on the street. He was supposed to have been mistaken for his cousin Alex Higgins who was active in the movement.

Many stories have been told and re-told about the burning of Clifden and the assassination of John Joe McDonnell. One story is about a young curate, Fr Kelly who was being sent on transfer to Ballyconneely. He stayed in Clifden that night. On St Patrick's morning he came on the body of John Joe and anointed all that was left of his mortal remains.

Another story is about people who came into town to go to Mass in St Joseph's Church. The Tans told them to kneel down outside the Central Hotel and kiss the blood of their hero. The burning of Clifden had ill-effects on many families in Clifden, not least my own. My father never really got over it. He was only fifty-two years when he died in 1930. My mother was a widow for forty years. She suffered through a lot of poverty in the thirties and forties. My brother James died at an early age of seventeen years. My brother Tom never reached mental adulthood.

Yet in spite of all this, my mother reared and educated her family. She saw them all settled in good jobs and married. She loved her grandchildren and enjoyed their company until her death in 1970.

When my sister Mary recalls the night of the burning, her saddest memory was to see the stable being burned with her pet purebred Connemara pony called 'Fanny' neighing as he was burned alive. The cows were also burned and the Tans put the burned carcasses of the animals in front of the house. One of the Tans kept playing '*God Save the King*' on our piano and then started firing bullets into the keys. Some of the other houses that were burned were Bartleys, P. K Joyce's, Mattie Joyce's, Lydon O'Neill's, Alex Higgins', Katie Guilfoyle's.

My uncle Pete Clancy was a member of the RIC. When he was stationed in Limerick, he was obliged to resign from the force because he got black fever. With his wife Nora, he joined his brother Pat in Clifden and worked in the business there. He was there on the 17th March 1921. The Black and Tans tried to burn Uncle Pat's house. Pat was not at home. He was attending a cattle mart in Dublin. Pete put out the fire. He was then taken out to the back yard and shot by one of the Black and Tans while his wife Nora looked on. One of them shouted at her 'You'll be a widow in the morning'. Pete got three bullets in the neck – one went within one-eighth of an inch of the jugular vein. The Tans thought he was dead but Dr Joe Casey who was a GP in Clifden came on the scene. Pete was rushed fifty miles away to the old Central Hospital in Galway where he underwent surgery. Dr Michael O'Malley from Killmikin saved his life. Pete later bought a house in Glann, Oughterard on the shores of Lough Corrib which he called 'Island View'. He got compensation, which was very little.

Pete was never the same after the shooting. His speech was impaired. He suffered from a bad back. In later years he was the victim of Parkinson's Disease. He died in Galway in his late fifties. His niece Bridie Cowley cared for him in his old age.

Written by Phyl Clancy

CLIFDEN'S PATRIOT SON

My sons of Connemara!
Cast off your slumbering thrall,
Arise! Your country needs you
And hearken to her all.

It's not the weak she wants of you
But the bravest and the best,
To march to Mountjoy prison
Where young Whelan lies at rest.

For the murder of Captain Henry –
On that bleak November day,
They arrested Tommie Whelan
When spies sold his life away.

The jury found him guilty
And then, alas! Did cry –
"Our hearts are, Lord, for Ireland's cause,
Let Tommie Whelan die".

Yes! Ireland has reared noble sons,
But none more brave and true,
And at the age of twenty one
He died for Róisín Dubh.

So, you sons of Connemara,
Hoist up your flag of green,
Be ready and be waiting
For the cause of Rosaleen.

Written by John Joyce

Kilmainham Jail. Tommy Whelan, Clifden (executed 14th March, 1921) with two prison wardens.

Soldiers of Destiny

Gerald Bartley was elected to the Galway County Council in 1924 on a Sinn Fein ticket. He was to serve on the Council until 1932. After the split at the Sinn Fein Convention in 1926, he stayed loyal to DeValera and joined Fianna Fail. He ran for election to the Dail in 1932. The 1932 election to the Dail was a very difficult election. There was a lot of bitterness and intimidation everywhere. You were either a Fenian or a Blueshirt. Many's the fight that broke out at dances in Clifden and some people were beaten up after Polling day when it was found out who they had voted for. Gerald had some very loyal and dedicated election workers, most notably Paddy Mannion and Petie Savage. Paddy Mannion had travelled all over Connemara with Gerald in the 1920s setting up local Fianna Fail Cumanns in the different parishes. Petie Savage was a great character. On polling day in 1932, he travelled out to Val Mahon Terrace in Clifden with a wheelbarrow to carry in an old woman who couldn't walk to the Polling Station. On another occasion he called to the house of an ardent Free State supporter in Errislannan. The man in question was still very bitter over the burning of Marconi's. And what would you be wanting today Petie" he said. Petie replied "I'm canvassing", to which Stephen enquired. "And who would you be canvassing for Petie?" "Gerald Bartley", replied Petie. "And who burnt Marconi Station", Stephen asked. "Ah there was only one mistake there, Stephen" answered Petie. "What was the mistake?" asked Stephen to which Petie retorted in no uncertain terms, "That they didn't feckin burn you as well". It was that kind of election, in many ways, the political re-enactment of the Civil War.

Gerald secured a resounding success over his main rival Josie Mongan. He got the bulk of his support from South Connemara, the Aran Islands, Renvyle, Leenane, Cornamona, Oughterard and on into Galway city. He got very little support in Clifden and was very disappointed about this. He received no support at all in the Errislannan, Ballyconneely, and Roundstone areas because of the burning of Marconi Station. He moved to Galway City to live in the 1940's because he felt he needed to establish a high profile in the city to secure his seat in Dáil Éireann. It was a clever piece of foresight on Gerald's part, as he went on to hold his seat until 1965, spanning four decades of Irish political life. Canvassing was a much more colourful phenomenon in those days than it is today. Large crowds would congregate outside Clifden Church on a Sunday morning to support their respective candidates. On one such occasion Josie Mongan addressed his supporters as follows, "When a Josie Mongan voter wants to get Josie Mongan, he can get him in his home in Carna, but when a Gerald Bartley voter wants to find Gerald Bartley he has to try to find his way fifty miles into Galway". Gerald found out about these remarks and in a subsequent speech in Clifden he answered his adversary with the following words "It was remarked here on a platform in recent days by Josie Mongan that you can get Josie Mongan at home in Carna while you have to go to Salthill to get Gerald Bartley. I can tell ye now, in 1916 and those years, you found Josie Mongan at home but you didn't find Gerald Bartley at home."

Gerald didn't see eye to eye with DeValera who kept him very much on the backbenches even though it was apparent to many that he had the ability to take on ministerial responsibility. There were some older supporters in Galway who urged him to go on an independent Fianna Fail ticket, maintaining that he would still be elected without any difficulty. However Gerald would never consider leaving the Fianna Fail Party over such matters. He reminded these supporters that he was among the founder members of Fianna Fail and that DeValera wouldn't always be there. In the years that followed he went on to serve as Minister for Lands and Fisheries, Minister for the Gaeltacht and Minister for Defence as well as serving a number of Junior Ministries. I always considered Gerald to be every bit as good a politician as he was a soldier. He was a good socialist who always tried to look after the weaker sections of Irish Society, the ordinary worker, the small farmer, the poor people and he got several bills passed to this effect. He was particularly knowledgeable on the economy and carried the most up to date information and figures to the many clinics he held all over Connemara.

John Mannion is the only politician from West Connemara who has been elected to Dáil Éireann since Gerald Bartley retired from political life in 1965. I feel that Councillor J. J. Mannion from Clifden could well be the next man to make it if he makes a good go of the Council. He is not a 'Soldier of Destiny' like myself, but I worked closely with him at the time of the plebicite on the proposed airstrip outside Clifden and I found him to be a man of great ability, particularly in the area of public speaking. It would be a great thing for this region to have one of our own back in Dail Eireann again, regardless of his/her political affiliation.

The desire to get into politics was always in me. I was inclined in that direction ever since Primary School. I've always loved helping people and doing things for people. I first joined Fianna Fail in 1945 and much later on when I returned from England after ten years, I quickly rejoined the local Fianna Fail cumann. As the 1974 County Council election approached, a lot of people in the cumann started saying to me "You'll go in the next Council election, you're the man we want". I agreed to let my name go forward. My main political opponent was Padraig Joyce, who had served as a councillor for nineteen years and was seeking re-election. Originally a member of Fianna Fail, he was now running on an Independent ticket and curiously enough he had the backing of my uncle Gerald who asked me if I would consider standing down. I remember saying to Gerald at the time,"You're gone a number of years out of it Gerald. I might stand down but the people of Connemara won't vote Padraig Joyce in". "They will if you get behind them" said Gerald, to which I replied "I don't think so Gerald, I don't think so". Shortly afterwards I met Padraig myself on the street in Clifden. He too asked me if I would stand down. I felt I had to stand my ground. "Padraig" I replied, "You must listen to me, You're an Independent, I'm Fianna Fail forever: it's very unfair of you to ask me that question here on the street today. If you were Fianna Fail, Padraig, I'd be right behind you and work hard for you". "Is that the way it is with you " he said. "Ara, I'll walk through you anyway", he added and walked off. When the counting of votes was finished on Polling Day I had received 1450 preferences to Padraig's 250 and I was duly elected on the first count. I wasn't happy about all the acrimony in the lead up to Polling Day, but politics is a precarious business and candidates have to be tough and uncompromising at times to succeed.

I served as a Fianna Fail councillor from 1974 to 1985 and they were eleven great years for me. I had very much the same socialistic approach to politics as my uncle before me. I became very involved with the islands issue. After the Inishturbot disaster in 1974, the people there became quite disillusioned and wanted to permanently leave their island. I arranged a meeting in the Celtic Hotel in Clifden to discuss the matter. There was a member from every house on the island present and that night we discussed the length and breadth of it. Marcus McNamara from Aillebrack gave me great assistance. I persuaded them all to sign a petition stating their deep desire to move to the mainland. I gave the petition to Bobby Molloy to bring to Dublin. He passed it on in turn to George Colley who was the relevant Minister and he then got the Land Commission to make out an official estimate. The cost of buying the land and building seventeen houses came to £400,000. Mr Colley allocated the money, the land was purchased and the houses were constructed in different parts of West Connemara. A lot of local builders wanted the contract but when I went to the Department to negotiate on their behalf I was told, "We want proper modern houses built and we're employing a professional contractor to do the job". Moy Contractors in Galway city were subsequently given the contract and the people were all off the island in about one year. They're all working now on the mainland driving cars and paying their taxes (which they didn't have to do on the island) so I'm pretty sure that the £400,000 is well paid back by now.

I always had great admiration for island people, the way they survived and carried on without any of the facilities or infrastructure that we mainlanders take so much for granted. My uncle Gerald said to me back in 1974, "You're elected to the Council now, don't neglect the islanders, those people all need looking after". I spent a lot of time subsequently trying to help the people of Inishbofin. After long delays, Jack Lynch was finally persuaded to allocate the necessary funding to renovate the school which was in a very sub-standard condition. Electric light was another contentious issue and I spoke out strongly on behalf of the island people at one Fianna Fail Ard Feis in Dublin. Afterwards Jack Lynch told me he'd go ahead with it and shortly afterwards generators were installed on the islands. The pier was always high on the agenda and I was forever pushing this issue. Eventually after meeting with Charles Haughey about it one day in Galway, I got some satisfaction. He told me to send him all the details in a registered envelope and that he would take it from there. Soon after it was announced publicly that one million pounds had been allocated for the development of the pier on Inishbofin. I also helped secure an ambulance for the island and I was able to get some extra funding for the renovation of the dispensary. I took great satisfaction from getting things done for the island people and they were always very good to me on polling day in return.

The upkeep of the roads appears to be a never ending sorry saga in West Connemara. In 1978 after a long struggle I eventually persuaded George Colley to allocate £95,000 for six different roads in the Renvyle area, but apart from that I had very little satisfaction on this controversial issue. I had a great deal more success in relation to planning permission. At that time, if the Council turned down a planning application, County Councillors could invoke Section 4 to overturn the decision. The councillor in question had to obtain three signatures from within the chamber. Having obtained the three signatures, the councillors then voted either for or against invoking Section 4. At that time a majority of one was sufficient to overturn a refusal. Over the years I invoked a lot of Section 4s for people in West Connemara who had been initially refused Planning Permission. Fine Gael's John Mannion worked side by side with me on many of them. I could nearly always depend on him to be one of the three signatories.

Getting elderly people fixed up with their proper entitlements was also an area within which I was able to get a lot accomplished in those years. I felt a deep obligation to do everything I could for the more senior members of the community and to ensure that they were not being exploited in any way. I was on the Hospitalisation Board which was a Recommendation Board and didn't have executive powers. This Board dealt a lot with people's entitlements to various allowances. Fuel for old people was an area in which it was necessary for me to become involved on several occasions. I remember one particular instance concerning an old woman who lived on her own in Renvyle. She had been refused a fuel allowance on the grounds that she had money of her own, and was therefore not entitled to free coal. I went to the woman and persuaded her to tell me how much she had in the bank. She explained to me that she had £250 on deposit. I asked her whether she would be willing to sign an official document to that effect and she indicated her agreement. I went back to Clifden that evening to make arrangements for the delivery of her coal entitlement. I ordered a bag of coal from Diamond's to be delivered to keep her going whilst I contacted the powers that be in Galway the following day. I explained to the person in the Galway office that the woman in question was in living in such dire circumstances that there was a grave danger of her dying if she did not receive her fuel allowance. Later that day, Willie Diamond received a phone call from the office in Galway instructing him to deliver a half tonne of coal to the woman without any further delay. In a subsequent conversation with Willie, he told me that I had worked wonders because he was well aware that the woman in question had been refused a fuel allowance on several other occasions.

I recall another case in which a woman in Kingstown had been refused on the basis that she owned cattle. When I went out to see her and to investigate the situation, I discovered that she had in fact only one animal. I took responsibility for ensuring that she received her entitlement, and shortly after my visit, a half tonne of coal was delivered to her door. I did a lot of this type of work during my time in office and I would consider that coming to the assistance of old people was probably the most rewarding aspect of my work.

I was a member of the Library Committee. The Council either owned or hired the libraries and it was also the Council who employed the Librarians. I used to always go to Sarah Smith, the Clifden librarian to find out her needs prior to a committee meeting. I would make a list of the type of books people were looking for and bring this list to the meeting. There were always a lot of parents looking for suitable children's books. I was also on the Sheep-Dipping Board. I remember going out to see Hugh Musgrave on Cleggan Farm before one particular meeting. I explained my position to him and asked him to educate me on matters pertaining to sheep. He was a great help to me. He informed me about a particularly dangerous winter dip which he felt should be banned from use. I pushed for this at the meeting and eventually, after extensive testing of the product, it was withdrawn. My main work on this committee was trying to obtain dipping boxes for different sheep farmers. I did my best but achieved very little overall. I was at that time the County Council representative on the Interview Board of Clifden Community School. I remember a Brother Sylvester who was teaching in Offaly, Inspector Mc Ginty from Galway and the Head Sister of the Convent of Mercy in Tuam were also on the board. It was a very difficult job one which I didn't relish but I was always a great believer in appointing the candidate with the best all round qualifications.

When I was first elected in 1974, travelling expenses for County Councillors were 40p a mile rising to 57p by 1985 – when I failed to secure the Fianna Fail nomination by five votes and decided to retire from politics. We also received £14 per meeting. We used to love a trip to Dublin but meetings in Dublin didn't arise too often. The expenses claim forms were always filled out at the Galway meetings and handed to a civil servant. It usually took a week for the cheque to arrive out. When I was out canvassing for re-election, I generally found people to be very well-mannered and helpful although there was always the odd one who would say "Ye're all the bloody same, we only see ye when there's elections". I remember being verbally abused once while canvassing in Renvyle. I was somewhat shaken by the episode and rang John Bradley, the Director of Electors, from a public house in the area. Within one hour he had organised for two plain clothes policemen to come out and keep me under surveillance. They informed me that the person in question was not a friend of theirs either and that they would sort him out if he stepped out of line again. They stayed close by me until I finished canvassing late that night. When I was canvassing, I always made a point of calling to houses where I knew I'd get no vote to show that I was a man for the people and that regardless of their political affiliations I was at all times, prepared to help them.

The job was very frustrating at times particularly in the area of securing entitlements for people. There could also be a fair bit of stress but not on a continual basis. I enjoyed the meetings, and involved myself in all the discussions. There were many heated debates during those years and I was inclined to lose my head a bit if confronted by arrogance. I was ejected from chambers on a number of occasions. My happiest political memory was getting elected the first time. It was a very proud feeling, to be carrying on in my uncle's footsteps. I have regrets also. There were times when I let some of my constituents down by not getting to the right person in time. I suppose my biggest regret is the fact that I didn't really look after my building contracting business properly during those eleven years. At one stage during the mid-1980s, I had £200,000 worth of work in operation but I didn't keep proper command of my work and in the end potential clients went elsewhere because I couldn't accommodate them properly. Still money isn't everything and I wouldn't swap my time in politics for anything. It was a very happy and valuable part of my life.

Remembered by Gerald Bartley and written by Paul Gannon

A Backroom Business

Francie Mannion

The Medium was unique to Claremorris and Clifden. It measured three-quarters of a pint, and the thick fluted pint glasses, which remained in use until the end of the 1950s, were very suitable for the pouring of a medium. The popularity of a public house was very often based on the size of its medium. The medium was the standard drink of the day because people were so poor they couldn't afford to be drinking pints. The pint cost 9d, the medium only 7d, the cheapest alcoholic drink a man could buy. If he had 7d, he had an entrance to the pub and once inside there was always the possibility that some tourist or perhaps some native person home from England on holidays, might arrive in and buy him a pint. The medium was an illegal sale because drink is supposed to be sold by standard measure. The medium was very consistent in its popularity. Ninety per cent of the customers preferred it to the pint because they were under the impression that it was better value than a pint. Medium clients, many of whom were pensioners, were an essential part of the clientele. However, during the 1960s the local Vintners Association decided to end the practice of selling mediums because the nature of the licensed trade business had changed so dramatically and it was time to move on.

My family had been in the licensed trade since 1932. In 1935 we bought the present premises from Lydon-O'Neills for £400. The licence fee was £4 a year and was to remain at £4 until the end of the 1970s. My earliest memories of the pub date back to 1939. The pub didn't really mean anything to a young boy of eleven except that instead of being off playing football with my friends, I might end up having to stand in behind the bar and help out for a few hours. The business was very small at the time. There was no such thing as a full pub. The pub was only a small part of a much larger business, grocery, drapery, hardware or in our case, a butcher's shop. It was only an adjunct, a room at the back where people could slip in for a drink when the shopping was done. My father was very much a landowner, a farmer and a butcher. He was never a serious publican. If he had to go behind the counter to fill drink, he'd fill it, but he was far happier working on the land. Our pub was always noted as being a Fine Gael pub but we always had customers of every political affiliation including old IRA fellows and World War veterans. There was hardly ever any hassle, as we were well known as being a very strictly run bar where everyone was welcome but messing wasn't tolerated. My father was a caring and considerate man who sometimes had to be very strict on customers who were over the limit, for their own protection.

Throughout the 1940s and 1950s the licensed trade was a thoroughly and utterly uncomplicated business. There were very few varieties of alcoholic drinks for sale. All the men drank Guinness. There was no draught beer or draught lager. The only beer available was a bottle of Bass. The Guinness came in oak barrels throughout the thirties and forties. Part and parcel of a barman's equipment that time was the bit and brace. The oak barrel was put on its side and bored with the bit and brace until the little tip at the top of the bit would come on the inside of the barrel and then the porter would ooze out slowly. The barman then got his tap and hammered it in with a mallet. The barrel was then lifted onto a stand and the porter was poured into big enamel jugs. The pints or mediums were served from these enamel jugs with a second glass being employed to hold back the froth. The Guinness maturing inside the barrel created its own gas, but as the barrel went down there was less gas and froth, and the barman could draw directly from the tap. This process continued until the mid 1950s, at which point Guinness's started sending out barrels with steel rings on them. All the barman was required to do thereafter was to hit the circular piece of timber inside the steel ring into the barrel and then hook up the tap. Guinness's persisted with the oak barrels until the late 1950s when they replaced them with steel barrels. There were two types of oak barrels, the kilderkin, which held sixteen gallons, and the firkin, which held eight gallons. The steel barrel had a capacity of eleven gallons. It was often remarked that the Guinness never tasted as good out of the steel barrel as it had tasted previously out of the oak barrel. Guinness's had a complete monopoly on

Paddy Mannion and P. K. Joyce in Clifden, 1950.

Outside 'Tommy's' 1952.

supply right up until the 1970s. Advance payment by cheque was always required with any order. There were no exceptions to this rule. Dispensers were introduced during the 1970s. A dispenser was a large cone-shaped apparatus, which was attached to the counter. It could hold about three gallons. Its primary function was to get the Guinness settled before pouring.

The other alcoholic drinks on sale in our pub prior to 1960 were whiskey, brandy, port, red rum and sherry. They all cost 10d each, sherry and port being a double measure. Sherry was the popular ladies drink and all the pubs in those days had a snug to facilitate women having a discreet drink. It was highly irregular for a woman to sit at the main bar with the men.

I did my leaving Cert in June 1947 and later that summer I was offered a scholarship to UCG on the basis of my results. I was interested in going to university and had notions of doing an engineering degree. My father however was very anxious for me to take over the family business and he eventually persuaded me to adhere to his wishes. At the tender age of nineteen, I was handed complete and utter control of the business. I could do whatever I felt necessary and my father never interfered in the management of the public house thereafter. It was very easy to run a pub in 1947. The whole scene was very uncomplicated and relaxed. I could close up the pub at the blink of an eye, any time of any day during the week, if I so desired, without fear of criticism from the general public. If I wasn't open, people would simply go to some other pub. I played a lot of football in those days and I could devote as much time as I liked to training. I think it would be fair to say that up until 1960 the whole institution that was the public house seemed to just trundle along without even being conscious of itself. It was merely an adjunct to a more important business, a sort of backroom sideshow. "We'll go into the back," they'd say. The men would sit around the fire on barrels; boxes even planks in some instances and break into easy conversation. The weather, the price of cattle, and fishing were the usual topics of conversation. The atmosphere was homely and pleasant, almost like being in one's own living room. Pubs were pretty run-down places in the late 1940s. They hadn't changed or developed in decades. There was no concept of competition between the various public houses nor was there any concept of "the local". Wherever a few people would happen to meet while doing their shopping, that was usually the place where they might go in the back for a drink. A "regular" was someone who might come in for a drink two or three times a week. There was no such thing as organised music. Cards and darts were the popular pub pastimes. The men played Twenty Five usually for a leg of mutton and they would practise for hours at darts. The Connemara Darts Championships were really big occasions and the overall standard of dart playing that time was streets ahead of what it is today.

Wednesday was pension day for the World War I veterans and usually a very busy day in the pub. Their pension was around ten shillings at the time. These ex-British servicemen, all natives of West Connemara were among my best customers at the time. They had all been very deeply affected by their experiences at the Somme, Verdun and in Mesopotania and even though it was customary for them to become very noisy and cantankerous, I still had great admiration for them because they were such a tough bunch of men, who had really been through the mill and suffered terribly. I spent many an hour listening to them describing their war experiences. In all my years as a publican I would have to rate Joe Bartley from Ballinaboy as being the best character that frequented my premises. Joe served in the RIC in Belfast from 1910 to 1922 before returning home to West Connemara to retire and draw his RIC pension which was quite substantial in those days. Joe was a natural storyteller who seemed to possess an endless supply of stories and his ability to tell a good yarn will probably never be equalled. According to the laws of the time, there was no drinking on Sundays unless one was a bona fide. A bona fide was a person who lived three miles or more from the nearest public house. He or she was entitled to a drink between 1 p.m. and 7 p.m. on the basis that they were travelling on a journey and were entitled to some refreshment. This peculiar law probably owed its origin to one of the old inn laws in England. It was eventually abolished in the 1963 Act. Ironically enough, Sunday morning after Mass was our busiest time of the week. Sunday was very much, the countrymen's drinking day. They'd slip in quietly through the back door and for two hours solid we'd be flat out behind the counter filling porter. This Sunday morning practice was something that was totally illegal, yet in those days it was the only time during the week that there was anything resembling a rush. Once the two hours were up, that was it. We closed up for the day and everybody went home happy.

The day of the Clifden Races was the biggest day of the year in those times. We always set up an open-air tent for selling drink and race day was probably our most profitable day of the year. There were also race meetings in Omey and Errismore and we used to always buy a licence to sell drink at these meetings. The Errismore meeting was usually held the week after the Clifden races. The Guinness was brought out the night before and left overnight in a house near the course. The open-air tent was a great novelty, particularly on a fine day but we always did tremendous business at the races, regardless of the weather. We did put our prices up a little in order to cover the cost of the licence and the cost of transport. The barrels of porter were emptied into a basin to give the Guinness a chance to flatten down and the pints were poured from enamel jugs. We never sold mediums at the races because the crowds were too large and it would only have complicated matters too much. It was a rough and ready operation but the people never complained. They were glad to get porter no matter how warm it might be. Apart from the races and general election nights, Christmas Eve and St. Stephens Day were the two busiest days of the year. There was no significance attached to New Year's Eve. We were not allowed to open on St Patrick's Day but this didn't prevent the drink from flowing illegally. We used to bring the porter out to the customers in jugs. They'd drink away all day out in the sheds at the back. I used to dread St Patrick's Day because there were always a lot of fights. It seemed to me at the time that all the disputes around the place, that had to be settled, were inevitably settled on St Patrick's Day.

'Keeping an eye'...Tommy Mannion enjoying a glass of stout.

There were no restaurants in Clifden during the 1940s and 1950s as far as I can remember. We often brought women into the kitchen for a cup of tea while they were waiting on their husbands to finish their drinks in the back. I remember an old lady named Mrs. Heffernan who lived across the street from us, where Fogarty's restaurant is today. She used to cook steak or chops for people who would bring the meat over to her after buying it from us. While the food was being prepared they would go in the back for a drink, before returning subsequently to Mrs. Heffernan to eat the meal she would have ready for them. She would charge them so much for the cooking and so much for the bread, butter and tea. I reckon this arrangement, which went on for many years, was unique to the town of Clifden. I doubt very much if a similar system operated anywhere else in Ireland. Public house opening hours around that time were from 10 a.m. to 10 p.m. The police raided every once in a while and I was up in court on a few occasions for late hours. I never attended the court myself because it was always a clean catch. The penalty for such an offence in those days was usually a ten-shilling fine. However when endorsements were introduced in the 1963 Act, the whole business of after-hours drinking became much more serious because three endorsements meant the loss of one's licence. Overall, I had a very good relationship with the Gardaí and often changed their monthly cheque for them. Clifden was a very quiet peaceful town where the most common misdemeanour was probably bicycle theft and the policeman's job was largely stress free.

As the 1950s neared their end I had no idea that the whole scene was about to change so dramatically. The advent of mass tourism in the 1960s was probably the single most influential factor in bringing about such a radical transformation within the industry. Clifden had always been a very popular destination down through the years for British people. Guinness's were very much the catalysts of all this change. They were determined to improve both the quality of licensed premises and the quality of the drink on offer. In 1960 they brought out a scheme whereby free architectural advice was given to any publicans who wished to avail of it. The publican told the architect how much he was prepared to spend on refurbishing his premises and the architect drew up the plans accordingly. It was a great scheme and many public houses in Clifden, including ourselves, availed of it. I feel that 1960 was a watershed, a defining moment, so to speak, in the history of the licensed trade in this part of the country, because it saw the first real change and development in the industry for possibly as much as one hundred years. My principal concern at the time was that

'Having the crack'. From left: Walter Flaherty, Henry Conneely, Martin V. Mannion and friends.

in our particular case, we wouldn't go overboard and lose the traditional ambience and atmosphere, which had always been our trademark down through the years. I was determined to get the balance right. Rural electrification also made a huge impact and by 1960 all public houses had refrigeration. From 1960 on the industry became much bigger and busier and all publicans had to become much more professional and businesslike in their attitude and outlook. The introduction of VAT, which was 2.5 per cent in the 1960s, meant that the authorities henceforth would know exactly what we were all selling. We had to make out VAT returns to get our percentage of the VAT back. Taxation and PRSI followed and all of these developments testified to the emergence of a new order in business. As Pearse once wrote, "Changed, changed utterly, a terrible beauty is born". The death knell had sounded for the old system. Publicans were left with two choices, to move with the times or get out altogether. Many publicans got out of the business because the scale of the change was too much for them and they felt they couldn't cope.

I had no regrets about participating fully in all the upheaval at the time because it was challenging and exciting and it brought increased prosperity. We had never employed any outside staff until well into the 1950s but the employment of staff became a big concern during the 1960s. Nowadays, the day is so long and so busy, that one has to employ two people, to keep one behind the bar at all times. In my opinion, the good barman is always on the move, always of busy appearance and always with an eye on the customers to see that they are happy. For a pub like ours to have gone so much into the food business in the last forty years is indicative of just how much things have changed. Food now caters for at least half of our business. After over fifty years in management I finally decided to retire although I still take a keen interest in the affairs of the pub. There was a vocational side to being a publican. I knew all my customers very well over the years and often discussed their problems with them. I suppose I often heard a lot of things that I'd rather not have heard but being a caring and understanding confidant to people was a very important part of my work. I've always believed that a publican will do a lot of harm to his business and his customers if he's not a caring individual. I never lent money to customers for the purpose of buying more drink because I knew it would have been very wrong of me to take advantage of a man's weakness and that I'd never have any luck for it. In some respects the public house was a bit like the doctor's surgery where a person might get a cure, a tonic or some good counsel. Many people confided in me about issues of a personal nature because I was acknowledged as being very discreet.

Admiring the Liam McCarthy Cup after Galway's All-Ireland win in 1988. From left: Mikey O'Donnell, Michael Pryce, Eoin Burke, Aine O'Neill, Catriona Mannion and May Mannion.

The most rewarding aspect of being a publican was meeting people. It was always a great experience to feel the adrenaline flowing on a busy night and to enjoy the buzz which came from creating and nurturing the right kind of atmosphere. We always had the reputation of having a good pint down through the years. I also enjoyed being my own boss, master of my own destiny, so to speak. It meant I had to put in many long, unsociable hours but at the end of the day I called the shots. My policy on not allowing any other type of music except traditional, has stood the test of time. Mannion's is still an establishment that the older, more conservative element like to frequent in contrast to younger people who are not as attracted to it because it is so traditional in its character. The Vintners Association reorganised during the 1940s and I was chairman for many years. Its main function was to foster co-operation among the publicans and to promote events which would be of benefit to all the publicans. It has been relatively successful over the years in achieving these objectives. My son now manages the business and I know he will be well able to cope with whatever changes or developments are necessary to bring the business into the next century. I must admit I do tend to be much more outgoing in offering him advice than my father ever was with me. It's mainly because I realise that managing a public house today is a much more sophisticated and complex business that it was in 1947, when my father handed over the running of this proud establishment to me.

Remembered by Francis Mannion and written by Paul Gannon

THE HALF BARREL OF BEER

Now listen to me and I'll sing you a song.
It ain't so interesting and it ain't very long.
It ain't well composed but it's fair for a start.
For I never went to school and I ain't very smart.
'Tis about a half barrel, a half barrel of beer,
That was bought in the Whitehouse exceedingly dear.

Now before proceeding with this batch of a song,
I must introduce you but that won't take long,
To the men who took charge of this joyful event
When a war torn world was bleeding and bent.

Mike McLaughlin, the Treasurer, a more trustworthy boy
Cannot be found in the province from here to Shanghai.
Bruddy, the Chairman, and Secretary Luke Nee,
For an undertaking like this there needs a sound Committee.
And then there was Wattie, I hear he was dark,
Tom Vallely, Joe Curley and O'Malley Mark.

So now that I have mentioned the principal men
Who worked for a week with pencil and pen,
To arrange this fine function that all did enjoy.
Still while some of them laughed, others did cry.

Now listen attentively to the rest of my ballad,
And I'll tell you the effects of the sweetcakes and salad,
Of the wine and the minerals that would give you the gout,
And the little half barrel of watery stout.

Paddy Heanue got courage, when he got a few jars,
And says he to Gregory 'shove up your spars'.
Be not like O'Sullivan but defend your old dial,
Or to carry you home we won't think it worthwhile.

Says Gregory anyways 'I do not give a fig',
'All the Heanues of Derryinver in one hour I'd swig'.
'Give over your humbug and aggravate not a man,
Who stood in Tullycross while other men ran.'

Then Paddy immediately got very quiet,
He went to the room and forgot about fight.
Says he to the barman, why spare the blessed stuff
If there's any good in it, it is in enough.

So Curley filled for him, a pint full of froth,
He took it and shook it, then you should see his wrath,
Says he 'What's the idea or what is the joke of a caper
like this on a poor thirsty bloke.'
So he went from the room, Gregory to seek,
Says he I will find him, if it takes a wet week.
But where did he find him but up drinking tea,
With his cup in his hand and his cap on his knee

When they came face to face, both of them cried,
Whilst the crowd cried with laughter,
They sobbed and they sighed.
Then Paddy got vexed and he said 'It's no joke',
He stepped back a pace then, an Irish citeog,
Caught Gregory's ear with a terrific clout,
And for the second time that night, there was a knockout.

So now I must finish, I wo not detain you long,
But I must give the finishing touch to my song.
No more will I mention the drink or of food,
But there came a few blokes that I must not exclude.

There came the two Wallace brothers from Creggauns,
And also, John Pete back Dawros Mór,
Then last but not least there comes Mr Jack,
Who runs a pavilion in Letterfrack
All heard of our time and came in full style,
With ivory rimmed specks and McWilliams hair oil.

Then the party being over, it was a queer sight,
To see a little hand cart being dragged through the night,
Filled with utensils that once were a full,
Up by Brughar Duba and the butcher's hill.

Empty cans, empty buckets, empty saucepans and bottles,
And men looking for a cure for dry thirsty trottles,
And the women in their wake with tablecloths and towels,
Spoons, knives and forks, cups, saucers and bowls,
'Twas like the evacuation of Belgium town,
When bombed and machine gunned,
Their dwellings crumbled down.

So now I'll conclude in an old Irish way
Le oíche bhreá againn is le cúnamh Dé
Sula nimeoinn an Samhradh is sula dtiocfaidh and Fhómhar,
Beidh oíche brea eile againn is uisce beatha go leor.

Author unknown
Given to me by Mary Roe

THE CURE

After a night on the beer and whiskey
The sea is my salvation, my redemption
After last night's racket in the Den
Thank you God for this ocean of nourishment
Injections of energy, shock waves to my system
Make me want to scream out in new found ecstasy
Bury my head in a wave
Kill the sickening pain with volumes of sea water
Wash away all the previous night's sins
Feel pure and feel free again
With clarity of mind and body equilibrium
Last night's futility all forgotten
I am rescued from the aftermath depression syndrome
Face the day with new courage and hope
Close last night's chapter and start a new one

Written by Paul Gannon

Educational Odyssey

Jenny Conboy

I grew up just outside Castlemaine in Co Kerry and it was there that I received my primary education. I attended the Catholic girls' school, which was separated from the boys' school by a high wall. We used to converse with the boys through cracks and holes in this wall at breaktimes. There were almost seventy children in each of the schools. There was also a Protestant school in Castlemaine with about thirty pupils. Before their school was built they used to attend our schools and were always let out in the yard to play at religion time. We always had good relations with our Protestant neighbours. Within our own school there was a sense of social order. We were from the country, the daughters of farmers, and somehow we felt that the daughters of guards and shopkeepers from the town were on a higher echelon than us. We never felt as well-dressed as them or as sophisticated and this resulted in us having a bit of an inferiority complex. Looking back now, a lot of it may have been in our own imagination. Out school subjects in the 1930s were English, Irish, Maths, History, Geography, Catechism, Singing, Cookery, Sewing and Knitting.

In English, apart from reading, the main emphasis was on penmanship. We seemed to spend all our afternoons doing transcription or dictation. Every weekend we got an essay to write. The teacher would give us the title and a few ideas and on Monday the essays would be read out. We learned poems like '*The Wayfarer*' by Padraic Pearse, off by heart. There was no emphasis on self-expression or on developing educated opinions about issues. I honestly do not know how children of the time ever learned to read, in the absence of graded readers, bridge readers, flashcards and, of course, phonics. The Clonard and St Brigid readers that we used were practically second level standard in some cases. Pupils had no books at home. We had to learn pages off by heart. It was drilled into us religiously and I suppose that is why so many learned to read in the end.

We always stood around in a circle for reading and spelling, not because there was a shortage of seats but because it was the done thing. The system was very hard on slow learners. If you were not able to read you were not able to read. The teacher was interested in the slow learner and wanted to help but there was no inservice training or material resources available. The concept of Remedial Education was still a long way off. It was in such circumstances that many teachers became frustrated and angry. Personally I have no recollection of ever finding it hard to read. I developed a great love of reading in 5th and 6th class and I would voraciously read anything I could lay my hands on including the daily newspaper which I used to bring home to my father every day after school. When the County Library service started, it seemed to open up a whole new world for me.

The main emphasis in Irish was on grammar. We did not speak Irish but we had a high academic standard. There was a great sense of equality between Irish and English in St Carthage's. We never felt that we had to learn Irish; we just took it for granted that we would do Irish the same as we would do English. My grandmother was a fluent Irish speaker and my father was also fairly fluent. I remember I knew all my prayers in Irish before I ever started school. Most of the work in mathematics was done on the blackboard. Children were called up in their turns to do various sums and solve different problems and this caused certain pupils a great deal of stress and fear.

Cookery was one of my favourite subjects. We often had to stay on after school to get things finished but we did not mind this because we always got to eat whatever we produced. I remember making homemade soups and pancakes, baking different types of bread and even cooking bacon and cabbage on one occasion. In singing class, we learnt songs by ear, all kinds of songs. We also used to practice the scale but there was no learning of musical instruments. History and Geography were taught in a traditional manner and were very much based around Ireland. However, despite these rigid structures we never had any sense as children that we were working within narrow parameters and that we were somehow missing out. We did not know any better so we had no grievance.

Before I started school my grandmother had already taught me to sew and knit. Ironically enough this was to most subject I grew to hate in school mainly because all we ever seemed to do was make small pieces for our scrapbooks. I could never see the point of making all these small pieces. We had to follow a certain programme: hemming, running, backstitching, darning and buttonholes. Everything went into the scrapbook to be scrutinised at the end of the year by the Sewing Lady. My outstanding memory of the

Pupils of Calla National School, 1930.

Sewing Lady is that she always wore a hat. We did not see many ladies with hats in those days. She had not a pleasant personality and was inclined to give out a lot. This turned a lot of us against sewing. After examining all our scrapbooks she would usually instruct certain pupils to demonstrate a particular stitch. We also had to wear a thimble and hold the needle in the correct fashion. The Sewing Lady also examined us in cookery. The teacher always decided what we would produce because she would have to buy all the ingredients.

The Catechism exam given by a priest from the diocese was always the cause of much trepidation. We would spend hours learning off answers to difficult questions. There was often hassle at home when we would struggle to remember answers for our father. I had good recollection of answers but I never understood what I was talking about. On the day of the exam the teacher had everything orchestrated, having arranged us, according to ability, in a special way for the Inspector! I used to feel sorry for the teacher on days like this. The stress and the strain she was suffering was very evident. I never associated learning the Catechism with the prayers that I used to say or with going to Mass. I felt that this Catechism was something different altogether. It is much better nowadays, because children understand what they are talking about. The only part of the religious programme that I really enjoyed was Bible history. I do not recall getting any money on my

Confirmation day. I remember we had to wear white dresses. My mother went to town to buy the dress and the only white dress she could get had a tiny purple mark on it. She got a discount off the price because of the mark. I remember on the day being so fearful of some other girl spotting the mark. There was a lot of competition dresswise and it was a rotten thing. There was no social fuss after the ceremony. I remember my sister had pneumonia and we were all dying to get home to see how she was. My father missed the ceremony because he had to look after her.

The priest used to visit us once a week. He was an oldish man and he was always talking above our heads. We never really understood whatever message he was trying to get through to us. Every week without fail, the guard also paid the school a visit to check the attendance. We were fearful of his very impressive physical presence. He was always so straight and immaculate yet we never liked him because he never spoke to us. Indeed he would hardly acknowledge our existence. We were children and we were not to be spoken to. We never asked him any questions. In contrast, the School Inspector, Mr McCurtain was a very humane man who talked to us and not at us. He was able to get the best out of us and we were always very responsive to him.

1938 was the year that all the folklore was collected nationally by primary school children. I remember there was a lot of excitement about it in our school. I visited a few elderly people and recorded the stories they told. The teacher compiled all we had collected into a book and we never heard anything else about it after that. We used to have great fun reading out our respective stories to each other in the morning while the teachers would be engaged in their customary big chat. I always felt that the folklore project was probably more work for the teacher than it was for us because I imagine she had to proof-read every story and copy them all in a much larger book in her own handwriting to be sent away.

The greatest part of school was the going and coming, the chat and banter when the teachers would be talking and, of course, playtime. Looking back on my primary school experience there was this great contrast all the between the dour negativity, the submissiveness and the almost unnatural silence inside the four wall of the classroom and the sheer exhilaration and freedom outside of those four walls. Skipping was our main form of sport at breaktimes. We had a great variety of skipping games. I can still recall a few lines from one of these games 'Cups and Saucers, Plates and Dishes. Here comes the man with the Calico britches'. We used to also play a game called 'Strides' which was something like the 'Simon Says' game which children play today. We never played football, except to kick the ball back to the boys if it ended up in our yard. We were always very active during our breaks. There was always a lot of movement involved in whatever we did. We were very imaginative and resourceful in play. The yard was very small but we adapted and nobody went in complaining to teacher because it just was not an option. I feel that too much is done for children today and that they do not have to organise themselves enough.

There are many negative memories of my schooldays, some of which deserve a mention. My worst memory is of the cane. It was used as liberally on us as it was on the boys in their school. Humiliation was another strategy often employed by the teacher. Sometimes students were forced to kneel on the floor facing the wall. The teacher always stood at the fire and on cold, wet days this used to seem so unfair to me. She used to call out the names of those families who had not yet brought a horse cart of turf to the school. I used to feel very embarrassed if ever my father's name was called out.

We all hated and feared the day the dentist would visit. Teeth were extracted there and then in the classroom, a practice that was very unhygienic and caused us great distress. I remember fainting in school once, the day after I had a tooth pulled. Mrs Kavanagh got very flustered and worried but there was still no way I could go home immediately. I just had to stick it out until three o'clock.

The boys and the girls walked to school together. Fights usually took place on the way home after school. Sometimes the mothers would intervene on behalf of their own offspring. In the last term we used to take a shortcut home through the fields and I remember a particular orchard of crab apples that we used to raid. There was also a particular spot where we could get wild strawberries close to the well which many families drew their water from. It used to often take us half the evening to get home because we would be so long saying goodbye to each other at various crossroads.

We would sit on fences and linger at crossroads and as we departed everyone would be excitedly looking forward to meeting up again the following morning. There were hardly any cars that time and, we used to have the whole road to ourselves. The only thing we were afraid of was one particular old lady who was very contrary. No fear of abuse or abduction. There was a great sense of camaraderie among us. We all looked out for one another. We were like one big happy family. If somebody was not feeling well we would usually make a chair with our hands and carry the sick person home between us. Adults were not really part of our world. We were left very much to our own devices. I found Mrs Kavanagh to be detached and aloof and I was afraid of her. It was the same for the other children and this had the effect of bringing us closer, almost like we were united against the teacher. I had a sense of equality with my mother that did not exist between my teacher and I.

Despite all the negativity in relation to adults at school, I still had a very positive impression of adults because of all my aunts, uncles, cousins and neighbours. We visited every house in the village and always on these visits we had free expression and communication with the adults. At school we always felt the adults were above us, that they were different, almost like a different breed. My aunt who was a teacher in Tipperary was very much the exception in my eyes. She was a lovely kind person, very positive and her enthusiasm for teaching was infectious. She was the same person inside the classroom as outside. I often used to compare her to my own teacher and I could never reconcile in my mind how both of these women could be in the same profession.

My aunt was one of the reasons for me pursuing a career in teaching, but there were other stronger reasons. I was the eldest in the family and spent a lot of time minding and teaching my younger brothers and sister. Along with certain other girls I had been asked on occasion by Mrs Kavanagh to take the class in school for the odd history or geography lesson and I enjoyed it. I enjoyed helping my younger brothers and sisters with homework. I was also a good organiser. A combination of all these factors led me to believe that I could be very happy teaching for a living. My parents did

Pupils of Clifden Christian Brothers' School, 1950

not mind what I did so long as I was happy doing it. After doing the Primary Cert I went to the Presentation Convent in Milltown and sat my Inter Cert after two years. I then went to the Presentation Convent in Tralee to study for my Leaving Cert.

A certain amount of pressure was put on me along with other girls to consider joining the Presentation Sisters. We were invited to parties and social gatherings organised by the nuns in the convent. I was part of a group that was invited on a regular basis. There was no question of refusing the invitation. I suppose we had a certain degree of interest in joining. We had heard so much about the nuns, about how they had such a fine life! At these gatherings they would not push a particular view on us. They just gave us tea and cakes and let us take everything in. It was a very subtle approach, a deliberate ploy to give us a very favourable impression of the whole set up. The Presentation College in Tralee was not a Preparatory College but having achieved four honours in my Leaving Cert I was still very confident of getting the call to training. I applied but I was turned down without any explanation. There were students from Preparatory College who did not achieve as highly as me in their Leaving Cert yet were called. This made me very bitter. I had aunts in America who wanted me to come over and go to night school but I was not ready to emigrate. Immediately after my Leaving I did substitute work here and there in different schools in Kerry. I was allowed to do so because I had achieved a high percentage in Irish in my Leaving Cert. I was officially known as a JAM (Junior Assistant Mistress). I spent three years as a JAM from 1946-1949. During this period I often thought about doing something else but another teaching job would always present itself and I would follow the work. I was paid every three months: £28 for the first month, £28 for the second month and £32 for the third month. I received no holiday pay. In 1949 I saw Lettergesh National School advertised in the *Irish Independent* and I decided to apply for it. It was a permanent position and I did not care about having to migrate to West Connemara. I would have gone anywhere for a job. A lot of teachers had come to Lettergesh during the 1940s and left after relatively short periods of time. The school manager Fr Connolly was desperate to find a teacher who would be prepared to give a long-term commitment. He is reputed to have said at the time: "The next one that comes to Lettergesh will come from Donegal or Kerry, she will be well used of mountains and she will have to stay". It was Fr Connolly who informed me by letter that I had the job. There was no interview. The numbers were down to twenty-eight mainly because all children from Mullaghgloss had switched to Tully School because of teachers not staying in Lettergesh. Fr Connolly was permitted to appoint a JAM to a full-time position in Lettergesh because the numbers were so low. The numbers would later rise to sixty during my time there.

I got a train from Tralee to Galway and then a bus out to Renvyle. When I arrived in Tullycross I was met by Fr Connolly who had lodgings arranged for me in Paddy McDonnell's house. The Principal of Salruck, the neighbouring school also stayed in this house. I was later to lodge in Patrick Kerrigan's; the principal teacher in Lettergesh was a man called Bertie Cunningham from Tuam. It took me a while to settle. I found the mountains so frightening and intimidating because they were so bare. I had looked at mountains all my life, my house being surrounded by the Macgillycuddy's Reeks on one side and Mt Brandon on the other, yet I still thought that the mountains of West Connemara were so huge. Every place seemed to bare and so rocky and there just were not enough trees. I can still vividly recall my first impressions of the school: the bare floor with all the holes in it, the old seats, the few pictures on the wall and, of course, the big old fireplace.

I found the Connemara children to be no different than the Kerry children. They had largely the same style, the same clothes and the same banter. I had to do my diploma during my first two years. My inspector's name was Mr Clerkin. He was a tall red-haired man with thick glasses. He came unexpectedly on one occasion. He had arrived in Letterfrack to inspect a teacher there, only to find that the particular teacher was absent through sickness. He decided subsequently to visit me. My principal advised me to agree to be examined even though I was not obliged to, not having received any notification. In fact I never received any notification for any of my inspections during those years. The Inspector always seemed to come to the area to see someone else yet he would invariably end up with me. In any case, I took Mr Cunningham's advice and it worked to my advantage because I was facilitating the Inspector. Mr Clerkin did not tell me anything. He was a quiet man and everything was always fine with him. In 1956 I was forced to retire from teaching because of the Marriage Ban. I accepted my fate without any acrimony or bitterness. It was procedure at the time. I was not really that sad or emotional about leaving, because there was an expectation that the Marriage Ban would soon be lifted. I remember the parents presented me with a bowl, which I still have to this day. I was paid a gratuity of £128 on leaving which I later paid back towards my pension when I resumed teaching. The Marriage Ban was lifted in 1960 but between 1960 and 1962 no suitable vacancy arose. I never expected to get back into Lettergesh School but in 1962 a vacancy arose. I applied and was given the job. I was immediately put on six months probation because I had been out for so long. My Inspector was the infamous Mr Donegan, a different kettle of fish entirely to Mr Clerkin. I remember receiving a letter just before Christmas informing me that that I would not be sanctioned by the Department because Mr Donegan had not deemed me deserving of such. He did not consider the pupils standard in Irish or Maths to be sufficiently high. He indicated that he would be back in a month. I was angry and disappointed. A fellow colleague at the time advised me that the only way to get on with Donegan was to stand up to him and to request him to demonstrate the correct way to instruct, if my own approach was not working. He arrived back in January, picked out an Irish lesson and started asking them questions. They had not a clue. I remember saying to him 'Did you expect that they would have Irish in a month? You tell me what I should do. Show me how to teach the Irish lesson.' He was in his glory then, explaining everything to me. He returned again in February and the students were powerful because I used the particular methodology he had advocated. This time I got my long awaited authorisation from him. I was very fearful of Donegan initially, like many other teachers at that time. Usually on arrival he would tell me that he wanted a boiled egg for his lunch. You can imagine this boiled egg over the big open fire, which would not be burning half the time. I remember one day sending my son Paschal, who was only five or six years of age, all the way back to our lodgings in Mullaghgloss to get an egg, a pea tin to boil it in, some salt and homemade brown bread. I had to write it down for him to give to Mary Kerrigan who was looking after my younger children in the house. Such was the authority and power vested in the school inspector at that time, I was prepared to go to such extremes to accommodate his wishes. Some teachers of course disagreed with him and did not get on with him thereafter. I found the best psychology was to put him up on a pedestal, to emulate his style and to act as if I was his apprentice. I had no problem with him after my probation ended. He had a very dour personality and could also be quite unpredictable. I remember one time myself and another teacher from the area went to An Gríanán in Dublin on a two day public speaking course. The course was held over Monday and Tuesday and we had sought and obtained permission from Inspector Donegan to attend. You can well imagine our state of shock when he arrived in our respective schools on the Wednesday morning. That was the type of man he was. The Divisional Inspector at the time, Mr Holland, was the most impressive inspector I have ever seen with children. I remember him arriving one day at about 2.30 p.m on a dull dark evening. He amazed me the way that he was able to get so much out of the children in such a short time, at that time of the day.

My style of teaching, was such that I always had to be very organised. I am still the same way today. We were very limited that time in our choice of textbooks compared to today. Catalogues would arrive from the Educational Company and from Browne and Nolan and you chose one or the other. We never really got a chance to preview the books. We would send off our order and the books would be posted out to us. There was no such thing as going into educational bookshops in Galway like they do today. Educational supplies, including copies also arrived by post. I was always the type of teacher who had to have things done correctly. I was not an out and out perfectionist but I did try to instill a desire to aspire to the highest possible standards, in my pupils. I had a great relationship with Mr Cunningham my principal. He taught me how to do the roll books, attendance books and registers. He also showed me how to do the salary returns every month. More importantly however, he gave me great advice as regards how to deal with children and their parents. He was often off school due to sickness and I spent many days running the school on my own at a time when the numbers were around fifty. His wife suffered from cancer and I often did jobs for him to enable him to spend more time with her.

My social life, as a single woman in the 1940s and 1950s was very uncomplicated. I played cards and I went to dances. Women were not to be seen in public houses in those years. My usual social companion was the teacher in Salruck. We usually played cards in Leenane on a Friday night. Sometimes we stayed overnight. We often cycled to Ballinrobe on a Saturday where we might do some shopping or get our hair done. Then it was back to Leenane on Sunday for the dance on Sunday night. We also went to country house dances in Mark Coyne's and Paddy (Bike) Coyne's. Poker schools in Cunningham's were also a regular thing and the priest would always join us on those nights. I first met my husband Malachy at a dance in Leenane. We married in 1955. Being married to a fellow teacher did have its advantages in that we were able to share problems but the downside was that there seemed to be no getting away from the job at times.

When the Cunninghams left the area in 1962 to go and live in Tipperary, Cáit Tunney became the new principal. She married in 1964 and moved on. There was an expectation that I would apply for the principalship but if truth be known I did not really want all the added responsibility. My children were young and I'd enough to do at home. I loved teaching the junior section of the school and I knew it would be expected of me to take the senior section if I became principal. Mary Joyce became the new principal and she was later succeeded by Mary Walsh. When Mary Walsh, left Salruck to take over in Lettergesh it failed the Department of

Education to find a replacement for her and this subsequently resulted in the amalgamation of Salruck and Lettergesh. We eventually had a new school built in 1976. When Mary Walsh decided to move to Dublin in 1977, I decided to apply for the principalship. At that stage, I had many years of experience behind me, I felt my children were the right age and I felt ready to run my own school. I remember we thought we would never get into the new school. Moving in was one of the best experiences of my teaching career. For the first time ever I did not have to put on layers of clothes to keep warm: we had lovely new carpets, lots of windows to let in so much more natural light and of course the luxury of electricity.

Throughout the 1950s and into the 1960s we used to have the free cocoa and bread. The cocoa was boiled in a big pot up on an iron bar over the open fire. The first job in the morning was always to get two buckets of water from the well for the cocoa. The fireguard would be put across the fire but this big pot bubbling away was still a great source of danger and such a phenomenon would be totally unacceptable in this modern era of fire officers and safety statements. Mick Flanagan from Clifden had the contract for delivering the free bread. I remember they were white loaves, unwrapped, inside a big bread bin. They were cut up on one of the tables without any regard for hygiene. The mixed fruit jam used to arrive in big crocks from Fruitfield. The free bread and jam was only given to areas that were considered congested or disadvantaged.

The parents were always a great support to me in a very unobtrusive way. In the 50s and 60s they very rarely came to the school apart from the two station masses each year in the school. The whole concept of fundraising was not born until the 1970's and when it did arrive the parent body embraced it wholeheartedly. Going back a lot further I can remember a time when we used to get about £15 each from the Department for the purchase of educational materials. I paid for a lot of school requisites out of my own pocket over the years.

The late '60s was a time of great anticipation in our profession. It was well documented that a new curriculum was on the way. I remember the kindergarten advisors coming to our school in the lead up to this new curriculum. I remember a Mrs O'Dwyer explaining to us about all the different types of copies that would be most suitable for juniors. On another such occasion I remember I had one particularly hyperactive child from the senior room planting a few cuttings for me in little boxes when one of the kindergarten advisors arrived unexpectedly. The principal had sent him into me because he was driving her mad and I had given him this activity to keep his mind occupied. I sent some of my own pupils over to work with him. When the

Principal Maureen Kelly with the pupils of Ballinaboy National School, March 1970.

kindergarten advisor arrived I got very stressed out because I was sure she would be less than impressed at this type of activity going on in the classroom. I was dumbstruck and somewhat relieved when I heard her say, 'Well, is not this lovely'. She was delighted to see the senior pupil working side by side with the juniors. I remember I had this sense at that stage that I'd love this type of activity to be formally part of the school curriculum.

The New Curriculum when it did arrive in 1971 was very much the teaching equivalent of Vatican II. It was a big change. We had inservice days, involving a lot of hard work but it was wonderfully liberating and for the first time in my teaching career I felt free to try anything. The stillness and silence of the classroom during the preceding decades was now replaced with the hustle and bustle of a child-centred approach. Learning became very much an active experience for the child, who was now allowed to move freely around the room and ask questions about a whole range of issues. The New Curriculum definitely facilitated a much higher quality of interaction between pupil and teacher. I found this to be far preferable to the pre-New Curriculum days of the class sitting passively as I gave instruction in a dictatorial manner. Gone also was the Primary Cert which really put a lot of pressure on both teachers and pupils. It was as valuable to some students in those times as the Leaving Cert would be today, but for other students the Primary Cert was synonymous with failure, resulting in a sense of low self-esteem and for this reason I was glad to see it go. Henceforth all pupils would progress at their own pace, at their own level and according to their own ability.

Prior to the introduction of the New Curriculum, Irish was always my favourite subject to teach. We were in the *BreacGaeltacht* and the children had a natural love for Irish especially for Irish songs. The *gaelachas* was inbuilt in them and they were very responsive during lessons. After 1971 I took a particular liking to Environmental Studies and Music. Teaching was a whole new experience for us all but the subsequent declining emphasis on key areas of the curriculum like tables and spelling did concern me.

Children today have too much. Everything is handed to them on a plate. Often times, they are continually brought to school in cars. Sometimes, because of the type of modern society we live in, this is sadly unavoidable. I do not believe that the children of today have the same freedom as we had growing up. They seem to me to be restricted all the time. They have to be watched and minded a lot more and I do not think they will ever really be as independent and resourceful as we were. I wonder was it respect we had or fear or are the two of them the same thing. I think it was more fear of authority in our day. When modern day children show respect, it is probably a more genuine sincere respect than what we had.

The parents of today are more educated that they were when I was going to school and because of this they have greater expectations for their children. In the '30s, '40s and '50s the mother was always at home and had more time to give to her children than the mothers of today have. It is probably not fair to compare the different eras. Back in the 1950s we had not the equipment or modern technology or even electricity. There was a lot of economic poverty. Nowadays children have everything that's going, both at school and at home, but I wonder are they any better off or are they able to learn any better. There is definitely more stress to teaching today in relation to trying to keep up with parental expectations and keeping with all the technological advances in education. The curriculum is overloaded and the management of time in school is a bit of a nightmare for teachers of today. Discipline is much tougher and the administrative workload for Principals has increased out of all proportion.

The only advice I could give to a young aspiring teacher is to go for it if its what you want and it makes you happy. I always say, as long as a person is happy doing a job then it does not matter what job it is. We do not have the right to tell another person to stay away from a particular job or profession because they might be very suited to it. It is down to whatever the person feels inside herself or himself. In my opinion, patience is the most important quality required for teaching. I have no regrets whatsoever about becoming a teacher. It was my vocation in life. Teaching is not like your straightforward nine to five job because there's always work to prepare when you come home and there's always plans, strategies and ideas going around in your mind. You cannot help it or control it. It is a mindset and a disposition that is part and parcel of being a teacher. Any person lacking this degree of application and dedication should not in my opinion be teaching at primary level. It was my whole life, all consuming, and always on my mind. We're not the island of saints and scholars that we used to be but our primary teachers are still held in high esteem mainly because, in Ireland, unlike many other countries, the job is still regarded as a vocation. It is my fervent hope that this will always be the case.

Remembered by Jenny Conboy and written by Paul Gannon

SIGN OF THE TIMES

(This is a copy of a letter received by the late Mrs. Alice Kennelly, N.T., Principal Teacher at Aillebrack N.S. 1930-1958, from the Office of National Education, Dublin, when she was assistant teacher in Ballinaboy N.S., with the late Patrick Casey of Clifden from 1921-1930. Ar dheis Dé go raibh a anam dilis. She previously taught at Streamstown NS (Clifden), Bray (Co. Wicklow) and Birmingham (UK).

Reverend Sir,
I am directed to remind you of the official letter addressed to you on the 28th April last, and to request you to be good enough to obtain and furnish at the earliest possible date, any statement that Miss McHale, assistant teacher, may have to offer, regarding the allegation that she has been assisting those in arms against the Government of the country. You should also furnish at the same time your own observation in regard to the matter.

(signed the Right Reverend Monsignor McAlpine, P.P., V.G.)

SURVEY

Statistics for West Connemara Primary Schools 1949

SCHOOL	PUPILS	TEACHERS
Leenaun	51	2
Lough Inagh	25	1
Ballinafad	30	1
Toombeola	30	1
Roundstone (Boys)	52	2
Roundstone (Girls)	50	1
Murvey	18	1
Calla	45	2
Cashel	62	2
Cushatrough	25	1
Ballyconneely	53	2
Aillebrack	45	2
Doonlaughan	20	1
Ballinaboy	20	1
Gowlane	21	1
Clifden (Boys)	50	2
Clifden (Girls)	125	5
Streamstown	25	1
Kingstown	47	2
Inishturk	10	1
Inishturbot	15	1
Omey	15	1
Inishbofin	37	2
Aughris	50	2
Cleggan	51	2
Moyard	45	2
Letterfrack	49	2
Tully	61	2
Eagles Nest	50	2
Lettergesh	48	2
Salruck	15	1
TOTAL	**1240**	**51**

Statistics for West Connemara Primary Schools 1999

SCHOOL	PUPILS	TEACHERS
Leenaun	15	1
Roundstone	38	2
Ballyconneely	70	3
Aillebrack	40	2
Clifden	220	9
Kingstown	34	2
Claddaghduff	36	2
Cleggan	40	2
Inishbofin	30	2
Letterfrack	70	3
Tully	45	3
Eagles Nest	37	3
Lettergesh	36	2
Cashel	58	3
TOTAL	**769**	**39**

Since 1949 seventeen of the area's thirty-one primary schools have closed. There has been a 40% decline in the number of pupils and a 25% reduction in the number of teachers employed.

Survey carried out by Eamonn Mac An Ríogh

Religious Instruction FOR Primary Schools

SACRED MUSIC.

All schools will be examined annually in the following programme:—1, Benediction Service. Salve Regina. 2. One Irish and One English hymn from the following: Ar nAṫair; Mo Ġráḋ-sa mo Ḋia; Ġile mo Ċroiḋe; Beannaċt Leat; Soul of My Saviour; Jesus, My Lord; Hail Queen of Heaven.

All teachers are earnestly requested to coöperate with the effort which is being made to promote Plain Chant throughout the diocese.

IRISH SPEAKING SCHOOLS.

1. The Provincial Synod (No. 136) says:—"We earnestly wish that Catechism be taught in the Irish language in every school in the whole province where it is understood by the Children."
2. Either Dr. MacHale's, or Dr. O'Flaherty's Irish Catechism may be used until the new Catechism has been translated. But, whichever Catechism be used, the amount of knowledge required in each standard will be that outlined in the above programme.

NOTES.

1. In every inspection by the Diocesan Examiner the pupils will be expected to know not only the programme for their own class but also the programme for the previous classes.
2. In explaining the Catechism Sacred Scripture may be drawn on to illustrate and vivify a large portion of the Catechism.
3. The short Bible Stories for the Junior Classes will be found in *The Child's Bible History*. (Knecht).
4. There ought to be a map of Palestine in each school.
5. Children of the 4th and higher standards should form the school choir and sing in a single group.
6. It is earnestly recommended that the work of the school should be concluded each day by the singing in common of the *Salve Regina* or some other hymn.
7. True education requires that the character of the pupils should be formed in accordance with the law of God, made known to us by Reason and Revelation. Not only then should the pupils receive adequate Religious Instruction but a religious spirit should animate the whole life and work of the school. The teacher should inculcate the practice of charity, truthfulness, justice, obedience of lawful authority, and all other virtues. The school day should begin by prayer.

✠ JOSEPH,

Archbishop of Tuam.

September, 1955.

THE OLD SCHOOL HOUSE

The schoolhouse, it stands by the roadside
Where our children have all gone to school
As we often watched them go over the road
With their schoolbags, their books and a rule

The views from the windows are lovely
As they gaze o'er that beautiful lake
And us parents sure we often wondered
In the years ahead what would be their fate

For soon they would grow into adults
And travel I am sure that they will
Far away from that lovely old schoolhouse
That stands near the foot of Doon Hill

They will travel to some foreign country
And walk around city and block
But someday I hope they'll return
To their own lovely village, Aillebrack.

Written by Penny O'Malley

The Beautiful Game

My father informed me that it was a man called Joe Curley from Tullycross who first brought a proper football to Renvyle in the late 1890's. The place he ordered the ball from in Galway actually sent him on a rugby ball by mistake and this was duly returned and a round ball sent on in its place. He organised a game on Flaherty's beach. The fact that there was massive interest locally can be gauged from the turnout. There were about thirty players on each side. There was no referee and no rules. There were no posts either. One team had to work the ball into the 'garraígainimh' (the sandy garden) on the west side and the other team had to work it as far as a couple of sand bunkers on the east side. It must have been a funny spectacle, the sight of sixty men all frantically chasing after the round ball with every man desperate to get a kick on it. It was no place for the fainthearted. Generally speaking the men wore bréidíns, patched up tweed trousers, tied round the waist with a string and báiníns, white flannen jackets without buttons, which could also be tied with string. Football jerseys, togs and boots were unheard of. These men would all have worn

Cashel footballers 1904. Front row l to r: Jack Kelly, 'Mona' Faherty; middle row l to r: Michael King, Pat "Fred' Nee, Jack Nee, Pat Conneely; back row l to r: 'Baker' O'Connor, Jimmy 'Tailor' Molloy, Pat King, Martin King, Pat Molloy, Joe Davin, Pat Mulkerrin, Tom Crean.

Lettergesh 1935. back row l to r: Patrick Coyne, Patrick Gibbons, Martin Kane, Martin Kerrigan, Thomas Conroy, Dan Coyne, Patrick Kane, Patrick Kerrigan, Tom Coyne, Pat Kelly; front row l to r: Petie O'Malley, Peter Faherty, Johnny Walsh, Patrick McDonnell, Peter Coyne, John Coyne, Michael Gibbons.

strong hobnail boots and if any man did not have a pair he'd borrow a pair from somebody looking on. Curley must not have been impressed at the general mayhem he surveyed that day, because he very soon wrote off for a book of rules which eventually arrived sometime later.

Shortly afterwards he formed the first ever Renvyle team. This team played its first match against Kylemore down by the White Strand in Renvyle. The Kylemore Team, which also had lads from Letterfrack, Ballinakill and Derryinver, used to practice in Ardigoole. Over one hundred years later Sr Benedict, farm manager at Ardigoole, would make this same piece of ground available to Renvyle GAA for training while the community pitch in Tullycross was under development. This first ever match between Kylemore and Renvyle was 21-a-side. There were posts at either end of the field but without crossbars. Goals were scored by kicking the ball between the posts and points were scored by kicking the ball outside either of the two posts. It was something similar to present day Australian Rules football. Joe Curley appointed John Conneely from Tully, captain of the Renvyle Team, and from that day on he was always referred to as the 'Captain'. The Renvyle team had bought a barrel of cider between them to share with the Kylemore Team after the match. They were surely well up-to-date if not ahead of their time in this laying on of post match refreshments.

The first game I remember seeing was in 1923: I was ten years old and

I went to the White Strand with my mother to see Renvyle play Lettergesh. Two of that Renvyle Team, Jack Gibbons (93 years) and Josie Coyne (95 years), are still alive today. Josie lives in America. The rest of the team that day was Eddie Diamond (goalie), Martin Stephen and Thomas Walsh, Josie and Tadie Salmon, Michael Lewis Connolly, Jim Canavan, Pahy Heanue and Austin O'Malley. The only Lettergesh players I remember were Jack and Pateen Gibbons. From the age of thirteen years onwards, I used to go down to the field behind Renvyle House Hotel and beside the lake on Sundays, when the men would be practising. The field is part of the golf course now. Like the other young lads I'd be hoping to get a few kicks on the ball. One sure way of getting a kick was to retrieve the ball from the lake whenever someone would take a stray or a wayward kick on it. This used to happen often. I remember it was a leather football all right but somehow it was not well made. Over a short period of time it would usually start to bulge out of one side. Its shape would get so distorted that it would nearly resemble a rugby ball and because of this it was nearly impossible to kick it accurately. It would never travel straight through the air and this used to spoil the enjoyment. Of course none of us had permission to be playing football in that place. It was private property and we were trespassing. I often remember Jack Wallace and Joe Ribbon chasing us off. They were herdsmen working for Mrs Gogarty in the Big House at that time.

I was seventeen years old when I played my first match in 1930. It would be something like a Minor match nowadays. We played a team from Letterfrack Industrial School on a field, which today is part of the Connemara National Park. We were brought to Letterfrack on Curley's open lorry. One of the Christian Brothers refereed the game and I remember three more of them played for the school team. Our team included Paddy Walsh, John O'Malley, Mikey Coyne, John Dinny Salmon, John Briany Salmon, John Heanue, Johnny Walsh, Pete Coyne and Stephen Sailor Flaherty. It was a very rough match: I remember getting a headbutt and being marked for weeks afterwards, just below my right eye. In any case, we won the game. There were no refreshments afterwards; we went straight home again on the lorry. In that same year I played my first ever game with the Renvyle adult team back on the field behind the hotel and beside the lake. It was also the first time that my brother Patrick, Mikey Coyne, Patrick Wallace and Pakie and Stephen Sailor played for the team. The older players included Jack Martin Kane, Pete Hyland, Tom Heanue, Martin Conneely, Michael Baker and Mick Fitzpatrick. I remember the following men played for Lettergesh. Phil Conroy, Paddy McDonnell, Peter Faherty, Pateen and

Michael Gibbons, Peter Coyne, Martin Coyne, Anthony Kane, Martin Kerrigan, Michael Kane and Pete O'Malley. We got the loan of currach oars to use as goalposts and we tied rope across for crossbars. Lettergesh won the game, mainly because Anthony Kane, the army man from Shanaveg, was such a good player. I remember him scoring a few goals with really powerful shots. The game was refereed by Michael Lewis who we all respected and was a very good referee. It was a rough, direct style of football. There was a lot of long kicking but hardly any passing. Players at that time were also allowed to footblock and this was a very dangerous practice. There was very little handpassing. We all had a habit of letting the ball pass down into our hands instead of jumping early to execute an overhead catch. Anthony Kane, having trained with the army in Galway, was an exception in that he was the only player there that day who was able to demonstrate to us the art of high fielding. We spent a lot of time after that practising this type of catch, trying to copy Kane's style. A lot of the players that day also had the habit of volleying the ball soccer style as it came towards them. Players were also inclined to pull on the ball first time instead of trying to pick it up, a bit like hurling players pulling first time on the sliotar.

There was a fellow called Martin Davis living in Cashleen at the time. His father was from Cashleen but he was born in Scotland where he spent many years. He was a great soccer player and we heard he had played for Shamrock Rovers in Dublin at one stage. We had great admiration for this man's skills and we used to try to copy these skills when we were playing football. There was no such thing as coaching in those days so all we could do to improve our own game was to try and copy any player we saw who had certain abilities that we did not. Anthony Kane and Martin Davis were two such players.

Renvyle footballers, 1938. Standing l to r: Mike Coyne, Michael Flaherty, Petie Walsh; sitting l to r: Michael Walsh, Stephen Salmon, John Diamond.

In 1930 Renvyle affiliated to the West Board. Credit for this goes to either Michael Lewis or Patrick Lydon. They were the only men I knew who had any bit of education and could write letters. Michael Lewis managed the first ever

Renvyle Team to play in a West Board Junior Championship Match. The match was against UCG's second team and was played in Clifden. The Renvyle Team lined out as follows.

Goalkeeper:	Tom Heanue	(Derrylough)
Full Backs:	Pete Hyland	(Cloonluane)
	Peter Canavan	(Ardnagreevagh)
	Jack Martin Kane	(Ardnagreevagh)
Half Backs:	Martin Davis	(Cashleen)
	Michael Lewis	(Rusheenduff)
	Paddy Baker	(Ardnagreevagh)
Midfielders:	Michael Baker	(Ardnagreevagh)
	Martin Conneely	(Ardnagreevagh)
Half Forwards:	Jim Kane	(Cloonluane)
	Anthony Kane	(Shanaveg)
	Pakie Salmon	(Ardnagreevagh)
Full Forwards:	John Thomas Kane	(Ardnagreevagh)
	Michael O'Malley	(Tullymore)
Captain:	Mikey Conneely	(Derryinver)

They had no jerseys or togs. I was not at the game but I heard that it was a very rough game and that one of the UCG. players was knocked out. Renvyle won the game but lost their second round match to Annaghdown in Oughterard. Clifden were playing a championship match there the same day and all their players agreed that Peter Canavan was the best player on the field in the Renvyle-Annaghdown game. There were no Lettergesh or Letterfrack lads on that team because there was not any of them

Mongan Cup Team 1948. Back row l to r: Paddy Hynes, Fr Ned Stankard, Fr Stevie Ludden, Tom Summers, Miko Collins, Joe Gibbons, Francie Mannion; front row l to r: Joe Conneely, Ulick Joyce, Sean Mannion, Paraic Joyce, Frank Casey, Paddy Joe Conroy, Peadar O'Toole.

playing to a high enough standard. However, during the 1930s, Paddy Nee and Eamonn Guy from Letterfrack and Patrick McDonnell, Pete O'Malley and Martin Kerrigan from Lettergesh did go on to make many a Renvyle team. We were a long time playing before we got our first jerseys. I remember going in to play Clifden in a challenge match in 1932. We had no jerseys or boots. However, the Cleggan team did, and somehow they found out about our game, and must have considered that we had a team good enough to give Clifden a good game of it, because they agreed to lend us their gear so as to improve our chance of winning. A man called Wallace from Inis Turbot brought the gear to Clifden travelling on horseback. He actually passed out the Renvyle lorry on the way in at Taobh-a-Locha. He stayed to watch the game and returned home with the gear afterwards. I remember we used to hold the odd dance in Curley's dancehall, which still stands in Tullycross today. Patrick Lydon would get permission from Mrs.Curley to use the premises and I can remember myself and my grandfather playing the music at one of these dances. It was with money raised from these dances that Patrick Lydon bought the first ever set of jerseys for the Renvyle club. They were blue with white cuffs and a white collar.

Throughout the thirties I played in many challenge matches for Renvyle against Letterfrack, Lettergesh, Clifden and Cleggan. I played three or four times against Cleggan back in Aughrismore. Sometimes we got over on Curley's lorry, sometimes we cycled over. We also played Cleggan five or six times over on Flaherty's Beach in Renvyle. We never lost to Cleggan as far as I can remember. However, in all the times I played 15-a-side against Clifden I was never on a winning team. We had footballers in Renvyle every bit as good as Clifden but they always seemed to have the more balanced team. Of course they were always able to strengthen their team with players who were not native to the town like guards or shop boys. We always felt that without these types of players they'd find it very hard to beat us. I played in the Mongan Cup against Clifden but never a Championship match.

Tom Connolly: Organiser, Secretary, Treasurer, and sometimes full forward for St Cáillín's GAA Club, 1957.

We were never drawn against them in those days. I remember playing against Roundstone in Gurteen Beach in a Mongan Cup match, which we won easily. I can also remember losing to Carna in a Mongan Cup match on Flaherty's Beach. I played in a challenge match for Letterfrack once, against a team from West Mayo called Kilmeena. This match was organised by a man called John Cummins from Kilmeena who worked in Letterfrack Industrial School as a carpenter. Two lorry loads of lads went down, the second lorry belonging to the Christian Brothers. I remember we were easily beaten, scoring only one point in the whole match. Afterwards, we went to Newport for tea and then on to Cummins' house in Kilmeena to a dance.

During the 1930s I played in several West Board Junior Championship matches for Renvyle without ever winning a single one. We lost to Killannin, Athenry, Éire Óg and Míchael Breathnach's, all in Oughterard. I recall we played Míchael Breathnach's in February. We had not practised since the previous summer and we were hammered by about thirty points. Oughterard had one of the best senior teams in the county at that time and some of their players watched our match. Afterwards they told us that they had been lucky to beat Míchael Breathnach's in a challenge match the previous week. We were unlucky to be beaten by Éire Óg, losing by one point. I remember going for a goal and their goalie going full length to deflect my shot over the crossbar. We travelled to all these matches in Oughterard on Diamond's open lorry. Carna defeated us one year in a Championship match in Clifden. The closest we ever came to winning a Championship match was in 1938 when we drew with Headford in Clifden. This match was played in Curraghmór. That day we had Paddy Nee from Letterfrack, Martin Kerrigan and Paddy Mc Donnell from Lettergesh

Renvyle v St Cáillín's, August 1957. This was the very first match ever played on the new sportsfield in Tullycross.

as well as Papy Gordan and Festy Feeey from Cleggan. Feeney was a great forward. I remember seeing him score 1-6 for Cleggan against Carna in a Mongan Cup match in Clifden. The full team that day was:

Goalkeeper:	Tom Heanue
Full Backs:	Paddy Walsh, Jack Martin Kane, Martin Kerrigan.
Half Backs:	Papy Gordon, Paddy Nee, Jim Kane.
Midfielders:	John Gannon, Mick Fitzpatrick,
Half Forwards:	Mikey Coyne, Paddy Mc Donnell, Stephen Salmon.
Full Forwards:	Pakie Salmon, Festy Feeney, John Diamond.

I remember having a point disallowed and there being a big row over it. The match was refereed by Pat Gibbons from Oughterard. The replay was in Oughterard. Patrick J. Salmon drove us down in Diamond's lorry. The Cleggan lads never showed up that day and this was a big reason for us losing that replay. I cannot recall any Championship matches being played during the war years. There was not any means of transport out of Renvyle. 1938 is also the only year back then when I can ever remember attending an official club meeting. It was held in the old Protestant Church overlooking Mortimer's Campsite today. There were only seven of us there with Patrick Lydon chairing the meeting from the altar. I remember Jack Martin Kane was elected treasurer, Patrick Lydon Secretary and Mikey Coyne Captain. There was not really any such thing as club meetings that time. When lads would meet at crossroads they'd talk about whatever match was coming up.

In 1937 Clifden made it through to the County Junior Final against Gort. It was to be played in the sports ground in Galway City. The Clifden manager was Patrick Joyce. He wrote a letter to our secretary Patrick Lydon looking for a certain few Renvyle lads to play with Clifden. Stephen Salmon, Mikey Coyne, Jim Kane and myself were asked and we all agreed to go. Our main reason for going was for the day out. We had never have been to Galway City before. We enjoyed a game of football but we were not too bothered whether Clifden won or not. I played in midfield, Jim Kane played halfback and Stephen Salmon and Mikey Coyne played in the forwards. We all played under false names: I played under the name of John O'Malley. I did not play very well. I remember my marker fouling me every time I went up for the ball. He had too much craft for me, never being pulled once by the referee. Gort won the match easily enough. They had some great players; I was surprised at their team being so good because I never thought there were any good footballers in Gort on account of the hurling being so strong there. We heard afterwards that a lot of the players who played that day were senior footballers from Clare. I believe a lot of that kind of thing went on in those days. Still we had a good day out. I remember we all stayed on afterwards to watch a hurling match between Galway and Limerick. It was my first time ever to see a hurling match and I have never attended another hurling match since.

Throughout the 1930's, seven-a-side competitions were very common. They were usually part of a sports day, in a particular place. I played in my first seven-a-side in June 1933 at the age of twenty. On this particular Sunday, I was part of a group of young lads, lying around on the green in front of the Grand Gate entrance to Renvyle House Hotel. We used to often pass the time this way on Sundays. I suppose if we had a football we would probably been playing football instead. Anyway, on this particular Sunday this new open lorry suddenly appeared. It had been driven by Maisie Davis from Tully, her father Patrick having just bought it. Maisie and her sister pulled up and asked us if any of us would like to go to the sports in Killmilkin. We all jumped in of course, even the lads who had no interest in sports. We had no notion at all of playing football; as far as we were concerned we were only going to watch. When we arrived at the sports we heard about the seven-a-side so we made up a seven. I can remember Tom Heanue, Steve Salmon, Martin Conneely, and Pakie Salmon being on that seven. We were knocked out in the first round, losing to Cornamona.

Leenane was a popular venue for the seven-a-side in those days; I played there a couple of times. We used to go in Diamond's lorry and I remember we always had to pay our own way; it might cost two shillings or a half-crown. I remember losing to Clifden and Clonbur on different days. In later years, after I had finished playing I used to go to Leenane to watch seven-a-sides. I remember one year a great Oughterard team beating Louisburgh in a final. Louisburg had two County players that day, Austin O'Toole and a fellow called Mulvey. However, Oughterard had Dinny, Eddie, Tom and Charlie Sullivan who all played for Galway, as well as Ned and Don Keogh. That day Renvyle were knocked out by Clonbur.

I played in a few Sevens Tournaments in Ardigoole in Kylemore. My fondest memory is from 1937 when we beat Clifden in the final. With four minutes left we were three goals down. Our manager Patrick Lydon moved me from midfield into full forward bringing Mikey Coyne out. I remember catching the first ball that came in and scoring a point. I caught the next delivery also and scored a goal. At this point I somehow figured we could win it. I moved myself out a small bit, caught the kickout, soloed in, drew the fullback and handpassed inside to Pakie Sailor who soloed in to score a goal. From the resulting kickout, I secured possession again and managed to again find Packie Sailor who scored his second goal. When the ball was kicked out, the referee John Heanue from Baunogues, who was a fine referee, blew for time. It was my happiest moment ever playing football and the only time in my life that I ever won a medal. I was later to lose the medal on Tullybeg beach, something I regret now, but did not think much about back then. The following year in Ardigoole, Renvyle and Clifden again reached the final, the other teams in the final being Ballinakill and Letterfrack. I remember that particular final because it was the only time I marked the great Connie McGrath. For some reason the Galway selectors would not pick him. He later joined the Garda Siochana, moved to Cork and went on to play not only for the Cork county team but also for Munster in the Railway Cup.

This particular day he had been marking Johnny Kane from Ardnagreevagh in the first half. We were losing badly at half time and knew we had to do something about McGrath. The other players that day were Tom Heanue (Goalie), Paddy Walsh, Mikey Coyne, Willie Diamond, John Diamond and Steve Salmon. Steve Salmon agreed to mark McGrath but Tom Heanue would not let him out of the full back line. Two or three others would not take on the job so in the end they asked me and I said I would give it a go. He was easily the best player I ever marked. I was not good enough to get the better of him and he was not fit enough to beat me either. By the end of the game neither of us had scored. We had cancelled each other out. Both of us were dead on our feet but I was happier because Renvyle had won the match. I remember myself and Connie McGrath did not speak or shake hands afterwards.

I remember a seven-a-side competition in Letterfrack during the War years. It was held in a field at the butt of the Diamond Hill beside the main road. I heard the College in Letterfrack was hoping to buy the same field from the National Park today. I had been out of football for a while and had only gone up that day to watch. Renvyle had a good seven, which included Steve Salmon, Mikey Coyne, John Diamond, Paddy Wallace, Willie Diamond and Johnny Kane. Lettergesh had a team, which included a couple of army lads. Ballinakill who had fine players in Malachy McLaughlin from Ballinew, John Coyne from Sheeauns and John Mullen were also represented as were Letterfrack themselves. I remember myself and my neighbour Jim Kane went to the sports on foot. On arriving we were asked by a group of young lads if we would make up a Renvyle B Team with them. This group of lads included Jack Nee, Paul Nee, Johnny 'Maura' Flaherty, Johnny Corcoran and Peter Sailor. We agreed to play and in the first round were drawn against Cleggan who were favourites to win out the tournament. Much to our own surprise we beat Cleggan. I can still remember one of the Cleggan lads saying afterwards 'Ye have us ruined, Renvyle's second team beating us'. We lost to Lettergesh in the semi-final. On the other side of the draw, Letterfrack beat Ballinakill only to lose in the semi-final to Renvyle A Team who went on to beat Lettergesh in the final.

I remember a seven-a-side in Rosleague one year. I went over to Tully after dinner where I met Paddy Heanue and John Diamond at Diamond's. We walked as far as Pakie Conneely's house in Tullycross where we were hoping to hire out his horse and sidecar for the day. Pakie was not available so we decided to run the rest of the way. As we neared Derryinver bridge we met a sidecar coming out the Derryinver road. It was Martin Connolly from Cashleen with his brother and two sisters. He stopped and brought the three of us to Letterfrack. We went to Freeney's Bar for a drink. I remember we had a bottle of stout each, bought by John Diamond. We left for Rosleague after this. There were four teams taking part that day, Renvyle, Letterfrack, Ballinakill and Clifden. I remember losing to Clifden in the final. Clifden would not ever compete unless they had a great team. They did not ever want to get beat. Renvyle had a different philosophy. They'd play with any sort of team, just for the fun of it.

I remember travelling to a seven-a-side on Omey Island in a sidecar belonging to Stephen O'Malley. It was my first time in Omey: I remember the tide being out and the tournament being played on the beach. There were only three teams that day. Clifden beat Cleggan in the semi-final and went on to beat us in the final. My final memory of seven-a-side football

St Cáillín's 1963, before a championship game in Pearse Stadium, Galway. Front row l to r: Michael J. Ferron, Eamon McBride, John Folan, Eamon Dobbins, John Wallace, Peter Veldon, Martin Burke, Tom Joyce (Pete); back row l to r: Mark McNamara, Michael Leonard, Bro. Paul, Tom Conneely, Joe Keane, Bro. Alban, Owen Reilly, Frank Leonard, Tom McDonagh, Joe King.

is losing to Oughterard in a tournament in Curraghmór near Clifden. I remember marking a fellow called Sean Donnellon. That Oughterard team also included Dinny Sullivan, Ned Toole, and Pat Gibbons. We had Steve Salmon, Tom Heanue, Pakie Sailor, Mickey Walsh and Mickey Coyne that day; Oughterard beat Clifden in a tight final.

As I look back on my football days, I have nothing but great admiration for Steve Salmon and Jack Martin Kane for the great service they gave to Renvyle. They played longer than any other players I knew during those years. Steve Salmon, was in my opinion, the most talented player in Renvyle at that time, mainly because he could play anywhere. I believe he was good enough to have played for the County in any of the full forward positions. He had two good feet, lots of clever tricks; he was very quick, very strong and very cool under any kind of pressure. My best Renvyle team from my time would have lined out as follows:

Goalie	Tom Heanue		
Full Backs	Paddy Walsh	Peter Canavan	Jack Martin Kane
Half Backs	Martin Kerrigan	Michael Lewis	Jim Kane
Midfield	John Gannon	Mick Fitzpatrick	
Half Forwards	Stevie Salmon	Mickey Walsh	Mikey Coyne
Full Forwards	Anthony Kane	Martin Davis	Paddy McDonnell

To conclude my story, I would just like to say that I enjoyed all the football I ever played.I never got down because of football. What was it anyway only an ould game. I just played for the love of it and did my best.We did not take it too seriously in those days. After all it was not a job of work. For us, at that time, it was without doubt a great way of socialising. I am sure it still is today. For me, the thing I enjoyed most was playing the game, the way it should be played, with plenty of high fielding and accurate kicking. I never worried too much about the winning or the losing. I played very little football once I turned thirty. I felt it was time for ould fellas like me to stand down and give the young lads coming up a fair chance.

I had enjoyed a good run of it and I will always be grateful for that. I still follow football with great interest today and my nephews keep me well informed on how Renvyle are doing each year. The players have a great new pitch to practise on, which is more than we ever had, but I am not bitter that we had no right opportunities in our time like the young men have today. I hope they knock great use of the new pitch and, please God, we won't have to wait too much longer for Renvyle to win it's first ever West Board Championship.

Remembered by John Gannon and written by Paul Gannon

THE MATCH

1991 WEST BOARD JUNIOR A CHAMPIONSHIP FINAL
(WINNERS PROMOTED TO INTERMEDIATE GRADE)
SPIDDAL 4-5 RENVYLE 0-5

The match was a wretched affair
I had played it long before it ever began
Played it in my dreams of glory
Played a blinder in my mind

Reality is a different affair
A reality of humiliation and shame
Stuck to the ground, awaiting inspiration
Management intervened, to put me out of my misery

Afterwards, the deathly silence of defeat
Weighed down heavily on a dressing room of despair
That evening I went to a quiet bar in Renvyle
To avoid the post-mortems.

Written by Paul Gannon

The Races

Nora McNamara

Horseracing was at the height of its popularity in West Connemara during the 1950s, when there were meetings held every summer at Lettergesh, Omey, Salerno, Roundstone, Clifden and Errismore. There has always been a great tradition of rearing horses in Errismore and the horseracing goes back as far as the 1890s. The Errismore races were held on Aillebrack commonage and in later years a few meetings were run off on Mannin beach. During the '50s the organising committee of Pakie Sweeney, Paddy McNamara, John Edward Coneys, Michael King and Bartley McNamara usually carried out a door to door collection every year throughout the region, in order to raise enough money to run the meeting. The response was always very difficult to predict. In some houses they used to get as much as five pounds, in others as little as a shilling. Insurance was not really an issue up to the end of the '50s. However in later years, the high cost of insurance became a major obstacle to overcome, and was probably one of the main reasons for this great annual event being eventually withdrawn from the West Connemara sporting calendar in the late 1960's.

Many families in Errismore were into horseracing. These included the Guys, the Coneys, the McDonaghs, the Conroys, the O'Neills, the Burkes, the Kings, the O'Malleys and the Courceys, as well as ourselves. The serious business of training the horses usually began about six weeks before the day of the races. Rival families were usually very secretive about how their training was going, and about who they had lined up as jockeys. Ambrose Coyne, Michael McNamara, John Mannion, Pat King, Matthias Conneely and Garnett Irwin were all popular jockeys of the day. Garnett Irwin was the best jockey I ever saw at Errismore races. She had such great style and technique and such a great command of the horse. All the respective families took their preparations very seriously and considered it a great honour to win a race. They were all very reluctant to divulge any

Paddy McNamara with 'Battleship' at Omey Races.

information relating to their preparations for fear of giving their rivals an advantage. There were many things to consider in order to get the best out of the horse on the day. Weight and diet had to always be given top priority. In our case, we always took our horses off the grass to thin them out. They were kept indoors and their stables cleaned thoroughly every day. We fed them a mixture of boiled potatoes and turnips. We also fed them a special type of crushed oats mixed with bran and flaxseed. The horses were fed three times a day early morning, midday, and early evening. We made sure that they drank plenty of water and we always gave them a good daily brushing to keep them feeling refreshed. To prevent their hooves drying up and cracking, we walked them in the sea every day. We walked and galloped them twice a day, and the day before the races, the jockey would arrive to do a few practice runs. Preparing horses for the races was difficult, time-consuming and sometimes frustrating

Paddy McNamara with 'Village Bell' at the Errismore Races.

CLIFDEN RACES

GATE receipts were up and entries were also at Clifden Races on Monday.

Results:

Connemara Pony Derby: 1, T. Guy's "Grey Dun"; 2, J. McDonagh's "Faulkeeragh Lass"; 3 ,M Walsh's "Sweet Maria."

Maiden Connemara Ponies: 1, M. Lee's "Dunloughan Lass"; 2, J. Conroy's "Foggy Dew"; 3, J. King's "Gay Going."

Clifden Plate: 1, M. McNamara's "Silver Pearl"; 2, J. McNamara's "Air Prince"; 3, A. Mulkerrin's "Black Swallow."

Connemara Ponies (confined to Clifden and Oughterard): 1, J B. Joyce's "Blonde Bombshell"; 2, J. King's "Gay Going"; 3, J. Conroy's "Foggy Dew."

Auto Race (Clifden Grand Prix): 1, P. Darcey; 2, S. King; 3, J McNamara.

Donkey Derby: 1, T. Wallace's "Gun Smoke"; 2, B. Conroy's "Clifden Bay"; 3, J. Coohill's "Rose."

Consolation Race: 1, J. McNamara's "Air Prince"; 2, A. Mulkerrin's "Black Swallow"; 3, T. Guy's "Black Tawn."

work, but if the horses performed to their full potential on race day, it made it all worthwhile. Over the years, my family were fortunate enough to have had some fine racehorses and we enjoyed a fair degree of success at various meetings with Silver Pearl, Pearl Diver, Village Bell, Battleship and Air Prince. Battleship who was over fifteen hands high and who raced from 1940 to 1958 was without doubt the best horse we ever had. In 1957 my husband Paddy bought his first ever thoroughbred, a horse called True Hindue for one hundred guineas at Goffs.

As race day would draw nearer there would be great excitement as well as a great sense of anticipation all around the neighbourhood. The races were the biggest day of the year in Errismore because there was no other excitement to look forward to in those times. A huge crowd would always turn up to cheer on their respective horses and to place a few bets with the two bookies who used to travel out from Galway. There were always two guards on duty also to ensure that everything would run in a smooth orderly fashion. Michael King from Bunowen had the job of race starter for many years and he started each race by dropping the flag. The first race was usually off at 2 p.m. with a further four races to follow at hourly intervals. Each race consisted of one and a half rounds of the course, a distance of about one and a half miles. There were usually four horses per race with prize money for the first three home. The prize money was usually £12 for first, £10 for second and £8 for third although there was always a feature race where the winner received £14. The feature race was always two full rounds of the course. The results were usually published in the *Connaught Tribune* the following week. I should add that it was all flat racing.

As well as all the local horses there were also many entries from other parts of Connemara. I remember Lees from Moycullen, Bolgers from Oughterard, Joyces from Clifden, Duanes from Moyard and McLaughlins from Cleggan all entering horses. I remember in particular a man from Renvyle named Tommy Lacey was a few years coming with a black horse without ever getting the opportunity to race it. I used to feel sorry for him because even though his horse stood no chance of winning, he was still

At the Clifden Races 1969. From left: Paddy Conneely with Silver Pearl; Michael Conneely with Prince Regent and Thomas Gorham with Air Prince.

very keen and enthusiastic, and hopeful of getting the horse entered each year. Then one year his opportunity finally arrived when there happened to be only two entries for one particular race. One of the horses belonged to Mattie Duane from Moyard and the other horse had been brought all the way from Killannin and was hotly fancied. None of the locals had bothered to enter their horses against these two because they were considered to be too well bred. Tommy Lacey was subsequently asked if he'd like to enter his horse just to make up the numbers and come in third. He was delighted to facilitate the organisers. The race duly commenced and by the end of the first circuit, the expected pattern had emerged. Lacey's horse was trailing well behind the front two who were neck and neck. The crowd were getting louder and more excited in anticipation of a close finish when by some unbelievable twist of fate, or maybe just divine intervention, didn't the two horses get sidetracked. As the crowd looked on in disbelief they suddenly ran off the course and continued on at great speed in a different direction, leaving the way clear for Lacey's horse to record a famous victory at odds of 10-1. It was a dream result for the bookies and also for one of the two guards on duty that day who had placed a bet of a pound on the unlikely winner.

Although the horseracing was undoubtedly the most important business of the day, there were also many side attractions to add to the occasion and to make the day more memorable. Currach racing and weight throwing were very popular. There were many fine oarsmen in the local village of Aillebrack. The three strongest pairings I remember were Padraig O'Malley and his brother Tom, Festus O'Neill and Tom McDonagh and Paddy McNamara and his son Bernard. Martin Conneely from Errislannon and Frank Duane from Silver Hill had many great battles in the weight throwing competition. There were usually a few novelty races on the day, bicycle

Waiting for the 'off', Clifden 1983.

races for men and women; a married men's race and a donkey derby. There was also tug-of-war in the evening between a local team from Errismore and Renvyle. All of these events help to keep the large crowd entertained between races and the organisers deserve great credit for having so much entertainment laid on. My favourite character at the races was Michael Conroy from Market Street in Clifden who was known as 'Crook'. He always brought his chequered roll of lino, with its black and white squares, to the races and we all used to toss for 'a penny a treat'.

As well as all the sport, the day of the races was a great social occasion. Many people met up on the day of the races, who might not meet again until raceday the following year. Old friends and acquaintances would talk about old times over a few drinks at Tommy Mannion's tent. Tommy would be all out of porter by early evening. It was one of his busiest days of the year.

Many years have passed since the last race meeting at Errismore and the old course is not so easily recognisable anymore. Those of us who were privileged to be part of the Errismore race tradition will always have so many happy memories to cherish. The races belong to a different era. They have run their course, but the love of horses among the people of Errismore lives on.

Remembered by Nora MacNamara and written by Paul Gannon

The Sale Of A Sire

On Saturday 6th September at sunset, there will be set up for sale and sold at Streamstown, a Sire the property of Seamus Shaughnessy, Shrule.

This Sire is a strong, staunch, steady, sound, stout, sinewy, safe, serviceable, strapping, supple, swift, smart, sightly, sprightly, spirited, sturdy, shining, sure-footed, sleek, smooth, spunky, well-skimmed, sized and shaped, a sorrel of superlative symmetry.

He is styled Shergar with snip, square-sided, slender-shouldered, sharp sighted, super-sexed and smart, showing a small star.

He steps singularly stately, free from strain, sprain, spavin, stringhaulets, staggers, scatagat, sallanders, surfeit, scouring, stranguary, sciatica, spasm, strangles, stams, stroumers, swellings, starfoot or scratches.

He is also free from splint, squint, squirt, scruff, sores, scars, scabs, scattering, shuffling, shambling, or any signs or symptoms of sickness of any sort.

He is neither stiff-mouthed, shabby-coated, sinew-shrunk, spur-galled, saddle-galled, shell-toothed, sling-gutted, surbated, skin-scabbed, short-winded, splay-footed or shoulder-slipped, and he is sound in the sword point and stifle-joint.

He has neither sick-spleen, sit fast, snaggle teeth, sand crack, staring coat, swelled sheath nor shattered hooves; nor is he sour, sulky, surly, stubborn or sullen in temper.

He is neither shy, sly, sluggish, slow, slouchy, skittish nor stupid and he never slips, skips, stalks, starts, stops, snarls, snuffles, snorts, shakes, stumbles, or stares in a stall or stable and scarcely or seldom sweats.

He has a showy, stylish, swish tail and is shod with a sound, safe set of shoes to stride on. He subsists on soil, stubble, sainform, sheaf-oats, straw, sedge, or scutch grass and is strong enough to carry sixteen stones in his stride with surprising speed over a six foot sod or stone stile.

His sire was Sly Sobersides out of a sister of Spindle Shanks by Silent Sampson, that sporting son of Sparkler, who won the Sweepstakes and Subscription Plate at Sligo last season.

Surely I have said sufficient to satisfy you that this splended sire should sell speedily for the specified sum of six-hundred-and-sixty-six smackers Sterling. Sin Sin.

Sean Kelly

STORIES THAT THE OLD FOLKS USED TO TELL

I often sat enraptured, and listened with delight,
To stories told by the old folks, around the fire at night,
Of brave deeds done, and victories won, on land and on the seas,
Of outlaws, smugglers, pirates, ghosts and giants as tall as trees.

Some of them told that hookers, by sturdy sailors manned,
Were split in two on Shennaghaus, about a mile from land,
No braver seaman took a deck, in hurricane or squall,
Since Grace O'Malley battered down old Curragh Castle's walls.

And Captain Sugan, smuggler king, from lands so far away,
Hauled down the flag to Cahir's saint while scudding up Clew Bay,
Then steered his course for Dawrosbeg, his cargo put on shore,
And slept the sleep of Baccus with the ghosts at Dooneen Mor.

King George's ships were chasing him, in hope to run him down,
And added another jewel to the British diamond crown,
In the way of straw-rope rigging, as though as ever grew
A Captain soaked in poteen and an Irish rebel crew.

But George's men were cowards, they turned about and fled,
From a speck upon the ocean's crest just inside Cleggan head,
A phantom white quadruped that was seen each seventh year,
For a day on Boffin Island and then would disappear.

Another told of outlaws bold, who tracked the mountainside,
But one was always spoken of, with reverence and pride,
That brave undaunted generous heart to you a landmark gave,
It's known to all, Scalp Johnnie was the famous outlaws' cave.

Cuchulainn dwelt on Dochrú, Finn Mac Cuumhaill on Diamond Hill,
And they threw the 'Smoothing Iron' to each other with a will,
But one day when Finn was hunting with his faithful stag-hound Bran,
It fell, and there it is today, called Leac a Bhodachán.

And Bran pursued a royal stag with all her canine skill
Among the cliffs near Lugnaneach and round the heath-clad hill,
Finn saw his hound in danger and called her back in vain
For she plunged off Léim na hEilite and was never seen again.

The stag was an enchanted prince, so runs the good old tale,
Sent over by the Danish King to kidnap Conal Maol,
It may be so, but this we know, it proved a sad mistake,
The stag and hound were never found, they perished in the lake.

From the bridge at Derryinver, away up to Lough Dix,
The dead help fairs three times a year and fought like hell with sticks,
Each faction showed the poteen round until the dawn of day,
And when the cocks began to crow, returned again to clay.

A Sassenach named Dixon, who loved the punch too well,
While riding by, a midnight fair, into the streamlet fell,
Then moved across the mountain his neighbours to oblige,
And they say he still stands at the bridge of Shanaveg.

My eyes are getting misty Bríd, I almost think I am back,
Among my old true friends once more in dear old Letterfrack,
And so astór just for awhile I'll say to you farewell,
Till I think of other stories that the old folk used to tell.

Written many years ago by a poet named Coen who lived in Letterfrack.

BEYOND THOSE HILLS

Beyond Maam Cross the friendly hills are waiting
As sunset streaks the countryside with gold
Westward we go into the heart of silence
Children once more returning to the fold.

Beneath the wooded hills Kylemore is silent
Only the thrushes singing in the brake
Here I have walked among the rhododendrons
And watched the shadows deepen on the Lake.

From Letterfrack to Ballinahinch and onwards
I've tried to single out the Pins in vain;
I've watched the fishing boats come in at Cleggan
And crossed to Inishbofin in the rain.

I've eaten crispy oven bread in Roundstone
And watched the village lads play Pitch and Toss
I've talked to Gypsies on the road to Cashel
And had my fortune told in Tullycross.

I've listened to the clamour of the shearing
The bleat of sheep and timid lambs new-shorn
The rumble of the turf-carts on the cobbles
The cuckoo's farewell call, faint and forlorn.

I've waited for the salmon fleet at twilight
Through Killary homecoming with its catch
I've danced at weddings until dawn was breaking
And rebel songs rang out beneath the thatch.

But I must not stay here idly dreaming
I've got many roads to wander – friends to see
But first I'll stand and watch those hills around me
And someone from the past might watch with me.

Written by Del Allen

A REVERIE

I wonder if the thrushes sing
In Drinagh as of yore
And if at night the curlews call
On Carna's lonely shore.

I wonder if the hoary thorn
That grew beside the road
Still bears, as in my schoolboy days,
It's ruddy autumn load.

I wonder if the Lurag stream
Still works its weedy way
Along the moor and past the school
To Cashel's shelter'd bay

I wonder if on Emlagh hill,
Beneath the moor's soft ray
The fairies still their revels hold
Till first grey light of day.

And – sweetest thought – I wonder if
My old friends speak of me
When gather'd round their cheerful hearths
In Cashel by the sea.

Written by Patrick Kelly (Bard of Connemara)

THE ROCKY RENVYLE SHORE

One day I am going back to the grandest place on earth
Where the mountains tower so high above the land God loves best
Where the people are so friendly and their smiles are to the fore
Where Atlantic waves are breaking on the Rocky Renvyle Shore.

There's Currachbawn and Cashleen, Ardnagreevagh and Gleanntán
Eagles Nest, Cloonluane and down to old Trábán
Derrylough and Derryinver, Derryherbert, Mullaghgloss
Tullymore and Gurteen and on to Tullycross.

The sea surrounds those heather hills where oft times I did roam
Where visitors from many lands have come to make their homes
The air is pure and healthy, sure who could ask for more
Than to breathe the gentle breezes from the Rocky Renvyle Shore

There Gran'dad played his fiddle whose music was divine
From his home upon the hillside, it rang out clear and wide
Jigs and reels and marches and melodies go leor
Could all be heard quite plainly by the Rocky Renvyle Shore

God bless you gentle people I love you one and all
You make me feel so welcome when ere I chance to call
And if I had but just one wish, there's nothing I would ask more
Than to live among you people grand, by the Rocky Renvyle Shore

Written by Pauline McDonnell

MY CONNEMARA

Lake, sea, land and sky,
Overall a glancing eye,
Bog, plain and mountains high,
Heaven now seems almost nigh!

Cottages, cairns and coral sands,
All welcoming like outstretched hands,
Castles too, with history filled,
Their gardens scented, air distilled.

Monuments to and age gone-by,
Spectacular against the sky,
Fisher-folk who know the sea,
Yet view with awe its rocky lea.

It's pathways, boreens, sounds of sheep,
A picture in my mind to keep!

Written by Margaret Mitchell

LINES WRITTEN ON TOP OF MWEELIN

My lonesome odyssey is complete.
I have enjoyed my voyage into the unknown,
Surrounded by the soft intimate sounds of Mother Nature.
Sludge scrunch – mountain solitude will save my soul.
I am on top now.
Sheep, transfixed by my presence.
Observe me with disdainful curiosity.
Down below I watch the Black Lake river's spectacular meandering.
As it heads off in search of the sea.
Rolling along through another sea.
A sea of bog.
So wet it reminds me of a giant sponge.
That could never be squeezed dry.
Far out the islands in silent splendour.
Sometimes there can be no words.
Just a deep-felt sense of privilege and appreciation.
From my vantage point, I see it all from yet another angle.
This mystical landscape that I am married to, yet will never understand.
This Paradise Lost that I will never leave.

Written by Paul Gannon

AND ANOTHER THOUGHT

Pray do not find fault with the man who limps
Or stumbles along the road,
Unless you have worn the shoes he wears
Or struggled beneath his load.

There may be tacks in his shoes that hurt
Though hidden away from view,
Or the burden he bears, placed on your back,
Might cause you to stumble too.

Author Unknown

This book is dedicated

to the memory of

John Gannon